RETHINKING FREIRE AND ILLICH

Rethinking Freire and Illich

Historical, Philosophical, and Theological Perspectives

EDITED BY ROSA BRUNO-JOFRÉ, MICHAEL ATTRIDGE, AND JON IGELMO ZALDÍVAR

UNIVERSITY OF TORONTO PRESS
Toronto Buffalo London

ISBN 978-1-4875-5043-1 (cloth)   ISBN 978-1-4875-5052-3 (EPUB)
                                  ISBN 978-1-4875-5047-9 (PDF)

Library and Archives Canada Cataloguing in Publication

Title: Rethinking Freire and Illich : historical, philosophical, and theological
    perspectives / edited by Rosa Bruno-Jofré, Michael Attridge, and Jon Igelmo Zaldívar.
Names: Bruno-Jofré, Rosa del Carmen, 1946– editor. | Attridge, Michael S., editor. |
    Igelmo Zaldívar, Jon, 1982– editor.
Description: Includes bibliographical references and index.
Identifiers: Canadiana (print) 20230477976 | Canadiana (ebook) 20230478026 |
    ISBN 9781487550431 (cloth) | ISBN 9781487550523 (EPUB) |
    ISBN 9781487550479 (PDF)
Subjects: LCSH: Freire, Paulo, 1921–1997. Pedagogía do oprimido. | LCSH: Illich,
    Ivan, 1926–2002. Deschooling society. | LCSH: Education – Philosophy. |
    LCSH: Religious education – Philosophy. | LCSH: Educational sociology. |
    LCSH: Critical pedagogy.
Classification: LCC LB880.F732 R48 2023 | DDC 370.1–dc23

Cover design: Will Brown
Cover image: (right) Ivan Illich leading a seminar at Centro Intercultural de Documentacion
(CIDOC), Cuernavaca, Mexico. James S. Roberts Photographs, Northwestern University
Archives. (left) CIDOC classroom with Paulo Freire. James S. Roberts Photographs,
Northwestern University Archives.

We wish to acknowledge the land on which the University of Toronto Press operates. This
land is the traditional territory of the Wendat, the Anishnaabeg, the Haudenosaunee, the
Métis, and the Mississaugas of the Credit First Nation.

This book has been published with the help of a grant from the Federation for the Humanities
and Social Sciences, through the Awards to Scholarly Publications Program, using funds
provided by the Social Sciences and Humanities Research Council of Canada.

University of Toronto Press acknowledges the financial support of the Government of
Canada, the Canada Council for the Arts, and the Ontario Arts Council, an agency of the
Government of Ontario, for its publishing activities.

 Canada Council for the Arts **Conseil des Arts du Canada**

 **ONTARIO ARTS COUNCIL** **CONSEIL DES ARTS DE L'ONTARIO** an Ontario government agency un organisme du gouvernement de l'Ontario

Funded by the Government of Canada   Financé par le gouvernement du Canada    Canada

Contents

Artist's Statement

ALAN WILKINSON

The six images in this collection of papers addressing the work of Paulo Freire and Ivan Illich all use contemporary techniques based on an infrequently utilized historic observational tool known as the Claude glass. The initial Claude glass technique, named after the French painter Claude Lorrain, was primarily used from the second half of the eighteenth century to the early nineteenth century by artists who chose to discern subject matter such as landscapes in moderately curved black glass mirrors. This technique changed how artists using a Claude glass perceived the world around them and prompted intense attention to many important components of what was being observed in the black glass, such as altered value ranges and compositional cropping facilitated by mirror edges.

The contemporary reflective photograph found at the beginning of each section is based on Claude glass procedures, and they have distinctive parallels to Scott Johnson's identification of what he sees as the "chief characteristic of these papers." Johnson's identification, in the epilogue to this volume, of a movement from "theory (as the historical-hermeneutical sciences, in Habermas's terms) to praxis (critical theory as action) and back again" broadly articulates the creative sequence undertaken in each image. Beginning with the efficacious, historic technique of reflection-based image creation via the Claude glass, an artist can be prompted to anchor configurative planning in the dynamic actualities of visual reversals, inversions, value modifications, picture plane angularities, and sectored compositions. Those dynamic actualities are transferred into completely new situations when innovative strategies are included, such as large-scale reflective surfaces, in situ mirror surfaces, thematic subject content, and emphasized distortion. The progression from the historic miniature black mirror origins to the reflective realities of modern urban environments provides artists with profuse opportunities to combine thematic content and image configuration.

It would be helpful for the viewer to note that these images were created without providing the camera lenses conventional linear access to the subject matter; the deployment of this assortment of on-site reflective surfaces that provide segmented views and alter the rendering of the scenes provide the viewer with an opportunity to examine the intricate and challenging ways in which we can encounter any view of our world. The cognizance of what one is perceiving is important from an empirical perspective, and this has important implications in education.

Freire's focus upon discernment is significant; if we consider discernment in the context of his meaningful assertion that human beings are part of reality, accurate analysis of what we are seeing becomes vital in processing visual data. Detecting and discerning elements of visual evidence in an image has a strong parallel to observing the outcomes of an experiment in a laboratory. Accurate discernment can facilitate the development of many meaningful conceptual structures. The discernment of the presence and nature of reflection-based renderings in this set of images is designed to communicate the value of intense observation.

Ivan Illich's aim to create educational methodologies for accurately focusing living people upon all aspects of reality without misusing historical filters or social templates is an essential curricular priority in meaningful learning. Concerns regarding the dominance of historically oriented methods could be very much present if templated methods requiring the carrying of ten-centimetre black mirrors in hinged silver cases were required. Instead, it is worth noting that implementing entirely new and often unanticipated methods of collecting visual image data does not trivialize a historic method, but instead augments it.

Alan Wilkinson
Ottawa, Ontario
15 October 2021

Part One: Historical Framework
sunrise engaging all
This photograph is a rendering that replicates the classic modifications to the value scale identified by the early Claude glass technique. Careful discernment of the image can reveal that secondary reflections are present and thus a second confirmation of this photograph being a reflection becomes clear. The dark-blue reflection generates a remarkably smooth value range in a setting that includes both dark areas and almost irrepressibly bright highlights.

Part Two: Theological Intersections in Freire's Work and Their Impact on Catholicism
sectoral vision presents

Encountering views of the world that are multifaceted by objects anchored in the ground yet visually connected to the sky can provide us with moments to think about how we make intelligible that which is encountered. Sectored views can require meaning to be explored.

Part Three: Freire and Illich and Contemporary Critical Issues in Education
window marching alone
Isolating a tool from anything that it can implement has an impact on results. This sole area of focus on the glass isolates the semi-reflective device in this night-time image, thus eliminating sharpness in both the non-reflected foreground and the reflected background. The only sharp focus in the photograph is on the dust and water stains attached to the glass. The seemingly large human figure is a small plastic soldier on a store shelf, and the background consists of commercial properties across the street.

Part Four: Freire and Illich and Indigeneity
dichroic yet clear
Dichroic mirrors reflect selected colours and transmit others. Settings with interacting dichroic mirrors provide ways of seeing unanticipated alignments of subject matter and set up relationships between elements in view that may have been ignored or dismissed. Black-and-white rendering of dichroic mirror reflections can intensify the subject matter by focusing on forms and themes.

Part Five: Freire in Attempts at Transformation in Asia in the Last Decades
navigation reversals invert
Reflective surfaces below or above subject matter deliver a second optical attribute in the form of inversion. Bodies of water are among the most common sources for the delivery of both reversed and inverted images.

Part Six: Epilogue
emerging presence continues
While Claude glass images that integrate the reflective and direct rendition of the artist's environment yield a clear overview of what process was in place regarding the transposition, one's perceptions from the initial, direct visual access to the final modified depiction, are seldomly narrow in scope. In this image the process of moving from direct rendition to reflective imaging is bridged by the large shadow in the foreground, with the right side of the shadow being rendered in direct representation and the left side being in reflection.

RETHINKING FREIRE AND ILLICH

Introduction

ROSA BRUNO-JOFRÉ, MICHAEL ATTRIDGE, AND JON IGELMO
ZALDÍVAR

This collection introduces the reader to the results of the symposium "Paulo Freire's Pedagogy of the Oppressed and Ivan Illich's Deschooling Society Fifty Years Later," which marked the fiftieth anniversary of two of the most influential books in modern educational and social theory: Paulo Freire's *Pedagogy of the Oppressed* (published in Portuguese in 1968, translated into English in 1970) and Ivan Illich's *Deschooling Society* (published in 1971 and drawn from articles written in the late 1960s and published in the editorial collections of the Centro Intercultural de Documentación, México). The event took place online through the auspices of the University of St. Michael's College (USMC) in the University of Toronto, the home of an internationally distinguished Faculty of Theology, a tribute to the Catholic underpinnings of these two public intellectuals, whose penetrating and prescient critiques have made an indelible impression, both within and beyond theological circles.

The symposium was funded by a Connection Grant from the Social Sciences and Humanities Research Council and gathered the members of the Theory and History of Education International Research Group (https://educ.queensu.ca/their). The event was led by the applicant, Rosa Bruno-Jofré, the Civic Culture and Educational Policies Research Team from the Universidad Complutense de Madrid (www.ucm.es/ccpe), members of the Institute for Research on the Second Vatican Council in Canada at USMC (http://dominicantoronto.org/institute-research-vatican-ii-canada/), and members of the Congregation of Our Lady of the Missions/RNDM women religious (http://www.rndmcanada.org/), who work with political refugees and join efforts with various NGOs in Canada and internationally such as Hospitality House Refugee Ministry (https://www.hhrmwpg.org/who-we-are).[1] Collaborators hailing from Australia, Canada, Chile, Spain, and the United States have generated an original and cross-disciplinary analysis of Freire's *Pedagogy of the Oppressed* and Illich's *Deschooling Society* to examine the books' intellectual and political roots and their lasting impact in educational theory and practice. The authors do not limit themselves to the two famous books, but instead broaden the enquiry to include other works by Illich and Freire, in particular how these other works are read by contemporary audiences. The contributors are in different stages of their careers. They include senior scholars who had the opportunity to meet and exchange ideas with Freire or attend a lengthy presentation by Illich in Mexico City, graduate students, and a member of a Catholic women's congregation who relates Freire to the congregation's spirituality and movement towards eco-spirituality.

A unique feature of this book is the fact that it treats Freire and Illich together, although not in a comparative way. Apart from a couple of dialogues/ interviews in the 1970s involving both authors, an IDAC (Institut d'action culturelle) document analysing and comparing them, and a known article, the literature celebrating each of their main works, by and large, don't relate the two.[2] That all said, the recent literature on Illich and Freire individually is extensive.[3]

Both Freire and Illich embody the critique of educational institutions that signalled the "long 1960s."[4] Freire developed over time a political ethics of social change, and his notion of a liberating education was linked to political action, while Illich offered a critique of schooling that would be a point of reference for alternatives such as homeschooling and forms of digital learning or even libertarian pedagogies. Both were Catholics. However, while Freire found inspiration in the social thinking of the Catholic Church that was dominant in the 1960s, in social and philosophical theories of the time, and then in Catholic liberation theology, Illich, a Catholic critical of the institutional church, was theologically orthodox and iconoclastic and had neo-medievalist views of the state.[5] For Illich, schooling (which subsumed education) was one of the certainties of modernity that imprisoned the search for knowledge, just as the church mediated the individual's free relationship with God. After his conflict with the Vatican from 1966 to 1969, exacerbated to an important extent by the publication in 1967 of "The Seamy Side of Charity" and "The Vanishing Clergyman" – the two pieces that questioned the institutional church and its policies – he moved from a critique of the Church as It (as institution) to a critique of schooling and the institutions of modernity.[6]

There were substantial differences with reference to the contextual elements of their writings. Freire's theories were rooted in adult education practices in Brazil and Chile in the 1960s within contextualized projects of society. Illich had created a network of centres in Cuernavaca in 1961 (as explained in chapter 1) that prepared Catholic missionaries with a commitment to incarnate in the culture, where they would give testimony rather than serve as agents of their own culture. By 1966, the Centre for Intercultural Documentation (CIDOC) was the only centre that remained – this time disconnected from ecclesiastical authorities. CIDOC became a hub for intellectuals and transformative thinkers who analysed the modern world, and many of them were concerned with education, including Paulo Freire, John Holt, Joel Spring, Paul Goodman, Augusto Salazar Bondy, and José María Bulnes, to name a few.[7]

Illich, through his writings, provided tools that nourished insightful critiques on education, energy, health, and critical digital literacy over time. He did not intend to articulate a learning theory or a pedagogical theory.[8] Furthermore, Illich, in spite of his questioning in the late 1960s of the institutionalization of values and of the church's political engagement with US projects for Latin America, would not engage in political action or even embrace liberation theology, seeing the church as a spiritual force.

Freire and Illich were good colleagues and allies in the 1960s. Freire had been introduced to Illich by the bishop of Olinda and Recife, Dom Hélder Câmara (the very notion of conscientization is attributed to the latter, probably in 1962).[9] Illich was familiar with what was happening in Brazil and with the Movement for Grassroots Education (or MEB), which had adopted Freire's literacy method, as well as with Freire's work and conceptions.[10] He actually mentioned the method in *Deschooling Society*.[11] Illich related later in an interview that he had intervened through Teodoro Moscoso, a high-profile Puerto Rican with connections in the US government, to obtain Freire's release from prison in 1964, after the coup against Brazilian president João Goulart.[12] Illich also hosted Freire at CIDOC in Cuernavaca for a couple of summers in the late 1960s and in 1970, and he acknowledged him in *Deschooling Society*.[13]

However, Illich and Freire followed different paths, particularly from the time Freire moved to the World Council of Churches. Although there was an exchange on 6 September 1974 in Geneva on the occasion of the fiftieth anniversary of the Geneva International School, in a seminar entitled "An Invitation to Conscientization and Deschooling: A Continuing Conversation," the distance between them in terms of their respective approaches to education and schooling was obvious. Freire pointed out that Illich had made an error when refusing to analyse the ideological question, since he separated the critique of the institution from the critique of the ideology.[14] Illich was not prepared to discuss the question of ideology at the time. Freire also said that Illich mythologized education and thought of the school as a diabolic instrument.[15]

Freire's conceptions had a presence across the world in educational reforms, albeit often stripped of their political transformative dimensions, an example being the case study in chapter 14, which looks at BRAC, a Bangladeshi NGO, and in struggles embodied in popular education projects. Freire's ideas were moved to the North and were at the core of critical pedagogy theorizations by Henry Giroux, Michael Apple, and Stanley Aronowitz, among others, and were present in projects of development education. For his part, Illich did not become a point of reference in critical pedagogy.[16] He inspired anarchist currents, land movements, the homeschooling movement (as examined in chapter 10, on the history of homeschooling/unschooling), as well as critical visions of energy, health, and the relationship between humans and technology.

Today, in light of the concerns with the rise of right-wing populist movements in various parts of the world and the presumed failure of education to achieve the purposes of democracy and democratic education, there is a search for a reformulation of democratic education and a consideration of the power of affective experiences.[17] It is interesting that Michalinos Zembylas, in his book *Affect and the Rise of Right-Wing Populism: Pedagogies for the Renewal of Democratic Education* (2021), relies on Freire's broad notion of pedagogy well beyond a teaching method and on the assumption that all pedagogy is political.[18] Meanwhile, one of the most distinguished contemporary thinkers, Boaventura de Sousa Santos, author of *The End of the Cognitive Empire: The Coming of Age of the Epistemologies of the South* (2018), places Freire in the Latin American anti-colonial and postcolonial thinking tradition, along with Roberto Retamar, Orlando Fals Borda, Aníbal Quijano, and Enrique Dussel, among others.[19] Santos praises dimensions of Freire's theory and marks the difference in objectives, writing, "whereas in Paulo Freire the major objective is the educational project, in the epistemologies of the South it is the ecologies of knowledge, from which the possibility of strengthening the social struggles against domination may emerge. In the latter case, it makes no sense to speak of educators; moreover, the postabyssal researcher must be a rearguard intellectual, never a vanguard intellectual."[20] As will be indicated in chapter 1, Freire has been the object of critiques from a gendered perspective, and by Indigenous scholars from North America, as conveyed in chapter 12 by Lindsay Morcom, who proposes a critical Indigenous pedagogy. Illich's book *Gender* generated an uproar among feminists in the early 1980s.[21]

Illich has become a point of reference when dealing with technology and energy. Thus, for example, decolonial scholar Walter D. Mignolo, who is in line with Gustavo Esteva's vision of sustainable economies, when discussing sustainable development or sustainable economies as an open question, goes to Illich's *Tools of Conviviality* and his call "for a reversal that puts the machine and current technology at the service of the user, re-establishing conviviality and the communal, rather than putting the user at the service of machines and technology under the goals of development, whether rough or sustainable."[22] *Tools of Conviviality* inspired chapters 7 and 8 in this collection in relation to energy and to digital tools.

Illich and Freire are being reread in this generation in light of contemporary issues and renewed searches for a good and just life and a reconstructed democratic education. However, we cannot neglect that both Freire and Illich led in different ways to a new manner of perceiving and understanding the concept of liberation as a human condition. They explored liberation in interplay with the historical context, against a theological background representing different temporalities and epistemologies. Their thought is thus nourished, critiqued (particularly in relation to gender), and indeed reconstructed with new voices.

The book makes a substantial contribution on various grounds. It offers a historical analysis using extensive primary sources and a wealth of original topics, some discussed for the first time. This is the case with the chapters on the influence of Freire's work on CELAM (Consejo Episcopal Latinoamericano y Caribeño, Episcopal Conference of Latin America), on the relationship of the Jesuits in Chile, on the creation of a digital tool, on the digital world and critical pedagogy, and on the reflections from an Indigenous perspective and related current approaches to education. There are also chapters dealing with concrete experiences, such as Freire's time in Bangladesh and in Timor-Leste in the post–new war period.

Part 1, Historical Framework, contains only one chapter, "*Pedagogy of the Oppressed* and *Deschooling Society* in the 'Long 1960s': A Contextualization," by historians Rosa Bruno-Jofré and Jon Igelmo Zaldívar. The chapter examines the characteristics of the context framing Illich's and Freire's lived experiences and intellectual roots, and explores the central points of their critiques of educational institutions. It traces the roots of Illich's anti-modernist and anti-state positioning, the complex intellectual background, and the influence of Maritain and Thomism. It also identifies existential intersections in Illich's intellectual and public life, going from his relationship with Cardinal Francis Spellman of New York, through his stay in Puerto Rico, to his network of centres in Cuernavaca. The authors argue that in *Deschooling Society*, "Illich brought a theological dimension to the analysis while placing the critique as a critique of modernity and the idea of progress." The work of Paulo Freire in his early years, discussed in the second part of the chapter, is examined in relation to his practice in Brazil at the intersection with the US modernization policy for Latin America through the Alliance for Progress and the Brazilian context that included a national developmentalist model, the movements of popular education, and the radicalization of sectors of the Catholic Church. The authors offer a political reading of *Pedagogy of the Oppressed*, written by Freire while in exile in Chile, taking into account Freire's radicalization and the influence of liberation theology. Overall, the authors argue that there is a line connecting the early thought of Freire and Brazilian pedagogues' interpretation of John Dewey's pragmatism. However, his literacy method and his conception of education generated an epistemological rupture in the political-pedagogical discourse of adult education and beyond.

Part 2, Theological Intersections in Freire's Work and Their Impact on Catholicism, explores themes of religion, theology, history, and Paulo Freire. It contains five chapters. In the first one, "The Reception of Paulo Freire at the Second Episcopal Conference of Latin America in 1968," Michael Attridge looks at Freire's work in relation to the historic conference of the Latin American bishops at Medellín, Colombia, in 1968 (known as CELAM II) – a topic that has never been studied. Attridge uses the theological category of "reception," that is, the way in which teachings are absorbed, assimilated, and even enculturated into the life of a community. In recent decades, Catholic scholars have most often applied this concept to how the Second Vatican Council (1962–65) has been received into the lives of people and been transformative for them. Attridge, however, applies it to Freire to ask how Freire's liberative educational approach was influential in shaping Medellín. To this end, he looks at the bishops and theologians who were most influential at CELAM II and, using historical research, concludes that indeed Medellín received Freire's work, especially in its section on education. This then opens the way for further research on the reception of Medellín's educational documents in the faith and life of the people in the generation that followed.

The second chapter in this section, "Paulo Freire and the Jesuit Intellectual and Educational World in Chile (1964–1969): A Collateral and Indirect Relationship," by Cristobal Madero, also situates Freire's research in a religious context in the 1960s, looking at his relationship with members of the Society of Jesus (Jesuits) in Chile. Using a historical approach, Madero traces points of contact as well as opportunities for interaction between Freire and the Jesuits, whether through the order's print periodical *Revista Mensaje*, its Latin American Institute of Social Studies, its Centre for the Economic and Social Development of Latin America, its Center for Research and Development of Education, or its network of elementary and secondary schools. Each of these were powerful venues for the transmission of ideas and the formation of human persons, so establishing connections helps us to understand Freire's spheres of influence. Supporting Madero's research are recent interviews with individuals connected to these institutes in the 1960s, which strengthen his conclusion that, overall, there can be no doubt of a strong connection between Freire and the Jesuits, even if it was, as he says, "collateral" or "indirect." Like with Attridge's work, Madero's discoveries invite further investigation into Freire's later years.

The next chapter in this section, "Lonergan and Freire: An Initial Conversation," by Darren Dias, also connects Freire and the Jesuit Order, but through a philosophical rather than a historical lens. Dias compares Freire's understanding of consciousness in his use of conscientization with Canadian Jesuit theologian Bernard Lonergan's work on consciousness in his *Method in Theology*.[23] Written around the same time as *Pedagogy of Oppressed*, Lonergan's work approaches the topic from a deductive, systematic theological approach, as compared to Freire's inductive, praxiological concerns. Using Lonergan's levels of consciousness, Dias argues persuasively that Lonergan's work complements, clarifies, and complexifies Freire's notion of conscientization. Freire situates his work in the concrete historical context of Latin America, whereas Lonergan develops a broader, acontextual, cross-cultural heuristic. Dias concludes that Lonergan complements Freire by "distinguishing consciousness and intentionality, horizons, realms of meaning, bias and conversion," where Freire has conflated these. At the same time, he suggests that Freire's strong, praxis-oriented concerns might contribute something of a direction for the development of Lonergan's work.

The fourth chapter in this section is entitled "'The Wolf Shall Dwell with the Lamb': Traces of Prophetic Judaism in the Concept of Love in *Pedagogy of the Oppressed*," by Gonzalo Jover and David Luque, which also focuses on a particular concept in Freire's work, namely, his understanding of love in *Pedagogy of the Oppressed*. The authors argue that Freire's use of the term was influenced by the works of Erich Fromm and Martin Buber, either directly or indirectly. Fromm and Freire met through Ivan Illich in 1966, and Fromm's concept of "biophilia" – the love of life – appears to have become important for Freire in his conceptualizing of the ideal relationship between the oppressed and the oppressor. As Jover and Luque write, the love of life for Freire is that which "activates the will for every human being to live a truly human life" – even if it is eschatological. Also influential was Martin Buber. Although the two never met, and Freire never cites Buber directly, Buber's I-Thou relationship, with its emphasis on dialogue, was also important for Freire in his understanding of love. The authors conclude that "Freire took from Buber the significance of loving dialogue in the mutual constitution of the I and the you." The question they pose in the end, which is an important one, is why Freire did not use the Catholic Christian concept of love, especially given his upbringing and his obvious connection to it.

Finally, this section closes with "Our Lady of the Missions and Paulo Freire: Weaving a Web of Life," by Veronica Dunne. Using the genre of storytelling and personal reflection, Dunne begins her work with a narrative to highlight the tension between Eurocentric ways of knowing and those of the other two-thirds of the world. Her chapter unfolds as a reflection on the influence of Freire on the work of the Sisters of Our Lady of the Missions (Religieuses de Notre Dame des Missions, or RNDM) in Canada and Peru, as well as on Latin American liberation theology, feminist liberation theology, and eco-feminist consciousness as sources of knowledge today. Dunne believes that Freire's work, together with that of liberation theologians Gustavo Gutierrez and Leonardo Boff, inspired the RNDM sisters in Canada and Peru in the post–Vatican II period in their ministries to the marginalized and disempowered. She also speculates that Freire was an influence for Pope Francis in his encyclical on creation, *Laudato Si'*, a work that closely aligns with the RNDM sisters today in terms of their own study, contemplation, and action. She concludes with a note of hope that Freire's disruptive, prophetic approach to the dominant narrative may continue to offer inspiration in the generations to come.

In part 3, Freire and Illich and Contemporary Critical Issues in Education, there are five chapters. The first, "Ivan Illich, Gender, and Energy," by historian Ruth Sandwell, goes to the thesis expounded by Illich in his books *Energy and*

Equity (1974), *Shadow Work* (1981), and the controversial *Gender* (1983),[24] in which Illich articulates, Sandwell writes, "the very high cost that high-energy-consuming societies have long been paying in terms of inequality and cultural alienation." Although Illich did not explicitly discuss catastrophic climate change as one of the negative polluting effects, the author argues that two aspects of Illich's work, his counter-narrative to the notion of "progress" through its high energy use, and his insistence "that changing gender roles have been among the most devastating results of the shift to fossil fuel use," demonstrate its importance. After analysing Illich, Sandwell moves to her own research, focusing on the ways that the nineteenth- and early twentieth-century household provides a focus and a scale to understand energy transition. She argues that the household is a foundational centre around which people organize their social and economic lives and through which energy flows in supporting those lives. The role of women is then explored, offering an interpretation of Illich's position in *Gender*, and of vernacular gender relations and the potential of the concept of "shadow work."

The second chapter in this section is "Building Convivial Educational Tools in the Twenty-First Century," by Ana Jofre, Kristina Boylan, and Ibrahim Yucel. It is grounded in Illich's understanding of "tools for conviviality" as tools that encourage individual creativity and expression and that can be adapted to people's needs and situations. The chapter describes the design of an interactive tool, CITE (Collaborative Interactive Tabletop for Education), being developed by Ana Jofre and her team at SUNY Polytechnic, which allows users to interact with digital data visualizations using hand-held tabletop objects. The novelty of this work lies in its accessibility and flexibility. Most tools of this type require expensive specialized hardware, but this system instead provides a set of instructions, along with open-access software, so that anyone can build it (and customize it) using easily available standard parts.

Next, Ina Ghita explores the possibility of applying Freire's critical pedagogy to digital learning environments in her chapter "In Support of Critical Thinking Education: Praxis and Dialogue in Digital Learning." The author's starting point is that critical pedagogy provides the tools and habits of mind to actively question theory, practice, and the belief of society, and to focus on how instructional design contributes, or not, to critical thinking. Ghita identifies "true dialogue" at the core of critical pedagogy and discusses how praxis, both in its active and reflective dimensions and dialogue, can support critical thinking in a digital learning environment. The author identifies dialogue not as the classic dialectic triad or a mechanical method but as a way of knowing, a way to participate in the "continuous construction and transformation of the world." She asks, "Is there sufficient dialogue in digital education today?" She writes that just as education cannot be neutral, it cannot be assumed that digital technology is neutral. Ghita's analysis shows that the versions of a public forum in most digital environments are not conducive to dialogue as a critical tool. The research is based on an analysis of programs and extensive interviews with students.

The next chapter in this section, by Jon Igelmo Zaldívar and Patricia Quiroga Uceda, is entitled "The Ideas of Ivan Illich in the History of Homeschooling/Unschooling Movement and his Intellectual Relationship with John Holt." The authors analyse how the ideas from *Deschooling Society* ended up providing the theoretical foundation for an anti-schooling movement through the mediation of John Holt's work. The authors explore three main frames of reference contextualizing the early reception of the ideas expounded in *Deschooling Society*: people's ideas related to technological developments, radical ideas related to the expansion of educational institutions, and organized parents rejecting schooling. After setting the stage, Igelmo Zaldívar and Quiroga trace Illich's intellectual influence on Holt, the central figure of the homeschooling/unschooling movement.

This section closes with "'The Time Has Come to Make the World Safe from Lifelong Education': John Ohliger, Ivan Illich, and Mandatory Continuing Education," by Josh Cole. The chapter examines an important yet neglected adult educator, John Ohliger, whose critique of what he called "mandatory continuing education" and its understanding as an attitude acquires new meaning in light of the close relationship between economy and education. The author analyses how Illich's thinking nourished Ohliger's analysis of adult education using a sophisticated, historically contextualized approach. This also takes the reader to the international development of adult education and its uses, which have led scholars to not only place Ohliger in this process but also to unfold current conceptions and policies on adult education.

Part 4, Freire and Illich and Indigeneity, has two chapters. The first is by philosopher and environmentalist Christopher Beeman and entitled "From *Nutrix Educat* to *Ju-jum Dakim*: A Possible Resolution for Ivan Illich's Forsaken Ritual." The chapter follows Illich into an etymological journey of *educare* and the phrase *nutrix educat* (wet nurse suckles) from Cicero, the latter being different from *docere* and *instruire*. *Educare* would mean to nourish. Beeman goes to Illich's intellectual journey to explain that the ritual of education is, in Illich's work, related to the ritual of the church. But Beeman builds an argument questioning Illich's notion of scarcity when he notes that Illich might not have thought of how abundant the world of learning is: "it extends not just into the more-than-human world, but to the relational epistemology that derives from and is understood to derive from knowing that is inseparable from a person's enacted relationship with the more-than-human." Out of his conversations with elders, Beeman comes up with the notion of *ju-jum dakim*, meaning "mother earth" or "land of ours," thereby bringing together the land with the idea of nourishment. This is placed within the context of Illich's encounters with the contradiction between a universal commitment to the public, a kind of faith and ritual, and its claimed value and the benefits coming from it, and Illich himself as a self-defined citizen of the modern West.

The second chapter in this section, "Reading *Pedagogy of the Oppressed* through the Lens of Indigenous Education: Reflections on Overlaps, Departures, and Social Developments," is by Indigenous linguist and educator Lindsay Morcom. Although Morcom acknowledges Freire's long commitment to education as a tool to dismantle oppression, she points out the limits of Freire's theory for decolonization and Indigenous education in settler colonial contexts outside of Latin America and the developing world. After exploring incongruences between Freirean and Indigenous education for conscientization and decolonization, she concludes by proposing a critical Indigenous pedagogy. Morcom sees a risk in essentializing the concept of liberation as a matter of class equality and in essentializing the processes of education and critical thought, as oppressed people and Indigenous people in particular may have other philosophies and strategies for critical education. In her view, *Pedagogy of the Oppressed* neglects the many ways in which oppression takes shape and is manifested. Morcom writes that the book treats class as a great divider, and she argues that failing to recognize the impact of colonization in the lives of Indigenous people could lead to recolonization. However, she points out Freire's concern with a program that fails to respect the world view of the people involved. She makes the case that Indigenous forms of power and knowledge are different from those of leftist (Western) understandings of political power. The questioning of the notion of progress is enlightening, as is dialogue within the Indigenous historical context. In her view, a critical Indigenous pedagogy would take into account insights from authors like Freire, while being receptive of Indigenous knowledges, norms, goals, and languages in the process of conscientization and decolonization.

Part 5, Freire in Attempts at Transformation in Asia in the Last Decades, has two chapters. The first one is "A Historical Analysis of the Application of Paulo Freire's Critical Literacy in the Design of the Rural Advancement Committee's Functional Education Curriculum in Bangladesh from 1972 to 1981," by Mohammad Abul Fateh. The author traces the literacy approaches taken by the Bangladesh Rural Advancement Committee (BRAC), an NGO that made use of Freire's method and theory in an attempt to develop human resources through education. The chapter focuses on BRAC's initiatives between 1972 and 1981, focusing on founder Dr. Fazle Hasan Abed's interpretation of Freire's adult literacy theory and his political intentionality. The author examines how BRAC emptied Freire's method of its transformative character and its empowering aim by depoliticizing it and limiting the scope of the BRAC projects to economic opportunities within the oppressive socio-economic structure supporting the rural production system. Although BRAC recognized that the landless poor were victims of exploitative social structures dominated by rural elites,

Fateh writes, it did not recognize and address the roots of poverty, corruption, and social injustice. Instead, Freire's methods and pedagogical theory were co-opted and used as a sign of the world of development.

The second chapter in this section is "The Influence and Legacy of Freire's Ideas on Adult Literary in Post–New War Timor-Leste," by historian of education Tom O'Donoghue. It traces adult literacy and Freire's influence during the period 1974–2004, when Timor-Leste (often referred as East Timor) went from being a colony of Portugal, to being colonized by Indonesia, to national independence as a post–new war society in 2004. O'Donoghue identifies the roots of the country's literacy movements as belonging to the Cuban Revolution and its literacy campaign, which, of course, predated the campaigns in Brazil and Freire's method. The author explores how education was used for many years by both the Portuguese and Indonesian administrations as an instrument of oppression generally, and especially of unique local cultures, thus ensuring segregation and subjugation. Bahasa Indonesia was the language of instruction. After independence, the Cuban-designed campaign *Yo, Si Puedo* (Yes, I can), for which the Cubans trained four hundred local tutors to work in Timor-Leste, and the use of a method called alphanumeric, based on a Freirean-style commitment to egalitarian humanism, combined with the writings of José Martí, became very successful. The language of instruction was also central; in particular, Tetum, although a multilingual approach, was difficult to implement. This unique chapter follows the various interpretations and adaptations of Freire's theory and literacy method in three historical moments – each with its own agendas – from early attempts to raise people's awareness of oppressive conditions under colonial rule, to the new intentionality in the struggle for independence, and finally as an independent nation.

The book closes with "From Theory to Practice and Back Again," by philosopher James Scott Johnston, who relies on Habermas's *Theory and Practice* (1972) and his notion of critical theory as a praxis that contains both social and political arms.[25] Johnston presents a large cross-section of the chapters in the volume to "use the opportunities provided by the respective authors to engage the dialectic of theory into practice and back again, with the goal of demonstrating how these chapters, taken together, embody the theory-practice continuum that Freire and Illich desire."[26]

NOTES

1   Connection Grant of the Social Sciences and Humanities Research Council, file no 611-2019-0427. Award holder: Prof. Rosa Bruno-Jofré (Queen's University). Co-applicants: Prof. Michael Attridge (USMC, University of Toronto), Prof. Elizabeth Smyth (University of Toronto), Prof. Jon Igelmo Zaldívar (Universidad Complutense de Madrid), and Dr. Veronica Dunne (Congregation of Our Lady of the Missions/RNDM).

2 See, for example, Pierre Dominicé and Rosika Darcy de Oliveira, *Freire, Illich, the Pedagogy of the Oppressed, the Oppression of Pedagogy*, IDAC Document #8 (Geneva, 1974); Paulo Freire, *Ivan Illich: La educación* (Buenos Aires: Galerna, 2002), 20; Paulo Freire and Ivan Illich, *La educación: Autocrítica* [Education: Self-criticism] (Buenos Aires: Ediciones Búsqueda, 1986).

3 John Baldachino, *Educing Ivan Illich: Reform, Contingency and Disestablishment* (New York: Peter Lang, 2020); Humberto Beck, *Otra modernidad es posible. El pensamiento de Iván Illich* (Mexico City: Malpaso, 2017); David Cayley, *The Rivers North of The Future: The Testament of Ivan Illich* (Toronto: Anansi, 2015); David Cayley, *Ivan Illich: An Intellectual Journey* (University Park: Pennsylvania State University Press, 2021); G. Esteva, *Repensar el Mundo con Ivan Illich* (Mexico City: La Casa del Mago, 2012); Samuel E. Ewell, *Faith Seeking Conviviality: Reflections on Ivan Illich, Christian Mission, and the Promise of Life Together* (Eugene, OR: Cascade Publications, 2019); Todd Hartch, *The Prophet of Cuernavaca: Ivan Illich and the Crisis of the West* (New York: Oxford University Press, 2015); Lee Hoinacki and Carl Mitcham, eds., *The Challenges of Ivan Illich* (Albany: SUNY Press, 2002); Jones Irwin, *Paulo Freire's Philosophy of Education: Origins, Developments, Impacts and Legacies* (London: Bloomsbury, 2012); Walter Omar Kohan, *Paulo Freire: A Philosophical Biography* (London: Bloomsbury, 2021); Peter Mayo, *Echoes from Freire for a Critically Engaged Pedagogy* (London: Bloomsbury, 2013); Raymond A. Morrow and Carlos A. Torres, *Reading Freire and Habermas: Critical Pedagogy and Transformative Social Change* (New York: Teachers College Press, 2002); J.M. Sbert, *Epimeteo, Ivan Illich y el Sendero de la Sabiduría* (Mexico City: Ediciones sin Nombre, 2009); Daniel Schugurensky, *Paulo Freire* (London: Bloomsbury, 2011); Michel Vandenbroeck, *Revisiting Paulo Freire's Pedagogy of the Oppressed Issues and Challenges in Early Childhood Education* (London: Routledge, 2020).

4 Arthur Marwick, *The Sixties: Cultural Revolution in Britain, France, Italy, and the United States, c. 1958–c. 1974* (New York: Oxford University Press, 1998).

5 Christian Smith, *The Emergence of Liberation Theology: Radical Religion and Social Movement Theory* (Chicago: University of Chicago Press, 1991), 20.

6 Ivan Illich, "The Vanishing Clergyman," *The Critic* 25 (June–July 1967), 18–25; Ivan Illich, "The Seamy Side of Charity," *America* 116, no. 21 (1967), 88–91; Ivan Illich, "Las sombras de la caridad," *CIDOC Informa* no. 67/3 (January–June 1967): 3/1–3/11. *Esprit* published a version in French entitled "envers de la charité," in March 1967, in its issue 35. See also Ivan Illich, "The Seamy Side of Charity," in *Celebration of Awareness: A Call for Institutional Revolution* (New York: Anchor Books/Doubleday, 1971).

7 We discuss this in Rosa Bruno-Jofré and Jon Igelmo Zaldívar, "The Center for Intercultural Formation, Cuernavaca, Mexico, Its Reports (1962–1967) and Illich's Critical Understanding of Mission in Latin America," *Hispania Sacra* 65, extra 2 (July–December 2013): 7–31.

8 Rosa Bruno-Jofré and Jon Igelmo Zaldívar, "Ivan Illich's Late Critique of *Deschooling Society*: 'I Was Largely Barking Up the Wrong Tree,'" *Educational Theory* 62, no. 5 (2012): 573–92.

9   According to a quotation of an oral comment made by Freire, he said, "It is gener-
    ally believed that I am the author of this strange term, conscientization, because it
    is at the core of my educational ideas. In reality, the term was created around 1964
    by a team of ISEB, among them philosophers Álvaro Pinto and Professor Guerreiro.
    When I heard this word for the first time, I immediately realized the depth of its
    meaning, because I am absolutely convinced that education, as a practice of freedom,
    is an act of knowledge, a critical approximation to reality. Since then, this word is
    part of my vocabulary, but it was Helder Câmara who was responsible for popular-
    izing it and for translating it into English and French." See Paolo Vittoria and Ana
    Maria Araujo Freire, "Dialogue on Paulo Freire," *International Journal of Education
    for Democracy* 1, no. 1 (2007): 112, https://scholarworks.iu.edu/journals/index
    .php/ried/article/view/115. The question has not been settled.
10 Marina Bandeira, "Movimento de Educaçao de Base," a report given to the Catholic
    Inter-American Cooperation Program (CICOP), Chicago, 23 February 1964, *CIF
    Reports*, vol. 3, April–December 1964. Reprinted in *CIDOC Cuadernos*, no. 38/1
    (Cuernavaca, Mexico: CIDOC, 1970), 1/12.
11 Ivan Illich, *Deschooling Society* (New York: Harper and Row, 1971), 18.
12 David Cayley, *Ivan Illich in Conversation* (Toronto: Anansi, 1992), 205–6.
13 Illich, *Deschooling Society*, xx.
14 Freire, *Ivan Illich*, 20.
15 Freire, 20. Also see Freire and Illich, *La educación*.
16 Richard Kahn and Douglas Kellner, "Paulo Freire and Ivan Illich: Technology,
    Politics and the Reconstruction of Education," *Policy Futures in Education* 5, no. 4
    (November 2007): 431–47, doi:10.2304/pfie.2007.5.4.431.
17 Michalinos Zembylas, *Affect and the Rise of Right-Wing Populism: Pedagogies for the
    Renewal of Democratic Education* (Cambridge: Cambridge University Press, 2021).
18 Zembylas, 211.
19 Boaventura de Sousa Santos, *The End of the Cognitive Empire: The Coming of Age of
    Epistemologies of the South* (Durham, NC: Duke University Press, 2018), 114.
20 De Sousa Santos, 261.
21 Ivan Illich, *Gender* (New York: Pantheon Books, 1982).
22 Walter D. Mignolo, "Sustainable Development or Sustainable Economies? Ideas
    Towards Living in Harmony and Plenitude," Socioscapes: International Journal
    of Societies, Politics and Cult 1, no. 1 (2019): 48; Ivan Illich, *Tools of Conviviality*
    (1978; London: Marion Boyars Publishers, 2001).
23 Bernard Lonergan, *Method in Theology* (New York: Searbury Press, 1972).
24 Ivan Illich, *Energy and Equity* (London: Marion Boyars Publishers, 1974); Ivan
    Illich, "Shadow Work," in *Shadow Work* (London: Marion Boyers Publishers, 1981),
    99–116; Illich, *Gender*.
25 Jürgen Habermas, *Theory and Practice*, trans. John Viertel (Boston: Beacon
    Press, 1973).
26 See the epilogue to this volume, p. 303.

PART ONE

Historical Framework

sunrise engaging all

Alan Wilkinson

1 *Pedagogy of the Oppressed* and *Deschooling Society* in the Long 1960s: A Contextualization

ROSA BRUNO-JOFRÉ AND JON IGELMO ZALDÍVAR

Contextualizing Illich and Freire in the Long 1960s

Freire's *Pedagogy of the Oppressed* and Illich's *Deschooling Society* are placed in the "long 1960s," a temporal designation coined by Arthur Marwick for a period characterized by social and cultural movements that changed the order of things from ca. 1958 to ca. 1974.[1] The end of the 1950s provided initial transformations that included demographic and economic changes, urbanization, mass communication, educational reforms, the rapid process of secularization, the civil rights protests, and processes of decolonization. The early 1970s brought an economic crisis, with post-Fordism and new market models signalling a new era.[2]

The "long 1960s" embodied a critical and transformational wave all over the world, albeit one characterized for its multi-directionality and the historicity of local and regional developments. The Cold War provided an embracing framework. It was the long decade of the Cuban Revolution and its inspirational influence in Latin America, and of the modernizing counteroffensive of the United States, with the Alliance for Progress launched in 1961 with a focus on education and the economy. For Catholics, it was the decade of the Second Vatican Council (1962–5, also known as Vatican II), which re-situated the church in light of contemporary conditions, and of the Medellín document (1968) produced by the Episcopal Conference of Latin America (Consejo Episcopal Latinoamericano, or CELAM), a reading of Vatican II influenced by liberation theology and seen through the eyes of a suffering Latin America.[3]

Two impactful critical books on education appeared amid all of this: Paulo Freire's *Pedagogy of the Oppressed*, published in English by Seabury in 1970, and Ivan Illich's *Deschooling Society*, published by Harper and Row in 1971.[4] The two authors were Catholics. Illich was an ordained priest, although he left his ministerial duties at the end of the 1960s while retaining his priesthood. On the occasion of the fiftieth anniversary of the publication of these two books, we will discuss the historical context framing their writing and their originality.

Our exploration is guided by three main questions: What were the historical characteristics of the context framing the authors' lived experience and their intellectual roots? What are the central points of their critiques? And in what ways do they differ?

Contextualizing *Deschooling Society* and Exploring Illich's Intellectual Roots

In an attempt to understand Illich's critique of schooling, we explore his intellectual background at the intersection with his life experience and how it formed his intentionality as a response to his context.[5] We also try to explain his shift from a critique of the Church as Institution to a critique of schooling as a certainty of modernity.[6]

Ivan Illich left the protective setting of the Vatican in 1951. He had graduated from the Université Gregoriana in Rome and earned a doctoral degree from the University of Salzburg, and had become an ordained priest.[7] At the Gregoriana, he was exposed to the orthodoxy of the *Magisterium Ecclesiae* – the official teaching of the church, which kept an anti-modernist position – and the intellectual framework known as neo-scholasticism.[8] At the time, Illich was also introduced to the emergent *nouvelle theologie* – which he did not embrace – and, a bit before this, to the pluralization of Thomism, both of these strands developed outside the Vatican walls.[9] Illich was familiar with phenomenology (Henri Bergson, Edmund Husserl), as is shown in his concern with the experience of lived reality in his understanding of the work with missionaries and in *Deschooling Society*; existentialism (Martin Heidegger, Karl Jaspers), as revealed in his quest for authenticity and the ontological being; and personalism, while his emphasis on the centrality of the human person and related responsibility relates his thinking to that of Emmanuel Mounier.

Jacques Maritain had a lasting presence within Illich's way of thinking.[10] Thus, he embraced Maritain's notion of an emancipatory engagement with the secular world, and Maritain introduced Illich to Thomas Aquinas's thought, which became an important frame of reference in his work, as reflected in *Deschooling Society*. Illich would pursue the line of moving beyond modernity and infusing society with the ancient ethos of the church. This explains his reluctance to identify himself with liberation theology or to link the church to any sociopolitical project. Illich's writing would be imbued, instead, with the notion of the church as the mystical body of Christ advanced by Belgium Jesuit Émile Mersch, and the vision that the life of Jesus on earth is prolonged in the church.[11]

There were important existential intersections in Illich's public and intellectual life that would influence his trajectory. One of these was his relationship with Cardinal Francis Spellman, archbishop of New York. In 1951, Spellman, whom Illich had met in Rome not long before, took Illich, who was then twenty-five years old, to his archdiocese. Soon after, Illich asked to be moved from the conservative Irish parish where he had been placed (Washington Heights) to the Incarnation Church, close to the George Washington Bridge, which ministered to Puerto Rican immigrants. As Cayley wrote, "Illich's sudden fascination with the Puerto Ricans was to shape the whole subsequent direction of his life,"[12] although it was a life of high contacts and important social and political relations.[13] Illich learned Spanish and ministered in a style that made sense to the community. As we have written elsewhere, "the experience at the Incarnation parish and his concern with cultural sensitivity was the first link in his journey that would take him to the experience in Cuernavaca."[14]

Spellman, known for his right-wing positions, connections to the CIA, and predatory sexual behaviour, protected Illich until days before his own death in 1967. The relationship is as fundamental as it is unexplainable in Illich's trajectory. In 1952, Spellman recommended Illich for an instructor position in the Faculty of Political Sciences at Fordham University; the same year, he appointed Illich as coordinator of the Hispano-American Office of the Archdiocese of New York; and in 1956, Spellman recommended that the thirty-year-old Illich be appointed vice-rector of the University of Puerto Rico and director of the Instituto de Comunicación Intercultural, also in Puerto Rico.[15] It was his experience in Puerto Rico that would define his thinking on education and schooling, and it was there that he met Everett Reimer and Leopold Kohr (precursor of the "small is beautiful" theory).[16] Reimer, a consultant to the Secretariat of Education on the Committee on Human Resources of the Commonwealth of Puerto Rico, had developed a critical view of the social function of the school.[17] Illich wrote in the introduction to *Deschooling Society*, "I owe my interest in public education to Everett Reimer. Until we first met in Puerto Rico in 1958, I had never questioned the value of extending obligatory schooling to all people."[18] A point of interest here is that, as per Illich's recounting, he and Reimer found many parallels in the problems of the church and the school.[19]

Illich had to leave his position in Puerto Rico due to his political statements. Upon his return to New York after his travels all over Latin America, he moved his attention to the creation of centres in Cuernavaca, Mexico, and in Anápolis, Brazil, in 1961, moving to Petrópolis in 1962, where he worked with Archbishop Helder Pessoa Câmara.[20] He established himself in Cuernavaca. The centres prepared missionaries until 1966 in response to John XXIII's 1961 call to religious congregations to send members to Latin America (and the Papal Volunteers for Latin America, or PAVLA, program) of 1960. These prospective missionaries were introduced to Illich's re-signification of the role of the missionary and his understanding of mission – rather than to the dictates of the Vatican. This was related to Illich's critique of the Church as It, or Institution, which he differentiated from the Church as She, as inspired by the spirit. The US Catholic hierarchy and the Vatican wanted to prepare missionaries working for the modernization of Latin America and within the Alliance for Progress. It was an ecclesiocentric approach. Instead, Illich thought that missionaries should reincarnate themselves in the local culture rather than becoming agents of their own culture, becoming like the people they were sent to adopt, with "poverty" being a central virtue.[21] He linked missionary poverty to feelings of weakness and dependency on the role of others. His was a reignocentric approach. Illich tried to construe a spiritual space with a strong emphasis on the teaching of language as well as authenticity; however, one cannot neglect to notice that there was no attention to Indigenous languages, just Spanish (Castellano), the colonial language. Illich's political manoeuvring becomes noticeable when analysing the creation of the centres. He inserted himself in the configuration of forces and ideas that were instrumental in the institutional response of the Catholic Church, in alliance with US policies, to social unrest in Latin America. It was also a reaction to the inspirational role of the Cuban Revolution in Latin America. Here, there are unanswered questions regarding his complex political relationship with the institutional US church, from which he got a great deal of cooperation and financial support to establish the centres to prepare missionaries – in particular, because we know that he wrote *The Vanishing Clergyman*, a very critical text, in Puerto Rico in 1959, although he did not publish it until 1967.[22]

Cuernavaca, the site of the centres in Mexico, was a refractive micro-cosmos, an experimental one, where powerful transformative characters interacted with a very conservative church. The centres became fluid spaces where a challenging way of making sense of reality generated a conceptual space of social positioning. A particular configuration of ideas emerged in which psychoanalysis had an important place. Illich became very close to Bishop Sergio Méndez Arceo, who had a transformative vision of the role of the church, and who started a liturgical and aesthetic *aggiornamento* before the Second Vatican Council.[23] There was also Gregorio Lemercier, prior of the Benedictine monastery of Santa Maria de la Resurrección, located near Cuernavaca, which was closed by the pope in 1967 over its use of psychoanalytic therapy. Erich Fromm, a neighbour and close friend of Illich, was a social psychoanalyst who attempted to frame Freud's discoveries in humanism by situating them as a search for criticism and uncompromising realism.[24] The preoccupation with psychoanalysis did not extend to gender issues or to questioning the patriarchal character of the Church as It, but instead focused on vocational issues and sexual concerns. Many distinguished theologians and social scientists participated in the life of the centres from very early on.[25] Although he opened space for liberation theology in the centres, Illich did not adhere to it because he believed in the spiritual role of the church.[26]

Key points in Illich's public trajectory were his decisions in 1964 to take control of the centres' reports, known as the *CIF Reports*, and to create the Centre for Intercultural Documentation (CIDOC) in 1963. These represented steps towards independence from the US church and its organizations, such as the Latin American Bureau of the National Catholic Welfare Conference, which financially supported the centres.[27] When, in 1966, CIDOC was moved from Chulavista, where CIDOC was originally placed within the Centre for Cultural Research (the centre that received missionaries to Latin America), to Rancho Tetela, it became an independent and self-sustained international intellectual hub. Illich cut ties with the Catholic hierarchy and the bureau. CIDOC was from 1966 to 1976 a point of convergence for Latin American transformative leaders and intellectuals, including Paulo Freire and writers and activists from other parts of the world.

Illich's process of radicalization in his approach to the church and missionary work reached a high point with the publication in February 1967 of "The Seamy Side of Charity," followed by "The Vanishing Clergyman" in June of the same year.[28] In the first, he made explicit his anti-imperialist position, critical of US interference in Latin America and of the alliance of the institutional Church with US policies and agendas, and the missionary project and papal volunteers. The Gospel should not, in his view, be in the service of capitalism or any other ideology. In "The Vanishing Clergyman," Illich questioned the institutional church, its bureaucracy and structure, and envisioned a future with "ordained laymen [sic]," with women kept outside the discourse. These publications led to an inspection in 1967 by the Episcopal Conference of Latin America and the conflict with the Vatican in 1968.[29] Illich had lost Spellman's protection when the cardinal died in December 1967. At this point, Illich left aside the critique of the church to critique the school as an institution of modernity.

There was a transition to *Deschooling Society* starting in 1968 with three texts on schooling published after Spellman's death. The first was "The Futility of Schooling in Latin America," published in *Saturday Review* in April 1968, which questioned the role of schools as an institutional model based on meritocracy in the movement towards "progress"; in Illich's view, this model served a modern middle class rather than the Latin American urban proletariat and landless rural masses.[30] He brought up again the question of the transplantation of people and institutions – raised in "The Seamy Side" – that left little space for creative local solutions.[31] The second text was "The School, That Old and Fat Sacred Cow: In Latin America It Opens an Abyss between Classes and Prepares an Elite and with Her, Fascism," published in August 1968 in the Mexican magazine *Siempre*.[32] In that article, Illich questioned the "liberal myth" that school was a panacea for social integration. The third text, "The School's Metamorphosis," was an address delivered at the graduation ceremony at the Universidad de Puerto Rico, Río Piedras Campus, in June 1969. The speech contains a sharp critique of schooling as a source of inequality and alienation from reality. Illich thought that the students' critique of teachers was similar to their grandparents' critique of the clergy, and he advocated for a space in which individuals could invent themselves.

Illich's writing on education marks a shift from a critique of the Church as Institution to a critique of schooling while using the church as an analogy. In the same way that he wanted to liberate faith from the mediation of the institutional church, he wanted to liberate education from schooling. The critique of schools and their function had attracted attention in the long 1960s, and it was a topic in the seminar organized by CIDOC in 1968. Social historians like Michael Katz interpreted the educational system as one that reproduced inequality and that failed to address the needs of minorities and the poor.[33] The launching of Sputnik in 1957 had moved the system to a functionalist-efficiency-oriented approach; the Cold War was also a cultural war. Paul Goodman, Jonathan Kozol, and John Holt had also denounced schooling as a source of inequality.[34]

Deschooling Society was published in Mexico in the *CIDOC Cuadernos* under the title *The Dawn of Epimethean Man and Other Essays*, a title that suggested a questioning of modernity. A publicist at Harper and Row, the book's US publisher, came up with the impactful title *Deschooling Society*, a line he found somewhere in the book. At the seminar in CIDOC and informally, Illich received comments, critiques, and suggestions from various people he mentioned, such as Paulo Freire, Peter Berger, Paul Goodman, John Holt, Joel Spring, Augusto Salazar Bondy, and others. Neither the topic nor the radical critique of education was new in the context of the long 1960s and the project to modernize Latin America steered by the Alliance for Progress. Everett Reimer's book *The School Is Dead* (1971) had a similar thesis; the author opposed compulsory schooling and advocated the separation of education from schooling. *Deschooling Society* is to an important extent the product of conversations with Reimer. What, then, is original about *Deschooling Society*?

Deschooling Society contained seven chapters: "Why We Must Disestablish Schools," "Phenomenology of School," "Ritualization of Progress," "Institutional Spectrum," "Irrational Inconsistencies, "Learning Webs," and "Rebirth of Epimethean Man." Illich brought a theological dimension to his approach to these issues. The church's long critique of modernity became one strand in his argument, as did the Thomist idea of agency and sensory experience enriched by his exposure to Freire's practices.

In *Deschooling Society*, Illich exhorted that education be liberated from schooling and from the monopoly of the state, and he denounced its semi-religious character. The analogy with his critique of the church is everywhere in the book: "The school has become the world religion of a modernized proletariat, and makes futile promises of salvation to the poor of the technological age."[35] Schooling had become an imposed necessity; following Thomas Aquinas, natural necessity was not repugnant to the will.[36] The school as an imposed necessity defined what was legitimate and what was not.[37] Educational institutions had played the role of powerful churches throughout history, serving as "repositories of society's myth, reproducing and veiling disparities."[38]

Illich's anti-statist and anti-modernist stand reveals temporal semantic layers of meaning, going back across timelines to early Christianity and neo-medievalist approaches.[39] Learning, in his view, had become a kind of merchandise or an institutional goal; the criteria for evaluation used in schools and the notion of a curriculum broken up into prefabricated blocks, were based on the myth of measurement.[40] Illich saw the disestablishment of schools as having the revolutionary potential to destroy the social order.[41] His critique of the nation state has something to do with Maritain as well. Maritain agreed with Georg Moenious that a natural political order would be deeply federalist and pluralist, respecting natural hierarchies and local power structures rather than being centralized.[42] Illich questioned the school not only as an institution, but as a societal ethos, as a cultural model that monopolized education. Thus, he asserted that it was not only education that had been schooled, but social reality as well, and that the institutionalization of values through schooling leads to a process of degradation and misery.[43] He introduced the idea that schooling leads towards the modernization of poverty through its hidden curriculum and does so along with the idea of self-perpetuating progress.

Illich's most controversial statement was that funding should be channelled to the beneficiary, in addition to his mentioning of Milton Friedman without any socio-economic consideration.[44] His alternative was grounded in the idea that people acquire most of their knowledge outside of school – schools being a place of confinement.[45] The use of educational webs offered a possible alternative within the context of an emerging counterculture and self-motivated learning; the technological revolution made this possible. One thread that runs throughout the book is the recovery of a sense of personal responsibility when teaching and learning, while questioning learning as merchandise or as an institutional goal. This is related to the Thomist idea of agency and to Illich's background in phenomenology and personalism, with some existentialist touches. "The Rebirth of the Epimethean Man" is an interesting final chapter, in spite of its apparent disconnection from the rest of the book, because it embodies Illich's conception of the modern human and questions the replacement of values – dear to traditional Catholicism – such as hope, faith, and love being replaced with expectation, planning, and charity.[46] Illich relates the ethos of consumerism to the fallacy of Prometheus.

The book exhibits a radical position. It condemns the school system and rejects any attempt at reforming the school.[47] Illich portrays the teacher as a secular priest who wears an invisible crown. The teacher, he says, pontificates as pastor, prophet, and priest, a guiding teacher and administrator of a sacred ritual.[48] Here, Illich neglects to consider negotiation, resistance, counter-hegemonic views, and localization.[49] He does not acknowledge transgressions in schooling or efforts at educational change, including experimentation in self-determination, or the development of critical consciousness. He does not envision schools as having their own social, cultural, and political contexts; he looks instead for a free encounter among those engaged in learning, just as he wants to liberate God's message from modernity. In addition, Illich's Thomism leads him to a universalist approach hovering over the social movements of the time, such as the civil rights movement, the feminist movement, and Indigenous movements, even if he makes limited references to the student movement.

So, where do we find originality in a book that has a lot in common with other books, and in particular with Everett Reimer's *The Death of the School*? Both Illich and Reimer wanted to separate schooling from the state, both wanted to stop compulsory schooling, and both embraced the web as a means to learning. Indeed, *Deschooling Society* was to an important extent the product of lengthy conversations with Reimer. However, Illich brought a theological dimension to the analysis while placing the critique as a critique of modernity and the idea of progress. He went back to the Thomist idea of agency and questioned the institutionalization of values, without engaging with a political project or vision.[50] He had critiqued the church for its involvement in imperialist projects in "The Seamy Side of Charity." With a Catholic background defined by Charles Taylor as both orthodox and iconoclast,[51] Illich's anti-state positioning was enriched by his analysis of how rules and regulations can imprison us (via the fetishization of rules); this would move Illich close to postmodernism, while making him appealing to anarchists and other critical thinkers. His concerns in *Deschooling Society* with the domination of the world market and big political powers made him appealing to those advocating alter-globalism. In his early search for the human beyond artificial limitations we can see the beauty of his thinking and the appeal of his radical words, even as we encounter his own humanity in our criticism.

In the 1990s, Illich critiqued the position he had earlier taken in *Deschooling Society*. He claimed he had been "barking up the wrong tree," and that, "much more important than the disestablishment of schools, I began to see, was the reversal of those trends that make education a pressing need rather than a gift of gratuitous leisure."[52]

Contextualizing *Pedagogy of the Oppressed* in Light of Freire's Intellectual Roots, Praxis, and Political Mediations

Paulo Freire carried out his early work in north-eastern Brazil in the 1950s and early 1960s, a time when currents of national developmentalism were dominant.[53] From 1961, these currents intersected with the Alliance for Progress, a program launched by US president John Kennedy in the midst of the Cold War and in the aftermath of the Cuban Revolution. National developmentalism, in line with import substituting industrialization and the notion of national consciousness, provided an ambiguous context for popular education centres and most popular education programs.[54] A number of intellectuals and authors engaged in actual state work, such as economist Celso Furtado, anthropologist Darcy Ribeiro, co-founder with Anísio Teixeira of the University of Brasília, and educators Anísio Teixeira and Paulo Freire; all of them converged from different directions with nationalist developmentalist principles.[55]

While Teixeira was the first coordinator of the National Institute of Educational Research, serving in that role between 1952 and 1960, and the leading force behind the 1962 National Plan of Education in the Federal Council of Education, under President João Goulart (1961–4), Freire presided over the National Commission on Popular Culture, convened in 1964 under the auspices of the Ministry of Education. The commission's mandate was to elaborate and apply a national literacy plan based on the project done in Angicos (Rio Grande do Norte).[56]

We will now trace Freire's pedagogical journey around his conception of adult education and his literacy method. His doctoral thesis, completed in 1959, "Educaçao e atualidade Brasileira" (Education and contemporary Brazil), not only shows Freire's intellectual roots, but also traces his reconstruction of the work of the previous generation of progressive educators, who happened to still be active.[57] Freire cited representatives of progressive education such as Anísio Teixeira, who fully embraced John Dewey's thought, and Fernando Azevedo and Lourenço Filho, who were close to the new education movement, as well as known thinkers linked to the developmentalist Higher Institute of Brazilian Studies (Instituto Superior de Estudos Brasileiros, ISEB), such as Alvaro Vieira Pinto and Hélio Jaguaribe.[58] Not surprisingly, Aldous Huxley and Karl Manheim were theoretical sources in his argument.[59] Dewey's *Democracy and Education* appears in the list of consulted works. The development of a critical consciousness, the relationship between education and cultural and social reality, and community involvement were central concepts.

Freire refers extensively in his thesis to his experience in the Department of Social Service of Industry between 1947 and 1957 in the Brazilian North-East, specifically in the state of Pernambuco. He talks of the way he expanded the dialogue with the community, his relationships with local families, a sense of national consciousness, and his understanding of development in relation to the consciousness of the masses. Freire's critique of schooling here is similar to the one developed by Teixeira and Azevedo, as he understands authoritarianism, verbalism, and lack of dialogue as part of "democratic inexperience"; he advocates an "ideology of development," obviously influenced by Vieira Pinto and Jaguaribe, which he sees as necessary for the progress of democratization. It is noticeable that Vieira paid particular attention to the growth of consciousness to understand the ideology of national development, which he conceived as an ongoing process.[60]

In his thesis, Freire engages with the notions of intransitive consciousness –
a lack of commitment to one's own existence – with the movement being first
towards a transitive, naive consciousness, and then a critical transitivity, characterized by depth in the interpretation of problems.[61] He was concerned with
fanatism and massification, and so relies on Aldous Huxley to confront "domestication" and massification, with mental attitudes leading to the "art of disassoci-
ating ideas"; this would generate a critical conscious position. He also draws from
Mannheim, and he would continue to do so. Mannheim was concerned with
mass mentality and the need to rediscover the educative effect of primary groups,
communal centres, health centres, etc.[62] Freire made the point that a philosophy
of education has to identify itself with the context in which it will be applied.

Those of the previous generation of Brazilian progressive educators still active in the 1960s, as we said, had become familiar with Dewey in the 1920s and
'30s. In their efforts to accommodate the modern world, these educators were
attracted by the notion of experience central to Dewey's conception of education, the role of education in social reconstruction, education and democracy,
and the social critique of the traditional school. In the context of the late 1950s,
these ideas gave rise to new meanings and conceptual constellations; there was
a movement from liberal forms of reformism to the project of nationalist developmentalism in the late 1950s and 1960s. It has been argued that developmentalism provided a fertile soil for Deweyan pragmatism, bringing to the fore the
inquisitive method as a scientific approach as a way to solve social problems,
experimentalism in schools, and the understanding of democracy as a way of
life.[63] Freire introduced new concepts and recreated others.

In his 1961 article "Escola primária para o Brasil" (Primary school for Brazil),
published in *Revista Brasileira de Estudos Pedagógicos*, Freire displayed, within
an economic developmentalist framework, central ideas that he would later
elaborate and reframe in relation to his experience with literacy in the field, in
Education as Practice of Freedom and even *Pedagogy of the Oppressed*.[64] For example, he refers to alienated societies, non-alienated authentic societies, critical
consciousness, domestication, society in transition (in particular, societies in
transition), the promotion of rationality and its relationship to democracy, the
clarification of popular consciousness, dialogue, integration over accommodation, and the clarification of the popular consciousness. Freire also made references to the need for agrarian reform and praised the Movement of Popular
Culture in Recife.[65] Furthermore, industrial and economic development, the relationship between school and community, the school as agent of social change,
and critical consciousness in the process of development are clear themes in this
important article. These were part of the developmentalist approaches of the
time embodied in the ISEB, and they were, by and large, in line with the ideas of
educational change espoused by Anísio Teixeira, Fernando Azevedo, and others
who continued to disseminate interpretations of Dewey's thought.[66]

There are features in the article and the article's bibliography that show the influence of Emmanuel Mounier's personalism, which was in the air among the Latin American Catholics of the time. One example is personhood, involving the free adoption of a set of values and communion with others, and the move away from an egotistic, inauthentic life. Mounier questioned the dehumanizing tendencies of communism and capitalism.[67] The influence of existentialism via Karl Jaspers is also evident (Vieira Pinto had translated Jaspers's work published by the ISEB).[68]

Freire, like any thinker, had started to work out a composite of ideas while drawing from his context. This context was rather confusing, given the tensions between socialist tendencies, social movements, processes of radicalization, and national developmentalism as a political model partly linked to the rural oligarchy.[69] The peasant movement in the North-East had become radicalized through the peasant leagues, while the Brazilian Communist Party supported developmentalism, as did the Catholic Church, although there was a rapid process of radicalization among the Catholic youth.[70]

Thus, the Movement of Popular Culture in Recife (a name modelled after the French movement Peuple et culture, or People and Culture) was initiated by the city's newly elected socialist mayor, Miguel Arraes (who served from 1960 to 1963), and by Professor Germano Coelho.[71] It was a project of communitarian popular education carried out by university students, artists, and intellectuals, and it aimed to spread literacy and basic education among the masses, thereby forming a political and social consciousness in preparation for political participation.[72] Professor Coelho, as quoted by Gaspar, said, "The Popular Culture Movement was born out of the misery of the people of Recife. From its mutilated landscape. From its mangroves covered with 'mocambos' (shacks built on stilts). From the mud of the hills and swamps, where illiteracy, unemployment, sickness and hunger grow."[73]

Within this confusing context, a number of popular education and literacy projects developed, by and large sponsored either by the government or by the Catholic Church, whose conservative sectors were alarmed by the convergence of Christianity and Marxism.[74]

After the success of the radio schools in the Archdiocese of Natal, Rio Grande do Norte's capital, which had provided a means to introduce Catholic ideology to young people and adults, in 1961, the National Conference of Brazilian Bishops – which had created the National Association of Catholic Radio Stations and aimed to expand that network – sponsored the creation of the Grassroots Education Movement (Movimento de Educaçao de Base, MEB) with financial help from the government.[75] MEB, at this point having assumed a developmentalist line, would take literacy programs and improvements to the rural population and provide literacy training so as to give people the actual right to vote; this was initially an attempt to reduce the influence of rural oligarchies and of the Left. MEB concentrated its efforts in the North, the North-East, and the Central-West region of Brazil, where the illiteracy rate reached 70 per cent.[76] The point here is that MEB became radicalized, grew in non-diocesan dependency, weakened the clerical oversight of the program, and got involved in unionization, and its literacy work was guided by the concept of "transformative action," which was further modified by the adoption of Freire's literacy method early in 1963.[77] As Elias said, Freire's literacy method contained the seeds of revolt, although that might not have been his objective.[78] Thus, the participants in his method thought about the structural causes of their poverty and ignorance, and became aware (conscious) of their situation within the system; the literary workers/facilitators did not attempt to integrate the participants in the existing social matrix. Developments among Catholics in Brazil favoured this approach. Already in 1960 ideas about grassroots Christian communities were spreading, and people had gathered to form such communities; the parishes would become networks of small groups of twenty to thirty people each.

The 1961 MEB annual report refers to "the integral development of the Brazilian people, taking into account the full dimensions of man [sic] and using all the authentic processes of conscientizaçao."[79] An article by Mariana Bandeira from MEB published in the CIF Reports refers to the use and meaning of the term "conscientization," which describes when a person is able to account for herself as a human being and for her problems, duties, and rights, including the right to fight for a just solution to her problems.[80]

In the midst of political wrangling, there were certain historical paradoxes, like Freire's literacy campaign in Angicos that took place over forty days in early 1963; Freire and his team were invited to undertake this campaign by the right-wing governor of Rio Grande do Norte, Aluisio Alves, and were financed by the Agency for International Development within the framework of the Alliance for Progress.[81]

The first forty hours of the literacy experience started in February and March 1963 with 380 adults in Angicos, a poor municipality with 9,540 inhabitants working in the local cotton fields or salt flats; while the process went on, the coordinators continued with their formation of the cultural circles in which participants could reflect on their practice. Many participants had to return to the field, while 150 adults completed the course, 135 of whom had been considered literate.[82] The New York Times published an article in June 1963 praising the achievement of literacy in forty hours in Angicos. It framed the successful experiment within the programs of the Alliance for Progress.[83]

The analysis of the experience was published by Freire in Revista de Cultura de la Universidad de Recife, under the title "Conscientização e alfabetizaçao – Uma nova visão do processo" (Conscientization and Literacy – A New Vision of the Process), in 1963;[84] other essays were included in the same issue describing the experience and the theoretical foundations of "Freire's system."[85] Freire wrote that human beings are not only inserted in reality, but they are with reality as relational and temporal historical beings, as they are able to distinguish "different existential orbits."[86] A key concept in the paper is integration, which Freire considers superior to accommodation; this is in line with his idea of being with the world, with reality, and the process of creating and recreating themselves that humans go through. He argues that integration is fundamental in the movement from a closed to an open society, a transition that he characterizes as a play of contradictions that should lead to something new; this implies moving away from a magical comprehension of reality. Freire also made clear an understanding that he would develop further in *Pedagogy of the Oppressed*: subversion is a concept that should be applied not only to those who don't have privileges and claim justice, but also to those who try to keep those privileges. This also pertains to external forces, and he is very critical here of the Alliance for Progress – in his words, a product of the struggle for world hegemony. He details the phases of the method used in Angicos that had as a background the distinction between the world of culture and the world of nature.

In contrast with Dewey's theory of human nature, which holds that human beings are continuous with the life process of other species ("human beings are more than non-human animals, but they do not cease being animals"),[87] Freire talks of a discontinuity inspired by Catholic thinking at the time. The discontinuity and differentiation of humans from the natural world, and the implicit anthropocentrism of such a position, are problematic in current thought. Furthermore, in Freire's work, human nature tends to be pure becoming, while in Dewey's, the ideal is to have both impulse – precariousness – and stability – habit.[88] The ontological vocation for Freire would be to be more than this, as humans discern, appropriate, and transcend their immediate world.[89] Reason is at the centre, as is personhood. Thus, with the foundation mentioned above, and from Freire's article in *Revista de Cultura de la Universidad de Recife*, in his view, humans would critically discover themselves as creators of the world of culture. This would be achieved by (a) studying the universal vocabulary of the group learning to read and write; (b) selecting generative words (based on the phonetic richness and the relation to local reality); (c) creating existential situations; (d) creating sheets with information for coordinators to use; and (e) registering phonemes deriving from generative words.[90]

The Freirean conception of adult education, the Popular Culture Movement to which Freire belonged, and the practice of MEB led to strategies of change from below, generating eventually an epistemological, discursive, and political rupture in the way literacy and education were conceived and understood. Freire was appointed by Minister of Education Paulo de Tarso to serve as president of the Comissão Nacional de Cultura Popular (National Commission of Popular Culture) within the Ministry of Education and Culture. This commission was in charge of preparing a national literacy plan (Decree 53,465/64).[91]

The military coup of April 1964 ended the project. Freire went to prison, then to Bolivia for a brief time, and then to Chile, where he stayed from November 1964 to April 1969, when he moved to a temporary position at Harvard University. During his time in Chile, Freire revised previous notes written while in prison and published them in book form in 1967 as *Educaçao como prática da liberdade* (Education as the practice of freedom).[92] The book returns to some of the themes discussed in his previous work, such as the movement towards an open society and the relevance of dialogue. It includes a critique of sectarianism that he would develop later in *Pedagogy of the Oppressed* and a reliance on Mannheim and his conception of fundamental democratization. Freire critiques massification in light of the need for economic development and avoids the false dilemma of humanism versus technology; his point of reference is Jacques Maritain. Freire makes special reference to the ISEB, known for its developmentalist positioning; in his words, the ISEB was "a moment in the awakening of the national conscience that was extended to the University of Brasilia."[93] Freire is referring here to a political consciousness leading to rational democratic participation, rather than massification in the sense described by Ortega y Gasset.[94] The chapter on education and conscientization goes back to his previous considerations on the magic conscience and on the movement towards a critical conscience (close to the notion of awareness), which he now considers in light of the phases of the literacy method; the book closes with an illustrated analysis of the method's application using elements of the cultural, social, and political environments of the students/participants in the curriculum. The bibliography includes authors consulted before in the course of his thesis and/ or articles, such as Alvaro Viera Pinto, Fernando Azevedo, Anísio Teixeira, Lourenco Filho, and Karl Mannheim, but also Jacques Maritain, Emmanuel Mounier, Gilberto Freyre, and in particular Erich Fromm, among others.

David Lehmann offers an interesting observation: "To compare *Education: The Practice of Liberty* with his later *Pedagogy of the Oppressed* is to compare two books with essentially the same message but a radically different set of footnotes: suddenly, in the second book, the names of Marx, Engels, Lenin, Lukács, Marcuse, Régis Debray make their appearance."[95] Our reading finds a continuity with his previous work, but also a theological and political shift that consolidates the epistemic rupture of Freire's approach to literacy and its political dimension.

Pedagogy of the Oppressed, written in Chile in Portuguese and published in 1968, and subsequently published in Spanish that same year and again in English in 1970, cannot be understood without a larger sense of the macro-context of the second half of the 1960s in Latin America and in a world going through decolonization.[96] At the micro-contextual level, the specific radicalization that was taking place in Chile, including in sectors of the Christian Democratic Party, informed parts of Freire's work and life.

Freire arrived in Chile in November 1964 and would stay until mid-1969. Eduardo Frei Montalva became the country's first Christian Democratic president on 4 November of that year. The Chilean Christian Democrat Party was influenced by Jacques Maritain and his notion of the social function of property.[97] Freire wished to pursue a reformist developmentalist agenda with the theme "revolution in liberty," a liberal democratic version of corporatism within the context of US investment in Chile and the Alliance for Progress, but he had to contend with a rapid process of political radicalization. The results of the election help to explain these developments: Frei and the Christian Democratic Party received 56 per cent of the vote with backing from the Right – the latter aiming to defeat the socialist candidate – while the leftist Frente de Action Popular (Popular Action Front), led by the socialist Salvador Allende, obtained 39 per cent of the vote with the backing of the Communist Party.

Meanwhile, Freire started doing consultative work for the Institute for Agrarian and Livestock Development (Instituto de Desarrollo Agropecuario, INDAP), the main body dealing with agrarian reform, whose executive vice-president was Jacques Chonchol. The reforms included the expropriation of haciendas and the organization of unions and cooperatives, and there were those from the Left and rebels from the Christian Democratic Party, such as Chonchol, who wanted to go further.[98]

By 1967, the municipal elections showed an erosion of support for the Christian Democrats, a hardening of the Right, and the parties of the Left gaining ground. Not only were sectors of the Left going through a process of radicalization, but sectors of the Democratic Party were as well. In fact, Chonchol, a leading rebel in the latter party, advocated "a non-capitalist way of development"; in 1968, he was ousted from the party leadership, and in November of that year he resigned as vice-president of INDAP. This was the political setting – along with growing mobilizations of peasants and seizures of urban and rural land – in which Freire conducted the training of rural literacy workers. The rebellions and the people working with Freire pointed to the limitations of the developmentalist reformist approach, and Freire had to question his philosophical and political frames of reference.[99]

In fact, Freire's context entered into a rapid process of radicalization. John Holst makes a strong argument that Freire's experience in INDAP (Institute of Agricultural Development), where he was in direct contact with young activists, and in ICIRA (Institute for Capacitation and Research on Agrarian Reform), where he led a team of young professionals investigating the thematic universe of peasants, played a central role in his political thinking.[100]

There is certainly a qualitative political change from *Education as a Practice of Freedom* (1967) to *Pedagogy of the Oppressed*, but we can argue that he moved liberation theology concepts to his pedagogy. Gustavo Gutiérrez, who had discussed the principles for a Catholic liberation theology for some time, published his *Teología de la liberación* (A theology of liberation) in 1971 in Peru, and mentioned Freire a few times in that book.[101]

We are doing here a political reading of *Pedagogy of the Oppressed* in the context of a time when the Left badly needed a pedagogical conception, and we find that Freire provided both a critique and a practice of education with a degree of hope. His questioning of the traditional Left was a feature of the "long 1960s" and had an intellectual counterpart and various expressions – one being the radical Left, with which Freire had become familiar in Chile. The language of oppressed/oppressor, albeit binary, facilitated a broader understanding of oppression at that point, even if Freire did not address specific situations of oppression. However, this binary understanding was reflected in the notion of education for liberation or domestication,[102] and it was also dominant in the language of popular education practices in Latin America: vertical/horizontal pedagogical relations, popular wisdom/scientific knowledge, state/civil society, among many others. This dualistic thinking was related to a theology that feminist the*logians started to question in the 1970s, being concerned with its anthropocentrism and a prevailing patriarchal and hierarchical view of the sacred.[103]

Pedagogy of the Oppressed is described by Freire "as a humanistic and libertarian pedagogy," as dialogical and problem posing[104] – the opposite to a banking method. The dialogue acts as a bridge. It is a pedagogy that leads students to question their reality, including the cultural constructions, systems, and structures. As such, it has two stages: in the first, the oppressed unveils oppression and commits to its transformation through praxis; in the second, reality has been transformed, and this pedagogy ceases to belong to the oppressed and becomes a pedagogy of every human being in a process of permanent liberation.[105] A pedagogy of the oppressed leads to the discovery that both oppressed and oppressors are dehumanized; a new human being emerges when the oppressed/oppressor binary is superseded.[106] Freire makes the point that the oppressors make the oppressed the object of their humanitarianism by means of a false generosity, an instrument of dehumanization. Illich made a similar point in "The Seamy Side of Charity" in relation to the politics of the North towards the South, the former represented especially by the Alliance for Progress.[107]

Freire's pedagogy embodies a social ethics of change and problem posing is conceived as a humanist and liberating praxis. At the core is Freire's almost theological argument that humans must fight for emancipation,[108] since freedom is the ontological vocation of a human being.[109]

Key elements of Freire's pedagogy include conscientization – through which humans enter the historical process as subjects who know and act; problem posing; dialogue – the word being essential and having dimensions such as reflection and action (praxis); and interaction – dialogue cannot exist without love and humility and an intense faith in humans.[110] These elements were present in his previous work. Relying on György Lukács and Rosa Luxemburg, key figures in Western Hegelian Marxism and quite popular in Latin America, Freire writes that the world and thought are dialectically interdependent: reality does not transform itself but requires critical intervention by people.[111] The reference to Hegel in his dialectical approach is not surprising.

In his reworking of his overall political and theoretical framework, Freire incorporated again elements of existentialism and the literature that informed those around him: Marcuse, Lenin, Mao, Marx, Fromm (with whom he was familiar), Fidel Castro, Che Guevara, and Louis Althusser, among others. The text is intertwined with a language of love and praxis that characterizes liberation theology and a move to denounce in order to announce. The analysis of what Freire called the people's "thematic universe" and their "generative themes" is revisited in light of limiting situations that conceal such themes; hence, the issues are not clearly perceived, and the task cannot be authentic and critical.[112] Particularly new is the focus of the last chapter of *Pedagogy of the Oppressed*, which refers to the theory of revolutionary action and the relationship between revolutionary leaders and the masses.

While he understands radicalization as a critical process leading to liberation (efforts to transform concrete, objective reality), Freire is critical of sectarianism, fanaticism (which is irrational), and of revolutionaries becoming fanatical prisoners of certainty.[113] Furthermore, if the new regime becomes a dominant bureaucracy, the humanist dimension of the struggle is lost and we can no longer talk of liberation.[114] He seems to refer to actual internal problems among the members of the Left, and on other occasions to situations deriving from agrarian reform.[115] He saw problems emerging, he explains, because of the identification of the oppressed with the oppressor, and the oppressed not having a "consciousness of themselves as persons or as members of the oppressed class and want[ing] agrarian reform [in order] to [themselves] become oppressors."[116] He interprets this as a fear of freedom.

Freire's approach was social in line with his communitarian Catholic tradition and his existential Christianity, and not individualistic, as it has been argued. Beyond his experience in Chile, we shouldn't neglect that the "long 1960s" was a time of global dissent, with processes and happenings that questioned the social and political order across space. A new contesting ethics was discussed. Freire's *Pedagogy of the Oppressed* came from reflecting on his praxis and his time, and this explains the extension of its influence, particularly in the popular education movement.

Freire's work has been praised and also critiqued; he was construed as an iconic figure and often used as a sign.[117] The critiques tend to be built around the theoretical tenets of his pedagogy in light of our own time. They refer to a lack of articulation of his Marxist ideas within his Catholic tenets; his decontextualization and abstract language; a lack of concern with the power of the teacher (in the case of the liberatory teachers); a lack of consideration of patriarchal privilege; a lack of critique of his own roots in modernist philosophy; his dualism (missing nuances); and the limits to his understanding of the relationship of Indigenous people to the land and their spirituality.[118] Decolonial authors Walter Mignolo and Catherine Walsh write that they understood pedagogy in Freire's sense "as a methodology grounded in people's realities, subjectivities, histories, and struggles."[119] Mignolo and Walsh go on to say that "social struggles for Freire are pedagogical settings of learning, unlearning, re-learning, reflection, and action."[120] These authors, albeit while granting the current relevance of Freire's pedagogy, acknowledge critiques, for example, from Native American author Sandy Grande, who argues that Freire's theoretical grounds and assumptions, which she refers to as Marxist, anthropocentric, and Western, are in tension with Indigenous knowledge and praxis.[121] We think that the praxis itself would renew these meanings – and even create layers of meaning – and show limitations, both at the theoretical and practical levels.

What was original in Freire's work? Although there is an initial thread connecting it with Brazilian pedagogues' interpretation of Dewey's pragmatism, Freire's literacy method and the educational conceptions sustaining it generated an epistemological rupture in the political-pedagogical discourse of adult education. His own praxis and experience in Brazil and particularly in Chile, as well as his engagement with liberation theology, saw him undergo changes in his political and theoretical positioning – away from developmentalism to a poorly defined radical democracy. Overall, his positioning and his literacy method emerged from a temporalized practice, although his pedagogy kept the central elements he had developed earlier.[122] Furthermore, as Bruno-Jofré writes elsewhere, "Freire brought a new element to the political discourse of the Latin American Left: the development of political consciousness from inside the political subject, rather than externally revealed by the party. The latter was a dominant position in the Marxist Left."[123]

Conclusion

Illich's *Deschooling Society* is an indictment of schooling and its mythologized ritual, which he said originated in the process of secularization. His analysis is placed within the context of a critique of modernity (modernity as the perversion of Christianity) and a neo-Thomist framework in an eclectic combination. A main feature is the recurrent analogy with the critique of the Church as Institution. It is an Illichean critique. His claims that the myth of schooling justifies the privileges of a few and that there was no difference between those who claim heritage and those who claim their status based on a degree (higher education) go straight to the core of meritocracy. It is interesting that Michael Sandel relates the situation of populism and Trumpism in the United States to the problem of meritocratic hubris.[124]

Pedagogy of the Oppressed was inspired by a social reading of the Gospel, Freire's own pedagogical practice with the oppressed in Brazil and Chile, and, while in Chile, by his political and intellectual familiarity with Marxist intellectual strands and liberation theology. Illich was a Thomist and saw the church as a spiritual force in society, somewhat in line with an ultramodernist position: neither capitalism nor communism, but a third way, that is, the infusion of Catholic values in society. Freire's conceptions and literacy methods, being grounded in the experiential context and an understanding of structures of oppression, were influential in advancing different reforms, were sometimes deprived of their political underpinnings, and had a life of their own in the popular education movement in Latin America in the 1970s and '80s. In 1975, Freire pointed out with reference to *Deschooling Society* that Illich erred in refusing to analyse the ideological question and thus could not understand the phenomenon in its entirety; he went on to say that Illich understood the school as an institution with a demonic essence that had to be suppressed or surpassed.[125] Freire, in contrast, believed that the ideological force behind schooling as a social institution could be changed and that reform efforts could work towards such ideological change. In his view, only a radical transformation of society could lead to a radical transformation of education.

Both Illich and Freire were engaged in a search to liberate humanhood, and both pursued a liberated ontological being. Freire's praxis was distinctive and provided the historizing moment, often co-opted of its liberating – utopian – social goal.

NOTES

1   Arthur Marwick, *The Sixties: Cultural Revolution in Britain, France, Italy, and the United States, c. 1958–c. 1974* (New York: Oxford University Press, 1988).

2   Rosa Bruno-Jofré, "The 'Long 1960s' in a Global Arena of Contention: Re-defining Assumptions of the Self, Morality, Race, Gender, and Justice and Questioning Education," *Espacio, Tiempo y Educación* 6, no. 1 (2019): 5–27.

3   Gregory Baum, "Vatican Council II: A Turning Point in the Church's History," in *Vatican II: Experiences Canadiennes – Canadian Experiences*, ed. Gilles Routhier, Michael Attridge, and Catherine E. Clifford (Ottawa: Presses de l'Université d'Ottawa/University of Ottawa Press, 2011), 360–77. See also François Houtard, "L'histoire du CELAM ou l'oublie des origins," *Archives de sciences sociales des religions 31e Année* 62, no. 1 (July–September 1986): 93–105.

4   Paulo Freire, *Pedagogy of the Oppressed* (New York: Seabury, 1970); Ivan Illich, *Deschooling Society* (New York: Harper and Row, 1971).

5   Quentin Skinner, "Meaning and Understanding in the History of Ideas," *History and Theory* 8, no. 1 (1969): 3–53.

6 The issues discussed in this part of the chapter have been developed at greater
   length in Rosa Bruno-Jofré and Jon Igelmo Zaldívar, *Fifty Years Later: Situating
   Deschooling Society in Illich's Intellectual and Personal Journey* (Toronto: University
   of Toronto Press, 2022).

7 Todd Hartch, *The Prophet of Cuernavaca* (New York: Oxford University Press,
   2015), 6; David Cayley, *Ivan Illich in Conversation* (Toronto: Anansi, 1992), 100–1.
   Illich left Rome in 1951, he stated, because he did not want to be part of the papal
   bureaucracy and in light of his disagreement with the Magisterium's preoccupation with
   doctrinal issues separated from world issues. We assume that he was referring
   to *Humani Generis*, or "Of the Human Race Concerning Some False Opinions
   Threatening to Undermine the Foundations of Catholic Doctrine." See Pius XII,
   Humani Generis, Of the Human Race, Encyclical (Vatican: Holy See, 12 August
   1950), http://www.vatican.va/content/pius-xii/en/encyclicals/documents/hf_p-xii_enc
   _12081950_humani-generis.html.

8 Neo-scholasticism lasted until the Vatican II Council; it was an interpretation
   of Thomism mediated by scholastic interpretations of the sixteenth century. It
   was an Aristotelic theology that defended an objective order of divine events and
   teachings, and a speculative theology not open to the realities of history. See Jürgen
   Mettepenningen, *Nouvelle Théologie/New Theology: Inheritor of Modernism, Precursor of Vatican II* (New York: T&T Clark International, 2010); Michael Attridge,
   "From Objectivity to Subjectivity: Changes in the 19th and 20th Centuries and
   Their Impact on Post–Vatican II Theological Education," in *Catholic Education in
   the Wake of Vatican II*, ed. Rosa Bruno-Jofré and Jon Igelmo Zaldívar (Toronto:
   University of Toronto Press, 2017).

9 The starting point of this theological current is usually placed in the article written
   by Dominican Yves Congar in 1935 entitled "Déficit de la théologie." He critiqued
   a theology that has become a little more than a technical matter. See also Mettepenningen, *Nouvelle Théologie*.

10 He attended Maritain's seminar during his time in Rome in the 1940s and also
   later in the United States, and Maritain was instrumental in generating in Illich a
   lifelong interest in Thomas Aquinas.

11 This is the concept that "the historical Christ is the same as the mystical Christ."
   See Émile Mersh, S.J., "La vie historique de Jesus et sa vie mystique," *Nouvelle
   Revue Théologique* 60, no. 1 (Jan 1933): 5–20.

12 David Cayley, "Part Moon, Part Travelling Salesman, Conversations with Ivan
   Illich," *Ideas*, 21 and 28 November, and 5, 12, and 19 December 1989, Canadian
   Broadcasting Corporation, transcripts, 3.

13 In New York, he was also part of the circle involved with *Commonweal Magazine*,
   in which Jacques Maritain, Dorothy Day, Thomas Merton, and Hannah Arendt
   had published, and he built a relationship with Dorothy Dohen, editor of *Integrity*,
   a popular Catholic monthly magazine that aimed at reorienting life to Christ, although it had a rather conservative theological tone. Illich published in the latter

an article about Puerto Ricans in which he is critical of the Church as Institution and its inability to adapt culturally to the Puerto Ricans. See Ivan Illich, "Sacred Virginity," *Integrity*, October 1955, reprinted in Ivan Illich, *The Powerless Church and Other Selected Writings, 1955–1985* (University Park: Pennsylvania State University Press, 2018), 32–5; Ivan Illich, "Rehearsal for Death," *Integrity*, March 1956, reprinted in Illich, *The Powerless Church*, 4–10; Ivan Illich, "The American Parish," *Integrity*, June 1955, reprinted in Illich, *The Powerless Church*, 5–16.

14 Bruno-Jofré and Igelmo Zaldívar, *Fifty Years Later*, chap. 1.

15 In August 1957, John XXIII, following a recommendation from Spellman, made Illich *camarero secreto de su santidad*. For an analysis of the relationship with Spellman, see Bruno-Jofré and Igelmo Zaldívar, *Fifty Years Later*, chap. 1.

16 Leopold Kohr (1909–94) was the precursor of the "small is beautiful" theory that would be developed by Ernst Friedrich Schumacher. Kohr believed that the modern economy of scarcity made it impossible to set ethical parameters in commercial relations.

17 Everett Reimer (1910–98) had been an adviser to state and federal agencies and had worked for the Atomic Energy Commission. He had done some work with universities, including the Survey Research Center at the University of Michigan, the Washington Research Center of the Maxwell School, and the University of Syracuse. In 1962, he left Puerto Rico and moved to Washington to work in the office coordinating the Alliance for Progress. In 1964, Reimer went back to Puerto Rico as adviser to the secretary of education, Angel Quintero.

18 Illich, *Deschooling Society*, xix.

19 David Cayley, *The Rivers North of the Future: The Testament of Ivan Illich as Told to David Cayley*, foreword by Charles Taylor (Toronto: Anansi, 2005), 142.

20 The network of centres included the Centre for Intercultural Formation (1960–67) based at Fordham University, New York, and linked to the church, which provided funding and support; the Centre of Cultural Research (Centro de Investigaciones Culurales, CIC; 1961–66) in Cuernavaca, which was the residence for prospective missionaries; and the Centre for Intercultural Documentation (Centro Intercultural de Documentación Intercultural, CIDOC; 1963–76). Both CIC and CIDOC were based in Cuernavaca, Mexico. The CIC counterpart in Brazil, located in Anápolis (1961–62) and later in Petrópolis (from 1962), was the Centro de Formaçao Intercultural (Centre of Intercultural Formation). In 1963, CIDOC was started within CIC. In 1966, CIDOC became the only functioning centre independent of the church. See Rosa Bruno-Jofré and Jon Igelmo Zaldívar, "Monsignor Ivan Illich's Critique of the Institutional Church, 1960–1966," *Journal of Ecclesiastical History*, 67, no. 3 (July 2016): 568–86; Rosa Bruno-Jofré and Jon Igelmo Zaldívar, "The Center for Intercultural Formation, Cuernavaca, Mexico, Its Reports (1962–1967) and Illich's Critical Understanding of Mission in Latin America," *Hispania Sacra* 66, extra 2 (July–December 2014): 457–87.

21 Rosa Bruno-Jofré and Jon Igelmo Zaldívar, "Ivan Illich, the Critique of the Church as It: From a Vision of the Missionary to a Critique of Schooling," in

Catholic Education in the Wake of Vatican II, ed. Rosa Bruno-Jofré and Jon Igelmo Zaldívar (Toronto: University of Toronto Press, 2017), 135–53; "Centre for Inter-cultural Formation (CIF), 1962–63," Cuernavaca, MX, Petrópolis, BR, Fordham University, NY, Cuernavaca, ME, manuscript, Daniel Cosío Villegas Library, El Colegio de México, Inventario 2007, folder 370.1996 C 397d.

22 Ivan Illich, "The Vanishing Clergyman," *The Critic* 25 (June–July 1967): 18–25; Ivan Illich, "The Vanishing Clergyman," in *The Celebration of Awareness* (Garden City, NY: Doubleday, 1971), 57–84. We read in the note published in *The Celebration of Awareness* that Illich wrote the first version in Puerto Rico in 1959.

23 Francine du Plessix Gray, *Divine Disobedience: Profiles in Catholic Radicalism* (New York: Alfred A. Knopf, 1970), 259–60.

24 Bruno-Jofré and Igelmo Zaldívar, "Ivan Illich, the Critique." Fromm was involved with the Frankfurt School. See Lawrence J. Friedman, *The Lives of Erich Fromm: Love's Prophet* (New York: Columbia University Press, 2013), 294. He wrote the introductions to some of Illich's work.

25 From 1964, when Illich took control of the *Reports*, we find articles by Marina Bandeira (MEB in Brazil), Hélder Camara (archbishop of Olinda and Recife and outspoken representative of liberation theology), peasant leader Francisco Juliao, Mexican writer Carlos Fuentes, Berkely sociologist Ivan Vallier, Mexican writer José María Sbert, Adolfo Gilly ("Camilo Torres: His Program"), Eduardo Galeano, and Gregorio Lemercier ("A Benedictine Monastery and Psychoanalysis," repro-duced from *Le Monde*). See also Bruno-Jofré and Igelmo Zaldívar, "Monsignor Ivan Illich's Critique," 579.

26 We also notice that, in 1964 and 1965 (in 1966, he closed CIC and concentrated on CIDOC), Illich invited theologians who would become international voices of liberation theology and radical leaders to deliver seminars, such as Gustavo Gutiérrez (leading theologian of liberation), Jesuit Juan Luis Segundo (Uruguayan liberation theologian), Argentinian Jesuit Alberto Sily (social activist), and American Michael Maccoby (anthropologist and psychoanalyst), among others. They gave seminars on social change in Latin America, medical services, etc.

27 Maryknoll Father John Considine had been chosen to head the Latin American Bureau of the National Catholic Welfare Conference (United States); he was in line with the Vatican, had the ear of the pope, and was very concerned with the shortage of priests and related the situation to Protestantism and communism. He was also a member of the trustees of CIF, based at Fordham, which had a degree of control over the centres.

28 Ivan Illich, "The Seamy Side of Charity," *America* 116, no. 21 (June 1967): 88–91; Illich, "Vanishing Clergyman." Both were later included in Illich, *Celebration of Awareness*.

29 See Tarsicio Ocampo, ed., *Mexico: "Entredicho" del Vaticano a CIDOC 1966–1969*, *CIDOC Dossier*, no. 37 (Cuernavaca, MX: CIDOC, 1969). The questions are on pages 4/83.

30 Ivan Illich, "The Futility of Schooling in Latin America," *Saturday Review*, 20 April 1968, 57–59 and 74–75.

31 Illich, "Futility of Schooling."

32 Ivan Illich, "La escuela, esa vieja y gorda vaca sagrada; en América Latina abre un abismo de clases y prepara a una elite y con ella el fascismo" (Cuernavaca, MX: CIDOC, 1968), 68/95. Originally published in *SIEMPRE Mexico*, D.F., 78 (789), 7 August 1968. Translation by the authors.

33 Michael Katz, *The Irony of Early School Reform: Education in Mid-Nineteenth Century Massachusetts* (New York: Teachers College Press, 2001).

34 Various authors had denounced the educational system from the late 1950s, including Paul Goodman, who was critical of programmed instruction, and published *Growing Up Absurd: Problems of Youth in the Organized Society* (New York: Random Books, 1960); Johnathan Kozol, who received the National Book Award for *Death at an Early Age: The Destruction of the Hearts and Minds of Negro Children in the Boston Public Schools* (New York: Bantam Books, 1967); and John Holt, proponent of homeschooling, who published *How Children Fail* in 1964 (New York: Dell Publishing).

35 Illich, *Deschooling Society*, 10.

36 St. Thomas Aquinas, *The Summa Theologica* (New York: Benziger Bros., 1947 ed.), translated by Fathers of the English Dominican Province, "Part I, Question 82," https://www.ccel.org/a/aquinas/summa/home.html.

37 Illich, *Deschooling Society*, 8.

38 Illich, 37–8.

39 Reinhart Koselleck, *The Practice of Conceptual History* (Stanford, CA: Stanford University Press, 2002).

40 Illich, *Deschooling Society*, 40–1.

41 Illich, 27.

42 James Chappel, *Catholic Modern: The Challenge of Totalitarianism and the Remaking of the Church* (Cambridge, MA: Harvard University Press, 2018), 36. It was a project of federalist anti-capitalism and an anti-modern form of politics; Gregory Munro, "The Holy Roman Empire in German Roman Catholic Thought, 1929–33: Georg Moenius' Revival of Reichsideologie," *Journal of Religious History*, no. 17 (1993): 439–64.

43 Illich, *Deschooling Society*, 2.

44 Illich, 6.

45 Illich, 18.

46 Illich, 105 and following.

47 Some authors relying on statements and writing from Illich later wrote that he did not suggest the complete elimination of schooling and therefore consider this as a misinterpretation. See, for example, Patricia Inman, "An Intellectual Biography of Ivan Illich" (PhD diss., Northern Illinois University, 1999). We are here discussing *Deschooling Society*.

48   Illich, *Deschooling Society*, 31.

49   Rosa Bruno-Jofré, "Problematizing Educationalization," in *Educationalization and Its Complexities: Religion, Politics, and Technology*, ed. Rosa Bruno-Jofré (Toronto: University of Toronto Press, 2019), 3–26, in particular 7.

50   See the introduction to Bruno-Jofré and Igelmo Zaldívar, *Fifty Years Later*.

51   Charles Taylor, *A Secular Age* (Cambridge, MA: Belknap Press of Harvard University Press, 2007), 737.

52   Ivan Illich, "Foreword," in *Deschooling Our Lives*, ed. Matt Hern (Philadelphia: New Society Publishers, 1996), viii.

53   The Freire component of this chapter was previously published in Spanish in Rosa Bruno-Jofré, "Paulo Freire y su Trayectoria Pedagógica Temprana," *Enfoques Educacionales*, Universidad de Chile, 18, no. 2 (2021): 101–19, https://doi.org /10.5354/2735-7279.2021.65395.

54   Roberto Leher and Paolo Vittoria, "Social Movements and Critical Pedagogy in Brazil: From the Origins of Popular Education to the Proposal of a Permanent Forum," *Journal for Critical Education Policy Studies* 13, no. 3 (2015): 145–62.

55   Lincoln de Araújo Santos, "A alternativa para o progresso: O nacionalismo-desenvolvimentista, seus intelectuais e o planejamento educacional nos anos 1960 no Brasil," *Revista Brasileira De História Da Educação* 19, no. 49 (2019): 3–18, https://doi.org/10.4025/rbhe.v19.2019.e057. Thus, Furtado, later active at CEPAL, Darcy Ribeiro, and Anísio Teixeira worked through the governments of Juscelino Kubitschek (1902–1976, president from 1956 to 1961), Janio Quadros (1917–1992, president from 31 January to 25 August 1961), and João Goulart (1918–1976, president from 1961 to 1964), and served in projects attempting to strengthen the internal economy, investments in science and technology, and universalization of education. See de Araújo Santos, "A alternativa para o progresso," 11.

56   De Araújo Santos, "A alternativa para o progresso." We will not delve into the complex political alliances and the Brazilian Communist Party strategy to support developmentalist projects as a stage. Suffice it to say that a nationalistic approach to developmentalism was quite dominant.

57   Freire, "Educaçao e atualidade Brasileira": this is the thesis he submitted for a competition for the professorship in history and philosophy of education in the School of Arts (Bellas Artes) in Recife in 1959, but he did not win.

58   Anísio Teixeira, *A educaçao e a crise brasileira* (São Paulo: Editora Nacional, 1956); Fernando de Azevedo, Afranio Peixoto, Doria Sampaio, Anísio Teixeira, et al., "O manifesto dos pioneiros da educação nova," *Revista Brasileira de Estudos Pedagógicos. Brasília* 65, no. 150 (May–August 1984): 407–25 (this is the 1932 manifesto accessed through Ibict Anísio Teixeira Virtual Library); Hélio Juaribe, *Condições institucionais do desenvolvimento* (Rio de Janeiro: ISEB, 1957); Fernando Azevedo, *A educaçao entre dois mundos*, 2nd ed. (São Paulo: Melhoramentos, 1958); and Donald Roderick Gaylord, "The Instituto Superior de Estudos Brasileiros (ISEB) and Developmental Nationalism in Brazil, 1955–1964" (PhD

diss., University of Tulane, 1991). This doctoral thesis by Gaylord shows the US vision of the ISEB.

59   Aldous Huxley, *El fin y los medios*, 2nd ed. (Buenos Aires: Editorial Sudamericana, 1944). This is the version cited by Freire. The English version was published as *Ends and Means* in 1937 by Chatto and Windus.

60   Alvaro Vieira Pinto, *Ideologia e desenvolvimento nacional*, 4th ed. (Rio de Janeiro: Ministério da Educaçao e Cultura, Instituto Superior de Estudos Brasileiros, Textos Brasileiros de Filosofia, 2, 1960), 19, 22. As Freire wrote in the thesis, the problems of naive consciousness and critical consciousness were debated by Vieira Pinto, Guerreiro Ramos, and Roland Corbisier.

61   Freire, "Educaçao e atualidade Brasileira," 30.

62   Karl Mannheim, *Diagnostico de nuestro tiempo*, 2nd ed. (Mexico: Fondo de Cultura Económica, 1946). This is the version used by Freire.

63   Ana Waleska, P.C. Mendonça, and Libania Nacif Xavier et al., "Pragmatism and Developmentalism in Brazilian Educational Thought in the 1950s/1960," *Studies in Philosophy and Education* 24 (2005): 471–98, doi:10.1007/s11217-005-1861-8.

64   Paulo Freire, "Escola primária para o Brasil" [Primary school for Brazil], *Revista Brasileira de Estudos Pedagógicos* (Rio de Janeiro, INEP-MEC) 35, no. 82 (April–June 1961): 15–33. Reproduced in *Revista Brasileira de Estudos Pedagógicos* 86, no. 212 (2005): 95–107.

65   Freire, "Escola primária."

66   Marcus Vinicius Da Cunha and Débora Cristina Cargia, "Pragmatism in Brazil: John Dewey and Education," in *Pragmatism in the Americas*, ed. Gregory Fernando Pappas (New York: Fordham University Press, 2011), 40–52; Waleska et al., "Pragmatism and Developmentalism in Brazilian Educational Thought."

67   Emmanuel Mounier, *Personalism* (Notre Dame, IN: University of Notre Dame Press, 1952).

68   Emmanuel Mounier and Erik Blow, *Existentialist Philosophies: An Introduction* (London: Rockcliff, 1948); Karl Jaspers, *Razão e anti-razão em nosso tempo*, trans. Alvaro Vieira Pinto (Rio de Janeiro: ISEB, 1958).

69   Leher and Vittoria, "Social Movements and Critical Pedagogy in Brazil," 145–62.

70   The peasant leagues gathered more than fifty thousand participants, mainly in the states of Pernambuco and Paraiba, with two of the best-known leaders being Francisco Juliao, founder of the Socialist Party, and communist José de Prazeres. For the political process, see Leher and Vittoria, "Social Movements and Critical Pedagogy in Brazil," 146.

71   Lucía Gaspar, "Popular Culture Movement (MCP)," Pesquisa Escolar Online, Joaquim Nabuco Foundation, Recife, last modified 7 March 2020, https://pesquisaescolar.fundaj.gov.br/en/artigo/popular-cultura-movement-mcp.

72   Germano Coelho, cited by Gaspar, "Popular Culture Movement." The movement opened a space for the arts, contributing to the development of a critical consciousness.

73 Gaspar, "Popular Culture Movement."
74 Michael Löwy characterized this convergence as one of "selected affinity," taking place in the Catholic University Youth and Catholic Student Youth groups, and, in particular, within Popular Action, which was a separated branch of the Catholic University Youth that brought Marxist-inspired concepts to the MEB. See Michael Löwy and Claudia Pompan, "Marxism and Christianity in Latin America," *Latin American Perspectives* 20, no. 4 (1993): 32; Andrew Dawson, "A Very Brazilian Experiment: The Base Education Movement, 1961–1967," *History of Education* 31, no. 2 (2002): 185–94, doi:10.1080/00467600110109276.
75 Marlúcia Menezes de Paiva, "A arquidiocese de Natal e as escolas radiofônicas (Rio Grande do Norte, Brasil)," *Revista Iberoamericana de Educación* 75 (2017): 133–46.
76 Dawson, "A Very Brazilian Experiment"; Kelly Ludkiewicz, "De la cultura popular a la transformacion social: Juventud estudiantil y movimientos de base en Brazil en los anos 1960," in *Globalizing the Student Rebellion in the Long '68*, ed. Andrés Payà Rico, José Luis Hernández Huerta, Antonella Cagnolati et al. (Salamanca: FahrenHouse, 2018), 15–22; Emanuel de Kadt, *Catholic Radicals in Brazil* (London: Oxford University Press, 1970).
77 Dawson, "A Very Brazilian Experiment," 187.
78 John L. Elias, "The Paulo Freire Method: A Critical Evaluation," *McGill Journal of Education/Revue des Sciences de l'education* 10, no. 2 (1975): 207–17, https://mje .mcgill.ca/article/view/7044.
79 De Kadt, *Catholic Radicals in Brazil*, 154.
80 Marina Bandeira, "Movimento de Educaçao de Base," a report given to the Catholic Inter-American Cooperation Program, Chicago, 23 February 1964. *CIF Reports*, no. 3 (April–December 1964): 1/12. Reprinted in *CIDOC Cuadernos*, no. 38 (Cuernavaca, Mexico: CIDOC, 1970).
81 As per the chronology prepared by Gadotti, on 3 December 1962, the agreement was signed by Freire, who was at the time director of the University of Recife's Cultural Extension Service (SEC), the Ministry of Education, the SUDENE (the Superintendencia do Desenvolvimento de Nordeste, or Superintendence of Northeast Development), and the State of Rio Grande do Norte and USAID (United States Agency for International Development), "within the purpose of the Alliance for Progress." David Lehmann wrote that the literacy project in Angicos was financed by an agreement between the state government of Rio Grande do Norte and USAID as part of a strategy to bypass SUDENE, presided over by Celso Furtado. See David Lehmann, *Democracy and Development in Latin America: Economics, Politics and Religion in the Post-war Period* (Oxford: Polity Press, 1990), 97.
82 Juan de Onís, "Brazil Conducts a Literacy Drive. Project Supported by U.S. Gains in Northeast," *New York Times*, 2 June 1963, 18. Gadotti indicated that the experience was also published in *Time Magazine*, the *Herald Tribune*, the *Sunday Times*, the Associated Press, and *Le Monde*. See Moacir Gadotti, "50 Years of Angicos and

of the National Literacy Program, Chronology," angicos50anos.paulofreire.org/en/cronologia. See also Carlos Alberto Torres, "Fifty Years After Angicos: Paulo Freire, Popular Education and the Struggle for a Better World that Is Possible," *Revista Lusófona de Educaçao*, no. 24 (2013): 15–34, https://www.redalyc.org/articulo.oa?id=34929705002.

83   De Onís, "Brazil Conducts a Literacy Drive."

84   Paulo Freire, "Conscientiçaçao e alfabetização – Uma nova visão do processo, estudos universitários," *Revista de Cultura da Universidade do Recife*, no. 4 (April–June 1963): 5–25.

85   Jarbas Maciel, "A fundamentaçao teórica do sistema Paulo Freire," *Revista de Cultura da Universidade do Recife*, no. 4 (April–June 1963): 25–60; Jomard Muniz de Britto, "Educaçao e unificaçao da cultura, estudos universitários," *Revista de Cultura da Universidade do Recife*, no. 4 (April–June 1963): 61–70; Aurenice Cardoso, "Conscientizaçao e alfabetizaçao – Uma visão prática do sistema Paulo Freire," *Revista de Cultura da Universidade do Recife*, no. 4 (April–June 1973): 71–80.

86   Freire, "Conscientização e alfabetizaçao."

87   Fred Harris, "Human Nature as Continuous or Discontinuous with Nature: A Comparison and Contrast of Dewey's and Freire's Philosophies of Human Nature and Education (PhD diss., University of Manitoba, 2009), 294–5.

88   Harris, 295.

89   Harris, 276.

90   Freire, "Conscientização and alfabetizaçao."

91   Rodrigo Lima Ribeiro Gomes, "A trajetória inicial de Paulo Freire: Do desenvolvimento e das tensões do seu método de alfabetizaçao de adultos (1958–1967)," *Movimento-Revista de Educação* 4, no. 7 (2017): 33–63. Catholic students from Popular Action linked to the national Union of Students exerted pressure to adopt the Freire method as part of a mobilization aimed at adult literacy.

92   Paulo Freire, *Educação como prática da liberdade* (Rio de Janeiro: Paz e Terra, 1967).

93   Freire, 98.

94   José Ortega y Gasset, *La rebelión de las masas* (Madrid: Editorial Alianza, 2005).

95   Lehmann, *Democracy and Development in Latin America*, 100.

96   The Medellín document was produced by CELAM in Medellín, Colombia, in 1968. It was influenced by liberation theology and took a clear stance in favour of the preferential option for the poor and denounced forms of oppression.

97   Lehmann, *Democracy and Development in Latin America*, 105.

98   Simon Collier and William F. Sater, *A History of Chile 1808–2002*, 2nd ed. (Cambridge: Cambridge University Press, 2004), 314.

99   At that point, life was framed by a less formal style and by the presence of the international social and cultural trends of the 1960s. New artistic expressions such as protest songs and a socially committed film industry developed. In 1967 and 1968, major universities in Santiago and Valparaiso went through considerable

upheaval, while the well-known right-wing intellectual Jaime Guzmán, rooted in Catholic integralism, took control of the student federation at the Catholic University. See Collier and Sater, *A History of Chile*, 322.

100 John Holst, "Paulo Freire in Chile, 1964–1969: *Pedagogy of the Oppressed* in its Sociopolitical Economic Context," *Harvard Educational Review* 76, no. 2 (Summer 2006): 243–70.

101 Gustavo Gutiérrez, *A Theology of Liberation* (New York: Orbis, 1973). The experimental work of Paulo Freire and his *Pedagogy of the Oppressed* together are characterized by Gutiérrez as "one of the most creative and fruitful efforts" (91).

102 Paulo Freire, "Education: Domestication or Liberation?" *Prospects* 2, no. 2 (Summer 1972): 173–81.

103 Joan Wolski Coon, ed., *Women's Spirituality: Resources for Christian Development* (New York: Paulist Press, 1986); Barbara Fiand, *Living the Vision: Religious Vows in an Age of Change* (New York: Crossroad Publication Company, 1990); Diarmuid O'Murchu, *Poverty, Celibacy and Obedience: A Radical Option for Life* (New York: Crossroad Publishing Company, 1999).

104 Paulo Freire, *Pedagogy of the Oppressed* (New York: Continuum 1983), 40.

105 Freire, 40.

106 Freire, 33.

107 Ivan Illich, "The Seamy Side of Charity," in Ivan D. Illich, *Celebration of Awareness: A Call for Institutional Revolution* (New York: Doubleday, 1971), 39–56.

108 Freire, *Pedagogy of the Oppressed*, 74.

109 Freire, 21.

110 Freire, 75.

111 Freire, 39.

112 Freire, 86 and 89. Freire also wrote, in Chile, *Extension or Communication?* See Paulo Freire, *Extensión o comunicación? La concientización en el medio rural* (Santiago, CL: ICIRA, 1969). This is a text in which he reflected on his rural practice. He also wrote in Chile some of the chapters compiled in Paulo Freire, *The Politics of Education: Culture, Power and Liberation* (New York: Bergin and Garvey, 1985).

113 Freire, *Pedagogy of the Oppressed*, 21.

114 Freire, 43.

115 As with any agrarian reform, its outcome in Chile was complex; thus, for example, the *socios* of the *asentamientos* almost "became a privileged class." See Collier and Sater, *A History of Chile*, 314.

116 Freire, *Pedagogy of the Oppressed*, 30.

117 A good analysis can be found in John Dale and Emery J. Hyslop-Margison, *Paulo Freire: Teaching for Freedom and Transformation* (Dordrecht: Springer Netherlands, 2010).

118 Kathleen Weiler, "Myths of Paulo Freire," *Educational Theory* 46, no. 3 (Summer 1996): 353–71; Paul Taylor, *The Texts of Paulo Freire* (New York: Open University

Press, 1993); John Elias, *Paulo Freire: Pedagogy of Revolution* (Melbourne, FL: Krieger Publishing Company, 1994); Jennifer Gore, *The Struggle for Pedagogies* (New York: Routledge, 1993). Daniel Schugurensky provides a concise and well-balanced account of critiques in relation to the reception and influence of Freire's work. See Daniel Schugurensky, *Paulo Freire* (London: Bloomsbury, 2019).

119   Walter Mignolo and Catherine Walsh, *On Decoloniality: Concepts, Analytics, and Praxis* (Durham, NC: Duke University Press, 2018), 88.

120   Mignolo and Walsh, 88.

121   Mignolo and Walsh, 89. Mignolo and Walsh also mention Maori anthropologist Linda Tuhiwai Smith, who argues that, quite often, paradigms deriving from Freirean approaches have obscured or negated the approaches of feminist theorists of colour, ethnic minorities, and Indigenous peoples. See Mignolo and Walsh, 89.

122   Rosa Bruno-Jofré, "Popular Education in Latin America in the 1970s and 1980s: Mapping its Political and Pedagogical Meanings," *Bildungsgeschichte. International Journal for the Historiography of Education* (successor of *Zeitschrift für pädagogische Historiographie*), no. 1 (2011): 23–39.

123   Bruno-Jofré, "Popular Education in Latin America." See also Rosa Bruno-Jofré, "Localizing Dewey's Notions of Democracy and Education: A Journey Across Configurations in Latin America," *Journal of the History of Ideas* 80, no. 3 (July 2019): 433–53.

124   Michael J. Sandel, *The Tyranny of Merit: What's Become of the Common Good?* (New York: Farrar, Straus and Giroux, 2020).

125   Paulo Freire and Ivan Illich, *La educación autocrítica* [Education: Self-criticism] (Buenos Aires: Ediciones Búsqueda, 1986).

PART TWO

Theological Intersections in Freire's Work and Their Impact on Catholicism

sectoral vision presents

Alan Wilkinson

2 The Reception of Paulo Freire at the Second Episcopal Conference of Latin America in 1968

MICHAEL ATTRIDGE

Introduction: Freire's Reception at CELAM II

The Second Episcopal Conference of Latin America (CELAM II) in 1968 was without a doubt the most important event for the Roman Catholic Church in Latin America in the 1960s. Its purpose was to guide the church in that region following the monumental changes that took place at the Second Vatican Council (1962–5) several years earlier. The idea for CELAM II originated in 1965 during the council's last session. At that time Pope Paul VI gathered the Latin American bishops to celebrate the tenth anniversary of the founding of the conference and asked them to reflect on the needs of the church in that region.[1] From this, Bishop Manuel Larraín of Talca, Chile, then president of CELAM, came up with the idea of a second meeting to consider the needs of the Latin American church in the light of Vatican II. The event took place three years later, from August 24 to September 6 1968 in Medellín, Colombia, and was entitled "The Church in the Present-Day Transformation of Latin America in the Light of the Council." Six preparatory meetings were held between June 1966 and August 1968 in six different cities in Ecuador, Argentina, Colombia, and Brazil.[2] At Medellín, 146 Latin American bishops participated, almost 25 per cent of the more than 600 at the time, in addition to religious women and men as well as laypeople.[3] Medellín was truly a landmark gathering. According to Latin American historian José Oscar Beozzo, "no other continent had an event comparable to Medellín."[4] It provided substance to such concepts as "the church of the poor, and a church committed to the liberation and full flourishing of the needy and abandoned." This new way of doing theology and of renewing church life would "become a major contribution of the Latin American church to the universal church."[5]

As the plans for Medellín were underway in the mid- to late 1960s, there was another force moving through Latin America, namely, the work of Brazilian educator Paulo Freire. Freire was born in Recife, Brazil, in 1921.[6] Despite his family suffering from financial hardship, he pursued studies in law and education, eventually obtaining a leadership position in education within the Brazilian government in the 1950s. In 1959 he completed his PhD and became a professor of history and philosophy of education at the University of Recife. At the same time, he was busy studying education among the poor and presenting his findings at national education conferences throughout the country. His work soon became known and appreciated by many progressive-minded Brazilians, including among Catholic clergy. When a military coup overthrew the Brazilian government in 1964, Freire was imprisoned. He and his family later fled to Bolivia, where they remained briefly before settling in Santiago, Chile. Among other things, Brazilian conservatives had become worried about Freire's literacy program because of its political and ideological implications; also, only those who were literate were allowed to vote.[7] As Chilean theologian Sergio Torres said, "the Brazilian military thought they were stomping things out. In reality they were only spreading it further – outside of Brazil."[8] Forcing Freire into exile meant that his work continued to spread across Latin America in the 1960s and beyond, especially through the publication of his first book, *Education: The Practice of Freedom* (1967), which he began during his imprisonment.[9] His second book, *Pedagogy of the Oppressed*, was published in 1968 in Spanish and translated into English in 1970.[10] *Pedagogy of the Oppressed* is the book that would bring him worldwide acclaim, influence many, and uniquely define him.[11] Today, Freire is known throughout the world and his methods have been taught on every continent. In 2018, the UNESCO Institute for Lifelong Learning co-organized a three-day congress focused on his work. According to the institute's website, Freire laid the foundations for a "new perspective on education and has shaped educators around the world."[12]

From the above description of these two major occurrences in Latin America in the 1960s, a question arises: Did Paulo Freire contribute to the conference in Medellín? By 1968 he was well known throughout Latin America and to some extent beyond. He was born and raised a Catholic and remained a person of faith, even if he was cautious of "religiosity" and had "grave concerns about the Church" and the lifestyle of many priests.[13] Without a doubt, at the heart of his educational work was a concern for human freedom and liberation. His 1967 book *Education, the Practice of Freedom* was noticed in Catholic circles, and he soon became closely associated with the emerging movement of liberation theology.[14] So, the question of his participation in the 1968 landmark Latin American conference is an important one to pursue.

At the same time there is a deeper question regarding Freire's contributions to CELAM II. In Roman Catholic theology over the past fifty years, especially in relation to the study of the Second Vatican Council, scholars have been focused on the theological question of "reception."[15] Reception entails the handing on of a good by one body to another, such that the good that is handed on benefits those who receive it. Reception is more than just a "coincidence"; there needs to be a direct connection from one to the other. For example, to demonstrate that the creation of an ecumenical commission in a Catholic diocese was the result of Vatican II, one would need to determine that the local bishop or another body did so directly because of it. Medellín is undoubtedly the reception of Vatican II.[16] But there were certainly other influences on CELAM II as well. Reception does not always have to be from a larger body to a smaller one. The Second Vatican Council itself is also an object of "reception" in that there were many voices that contributed to the resulting documents in their final form. For example, as the council was winding down, theologian Yves Congar listed in his diary the places in the final documents that are the result of his work.[17] So, we can say that Vatican II "received" Congar. But can we say the same about Medellín as having received the work of Paulo Freire? Little to no attention has been given to this question.

In what follows, I first offer a brief explanation of the development of the understanding of reception in order to clarify its meaning. I then offer some brief biographical information on four prominent Latin American Roman Catholic bishops in the 1960s who were influential at Medellín and who either had contact with Freire prior to the conference or who we could reasonably assume did have contact with him. I then turn to CELAM II, its preparations, and relevant parts in its conclusions, especially the fourth part on "Education," to show connections between the text of Medellín and Freire. Finally, I conclude with some observations and recommendations for further study in light of the question of Medellín's "reception" of Paulo Freire. In this way I intend to make a contribution to our understanding of the importance of Freire in celebration of the fiftieth anniversary of the English translation of his book *Pedagogy of the Oppressed*.

A Theology of Reception

Within a few years of the close of the Second Vatican Council in 1965, theologians began discussing the theology of reception. One of the first was the German scholar of early Christian literature Alois Grillmeier, who studied it in relation to the Council of Chalcedon in 451 CE. For Grillmeier, reception meant "the acceptance or adoption of some 'good' by a group of people that did not itself create the 'good.'"[18] However, he added, it was more than just the thing received that needed to be considered; the process of receiving was also important, and this could take many years to complete.[19] Two years later, theologian Yves Congar responded by arguing that Grillmeier's approach was too narrow. According to Congar, reception is "the process by which an ecclesial body truly makes its own a determination that it did not give to itself, by recognizing, in the promulgated measure, a rule that agrees with its own life."[20] Congar distinguished "obedience" from "reception or consent." The former was the understanding of the Scholastics in the Middle Ages, and it was tantamount to submission to authority. The latter, which was Congar's own view, is a process that involves the entire life of the community and draws on its own spiritual resources in the process of receiving the good. In other words, in comparing Grillmeier and Congar, we see that Congar's contribution is to emphasize that reception also involves a recognition by the receiver that that which is received is needed and accords with the receiver's own life.

Without reviewing the entire body of scholarship on this issue since 1972, there is one other important work to highlight, that of theologian Gilles Routh-ier. In 1993, Routhier produced a monograph-length study of reception in rela-tion to Vatican II; he was one of the first to do so. For him, reception is "a spiritual process by which the decisions proposed by a council are welcomed and assimi-lated into the life of a local church and become for it a living expression of the ap-ostolic faith."[21] It is not a top-down application, imposition, or implementation. Instead, he insists, it entails "assimilation," "actualization," "appropriation," or "inculturation" by the receiver.[22] Furthermore, he adds, "the appropriation and assimilation involve the receiving party [in such a way that] the good assimilated is necessarily transformed. It is not just the one who receives it who is affected by the exchange, but also the *bonum recipiendum* (the good received)."[23]

If we take the earlier work of Grillmeier and Congar and consider it along-side that of Routhier, we arrive at both a broader and a richer understanding of reception in relationship to Freire and Medellín. When considering whether Freire's work was received at Medellín, one needs to attend primarily to the local context in all of its distinctiveness and particularities – social, economic, political, cultural, and religious. As Routhier says, reception involves the as-similation and inculturation of the good that is received by the community. In this way the situation of the receiver is more important than the authority of the sender. Moreover, as the good is assimilated into the local culture, it is transformed according to the terms and expressions of the community, such that it becomes meaningful and operative for them. According to this, there are two broad considerations guiding this analysis of Freire and Medellín, namely, whether it can be established that Freire's work contributed to the conference and the fourth part of its conclusions, and whether in the process of receiving it, the conference assimilated it and made it its own. We return to these questions at the end of this chapter.

Influential Latin American Roman Catholics in the 1960s

In order to consider Paulo Freire's involvement at Medellín, we need to look at those who were around him, especially those who were influential at CELAM II in 1968. In this respect, sociologist of religion Christian Smith offers some assistance. Smith argues that, among other things, the emergence of progressive Latin American bishops in the mid-twentieth century helped to shape the form of Catholicism that developed on the continent in the 1960s.[24] Along these lines he identifies fourteen Catholic prelates from seven different countries: Argentina (Eduardo Pironio and Enrique Angelelli); Brazil (Hélder Câmara, Avelar Brandão, Cândido Padín, Eugênio Sales, and Paulo Evaristo Arns); Chile (Manuel Larraín and Raúl Silva Henríquez); Ecuador (Leonidas Proaño and Pablo Muñoz Vega); Mexico (Sergio Méndez Arceo); Panama (Marcos McGrath); and Peru (Juan Landázuri Ricketts).[25] Although this is a small number in comparison to the more than six hundred Latin American bishops at the time, Smith says these individuals formed a powerful group of "high caliber" progressive bishops. He writes, "Most of them were intelligent, aggressive, and organized. They knew what they wanted and how to get it."[26] These were the individuals who shaped the Catholic Church in Latin America in the 1960s, and most of them were at Medellín. Although it would be interesting to study all of them, we will look at only four for connections to Paulo Freire – Marcos McGrath, Manuel Larraín, Raúl Silva Henríquez, and Hélder Câmara.

Marcos McGrath

Marcos McGrath was born in Panama City in 1924. He joined the Congregation of Holy Cross, was ordained to the priesthood in 1949, and became auxiliary bishop of Panama in 1961. He attended all four sessions of Vatican II and participated notably in the formulation of *Gaudium et Spes*. During the first session of the council, he was elected to its doctrinal commission as one of three Latin American prelates, which meant that he travelled to Rome every three months from 1962 to 1965.[27] From 1964 to 1969 he was the bishop of the Panamanian diocese of Santiago de Veraguas, and in 1969 he was appointed archbishop of Panama. While studying in the United States, France, and in Rome throughout the 1940s and '50s he encountered the works of Yves Congar, Henri de Lubac, Karl Rahner, and Romano Guardini. He was influenced by the biblical and liturgical movements as well by personalism and Christian humanism, which served him well at the council, where these theologians and movements were embraced.[28]

There is evidence to support the claim that McGrath knew of Freire's work by the early 1960s through his involvement in the base ecclesial community (BEC) movement in Panama. BECs began in north-east Brazil in the late 1950s. According to Smith the catalyst came in 1956, when a parishioner complained to a local bishop, Agnelo Rossi, that the protestant churches were full at Christmas but the Catholic church was closed because there was no priest.[29] In response, Rossi trained catechists to work in the parishes where there was no pastor. Within a year, 372 lay associates had been trained, and by 1960 there were 475 BECs in the area. In 1963, under the leadership of McGrath, the idea was brought to Panama, to the San Miguelito slum of Panama City. McGrath was the auxiliary bishop there. The main purpose of BECs was to address the problem of a shortage of priests across Latin America. But the catechists were also being trained in pedagogical method, specifically Freire's method of con-scientization, which taught them to be more aware and to think critically about social circumstances.[30] If McGrath was not aware of Freire beforehand, he cer-tainly would have come into contact with his work by 1963.

Manuel Larraín and Raúl Silva Henríquez

Manuel Larraín and Raúl Silva Henríquez were both bishops in Chile when Freire arrived there in the fall of 1964. Larraín was born in Santiago in 1900 and studied law at the Pontifical Catholic University of Chile. He later entered the seminary and completed his training at the Pontifical Gregorian University in Rome. He was ordained in 1927 and appointed coadjutor bishop of Talca in 1938 and then bishop of the diocese the following year; he would remain in Talca un-til his death. According to a 1988 interview that Smith conducted with Chilean theologian Fr. Renato Poblete, "Larraín was a pioneer of social action." Others speak of him as worldly, up to date on the theological movements in Europe, and very concerned with social issues.[31] Larraín was a teacher in the seminary in Santiago, which put him in contact with the future archbishop of Santiago, Raúl Silva Henríquez. Together with several other Latin American bishops, he was one of the most forceful protagonists at the Second Vatican Council, which he attended for all four sessions. He was also instrumental in the calling of CELAM II in Medellín in 1968, even if he died two years before it occurred.

Raúl Silva Henríquez was born in Talca, Chile, in 1907. He joined the Sale-sians of Don Bosco in 1930 and was ordained to the priesthood in 1938. He taught in Chile from 1939 to 1945 and then became director of the Salesian College. From 1951 to 1959 he headed Caritas Chile, through which he worked with migrants and refugees, the elderly, the unemployed, as well as prisoners. Under his leadership Caritas provided aid to some 700,000 people, "regardless of creed or political affiliation."[32] In 1959 he was named bishop of Valparaíso, and in 1961 he was appointed archbishop of Santiago de Chile. Silva Henríquez also attended all four sessions of the council. According to Smith's earlier-mentioned 1988 interview, Poblete said that Silva Henríquez and Larraín were "very good friends." As archbishop and head of the Metropolitan See of San-tiago he became "the voice of others" at Vatican II, and especially of Larraín.[33]

Considering the prominence of these two bishops as church leaders, their concern for justice and liberation, and the fact that they were in the same ge-ographical area as Freire in 1964, it is difficult to imagine they did not know him. This is even more so the case given that all three of them were involved in the Chilean land reform program in the 1960s.[34] The program, which began in 1962 under Chilean president Jorge Alessandri as an agrarian reform bill and continued after his defeat to Eduardo Frei in 1964, saw the distribution of state-owned lands to Chilean workers and peasants. In the first two years, 60,000 hectares were redistributed, 40,000 of which were in Talca.[35] The Chilean church's position on this program was made clear early on in two pastoral letters denouncing liberal capitalism and stating that church supports "authentic agrarian reform."[36] To put its commitment into action, the Archdiocese of Santiago under Silva Henríquez and the Diocese of Talca under Larraín partnered in the creation of an Institute for Agrarian Promotion (Instituto de Promoción Agraria, or INPROA). Its purpose was to demonstrate the "necessity and urgency" of land reform in Chile and to "counter-arrest many of the prejudices against it."[37] Through INPROA, the dioceses distributed their lands to the rural workers.[38] At the same that this was happening, Paulo Freire was also involved in the project through the Chilean government. Within days of arriving in Santiago in November 1964, he met with Jacques Chonchol, a leader within the government's agrarian reform agency (the Institute for Agrarian and Livestock Development/Instituto de Desarrollo Agropecuario, INDAP).[39] Freire became involved in INDAP by training literacy workers and agrarian technicians, and soon his pedagogical methods were well known.[40] While he would become involved in other projects during his time in Chile, John Holst maintains that Freire's consultancy with INDAP represents his "most sustained work" in the country.[41]

Hélder Câmara

Hélder Câmara was born in 1909 in north-east Brazil. He was educated in local Catholic schools and entered the seminary in 1923. In 1931 he was ordained and in 1952 named auxiliary bishop of Rio de Janeiro. In 1964, Paul VI appointed him archbishop of Olinda e Recife, where he remained until 1985. Câmara was active in the formation of the Brazilian Bishops' Conference in 1952 and served as its general secretary until 1964. At Vatican II he attended all four sessions and aided in the formulation of *Gaudium et Spes*. After the council he guided the Brazilian church in its criticism of the country's military dictatorship (1964–85). According to a 1988 interview with one of his close associates, Marina Bandeira, Câmara was a dynamic and charismatic individual – "the bishops trusted him."[42] He was a talented leader and organizer, which made him even more famous in the country – "people wanted to see this bishop who had created some order in Brazil." In an interview with Thomas Quigley from the United States Conference of Catholic Bishops, Quigley said that Câmara was not just an organizer; he "had a way of importuning people until they did things."[43] He and Manuel Larraín were very good friends.[44]

Of the four bishops mentioned above, there is no doubt that Câmara was the closest with Freire. In fact, they are described as having a close and deep friendship for much of Freire's life.[45] Early on, Freire had been involved in the lay organization Catholic Action, which was promoted in Latin America through the work of Jacques Maritain.[46] Although he eventually stopped his involvement with the organization, it did bring him into contact with Hélder Câmara.[47] In 1947, Câmara had been made the national chaplain of Catholic Action, and through it had become a mentor to Freire. Their relationship grew from there. By the early 1960s Câmara was using Freire's educational methods. As Smith says, Câmara was influential in the Basic Education Movement (Movimento de Educação de Base, MEB) of the 1960s, which "sought to conscientize the masses through church radio programs." The MEBs followed a method that was based on Freire's "literacy training method." Through it Câmara fought against poverty and called for the conscientization of the poor.[48] Câmara continued to promote Freire and his work in the years that followed.

Beyond Individuals: Emerging Networks

The examples above begin to show the growth of a network of progressive intellectuals and church leaders in the 1950s and '60s. However, this was only the beginning; the interconnectedness of the community was much more widespread. Smith describes a "communication network" of theologians and bishops that facilitated the flow of information throughout Latin America and ultimately aided in the work of Medellín.[49]

First, in the 1950s air travel was still in its infancy, so "new ideas took years to move to other parts of the continent."[50] But within a decade travel by plane was so common that it would only take a week. Thus, meetings could happen more quickly, and information could be shared more easily.

Second, the brightest young priests were sent to the universities in Europe, where they met and studied together. As Smith points out, the early liberation theologians included "Gustavo Gutiérrez from Peru, Juan Luis Segundo from Uruguay, Enrique Dussel from Argentina, Rubem Alves and Hugo Assman – both Brazilian, and José Comblin – a Belgian-turned-Brazilian."[51] They either knew one another personally or were reading one another's publications. Gutiérrez and Segundo first met in Louvain in 1952; Dussel met Gutiérrez in Milan in 1962; Comblin met Dussel in 1959 when he read Comblin's critique of Catholic Action; Segundo met Dussel in Paris in 1963; and Gutiérrez, Comblin, and Dussel all attended Vatican II – "along with many others who became liberation theologians."[52] One of the earliest meetings was organized in 1964 by Ivan Illich and held at the Centro de Formação Intercultural in Petrópolis, Brazil. It was there that a program for liberation theology began to coalesce. As Edward Cleary describes it, "The inner circle that began at Petrópolis expanded through a series of informal meetings over the next four years. In 1965 alone, the group (which had flexible boundaries) met in June at Bogotá, and in July at Cuernavaca and Havana."[53] While this was happening, it is also worth recalling that many of the fourteen bishops mentioned above were also at Vatican II in the mid-1960s, which would certainly have helped to further develop this Latin American network of communications.

Finally, a third thing that facilitated contact was CELAM itself. The conference began in 1955 and its first president was Jaime de Barros Câmara, who "aligned himself with conservative forces" in the church.[54] However, within a few years things changed significantly. From 1959 to 1964, the president of CELAM was Miguel Dario Miranda, archbishop of Mexico City, who was a progressive. In 1964 Manuel Larraín became president and Hélder Câmara became vice-president. Until then, there had only been two departments in CELAM: Catechetics and the Committee on Faith. The new leadership expanded this to nine.[55] They also spread the work of CELAM out across the continent. In Quito, Ecuador, they created the Institute of Pastoral Liturgy and the Pastoral Institute for Latin America, and in Santiago, Chile, and in Manziales, Colombia, they created in each an Institute on Latin American Catechetics. To the various commissions they appointed many of the bishops and theologians already mentioned, including Marcos McGrath, Leonidas Proaño, Eugênio Sales, Cândido Padín, Pablo Muñoz Vega, Eduardo Pironio, Samuel Ruiz García, Luciano Metzinger, Segundo Galilea, Cecilio de Lora, Gonzalo Arroyo, Pierre Bigo, and Edgar Beltrán. When Larraín died suddenly in 1966, Avelar Brandão took over as president, Pablo Muñoz Vega became first vice-president, Marcos McGrath became second vice-president, and Eduardo Pironio became secretary general.[56] With this network of progressive prelates in place, there can be little doubt that Freire and his work were by then well known throughout the conference.

Medellín and Its Connections to Freire

Preparations for Medellín

As mentioned above, the idea for a second CELAM meeting was proposed by Manuel Larraín shortly after the Latin American bishops met with Pope Paul VI in the fall of 1965. Larraín saw it as an opportunity to communicate the theological results of the council to the church in Latin America. Six preparatory meetings were held in four different countries starting shortly after the close of Vatican II. Each had its own theme: "Education, Ministry and Social Action" (5–6 June 1966 in Baños, Ecuador); "Development and Integration in Latin America" (11–16 October 1966 in Mar del Plata, Uruguay); "The Mission of Catholic Universities in Latin America" (12–25 February 1967 in Buga,

Colombia); "The Pastoral of Missions" (20–7 April 1968 in Melgar, Colombia); "Church and Social Change" (12–19 May 1968 in Itapoan, Brazil); and "Catechesis" (11–18 August 1968 in Medellín, Colombia).[57] As Smith notes, in addition to these more formal preparatory sessions, the theologians also got together for informal consultations. One example was in Santiago, Chile, in July 1966 when Gustavo Gutiérrez, José Comblin, Juan Luis Segundo, and José Severino Croatto gathered to consider the theme of the "Word and Evangelization."[58]

During the time that preparations for Medellín were underway, Freire was busy teaching at the university in Santiago, working with the poor in Chile on literacy, and writing. As mentioned earlier, his first book, *Education: The Practice of Freedom*, was published in 1967, and his second book, *Pedagogy of the Oppressed*, which would be published in 1968, was also well underway at the time.

Whether it was through his fieldwork in education, his writings, or through his connections with Câmara and other bishops in Latin America, there is no doubt that Freire influenced the planning of Medellín. Gustavo Gutiérrez says that the preparatory meeting held on Catholic universities in Buga, Colombia, in February 1967 addressed the experience of popular education, especially in Brazil. He doesn't say whether Freire was present in Buga, but he does confirm that his "innovative work ... was an especially important influence" at the meeting.[59] Brazilian scholar Martinho Condini also points out that during the preparations for CELAM II, Cândido Padín and Hélder Câmara were responsible for the Department of Education for CELAM. Again, without specifying any details, he does state clearly that "Paulo Freire participated in the preparation of the Medellín Conference."[60]

CELAM II and the Presence of Paulo Freire

CELAM II took place from 26 August to 8 September 1968, with about 25 per cent of the Latin America bishops in attendance. Seven of them – McGrath (Panama), Pironio (president of CELAM), Sales (Brazil), Ruiz García (Mexico), Muñoz Vega (Ecuador), Henríquez (Venezuela), and Proaño (Ecuador) – opened the conference.[61] The final document of Medellín was divided into three sections: "Human Promotion," "Evangelization and Growth in Faith," and "The Visible Church and Its Structures."[62] The first section was further divided into five subsections, the second into four, and the third into seven. Thus, there were sixteen topics in total.

Scholars as well as journalists, church leaders, and theologians have pointed out the influence of Freire on the final text of CELAM II. For example, in his biography of Freire, American scholar James Kirylo writes that in the documents of Medellín, a "Freirean influence was apparent," especially through his concept of conscientization.[63]

In her 1977 award-winning book *Cry of the Poor*, the American journalist Penny Lernoux says that Medellín advocated for new educational programs "based on the pioneer work of Brazil's educational philosopher, Paulo Freire."[64] Freire's methods were developed in the late 1950s, and he continued to hone these ideas during his time in Chile from 1964 onward. While some churches, especially in Brazil, were using them, "it was not until Medellín that the Church adapted and expanded consciousness-raising techniques to include religious as well secular education."[65]

The Brazilian cardinal Paulo Evaristo Arns also agrees that Freire's work influenced Medellín. Arns was a participant at CELAM II and also the auxiliary bishop of São Paulo at the time. In a 1995 interview with educational scholar Peter Mayo, Arns said that "Freire not only changed people's lives but also the Church," referring to "the effect of his thinking on the Episcopal Conference of Medellín, 1968."[66]

The well-known Latin American liberation theologian Clodovis Boff provides further details of Freire's influence in the final texts of Medellín. He writes that the fourth part of CELAM II, focusing on education, "is one that explains more strongly the theme of liberation. The words: 'liberation,' 'liberate,' and 'liberator' appear there seven times. One paragraph (no. 8) makes explicit the content of what the document calls 'liberative education.' It defines it as 'that which transforms the student into the subject of his or her own development and is seen as a key means for the liberation of all people from all slavery (no. 8).'" In Boff's view "it is impossible to hide here the strong influence of the *Pedagogy of the Oppressed* by Paulo Freire."[67]

Moacir Gadotti and Carlos Alberto Torres, the founding directors of the Paulo Freire Institute in São Paulo, Brazil, also address Freire's influence on Medellín as well as on liberation theology. In their article "Paulo Freire: Education for Development" they write that, "Because of the impact in Catholic circles of his first book entitled *Education, the Practice of Freedom*, and particularly his concept of education for liberation which influenced the Medellín documents of 1968, Freire is associated with the emerging movement of Liberation Theology and is seen as one of its founding intellectuals."[68]

Finally, Osvaldo Mottesi makes the same claim about the connection between Freire's first book, the Medellín meeting, and the notion of liberation. In his 1986 doctoral dissertation he writes, "The first edition of Paulo Freire's first book *Educação como Prática da Liberdade* (Rio de Janeiro: Paz e Terra, 1967), the fruit of various years of pedagogical experiences in the popular movement of adult literacy in Brazil, appears approximately one year before the Second CELAM, Medellín. Freire's influence is evident in the conclusions of Medellín, especially in the document 'Education,' which speaks clearly of 'liberating education.'"[69]

While these individuals point to the influence of Freire's work in the final documents of Medellín, none of them undertake the work of analysing the texts. However, Irwin Leopando, in his doctoral dissertation entitled "A Pedagogy of Faith: The Theological Dimension of Paulo Freire's Educational Theory and Practice," does just that.[70] The main purpose of his research is not to demonstrate Freire's influence on Medellín, so the section that does so is just ten pages in length. In any case it's sufficient to show Freire's influence, especially if we also consider the many other voices described above, and in particular those of Gutiérrez and Arns, who directly participated. I will not reproduce all of Leopando's research here. Instead, I will focus on four points.

First, according to Leopando, one sees an influence of Freire even in the opening lines of the fourth Medellín document, "Education." Describing the Latin American educational landscape, the bishops speak of those "on the margin of culture, the illiterates" who are deprived of the basic benefits of communication through a common language. Their ignorance makes them a slave to others and their freedom is the responsibility of all. They must be freed from their "prejudices and superstitions," "their fanaticism," "their fatalistic attitude," and "their fearful incomprehension of the world in which they live."[71] Leopando writes that this introduction "could hardly be more Freirean."[72] The bishops' concern for those silenced, illiterate, and on the "margin of culture" was certainly shared by Freire. But their lament of "superstitions," "fatalistic attitude," "passivity," and "fearful incomprehension of the world," according to Leopando, reflects Freire's concept of "magical consciousness" where people attribute facts to a superior power.[73]

Second, the bishops call for an educational campaign to address their current situation. They say that the remedy is not to incorporate them "into the cultural structures existing around them, which can be oppressive, but into something much deeper." The people need to be equipped so that they can be "authors of their progress," and "develop in a creative and original way a cultural world of their own" that is "the fruit of their own efforts."[74] For Leopando, this proposal is "unmistakably Freirean," reflecting his conviction that "conscientizing education enables illiterates to 'begin to dynamize, to master, and to humanize reality.'"[75] Those affected "come to see the world not as a static reality, but as a reality in process, in transformation,"[76] and begin to realize that "they too, 'know things.'"[77]

Third, the bishops reject educational practices that support "dominant social and economic structures," and they criticize pedagogies that focus exclusively on "professional formation." To them, these approaches sacrifice "human excellence on the altar of pragmatism and immediacy in order to adjust to the demands of the labour market." Instead, they say that conscientizing education "converts [learners] into the subject of [their] own development."[78] To Leopando, the bishops' statement reflects Freire's "insistence that all human beings, regardless of their socio-economic status or literacy level must be invited to realize that they are already capable of shaping the world through shaping culture."[79]

Finally, the bishops offer a critique of the Latin American school curriculum. They write that in general the course content is "too abstract and too formalistic." Methods are more concerned with "the transmission of knowledge than with the creation of a critical spirit." The model is ineffective in people discovering "their proper being." Its orientation is "towards sustaining an economy based on the desire 'to have more' ... [rather than] 'to be more.'"[80] To Leopando, this appraisal is reminiscent of Freire's critique of Brazilian schooling as "disconnected from life, centered on words emptied of the reality they are meant to represent, lacking in concrete activity." The abstract disconnection from the reality of life stems from a lack of a "theory of intervention in reality, the analytical contact with existence."[81] Lastly, the bishops' exhortation for Latin Americans to "discover their proper being" was the same as Freire's call for them to stop looking for Western models for "prefabricated solutions" and to resolve their own problems.[82]

Conclusions

Two questions were posed at the beginning of this chapter: First, did Paulo Freire's work contribute to Medellín? And second, what does this mean in terms of a theology of "reception"? The first is simply a historical question of whether there's evidence that he influenced the meeting; and as already shown, there is. The statements by Arns and Gutiérrez in particular are sufficient, given that they were both at the conference. The affirmations of Boff and the analysis of Leopando, however, offer further details regarding where and how Freire's work was integrated. This is not surprising. Freire was a significant influence on human liberation in Latin America by the 1960s – through his work among the poor, his research and teaching in the university, and his roles in government. Moreover, his contact with some of the more prominent progressive theologians and bishops, like McGrath, Larraín, Silva Henríquez, Câmara, etc., meant that he was already connected to the network that would influence CELAM II. A future project could be to research the various archives to find out more details, precise historical links such as his personal involvement, discussions at meetings, and redaction histories of preparatory texts and the final documents of CELAM II.

The second question concerning Freire's theological reception, however, requires a bit more analysis and a review of the earlier contributions of Grillmeier, Congar, and Routhier. For Grillmeier, it was important to recall that reception is an ongoing process, one that may take many years. Congar emphasized that the thing received becomes a part of the receiver because it accords with the latter's own life. In other words, the thing received must be a good that fits with the community that receives it. To both of these Routhier insists that the receiving community is the pre-eminent concern and must be considered over and above the sender and its authority. The community must welcome the good, which means that it must understand it. Once it does so it can assimilate it into its own life, transforming and enculturating it according to its own needs.

With this in mind, there is no doubt of the influence and reception of Freire at Medellín, especially with respect to the conference's document on education. Leopando points to the bishops' statements regarding the problem of education in Latin America, where the poor and illiterate are held on the margins and enslaved to power. They are critical of the socio-economic structures and the prevailing pedagogies that focus on pragmatic outcomes for the sake of material gain. They proffer that the school system is too abstract and more interested in transmitting knowledge than cultivating critical subjects and enabling them to discover their own voices. Finally, their solution is not to educate by drawing people further into the existing oppressive structures. Instead, the solution is to make them agents of their own liberation, allowing them to develop their own cultural world through their own efforts – to conscientize them, transforming them into the subject of their own development. Leopando asserts that this analysis and these solutions are Freire's. The bishops may have transformed or reformulated his language in the process of making it their own at Medellín and according to their needs. But the work is Freire's.

All of this raises a new question, but one for another project. Given the incorporation of Freire's work in CELAM II – the meeting that drew the church's attention to the poor, that fought for liberation and the "full flourishing of the needy and abandoned" – what was its impact on the transformation of Latin America's education system in the years that followed it? In other words, how was Medellín received, especially with respect to education?

NOTES

1   Paul VI, "Discorso di Paolo VI nel X Anniversario del CELAM," Vatican, 23 November 1965, http://www.vatican.va/content/paul-vi/it/speeches/1965/documents/hf_p-vi_spe_19651123_celam.html.

2   Christian Smith, *The Emergence of Liberation Theology: Radical Religion and Social Movement Theory* (Chicago: University of Chicago Press, 1991), 152.

3   Enrique Dussel, *A History of the Church in Latin America*, trans. Alan Neely (Grand Rapids, MI: William B. Eerdmans, 1981), p. 145.

4   José Oscar Beozzo, *A Igreja do Brasil no Concilio Vaticano II: 1959–1965* (São Paulo: Paulinas, 2005), 537. Unless otherwise noted, all translations from the Portuguese are my own.

5   Rafael Luciani, "Medellín Fifty Years Later: From Development to Liberation," *Theological Studies* 79, no. 3 (2018): 567.

6   An excellent biography and overview of Freire can be found in James D. Kirylo, *Paulo Freire: The Man from Recife* (New York: Peter Lang, 2011). An older but equally strong biography of Freire is Denis E. Collins, *Paulo Freire: His Life, Works, and Thought* (New York: Paulist Press, 1977).

7   Kirylo, *Paulo Freire*, 52.

8   August 1988 interview with Sergio Torres in Santiago Chile, as reported in Smith, *Emergence of Liberation Theology*, 115.

9   Paulo Freire, *Education as the Practice of Freedom* (London: Writers and Readers Publishing Cooperative, 1973). The original was published as *Educação como prática da liberdade* (Rio de Janeiro: Editora Paz e Terra, 1967).

10 Paulo Freire, *Pedagogy of the Oppressed* (New York: Continuum, 2000). Due to the situation in Brazil in 1968, the book was first published in Spanish in 1968, in English in 1970, and in Brazilian Portuguese in 1975.

11 Kirylo, *Paulo Freire*, 65.

12 "The Relevance of Paulo Freire's Work in Today's World," UNESCO Institute for Lifelong Learning, 16 November 2018, https://uil.unesco.org/adult-education/relevance-paulo-freires-work-todays-world.

13 Kirylo, *Paulo Freire*, 278.

14 Moacir Gadotti and Carlos Alberto Torres, "Paulo Freire: Education for Development. Legacies: Paulo Freire," *Development and Change* 40, no. 6 (2009): 1256n3.

15 Some of the important studies include Alois Grillmeier, "The Reception of Chalcedon in the Roman Catholic Church," *Ecumenical Review* 22 (1970): 383–411; Yves Congar, "La 'Réception' comme réalité ecclésiologique," *Revue des Sciences philosophiques et théologiques* 56, no. 3 (1972): 369–403; Gilles Routhier, *La reception d'un concile* (Paris: Cerf, 1993). In 1996 a colloquium was held on "reception" at the University of Salamanca at which more than thirty scholars gave papers in English, French, Italian, and Spanish. The original papers were published as Hervé Legrand, Julio Manzanares, and Antonio García y García, eds., *La Recepción y la Communion entre las Iglesias* (Salamanca: Departmento de Publicaciones de la Universidad Pontificia, 1997), and translated and published in English in a special issue of *The Jurist* 56 (1997). See also Richard Gaillardetz, "The Reception of Doctrine: New Perspectives," in *Authority in the Roman Catholic Church: Theory and Practice*, ed. Bernard Hoose (Burlington, VT: Ashgate 2002), 95–114; and in 2020 the journal *Theological Studies* published an article drawing attention to the contributions it alone has made to the reception of Vatican II over the fifty year period (1966–2015): Gerald O'Collins, "*Theological Studies* and the Reception of Vatican II," *Theological Studies* 81, no. 1 (2020): 26–39. In that article, O'Collins draws attention to more than four dozen other articles on the subject.

16 Cf. Rafael Luciani, "Medellín Fifty Years Later: From Development to Liberation," *Theological Studies* 79, no. 3 (2018): 566–89. See also José Oscar Beozzo, *A Igreja do Brasil no Concilio Vaticano II: 1959–1965* (São Paulo: Paulinas, 2005).

17 Yves Congar, *Mon journal du concile* (Paris: Cerf, 2002), 2:511.

18 Grillmeier, "Reception of Chalcedon," 386.

19 For Grillmeier, reception occurred on the three levels: the kerygmatic, the spiritual, and the theological. These corresponded approximately to three communities in the church: the bishops, the faithful, and theologians.

20 Congar, "La 'Réception' comme réalité ecclésiologique," 370. Unless otherwise noted, all translations from the French are my own.

21 Routhier, *La reception d'un concile*, 69.

22 Cf. Routhier, 26, 94, 183–5, 197–8. See also Derek Sakowski, *The Ecclesiological Reality of Reception Considered as a Solution to the Debate over the Ontological Priority of the Universal Church* (Rome: Editrice Pontificia Università Gregoriana), 151–6.

23 Routhier, *La reception d'un concile*, 128.

24 Smith, *Emergence of Liberation Theology*, 90–103.

25 Smith, 101.

26 Smith, 102.

27 Robert S. Pelton, "CELAM and the Emerging Reception of the Bridge Theology of Pope Francis: from Marcos Gregorio McGrath to the Latin American Church Today," *Horizonte: Revista de estudos de teologia e ciências da religião* 16, no. 50 (2018): 462.

28 Pelton, 458.

29 Smith, *Emergence of Liberation Theology*, 106.

30 Smith, 107.

31 Smith, 102. See also Edward Llewellyn-Jones, "Bishop Larraín and His Relationship to Liberation Theology," *Eras Journal* 6 (November 2004), https://www.monash.edu/arts /philosophical-historical-international-studies/eras/past-editions/edition-six-2004 -november/bishop-larrain-and-his-relationship-to-liberation-theology.

32 Mario I. Aguilar, "Cardinal Raúl Henriquez, the Catholic Church, and the Pinochet Regime, 1973–1980: Public Responses to a National Security State," *Catholic Historical Review* 89, no. 4 (2003): 716.

33 Smith, *Emergence of Liberation Theology*, 102.

34 For more on the Chilean land reform program, see Cristóbal Kay and Patricio Silva, *Development and Social Change in the Chilean Countryside: From the Pre-land Reform Period to the Democratic Transition* (Amsterdam: CEDLA, 1992); Brian Loveman, *Struggle in the Countryside: Politics and Rural Labor in Chile, 1919–1973* (Bloomington: Indiana University Press, 1976). For an excellent history of Chile, see Simon Collier and William F. Sater, *A History of Chile, 1808–2002*, 2nd ed. (Cambridge: Cambridge University Press, 2004).

35 Hannah W. Stewart, "The Role of the Catholic Church in the Chilean Countryside, 1925–1964," (PhD diss., Duke University, 1985), 190.

36 Stewart, 198.

37 Stewart, 204.

38 Stewart, 205.

39 John D. Holst, "Paulo Freire in Chile, 1964–1969: Pedagogy of the Oppressed in Its Sociopolitical Economic Context," *Harvard Educational Review* 76, no. 2 (2006): 251.

40 Holst, 252.

41 Holst, 253. For a study on Freire, his pedagogical work in Chile, and its relation- ship to agrarian reform, see Andrew J. Kirkendall, "Paulo Freire, Eduardo Frei,

Literacy Training and the Politics of Consciousness Raising in Chile, 1964 to 1970," *Journal of Latin American Studies* 36 (2004): 687–717.

42 Smith, *Emergence of Liberation Theology*, 102.

43 Smith, 102.

44 Smith, 101.

45 Cf. Martinho Condini, *Fundamentos para uma educação liberatora: Dom Hélder Câmara e Paulo Freire* (São Paulo: Paulus, 2014). Kindle. See also Kirylo, "Paulo Freire," 40.

46 Kirylo, *Paulo Freire*, 40.

47 Daniel Schugurensky, *Paulo Freire* (New York: Continuum, 2001), 17.

48 Smith, *Emergence of Liberation Theology*, 16. In a later footnote, Smith explains that "conscientization (consciousness raising) is a pedagogical method, popularized by Brazilian educator Paulo Freire in the late 1950s, which used daily life experiences of the poor to promote literacy and foster a critical awareness of social reality." Smith, 106n27.

49 Smith, 108.

50 1987 interview with Edward L. Cleary, quoted in Smith, 108.

51 From its beginnings the liberation theology movement was ecumenical. While Gutiérrez, Segundo, Comblin, and others identified as Roman Catholic, Rubem Alves, for example, identified as Presbyterian. The commitment to liberation for them transcended ecclesial boundaries and commitments.

52 1988 interview with Dussel, quoted in Smith, 108.

53 Edward L. Cleary, *Crisis and Change: The Church in Latin America Today* (Maryknoll, NY: Orbis Books, 1985), 35.

54 Frederick C. Turner, *Catholicism and Political Development in Latin America* (Chapel Hill: University of North Carolina Press, 1971), 181.

55 The departments were Vocations and Ministries; Education; University Pastoral; Pastoral of CELAM; Public Opinion; Lay Apostolates; Liturgy; Seminaries; and Social Action. Cf. Smith, *Emergence of Liberation Theology*, 108. See also Turner, 181,

56 Smith, *Emergence of Liberation Theology*, 156.

57 Smith, 152.

58 Smith, 258n3. See also Osvaldo Luis Mottesi, "An Historically Mediated 'Pastoral' of Liberation: Gustavo Gutierrez's Pilgrimage Towards Socialism," (PhD diss., Marquette University, 1986), 36.

59 Gustavo Gutierrez, *The Density of the Present: Selected Writings* (Maryknoll, Orbis, 1999), 78.

60 Condini, "Fundamentos para uma educação liberatora," 91.

61 Dussel, *A History of the Church in Latin America*, 145.

62 CELAM II, *The Church in the Present-Day Transformation of Latin America in the Light of the Council, Conclusions*, 2nd ed. (Washington, DC: Division for Latin America – USCC, 1973).

63   Kirylo, *Paulo Freire*, 197.

64   Penny Lernoux, *Cry of the People: United States Involvement in the Rise of Fascism, Torture, and Murder and the Persecution of the Catholic Church in Latin America* (Garden City, NY: Doubleday, 1980), 40.

65   Lernoux, 374.

66   Peter Mayo, "The Roots of Paulo Freire's Praxis," *International Journal of Lifelong Education* 37, no. 4 (2018): 514.

67   The original Portuguese reads as follows: "O Documento IV, relativo à 'Educação' é um dos que explicitam de modo mais forte o tema da libertação. Sete vezes aparece aí a palavra 'libertação,' 'libertar' ou 'libertador.' Há inclusive todo um parágrafo (n. 8) que explicita o conteúdo do que chama com todas as letras a 'educação libertadora.' Define-a como a que 'transforma o educando em sujeito de seu próprio desenvolvimento' e é vista como 'o meio-chave para libertar os povos de toda escravidão' (n. 8). Impossível esconder aqui a forte influência da 'Pedagogia do Oprimido' de Paulo Freire." Clodovis Boff, "A originalidade histórica de Medelín," Servicios Koinonía: De la Agenda LatinoAmericana, accessed 16 February 2023, https://servicioskoinonia.org/relat/203p.htm.

68   Gadotti and Torres, "Paulo Freire," 1256n3.

69   Mottesi, "An Historically Mediated 'Pastoral' of Liberation," 156n22.

70   Irwin Ramirez Leopando, "A Pedagogy of Faith: The Theological Dimension of Paulo's Freire's Educational Theory and Practice" (PhD diss., City University of New York, 2011), 141–50.

71   CELAM II, *The Church in the Present-Day Transformation*, 80, quoted in Leopando, 142.

72   Leopando, "A Pedagogy of Faith," 142.

73   Paulo Freire, *Education for Critical Consciousness* (New York: Continuum, 2005), 39, quoted in Leopando, 142.

74   CELAM II, *The Church in the Present-Day Transformation*, 80-81, quoted in Leopando, 143.

75   Freire, *Critical Consciousness*, 4, quoted in Leopando, "A Pedagogy of Faith," 143.

76   Freire, *Pedagogy of the Oppressed*, 83, quoted in Leopando, 143.

77   Freire, *Pedagogy of the Oppressed*, 63, quoted in Leopando, 143.

78   CELAM II, *The Church in the Present-Day Transformation*, 81-82, quoted in Leopando, 143.

79   Leopando, "A Pedagogy of Faith," 143.

80   CELAM II, *The Church in the Present-Day Transformation*, 81, quoted in Leopando, "A Pedagogy of Faith," 145.

81   Freire, *Critical Consciousness*, 33, quoted in Leopando, 145.

82   Freire, *Critical Consciousness*, 26, quoted in Leopando, 145–6.

3 Paulo Freire and the Jesuit Intellectual and Educational World in Chile, 1964–1969: A Collateral and Indirect Relationship

CRISTÓBAL MADERO

Introduction

Between 1964 and 1969, Paulo Freire lived in Chile after being exiled by the Brazilian dictator Humberto de Alencar Castelo Branco. In 1969 he moved to the United States, returning to Chile in 1972 and again in 1992 for a limited time. During his exile in Chile, he worked for the Ministry of Agriculture, the Ministry of Education, and the Institute of Training and Research of Agrarian Reform (Instituto de Capacitación e Investigación en Reforma Agraria, or ICIRA). This last institution was run by the United Nations and the Chilean government. Freire's life and work during those five years in the 1960s took place in an atmosphere of social, ecclesial, cultural, and political upheaval. His academic and political connections during those years and his contributions to and tensions with Chile's so-called Revolution in Freedom program[1] are collected in excellent articles.[2] However, less known is Freire's relationship with specific power groups in Chilean society during those years. This chapter explores Paulo Freire's relationship with one of these groups: the Society of Jesus, also known as the Jesuit Order, or simply the Jesuits.[3]

During the twentieth century, the Society of Jesus in Chile operated as an intellectual beacon for Chilean society in general and the Christian social world in particular. The Jesuits did this most emphatically from the 1940s on, when the Bellarmino Centre, the name of the Jesuit community that brought together Jesuit experts in sociology, economics, anthropology, and theology, began operating. However, it was not until the 1960s that new *think tanks* of the Society of Jesus emerged from the Bellarmino Centre to address critical problems in Chilean society. "The Bellarmino Centre functioned as an active arm of the Catholic social militancy and had a visible influence on the growth of the Christian Democratic movement in Chile. The favourable environment for social reform and concern about the rise of communism, which had deepened with the Cuban Revolution, had unified the Catholics around the need to develop an alternative platform to Marxism. Jesuit experts were needed more than ever."[4] The journal

Revista Mensaje, and the Latin American Institute of Social Studies (Instituto Latinoamericano de Doctrina y Estudios Sociales, ILADES), were two representative institutions of this Jesuit intellectual initiative. Educational institutions also joined this intellectual enterprise through the Centre for Research and Development of Education (Centro de Investigación y Desarrollo de la Educación, CIDE) and their traditional work in k–12 schools run by the Jesuit Order.

In these years of fervour (1964–9) and later, it is unthinkable that Paulo Freire did not enter into some contact with this intellectual and educational world that so profoundly marked the political and social life of the country, notwithstanding the fact that, to our knowledge, there are no studies that show that contact. As we will see throughout this chapter, Freire did meet Jesuits and interact with Jesuit institutions during these years. Even more, he participated actively in some of those institutions, advising, writing, teaching, and speaking. However, it cannot be claimed that Freire directly impacted the Jesuits or their institutions. Instead, he had what I call a collateral and mostly indirect impact on some Jesuit institutions in the 1960s and later.

In the first part of this chapter, I summarize the activities of Paulo Freire during the years 1964–9, and during his short stay in Chile in 1972. In the second part, I examine his participation in different Jesuit institutions in Chile. The third and final part assesses the relationship between Paulo Freire and the Jesuits in the Chilean province.[5]

Although I am looking at Freire's interaction with a Catholic religious group, this chapter's goal is not to delve into possible religious interactions in Freire's personal life. I have already, to some extent, referred to that topic before.[6] This chapter does not assess the impact of this period on Freire's biography either; such an endeavour has been done by other authors already.[7] Instead, I aim here to expose a lesser-known dimension of one of the most influential intellectuals and educators of all time. At the same time, this study is relevant insofar it reveals direct testimonies of key informants who worked with Paulo Freire during and after his exile in Chile.

Paulo Freire's Work in Chile

The coup d'état that overthrew João Goulart in Brazil in 1964 caused the exile of thousands of people, among them Paulo Freire and his family. Chile received Freire along with many other Brazilian intellectuals. Although Freire had already made a critical intervention in education, particularly with his adult literacy program, his reputation in the 1960s was not extended beyond the Brazilian North-East in the way it was from 1970 onward. His years in Chile marked the beginnings of the Freire that we know today: a more public, more international, and more universal Freire.[8]

Freire landed in Chile in November 1964, the same month the Christian Democrat Eduardo Frei Montalva (1964–70) was inaugurating his presidency with a program called Revolution in Freedom (*Revolución en Libertad*). Although Brazil did not have an equivalent party, the Christian Democratic Party in Chile had ties to Brazil. Those ties allowed Freire to assume a job once he arrived in Chile. Particularly, the relationship between Jacques Chonchol (incoming president Eduardo Frei's choice as head of the Institute of Agricultural Development) and Paulo de Tarso (Brazil's former minister of justice, who was also in exile in Chile) made it possible for Freire to work for the Ministry of Agriculture at the Institute of Agricultural Development. As Kirkendall rightly points out, Freire had to work for a government that, although pushing a process of agrarian reform initiated by the previous government, was ideologically distant from the more left-wing principles embraced by Freire.[9]

The government program of the Christian Democratic Party included a project of popular promotion (*promoción popular*) whereby the peasants[10] had to transform themselves into new people capable of acting with self-awareness and conceiving of themselves as subjects (not objects) of history. To this end, organization among themselves became necessary. Illiteracy was an obstacle on the way to completing such a task. These ideas, generally attributed to Freire, were already in the government program of President Frei. Paulo Freire was hired to collaborate in a project that had already started at the Institute of Agricultural Development and the Ministry of Education with the concrete technique known as psychosocial method (*método psicosocial*). Waldemar Cortés, responsible for the Ministry of Education's adult literacy program, came to know this technique and decided to incorporate Freire into his team.

As part of the literacy campaign, Freire, Chonchol and Cortés witnessed the peasants' change of attitude and perspective on their reality: a process of awareness was set in motion, affirming that the agrarian reform was not fundamentally about productivity as much as the transformation of human beings.[11] However, that same awareness, which was the ultimate goal of the agrarian reform, also led people to turn against the government. As consciousness grew, peasants and other social forces demanded more immediate structural social changes.[12]

Frei's government advocated change, but of a more gradual kind. Intentionally or not, it was a reform that maintained a paternalistic pattern in its forms. By the beginning of his government in 1964, Frei wanted to eradicate illiteracy by the end of his term. By 1967 the goal was to reduce it from 16 per cent to 7 per cent. The Ministry of Education slowed down the literacy campaign, and the Ministry of Agriculture focused more on technology than on land distribution. Things became tense between Freire and the government as his intellectual path led him to embrace more left-wing ideas, causing strain in his relationship with the Christian Democratic government. After working there for just over three years, he eventually left the government. He joined ICIRA, a joint organization of the Food and Agriculture Organization of the United

Nations and the Chilean government. Many of his collaborators left the government and followed him to ICIRA, of which the Christian Democrat Party was critical. In the official magazine of the Ministry of Education, *Revista de Educación* (Journal of education), Kirkendall notes that Freire's name disappeared from the report on the literacy campaign between 1968 and 1969.[13] In other words, he was erased from the official history of the campaign.

Between 1968 and 1969, Freire worked at ICIRA. During this period, he had more time to reflect and write. He translated into Spanish the text of *Education as a Practice of Freedom*[14] *and* wrote *Extension or Communication*[15] and the essential texts of what would later become the *Pedagogy of the Oppressed.*[16] According to Holst, these texts, together with *On Cultural Action*[17] and the first eight chapters of *The Politics of Education,*[18] contain Freire's most important contributions to educational theory and practice. Holst argues, "He wrote about some of his most enduring concepts, such as banking education, problem-posing education, generative words, cultural circles, culture of silence, cultural action, and thematic universe. While it is clear that his initial work in Brazil was foundational for the development of many of these concepts, it is widely ignored that they were further developed for publication in Chile and that his work in Chile allowed him to reflect on his initial work in Brazil and develop many of the necessary theoretical foundations for it."[19]

Freire's Relationship with the Jesuit World in Chile

In what follows, I present the different points of contact between Paulo Freire and the Jesuits in Chile. I explore primary and secondary literature, archives, and most importantly, unstructured interviews with key informants. Below, I indicate the names of each informant and the institution in which he or she participated at the time of working or meeting with Freire: Marcela Gajardo (ICIRA), Juan Eduardo García-Huidobro (CIDE), Gabriel Salazar (CIDE, Colegio San Ignacio), Francisco López (ILADES), Adriana Delpiano (CORA),[20] Rolando Pinto (CORA), José Antonio Viera-Gallo (ILADES), Martín Miranda (CIDE), Luis Bustos (CIDE), and Francisco Álvarez (CIDE). These interviews took place between February and May 2021. When quoting from them below, I introduce the interviewee explicitly or include their name in parentheses.

Revista Mensaje. A Powerful Intellectual Journal

In 1951, the Jesuit priest Alberto Hurtado founded *Revista Mensaje*. In a poor country and distant from the intellectual debates on theological, cultural, and political matters of the world, *Mensaje* was an institution dedicated to the reflection and dissemination of Christian thought. At the end of a lifetime devoted to the social apostolate in the country, Hurtado pointed out to his religious superiors the need for a publication to comment on religious, social, and philosophical matters. Hurtado envisioned *Mensaje* as a testimony of the church's presence in the contemporary world. It would not be literary, nor would it be pious; it would, rather, address a broader range of issues. It should respond to the urgency of significant disorientation, especially among the youth. "No journals were filling such need in Chile. Foreign journals are inaccessible to the vast majority. There is a hunger for religious and social culture in university settings."[21] In 2021, the same year that Freire would have turned one hundred, the Jesuit journal celebrated its seventieth anniversary.

Since its foundation, and particularly during the second half of the 1960s, *Mensaje* was a beacon for the Christian world and a reference point for the intellectuals in Chile. Although a national journal, *Mensaje* has always included an array of international commentators. Frequently, authors such as Jean-Paul Sartre, Hans Küng, Jaques Maritain, Yves Congar, Gabriela Mistral, Karl Rahner, or Noam Chomsky were given space in its pages. In the second half of the 1960s, it was one of the publications with the most circulation in Chile, reaching about sixty thousand readers per year by 1969.[22]

In 1965, in the September issue, Paulo Freire wrote the article "Alfabetización de Adultos y 'Concientización'" (Adult literacy and "conscientization").[23] There he developed for the first time in Spanish experiences related to adult education in Brazil. He was particularly interested in developing the theoretical bases and the results of his literacy method in his beloved Brazil. As he clarified in the article, these were the experiences "that cost us prison, distance from our university activities and exile."[24] The article exposed the ideas that gave rise to literacy's critical moment, such as fundamental democratization, humanism, and the reflexive organization of thought.

Freire moved from ideas to practice, exposing literacy as a creative act (awareness of nature and culture) and the well-known uprising of the vocabular universe and the selection of generative words. Freire ended the article exposing the practical results achieved in Brazil until his departure and offering a projection of the economic costs of a campaign like that. He concluded that "This is all over. Painfully it was over . . . but without having left us in bitterness or despair. We continue to be hopeful and confident in man, whose destiny is not to 'become accustomed,' but to humanize himself."[25]

Freire had been in Chile for less than a year when his article appeared in *Mensaje*. The editor of the magazine between 1976 and 2017, Ernesto Espíndola, points out that Paulo Freire was becoming better known to the readership of the journal, but not only for the article in question: "he was often quoted in articles on literacy and popular education" (Ernesto Espíndola).

Mensaje published an obituary upon Freire's death in which it praised him as "one of the most well-known, creative and influential thinkers in Latin America and a universal figure of education ... committed to the cause of an education put at the service of the construction of more just, equitable, and solidary societies."[26]

Alfabetización de adultos y "concientización"

Paulo Freire

Introducción

En este artículo, que en parte reproduce estudios publicados anteriormente en el Brasil, trataremos de exponer los fundamentos de nuestra experiencia educacional, particularmente en el campo de la educación de adultos. Experiencias que nos costaron prisión, alejamiento de nuestras actividades universitarias y exilio. Experiencias y realizaciones de que no nos arrepentimos y que nos valieron también comprensión y apoyo no sólo de intelectuales y estudiantes, sino también de hombres sencillos del pueblo. Comprensión que habría significado para nosotros mucho más que las incomprensiones, las distorsiones y persecuciones de que fuimos objeto.

Este artículo, por lo tanto, no será el desabogo de un resentido, ni el grito de un desesperado. No somos ni una ni otra cosa. Nos interesa solamente exponer aquí, en síntesis, las bases teóricas y los resultados de nuestro trabajo con el cual se estaba consiguiendo en Brasil, algo más que una pura alfabetización mecánica de adultos.

Brasil — Una sociedad en tránsito

El Brasil vivía exactamente el tránsito de una a otra época. El paso de una sociedad "cerrada" a una sociedad "abierta". No era más una sociedad totalmente "cerrada", ni tampoco era ya una "abierta". Era una sociedad abriéndose. El tránsito era precisamente el eslabón entre una época que se desvanecía a otra que se iba conformando. Por ello tenía algo de prolongación y algo de adentramiento. De prolongación de aquella sociedad que se desvanece, y en la que se proyectaba, queriendo preservarse. De adentramiento en la nueva sociedad que anunciaba y que a través de él, se engendraba en la vieja.

Esta sociedad brasileña estaba sujeta, por eso mismo, a retrocesos en su tránsito, en la medida en que las fuerzas que encarnaba aquella sociedad, en la vigencia de sus poderes, consiguiesen sobreponerse de uno u otro modo, a la consubstanciación de la nueva sociedad. Sociedad nueva que se opondría necesariamente a la vigencia de privilegios, cualquiera que fuesen sus orígenes, contrarios a los intereses del hombre brasileño.

Democratización fundamental

Entrando a la sociedad brasileña en transición, se había instalado entre nosotros el fenómeno que Mannheim llama de "democratización fundamental", que implica una creciente activación del pueblo en su proceso histórico.

El pueblo se encontraba en la fase anterior de enclaustración de nuestra sociedad, inmerso

494

Figures 3.1a and 3.1b. *Mensaje* (Message) magazine edition and article on adult literacy and "awareness" of Paulo Freire.
Source: Virtual Library Revista Mensaje, 2021.

CIDE: Inspiring Practice and Educational Research

CIDE was founded in 1965 as a response of the Society of Jesus to Chile's educational challenges. Its founder, the Jesuit Patricio Cariola, served simultaneously as the director of CIDE and of the Federation of Institutions of Private Education (Federación de Instituciones de Educación Particular, FIDE). CIDE sought to be a space where people could think about the incorporation of Catholic schools in the educational reform of 1964, amid the social and ecclesial events of the 1960s: the celebration of the Second Vatican Council (1962–5), the Medellín Conference (1968), and the emergence of liberation theology, mainly under the influence of Gustavo Gutiérrez.[27]

CIDE was structured in two areas that more than a few of CIDE's former employees define as two souls. One soul was the development of educational research, mainly studies around the sociology of education. The other soul was the work in popular education. As Cariola's biographers point out, "between 1967 and 1968 is when experiences with popular groups are developed. The thought of Illich and Freire inspired the source of those experiences[28]." Patricio Cariola "constantly promoted the creation of actions, projects, and interventions where education was an opportunity for meeting, reflecting, and developing. Patricio was an innovative teacher who promoted the practice of popular education."[29] During the 1960s CIDE was a space where social, cultural, and ecclesial points of view were merged in a progressive sphere. One of CIDE's founding members, Martín Miranda, recalls that the centre "was an institution dedicated to education in the context of a progressive church … without Patricio [Cariola] being especially progressive in his beginnings."

From his role as director of FIDE, Cariola collaborated to develop the concept of the school community, meaning all those who integrate the educational process that takes place in a school: teachers, students, parents, and others. "The school community encourages each school to make a diagnosis of itself, to explain the concept of education with which it operates and to give a participatory organizational model. Specifically, it proposes the existence of democratic bodies in the school institution, such as parents, boards, student councils, teacher councils, and a board of directors composed of representatives of those organizations."[30] Some questioned whether the guiding philosophy of this conception of the school community was Marxist rather than personalist, the traditional philosophy that inspired the approach of Catholic educators in general and Cariola in particular. Cariola was advancing a concept aligned with the liberating education guidelines, ratified by the Second Episcopal Conference of Latin America (CELAM II) in Medellín and previously enunciated by Paulo Freire. In this way, Cariola "was at the forefront of educational thought, but aligned with his Church."[31]

Paulo Freire caused, by affiliation or rejection, a significant impact on the educational scene during the second half of the 1960s in Chile, the same period when CIDE was founded. Unquestionably, Freire's influence was inspirational among CIDE's rank and file. They joined CIDE sharing Freire's educational ideology: "It was vital that those who accompanied Patricio from the beginning of the creation of CIDE knew Paulo Freire, shared his criticisms of traditional education, had appropriated the principles, attitudes and values that promote a liberating *education*, as the Brazilian educator called it" (Martin Hurtado). Indeed, embracing Freire's pedagogical and educational ideas meant that CIDE was created not from scratch but with professionals and educators who shared a solid common ground. Again, it's not just Freire's ideas, but the impact that those ideas had on a group of professionals breathing the air of a progressive church in the larger context of significant social change.

Juan Eduardo García-Huidobro, one of Patricio Cariola's closest collaborators and one of the most influential researchers and public intellectuals from the 1960s to the present day in Chile, points out that each of the researchers and educators entering CIDE carried the Freire "chip." He also suggests that Freire's meetings with Patricio Cariola, Martín Miranda, Juan José Silva, and other members of CIDE were relevant. Marcela Gajardo, who was undoubtedly the closest person to Freire in Chile during his years of exile, says she participated in those meetings in which CIDE was shaped once Cariola dedicated himself entirely to its direction between 1968 and 1969. According to Gajardo, "Patricio Cariola always asked him [Freire] for meetings when we were at ICIRA to know a little more about what we were doing in Chile and with other Latin American countries."

Between January 1968 and April 1969, Paulo Freire was at ICIRA devoted to producing the following texts: (i) Adult Literacy; (ii) The Role of the Social Worker in the Process of Change; (iii) The Commitment of the Professional to Society; (iv) About the Generating Theme; (v) The "Banking" Conception of Education; (vi) Dehumanization, Problematizing Conception and Humanization; (vii) Settlement as a Whole; (viii) Agrarian Reform and Cultural Action; (ix) *Community Development*; and (x) *The Peasant Can Also Be the Author of His Own Reading Texts*. An observant reader will realize that many of these texts are part of what will later become *Pedagogy of the Oppressed*.[32] At ICIRA[33] he also translated the text of *La Educación como práctica de la libertad*[34] and wrote *Extensión o comunicación*.[35] Knowing the breadth of Freire's production, Cariola invited him to be the keynote speaker at the now traditional FIDE annual conference in 1968. This organization brought together hundreds of private schools in Chile. The theme of the day was "Liberating Education," and it was held in the coastal city of San Antonio.

CIDE, through its director Patricio Cariola and his closest collaborators, had interactions with Paulo Freire during his years in Chile and later. In 1972, Freire returned to Chile. Martín Miranda recalled "a meeting between Juan Eduardo García-Huidobro, Luis Brahm, and I with Paulo at CIDE on his visit in June 1972 where he made us see the need for criticism of our mutual naivety. Vital for the historical moment. A year before everything collapsed." In 1972, Freire realized the historical moment and recognized that the ideas he shared with CIDE must be revisited. Less than a year after that meeting, the Chilean historic project collapsed: a coup d'état resulted in the overthrow of Salvador Allende, and a bloody dictatorship was installed that would last for the next seventeen years.

The years of the Pinochet dictatorship (1973–90) saw the deployment of CIDE's principles and educational practice. Under CIDE, "popular education" came to be used as a pseudonym for "liberating education." The idea of liberation, strongly linked to Freire's pedagogical ideas, was camouflaged given the context of dictatorship. This meant that one of the most impactful of CIDE's programs, the Popular Education Workshop (Taller de Educación Popular, TEP), was closed. The National History Prize winner, Gabriel Salazar, worked at TEP between 1986 and its closure in 1992. Salazar points out how symbolically Paulo Freire entered Chile and CIDE, not in the 1960s but the 1980s: "Freire was *Chileanized* with Pinochet." This assessment comes from Salazar's judgment that Freire was an elite intellectual during his time of exile in Chile. Although he participated in literacy campaigns and worked directly with peasants, his entry was from above, and his ideas were not settled. Quite the opposite happened in a context of self-awareness and facing the need for unity to overthrow a dictator. Moreover, "Chile was no longer rural or illiterate in the 1960s, so Freire's literacy-based program was not essential," Salazar emphasizes.

In addition to TEP, the Open Centre for Popular Education (Centro Abierto de Educación Popular, CADEP), which operated between 1984 and 1992, was equally important. Luis Bustos, a popular educator at CADEP, confirms Gabriel Salazar's judgment that Freire´s ideas made more sense under a dictatorship. He also confirmed the tension between the two souls of CIDE, which only increased in the 1980s and '90s, the "one [marked] by the intellectual wing linked to the Catholic University of Leuven, the sociology of Basil Bernstein, and the European intelligentsia in general, and the other to Freire's popular education."

When democracy was restored in 1990, CIDE mostly abandoned its popular education dimension. Many of its members became part of the first and successive Ministries of Education under the transitional democratic governments during the 1990s. Also relevant to this history is the foundation of the Jesuit university in Santiago in 1997 (Alberto Hurtado University). The newly created university included CIDE in its organization. Under the university's statutes, CIDE was required to enhance its academic dimension rather than pursue popular education. Luis Bustos points out that "by 1990, some CIDE researchers said that Freire was pure past."

By 1977, CIDE was a founding member of the Latin American Network for Information and Documentation in Education (Red Latinoamericana de Información y Documentación en Educación, REDUC). It was a cooperative effort of twenty-two study centres in eighteen countries in Latin America. From its creation until 2006, CIDE coordinated REDUC. As Juan Eduardo García-Huidobro points out, REDUC's interest was to "rescue Latin American

Figures 3.2a and 3.2b. *CIDE* magazine editions.
Source: Virtual repository Universidad Alberto Hurtado, 2021.

languages in education."[36] Paulo Freire also appeared relevant to this enterprise. As noted by the former CIDE researcher and later minister of education (1994–2000), Ernesto Schiefelbein, "One of the common goals was to make the local language and historical roots a valuable source for the educational experience. Paulo Freire's role in this field, as in others, was highlighted. The rigid organization of social classes, inherited from the Hispanic colonial era and reinforced by industrialization, may have stimulated the interest in analysing education problems from a sociological angle and not from an educational one."[37]

Since its beginnings, CIDE published material that reflected CADEP's connection with the thought of Paulo Freire in different ways. *Cuadernos de Educación* and *El Mensajero* were just two of these publications. In June 1972, Martín Miranda and Juan Eduardo García-Huidobro interviewed Freire during his visit to Chile in June. The interview appeared in one of the *Cuadernos de Educación* issues that year.

ILADES

On 27 September 1965, Raúl Silva Henriquez, archbishop of Santiago, Bishop Manuel Larran, and the Jesuit Pierre Bigo agreed to create an institute "oriented to the elaboration, teaching and dissemination of the Social Doctrine of the Church. Silva Henriquez asked the Jesuits of the Bellarmino Centre to manage the Institute."[38] ILADES was therefore constituted in the fierce second half of the 1960s as a place where professionals with a profound sense of Christian teaching and the spirit of the Latin American church and society were taught and trained. Its principles were the preferential option for the poor, a solidarity based on a conception of the human being in interdependence with others, and the defence and promotion of life, dignity, and the human person's rights.

ILADES, *Revista Mensaje*, and the Centre for the Economic and Social Development of Latin America (Centro para el Desarrollo Económico y Social de América Latina, DESAL) – founded by the Jesuit Roger Veckemans – were the vital institutions of the Bellarmino Centre. It was the closest thing to a set of very influential think tanks when none existed. They were beacons of Christian thought because of their own merits and the fact that they did not maintain any rivalry with each other.

By 1969, a good part of the professionals and academics of the CADEP had become radicalized, considering themselves Marxist Christians. This trend led the Catholic Church in Santiago, the CELAM, and especially the Conference of German Bishops, who financed ILADES, to take away support and thus accelerate its closure, or, as some say, "its reduction to a minimal expression." What happened in those five years that saw ILADES become immersed in this crisis? Undoubtedly the social, cultural, and political changes that took place in the 1960s affected every aspect of Chilean society. According to Francisco

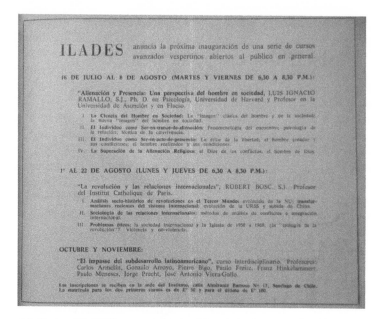

Figure 3.3. Poster of ILADES courses in *Revista Mensaje*. Paulo Freire is listed here as a professor of the interdisciplinary course "The Impasse of Latin American Underdevelopment."
Source: Virtual Library Message Magazine, 2021.

López, sociologist and part of the founding team of ILADES, "the bloody coups d'état in Latin America led to the exile of not a few left-wing intellectuals. The immediate consequence was that many scholars took refuge in Chile and were accepted into academic and university bodies such as ILADES due to their humanist and democratic inspiration. Among the professionals who left Brazil and sought refuge in Chile, Paulo Freire, Paulo de Tarso, and Fernando Henrique Cardoso arrived as professors or guest researchers at ILADES and DESAL."[39] In this regard, Cabaluz and Areyuna-Ibarra point out that the Jesuit Order in Chile, through the Bellarmino Centre, played an essential role in securing asylum for Brazilians in the country, and particularly Paulo Freire, as they had a significant influence on the upper hierarchy of the Christian Democratic Party and over organizations such as the Institute of Rural Education and the ILADES.[40] "The Jesuits were aware of the educational work developed by the Brazilian grassroots education movement and Freire's proposal."[41]

Marcela Gajardo confirms that Paulo Freire entered the sphere of the Bellarmino Centre during this period, both in ILADES and DESAL, as a professor and lecturer. As evidenced by an article in *Revista Mensaje* in July 1968, Freire offered an interdisciplinary course in ILADES on "the Impasse of Latin

American Underdevelopment." Similarly, Armand Mattelart, a sociologist who served as a professor at ILADES and a researcher at ICIRA, points out that in the 1960s ILADES received Brazilian exiles: "There was also the pedagogue Paulo Freire, whose book on the 'banking' conception, not dialogical, of the transmission of knowledge, we soon to be publish."[42]

Towards the end of the 1960s, a key figure in the recovery of democracy, the lawyer José Antonio Viera-Gallo, was part of the faculty of ILADES, and he remembers how that group of Brazilians who taught at ILADES collaborated decisively in the institutional crisis that gripped that body. Sharing a Christian matrix, Brazil did not have a Christian democratic party, unlike Chile. According to Viera-Gallo, this caused the Social Doctrine of the Church, the centre of ILADES's mission, to be increasingly replaced by Marxism. "Freire was not explicitly a protagonist in this crisis, but he was so implicitly. And this given that his methods of awareness and criticism, of becoming aware of one's place in history, permeated deeply in the group of intellectuals at ILADES. He certainly contributed to a moment of crisis at the institute. Freire and his critical conscience despaired Pierre Bigo, director of ILADES," says Viera-Gallo.

Traditional Jesuit K–12 Schools

Starting in the 1960s, Jesuit k–12 schools were strongly influenced by the Second Vatican Council, the 31st and 32nd General Congregations of the Society of Jesus (1965–6 and 1975), and CELAM II (1968). The social, cultural, and religious changes brought by these events "caused the educational apostolate of the society to undergo revisions."[43] Rolando Pinto has studied how Freire's ideas influenced the work of the Jesuits. While it is challenging to isolate Freire's direct influence from the impact of Medellín or liberation theology, it cannot be dismissed as an indirect impact.

I have already mentioned the permanent contacts between Patricio Cariola and Freire and the Freirean inspiration on a good part, if not the whole, of the team at CIDE. Most likely, all the educators and to some extent all the administrators of Jesuit schools in Chile (in those years, all Jesuit priests), participated in the FIDE event in 1968 dedicated to the theme of "Liberating Education." Teachers in these schools certainly knew about Freire's presence in the country and had had access to his article in *Revista Mensaje* on adult literacy.

In 1968, the Jesuit Santiago Marshall directed the Colegio San Ignacio El Bosque, one of the two Jesuit schools that served the upper and upper-middle classes in Santiago, Chile's capital city. Two antagonistic history teachers were hired to diversify the teaching of history in the school: Julio Retamal and Gabriel Salazar. If the former placed his concerns in Chile's founding families, or wondered whether the West still existed, the latter studied popular political violence and the relationship of intellectuals, the poor, and power. Salazar, who later worked at CIDE, took over Retamal's chair in the school. He recalls the time Paulo Freire accepted an invitation to meet with teachers of the school to share his ideas: "It was in the yard because many people would come, but it wasn't that many in the end." Freire gave a lecture, which, in Salazar's words, "did not impress greatly by its educational contents." What impressed Salazar was that both Freire and Marshall, the rector, were publicly questioned by some teachers who thought that Freire's Marxist ideas should not be exposed in a Catholic school. In the words of Marcela Gajardo and Martín Miranda (the latter also a professor of history at the school and a member of CIDE), this action angered Freire, who left the room. It was a space "where they told Freire many things, and he came out of the meeting very upset. I know because I accompanied him," said Gajardo. Many considered his presence a provocation in the context of the polarization then gripping the country. We recall that Freire was no longer the Freire of the 1965 article in *Mensaje*, the man who worked as an official of a Christian Democrat government. He had had the time to delve even deeper into the political dimension of his ideas, which were fed more and more with intellectual Marxist thought.

After considering the case of CIDE and ILADES, it is difficult to establish a relationship between Freire and k–12 Jesuit schools. However, Pinto thinks it is possible to show that Freire joined other forces to change the way Jesuits approach k–12 education.[44] For example, Cox and Imbarack show how the curriculum of Jesuit schools from the 1960s was distinguished from other networks of schools owned by Catholic congregations in Chile in three fundamental aspects. First, Jesuit schools more consistently reflected upon the issues of poverty, social inequity, and social injustice in their curriculum. Second, this curriculum emphasized the positive relationship between faith and culture to a greater degree than the other three networks studied by them. Faith had to do with culture not being enclosed, but it could also be impacted by culture in a double movement. Finally, the Jesuit curriculum emphasized a more significant political commitment to society in the formation of students.[45] Each of these findings resonated with the progressive context of the time, and especially with Paulo Freire's ideas about the purpose of education. Again, not Freire as a univariate explanation, but as one of many variables.

Balance of the Relationship between Freire and the Jesuits in Chile

The second half of the 1960s was, for both the Jesuits in Chile and for Paulo Freire as an individual, highly turbulent years. The Jesuits were influential intellectually and symbolically in the country, with a vast influence over the country's social and political life. Freire managed to grow intellectually and to produce essential pieces of writing during these years. Indeed, those works would bring him renown over the next three decades. It is not odd to presume that Brazilian intellectuals and the Jesuits encountered each other within various institutions during this time.

As I mentioned at the outset of this chapter, it is clear that Freire's impact on these spaces of encounter with the Jesuits (the central question of this study) was not essential, but rather collateral or indirect. Freire indeed wrote for the Jesuits' journal in 1965, but he did so only once. Neither was he asked to submit any further articles for review (and to the best of our knowledge, he did not try). This is not to say that this was not a meaningful relationship, or that Freire's article was not impactful; in fact, the journal dedicated many issues and numbers to educational topics, many of which referenced Freire.

Freire's influence could also be described as collateral in the case of CIDE. The value of Freire's presence and thought for the professionals who worked on popular education and the generation of knowledge that guided this work was instrumental to the mission of the CIDE. But CIDE was never focused solely on popular education. Some criticized Freire or saw him as an intellectual has-been. And perhaps most importantly, Freire never worked at CIDE. Knowing Patricio Cariola's vision and sense of opportunity, he would not have missed the chance to invite him to work more closely if he had been convinced of Freire's essential value. Again, as Marcela Gajardo says, this does not lessen the value of the several conversations between Cariola and Freire.

José Antonio Viera Gallo points out that Pierre Bigo, director of ILADES, ended up in a position that was at odds Freire and the other Brazilians. This tension added volume to an already loud dispute and undoubtedly was instrumental in the institute's closure. However, Freire was welcomed there as a professor. Was there a relationship between Freire and ILADES? Of course there was. Was it essential? In light of this study, we can say that it was not.

Concerning k–12 schools, the most extensive educational work of the Jesuits in Chile, Freire's contact seems marginal. Freire was more focused on adult education, which became a natural barrier in the world of schools. This apostolate, who kept the middle and upper classes on one side, and children and young people on the other, makes this relationship tenuous. He aroused passions in his one visit to a Jesuit school, but perhaps it would have been the same if another left-wing figure would have visited.

Paulo Freire is undoubtedly one of the most influential thinkers in education from the 1960s to the present day. Chile benefited from his presence. He also, amid the harsh conditions of his political exile, benefited from his time in Chile. In particular, the Jesuit Order overall benefited collaterally from its contact with the Brazilian. He was a supporting actor, but important (like all supporting actors) as someone who helped steer the Society of Jesus and the people who worked inside its institutions. In sum, Paulo Freire was collaterally associated with the Jesuit intellectual and educational world of the last five years of the 1960s and beyond.

NOTES

1 The Christian Democratic president Eduardo Frei Montalva governed between 1964 and 1970 with a program called Revolución en Libertad (Revolution in Freedom)

2 Fabian Cabaluz and Beatriz Areyuna-Ibarra, "La ruta de Paulo Freire en Chile (1964–1969): Alfabetización popular e influencias del marxismo heterodoxo," *Revista Colombiana de Educación* 1, no. 80 (August 2020), https://doi.org/10.17227/rce.num80-11066; Rolando Pinto Contreras, "Paulo Freire: Un Educador Humanista Cristiano En Chile," *Pensamiento Educativo* 34 (2004): 234; Marcela Gajardo, *Paulo Freire: Crónica de Sus Años En Chile* (Santiago, CL: Educación en Ciencias Basada en la Indagación, 2019), http://www.ecbichile.cl/home/download/paulo-freire-cronica-de-sus-anos-en-chile/; John Holst, "Paulo Freire in Chile, 1964–1969: Pedagogy of the Oppressed in Its Sociopolitical Economic Context," *Harvard Educational Review* 76, no. 2 (July 2006): 243–70; Andrew J. Kirkendall, "Paulo Freire, Eduardo Frei, Literacy Training and the Politics of Consciousness Raising in Chile, 1964 to 1970," *Journal of Latin American Studies* 36, no. 4 (November 2004): 687–717; Carlos Alberto Torres, *Paulo Freire En América Latina* (Mexico City: Editorial Gernika, 1980).

3 Founded in 1540 in Rome, by 1556 the order had members on all continents. In 1593, the Jesuits arrived in Chile, where they founded one of the first schools and universities in the country, along with other educational institutions such as libraries. John W. O'Malley, *The First Jesuits* (Cambridge, MA: Harvard University Press, 1993); John W. O'Malley, *The Jesuits: A History from Ignatius to the Present* (Lanham, MD: Rowman & Littlefield, 2014); Andre Ravier, *Ignatius of Loyola and the Founding of the Society of Jesus* (San Francisco: Ignatius Press, 1987).

4 Fernanda Beigel, *Misión Santiago. El Mundo Académico Jesuita y Los Inicios de La Cooperación Internacional Católica* (Santiago, CL: LOM Ediciones, 2011), 84. Unless otherwise noted, all translations are my own.

5 The Society of Jesus is organized territorially into provinces. The Chilean province includes the entire national territory of Chile. This is not the case, for example, for the national territory of the United States, which is composed of four provinces, or that of Argentina and Uruguay, which combined make up a single Jesuit province.

6 Cristóbal Madero, "Theological Dynamics of Paulo Freire's Educational Theory: An Essay to Assist the Work of Catholic Educators," *International Studies in Catholic Education* 7, no. 2 (2015): 122–33; Madero, "Freire and Religion: Myth, Callings, Liberation and Communion," in *Wiley Handbook of Paulo Freire*, ed. Carlos Alberto Torres (Hoboken, NJ: Wiley, 2019), 431–44.

7 Holst, "Paulo Freire in Chile, 1964–1969."

8 Kirkendall, "Paulo Freire, Eduardo Frei, Literacy Training and the Politics of Consciousness Raising in Chile, 1964 to 1970," 688.

9 Kirkendall.

10 In 1960, 31.8 per cent of the Chilean population was considered rural.

11 Kirkendall, "Paulo Freire, Eduardo Frei, Literacy Training and the Politics of Consciousness Raising in Chile, 1964 to 1970," 697.

12 Behind the concept of awareness is Freire's search for the emergence of a woman and a man with a new consciousness, who respond to the vocation to be completely human. The situation of poverty and inequality in Latin America, and Freire's readings of personalist, Marxist and neo-Marxist authors, made him affirm that it is the social structure that must provide men and women with a context in which to carry out their vocation. To achieve this, men and women must free themselves from an ideology of oppression through the process of conscientization. This process responds not only to the call to become aware of one's own situation, but also the context, the ideology behind the oppressed-oppressive relationship, and one's own incompleteness. Awareness can be fostered, Freire thought, in an educational context, and that is why the teacher plays a preponderant role, not just in the mere transmission of content, but also in the promotion of a new humanity. The problem of education – its disease as Freire himself called it – is that was established on a banking conception of education: a model whereby teachers simply deposit knowledge in students as if they are empty receptacles. On the contrary, Freire believed in an education that questions that which is otherwise taken for granted. This requires teachers to enter a new dimension of education. Throughout many of his works, Freire is insistent on certain characteristics and attitudes that teachers must have in the face of their most radical function. The root of this was certainly to be found in his intellectual training, but particularly in his own life experience.

13 Kirkendall, "Paulo Freire, Eduardo Frei, Literacy Training and the Politics of Consciousness Raising in Chile."

14 Paulo Freire, *La educación como práctica de la libertad, La educación como práctica de la libertad* (Santiago, CL: ICIRA, 1969).

15 Paulo Freire, *Extensión o comunicación?*, Publicaciones del instituto de capacitación e investigación en reforma agraria (Santiago, CL: ICIRA, 1969).

16 Paulo Freire, *Pedagogia do oprimido* (Rio de Janeiro: Paz e Terra, 1970).

17 Paulo Freire, *Sobre la acción cultural, Sobre la acción cultural* (Santiago, CL: Instituto de Capacitación e Investigación en Reforma Agraria, 1969).

18 Paulo Freire, *The Politics of Education* (Westport, CT: Bergin & Garvey, 1985).

19 Holst, "Paulo Freire in Chile, 1964–1969," 244.

20 CORA is the Corporación de la Reforma Agraria, or Corporation of Agrarian Reform.

21 "Sobre nosotros – Revista Mensaje," *Revista Mensaje*, accessed 17 February 2023, https://www.mensaje.cl/sobre-nosotros/.

22 Antje Schnoor, *Santa Desobediencia. Jesuitas Entre Democracia y Dictadura En Chile 1962–1983* (Santiago, CL: Ediciones UAH, 2016).

23 Paulo Freire, "Alfabetización de Adultos y 'Concientización,'" *Revista Mensaje* 14, no. 142 (1965): 494–501.

24 Freire, 494.

25 Freire, 501.

26 Marcela Gajardo, "El legado de Paulo Freire," *Revista Mensaje* 46, no. 459 (1997): 23–24.

27 Gustavo Gutiérrez, *A Theology of Liberation: History, Politics, and Salvation*, trans. Caridad Inda and John Eagleson (Maryknoll, NY: Orbis Books, 1988).

28 Josefina Rossetti, Francisco Álvarez, and Cecilia Cardemil, eds., *Patricio Cariola Barroilhet. Jesuita Innovador En Educación y Creador de Consensos* (Santiago, CL: RIL editores, 2019), 200.

29 Rossetti, Álvarez, and Cardemil, 168.

30 Juan Cristóbal García-Huidobro, "CIDE, 50 Años Contribuyendo a La Educación," *Cuadernos de Educación*, special issue (2015): 34.

31 Rossetti, Álvarez, and Cardemil, *Patricio Cariola Barroilhet. Jesuita Innovador En Educación y Creador de Consensos*, 193.

32 Freire, *Pedagogia do oprimido*.

33 The office Paulo Freire used for his work at ICIRA was, according to Luis Bustos, on the second floor of the Bellarmino Centre. Juan José Silva, working for CIDE, used to work in the joint office.

34 Freire, *La educación como práctica de la libertad*.

35 Freire, *Extensión o comúnicación?*

36 Juan Eduardo García-Huidobro, *La Experiencia REDUC (Red Latinoamericana de Información y Documentación En Educación)* (Santiago, CL: SIDOC, 2007), http://repositorio.uahurtado.cl/handle/11242/9698.

37 Ernesto Schiefelbein, "Tendencias de la investigación en América Latina: 'Seminario 80,'" *Perspectivas* 11, no. 3 (1981): 401–4.

38 Francisco Lopez, *Ilades. Testimonio de Una Historia 1965–1998* (Santiago, CL: Ediciones UAH, 2013), 49.

39 Lopez, 33.

40 Fabian Cabaluz and Beatriz Areyuna-Ibarra, "La ruta de Paulo Freire en Chile (1964–1969): Alfabetización popular e influencias del marxismo heterodoxo," *Revista Colombiana de Educación* 1, no. 80 (2020), https://doi.org/10.17227/rce.num80-11066.

41 Cabaluz and Areyuna-Ibarra, 298.

42 Beigel, *Misión Santiago. El Mundo Académico Jesuita y Los Inicios de La Cooperación Internacional Católica*, 178.

43 Germán Villarroel and Juan Cristóbal García-Huidobro, *Décadas de Articulación y Renovación. Evolución Histórica Del Área de Educación Escolar de La Provincia Chilena de La Compañía de Jesús* (Santiago, CL: Mensaje, 2020), 19.

44 Rolando Pinto, "Paulo Freire: Un Educador Humanista Cristiano En Chile," *Pensamiento Educativo* 34, no. 1 (June 2004), 234–58.

45 Cristián Cox and Patricia Imbarack, "Catholic Elite Education in Chile: Worlds Apart," in *Catholic Education in the Wake of Vatican II*, ed. Rosa Bruno-Jofré and Jon Igelmo Zaldívar (Toronto: University of Toronto Press, 2017).

4 Lonergan and Freire: An Initial Conversation

DARREN DIAS

Introduction

The English edition of *Pedagogy of the Oppressed* appeared in 1970, two years after its original publication in Portuguese. It has since been translated into numerous languages, and its author, Paulo Freire, has become one of the most cited thinkers in the field of educational theory.[1] One year later, in 1971, the Canadian philosopher and theologian Bernard Lonergan published *Method in Theology*. Lonergan is one of the most influential theologians in English-speaking North America, and the subject of an incredible volume of scholarship.[2] In this chapter I will bring key themes found in *Pedagogy of the Oppressed* and *Method in Theology* into what I hope will be a constructive dialogue. As a student of Lonergan, I will limit myself to what I suspect he can contribute to Freire's thought. Scholars of Freire's thought will have to judge if this is a helpful contribution.

Bernard Lonergan was born in Buckingham, Quebec, not far from the Canadian capital of Ottawa, in 1904. He entered the Society of Jesus in 1922, in which he enjoyed a classical humanist and theological education typical of Jesuit formation. After studies in philosophy, languages, and math at Heythrop College, London, he completed his doctoral studies in theology with a dissertation on grace and freedom in the thought Thomas Aquinas at the Pontifical Gregorian University in Rome. Lonergan taught at College de l'Immaculée Conception (Montreal), Regis College (Toronto), and the Gregorian, and was visiting professor at Harvard University and Boston College. His most significant early work, *Insight: A Study in Human Understanding*, was published in 1957. *Method in Theology* represents his more mature thinking.

Paulo Freire was born in Recife, in the Brazilian state of Pernambuco, in 1921. As a result of the Great Depression, Freire's family was plunged into poverty. After studies in law and education, Freire wrote his doctoral dissertation on adult literacy. In 1963 he was appointed director of a national literacy program.[3] In 1964 he was forced to seek exile in Chile following a coup d'etat in Brazil. He completed *Pedagogy of the Oppressed* while in exile. In 1970 Freire took up a position in the Office of Education of the World Council of Churches in Switzerland. He was particularly interested in decolonization in Africa. In 1979 he returned to Brazil, where he continued his work in popular education and political activism.

Framing the Dialogue

There are clear differences in discipline, context, and method between Lonergan and Freire. For example, Lonergan is concerned with mid-twentieth-century Roman Catholic theology and its place in the modern church and university, while Freire's concerns relate to the concrete liberation of the politically, socially, and economically oppressed. Lonergan's method is systematic and deductive while Freire's is inductive and rooted in praxis. However, there are also common themes in the two men's work. For example, economic analysis plays an important role in their social thought. Like Freire, the experience of the Great Depression shaped Lonergan's thinking. Lonergan was already teaching in Montreal by 1940. But his belief in the importance of economics because of the experience of the Depression is found in his early writings[4] and in a series of articles he wrote for the *Montreal Beacon* and the *Canadian Register* in the early 1940s. Chapter 7 of *Insight* explores economic and political systems, capital, technology, class and class conflict, capitalism, liberalism, and totalitarianism.[5] Near the end of his career, Lonergan considered returning to the study of economics because of the questions emerging from liberation theology. Freire's experience of the Depression as a child was acute and personal, as his family was forced to exchange their middle-class existence for poverty. In addition to the socio-economic situation of poverty in Brazil, this existential experience affected every aspect of his childhood and subsequent scholarship and commitments. Using liberation theology as a middle ground on which to compare Lonergan and Freire could be a fruitful avenue for discussion. Not much scholarship on the relationship of either scholar to the liberation movements that were growing in the 1970s and '80s has yet been undertaken.[6]

Another possible point of intersection in a dialogue between Lonergan and Freire would be a philosophy of education. Although Lonergan himself did not write explicitly on the topic of education, he did nonetheless give an important and influential workshop on Catholic education in Cincinnati, Ohio, in 1959. The workshop consisted of lectures in the mornings and then dialogues and questions around praxis among participants in the afternoons. These are published as *Topics in Education*.[7] Contrary to any romantic notion of education for its own sake, Lonergan clearly links education to the common good. According to Paddy Walsh, Lonergan outlines six requirements for a Catholic philosophy of education: a philosophy of education must be thought out in its concrete situations, not its abstractions; it is contemporary and not timeless; it must include theology; it must carry existential meaning for both student and teacher; it must engage the other human sciences; and it concludes with an "awareness of our responsibility for our human situation and future ... to exercise responsibility."[8] Judging from these requirements, a conversation between Lonergan and Freire on the philosophy of education would be fruitful.

In addition to bringing these two thinkers into dialogue around liberation theology and educational theory, another potentially rich area of overlap would revolve around Lonergan and Freire's theological world views and conceptions of spirituality, rooted as they are in the Roman Catholic Christian tradition. Lonergan's religious commitments are more overt and clear, for obvious reasons. Freire's theology and spirituality is to be found peppered throughout his work, often latently, whether due to his personal faith, religious-cultural context, or early experiences with activism, such as that practised by Catholic Action. His religious commitments are more obvious in his later writing.[9] Theological tropes that could be compared and contrasted in Lonergan and Freire are legion, at least from a theologian's perspective. Some of these include phenomenology; social ethics; sin and grace; history and eschatology; Christian humanism; and theological anthropology. Theological anthropology asks such questions as, what does it means to be human? And what does human flourishing look like?

Lonergan's anthropology is explicitly and clearly theological, rooted in the openness of the human person to question and the capacity to know and to love God. Freire's equally positive anthropology is grounded in what Stanley Aronowitz calls a "secular liberation theology"[10] with its categories of "authenticity, humanization, and self-emancipation."[11] At the heart of these anthropologies is the human capacity for self-awareness, self-transcendence, and the ability to shape history. It is beyond the scope of this brief chapter to make a fulsome comparison and contrast of Freire and Lonergan's anthropologies, however beneficial such a contribution would be. Instead, I will focus on one particular, and central, aspect of both their anthropologies, namely, "consciousness." I will draw on Lonergan's in-depth treatment of consciousness to help complement, clarify, and complexify Freire's concept of "conscientization." Likewise, I will draw on some of Freire's praxiological concerns to signal directions for development in Lonergan's thought. I compare and contrast consciousness, here understood to be self-awareness or critical self-appropriation and famously termed "conscientization" in Freire and "transcendental method" in Lonergan. In this fiftieth-anniversary year, I will limit myself primarily to the classic texts of *Pedagogy of the Oppressed* and *Method in Theology*.

Freire on Consciousness

Freire rarely speaks of consciousness alone. He employs the term either in its verbal form (*conscientizacao*/conscientization), or as a process of critical consciousness. *Conscientizacao*, according to Freire, "refers to learning to perceive social, political, and economic contradictions, and to take action against the oppressive elements of reality."[12] This is a "process of developing a critical awareness of one's social reality through reflection and action. Action is fundamental because it is the process of changing the reality ... We all acquire social myths which have a dominant tendency, and so learning is a critical process which depends upon uncovering real problems and actual needs."[13] Conscientization is a complex process whereby one comes to know reality and to shape one's history.

Freire outlines four levels of consciousness. The first level is *intransitive consciousness*, where people are concerned with meeting their "most elementary needs" and are marked by a "near absence of historical consciousness."[14] The second level is *magical consciousness*, which is evident in "closed societies" where people's social situation is taken as a "given." "This form of consciousness is characterized by a fatalistic mentality" and "self-deception ... for people have internalized the negative values that the dominant culture ascribes to them."[15] *Native* or *popular consciousness* is the third level. This is where a questioning of the "givenness" of a situation begins as well as an affirmation of subjects' agency in history. This is in spite of the "danger of manipulative populist leadership" that tries to convince the oppressed that there is no alternative to the way things are.[16] *Critical consciousness* is the highest level of consciousness and is achieved through "conscientization." This level is characterized by questioning and dialogue and a "depth in interpretation of problems, self confidence in discussions, receptiveness, refusal to shirk responsibilities."[17] It is accompanied by a "radical denunciation of dehumanizing structures ... [and an] announcing of a new reality to be created by men" so that they can shape their destinies.[18]

Critical consciousness is not a static, once-and-for-all achievement, but a dynamic and ongoing process in which one reflects upon and becomes aware of one's real situation. According to John Elias, conscientization is "the development of critical awareness achieved through dialogical educational programs associated with social and political responsibilities."[19] Critical consciousness brings about an awareness of oppression and dehumanizing situations and results in the will to transform these situations. Hence, beyond merely cognitive and epistemological awareness, the concept of conscientization includes the capacity to transform one's situation by moving circuitously from an analysis of the oppressive situation to critical reflection, engagement, and finally transformation.

Critical consciousness emerges from the cycle of critical reflection. According to Alexis Jemal Freirian, critical reflection includes the following:

1. Thinking critically about accepted beliefs, thoughts, feelings and assumptions;
2. Detecting the hidden interests underlying personal and social assumptions and beliefs;
3. Identifying how history impacts the present and details of everyday life and ways of thinking and feeling serve to maintain and perpetuate systems of inequality.[20]

Ongoing critical reflection leads to an awareness of reality and results in a deeper commitment to act in order to change oppressive social, political, and economic conditions.[21] Freirean pedagogy loops social action "back into analysis and dialogue such that reflection and social action merge to form praxis, the foundation for revolution."[22]

In his assessment of recent literature that engages Freire's legacy, Jemal refers to some critiques of critical consciousness that characterize it as "unidimensional" – for example, as a "purely cognitive state that derives from the critical analysis of sociopolitical inequity."[23] Thus, critical consciousness overcomes a false consciousness by achieving a critical awareness of oneself and one's relationship to the world. Another "unidimensional" charge regards the nature of the relationship of "awareness and action."[24] What exactly is the relationship between cognitional acts and the "skills that facilitate effectively addressing issues of social injustice?"[25] Or what is the relationship between critical consciousness, praxis, and liberation? And what is the relationship between the lower level of intransitive consciousness and higher levels of critical consciousness and finally liberative action?

Citing the work of Baker and Brookins, Jamel reports, "Despite the research on CC [critical consciousness] that has contributed to our understanding of CC and the wide usage of CC, the CC construct and theoretical framework remains vague, ambitious and fragmented."[26] He goes on to say, "Definitions differ on whether CC is an outcome or a developmental process and confuse CC, conscientizacao, praxis and the tools, strategies or techniques of the consciousness-raising process."[27] I propose that dialogue with Lonergan's work can assist us in thinking through what remains vague and fragmented in Freire, especially when we examine Lonergan's detailed heuristic of consciousness, and in particular Lonergan's exploration of patterns of experience, transcendental method, horizon, realms of meaning, bias, and conversion.

Lonergan on Consciousness

An initial dialogue between Lonergan and Freire is found in Robert M. Doran's opus *Theology and the Dialectics of History*. In that work Doran is interested in exploring what the Kingdom of God could look like on earth using insights from Lonergan, depth psychology, and liberation theology. According to Doran, Freire is concerned with the "liberation of consciousness":

> What Freire was actually *doing* with illiterate and oppressed peasants held captive in a system of economic and political oppression entailed helping them to claim as their own precisely the native capacities of human intentionality that Lonergan has disengaged in a more general heuristic fashion.[28]

Lonergan provides a heuristic to understand Freire's project. This includes a heuristic for understanding consciousness.

Doran focuses his attention on what Lonergan terms "patterns of experience." These patterns are governed by experiences we have appropriated and so made our own.[29] According to Doran, Freire demonstrates that such a "pattern can be a function not only of one's own self-determined interests and concerns, but also of psychological, social, economic, political, and linguistic conditioning."[30] They are the product of psychological and social determinisms that purport to be the way things have to be, with no alternative. Freire's method promotes the awareness that the experiences of the oppressed are conditioned by patterns that benefit the oppressor. Freire's pedagogy helps the oppressed "recognize that they can reach an understanding of their experience outside of the conditioned pattern and that launches a possibility of a new interpretation and a new pattern by setting one on a process of further questioning."[31] Doran calls this "the power of raising questions."

In *Learning to Question: A Pedagogy of Liberation*, Freire and Faundez claim that even in the context of ideology and alienation, the human subject's "persistent questioning ... reveals one's capacity for self-transcendence."[32] Questioning is, according to the authors, "essentially democratic and for that very reason anti-authoritarian."[33] Likewise, for Lonergan, questioning is the hallmark of human development that leads to self-transcendence. Freire's anthropology adds a contextual dimension to Lonergan's heuristic. Doran speaks of

> a heightened recognition that the constitution of consciousness in its capacity for insight and reasonable judgement has a liberating potential, especially when it is not just exercised but also claimed as one's own ... To be deprived of this power by a cultural conditioning and determinism is to be deprived of a constituent of the *humanum*. To claim and exercise this power is a source of liberation from other deprivations of the *humanum* as well.[34]

Thus, the questioning that is constitutive of the capacity of the human consciousness for insight and reasonable judgment is a powerful ingredient in human freedom and liberation.

Transcendental Method

Lonergan provides a thorough account of human consciousness, first by distinguishing between four levels of consciousness that are related and successive, and then by distinguishing between "consciousness" and "intentionality."[35] The first level of consciousness is the empirical level: the level of experience, sense, perception, imagination, feeling, etc. Next comes the intellectual level of enquiry and insight into the data of experience. The third level is rational: reflection, deliberation, and judgment; when one weighs the evidence gleaned in understanding in order to make a judgment of fact. The last level is that of

responsibility: the existential moment when one decides if one will live according to what one has affirmed to be true in the previous level.

Lonergan describes this process as spontaneous since it is constitutive of all
human knowing:

> Spontaneously we move from experiencing to the effort to understand; and the
> spontaneity is not unconscious or blind; on the contrary, it is constitutive of
> conscious intelligence ... Spontaneously we move from understanding with its
> manifold and conflicting expressions to critical reflection ... [Spontaneity] is con-
> stitutive of our critical rationality, of the demand within us for sufficient reason, a
> demand that operates prior to any formulation of a principle of sufficient reason
> ... Spontaneously we move from judgments of fact or possibility to judgments of
> value and to the deliberateness of decision and commitment ... It constitutes us as
> conscientious, as responsible persons.[36]

The relationship between the levels of consciousness is not the result of learned
skills, but rather arises spontaneously in human consciousness. It is constitutive
of the process of human knowing, independent of culture, historical development, age, or stage of life. As it is constitutive of human knowing, it is present
in any learner.

Levels	Operations	Transcendental Precepts
Empirical	Experience	Be attentive
Intellectual	Understanding	Be intelligent
Rational	Judgment	Be reasonable
Responsible	Decision	Be responsible

Each level has a corresponding operation and precept. At the empirical level,
the subject is invited to be attentive to the range of data he or she experiences.
At the intellectual level, the subject is invited to be intelligent in attempting to
understand the data of experience. At the rational level, the subject must weigh
various understandings and hypotheses and make a judgment of fact: Is this
or that understanding correct? At the level of responsibility, one must decide
if one will act in accordance with what one knows to be true and valuable.
Lonergan explains that "Our consciousness expands in a new dimension when
from mere experiencing we turn to the effort to understand what we have experienced."[37] Further, rationality "emerges when the content of our acts of understanding" are not merely a "bright idea" but "what is really so."[38] In judgments
of fact or value, the meaning is independent of the subject: judgments of fact
state what is or is not so, and judgments of value what is truly good or better.[39]
The fullness of judgments of value stems not from merely knowing the good

but from doing it as well. There is in such judgment a performative aspect. In a judgment of fact, one can know the good without doing it. A judgment of value, on the other hand, is constitutive of moral self-transcendence. Judging what is really so, what is fact and value, is followed by deliberation for action.

While consciousness is the dynamic process of moving from experience to understanding to judgment to decision, "intentionality" is the objectification of this process. The process can be heightened by intentionally adverting to and objectifying consciousness; thus, what is conscious can be intended. With regard to the conscious intentionality that constitutes his transcendental method, Lonergan states the following:

> To apply the operations as intentional to the operations as conscious is a fourfold matter of (1) experiencing one's experiencing, understanding, judging and deciding, (2) understanding the unity and relations of one's experienced experiencing, understanding, judging and deciding, (3) affirming the reality of one's experienced and understood experiencing, understanding, judging and deciding, and (4) deciding to operate in accord with the norms immanent in the spontaneous relatedness of one's experienced, understood, affirmed experiencing, understanding, judging and deciding.[40]

For example, one can see or hear something without intentionally adverting to the internal processes of seeing and hearing. One can also intentionally bring to consciousness an awareness of one's process of seeing and hearing. Lonergan's transcendental method poses three basic questions: "What am I doing when I am knowing? Why is doing that knowing? What do I know when I do it? The first answer is a cognitional theory. The second is an epistemology. The third is a metaphysics, where, however, the metaphysics is transcendental, an integration of heuristic structures, and not some categorical speculation that reveals that all is water, or matter, or spirit, or process, or what have you."[41]

The transcendental method has several functions germane to a dialogue with Freire's critical consciousness. First, transcendental method is normative because the precepts have a "prior existence and reality in the spontaneous, structured dynamism of human consciousness."[42] It is not exclusive to elites or academics, philosophers or priests, but in all human persons. It is a constitutive feature of being human that simply cannot be taken away by the force of the powerful. Transcendental method is a point of departure for dialogue between different groups. There is also a critical function in the relationship between cognitional theory, knowing, and reality. What is known is not an illusion, or hegemonically determined. The human person is capable of becoming aware of his/her situation *as it really is*, not as it may be imagined or constructed by others. Lastly, there is a heuristic function whereby "every inquiry aims at transforming some unknown into a known. Inquiry itself, then, is something between ignorance and knowledge. It is less than knowledge, else there would be no need to inquire."[43] Knowledge is not a given, but something discovered and grown and acquired in ongoing dynamic processes.

Horizon

Another aspect of Lonergan's heuristic of human consciousness has to do with context or horizon. Human enquiry takes places within a historical, social, cultural, religious, and linguistic context that Lonergan names "horizon." Horizons "are the sweep of our interests and of our knowledge; they are the fertile source of further knowledge and care; but they are also the boundaries that limit our capacities for assimilating more than we already have attained."[44] Differences in horizon may be complementary, genetic, or dialectical. Complementary horizons work together for the functioning of society. Genetically different horizons may indicate a difference in stages of development. Horizons that are dialectically opposed may be contrary or contradictory. Those that are contrary may be able to be integrated into a higher synthesis while those that are contradictory remain opposed. Navigating these differences in horizon enables one to clarify one's position and to dialogue in spite of, and perhaps because of, personal, social, cultural, and religious differences.

Although horizons signal limits and boundaries, they are also the springboard to expansion, development, and growth. We are not trapped within a horizon, or a perspective within a given horizon. Following Joseph de Finance, Lonergan distinguishes between the "horizontal" and "vertical" liberty or exercise of freedom. "Horizontal liberty is the exercise of liberty within a determinate horizon and from the basis of a corresponding existential stance. Vertical liberty is the exercise of liberty that selects that stance and the corresponding horizon."[45] The exercise of horizontal liberty is the movement within a given horizon to another. For example, one can move from being a culture warrior Roman Catholic to a social activist Roman Catholic, all the while remaining a committed Catholic. Vertical liberty is more radical than a change in perspective: it is a new way of situating oneself in the world. No one person or group is determined by their horizon, which is constantly shifting because of new and emerging data, understandings, judgments, and decisions.

Realms of Meaning

Lonergan posits that meaning is communicated in various ways, through various carriers, and with various functions. Different realms of meaning are distinguished by the emergence of different exigencies. Lonergan explicitly enumerates three realms of meaning in *Method*, and more latently posits a fourth. While these realms have unfolded historically in Western history, they are simultaneously present and operative in a world mediated by meaning. The first is the realm of common sense – of "persons and things in relation to us. It is the visible universe."[46] The world of immediacy is like the world experienced by a child. The child's world is constituted by those people and things that are subject to his/her direct experience (food, toys, parents, etc.). We know this realm simply by experiencing it. But in the realm of common sense emerges questions that probe beyond the world of immediacy and that cannot be answered from within the realm of common sense. Asking and attempting to answer these questions gives rise to another stage of meaning: theory.[47] The realm of theory attempts to explain the relationship of things not in relation to the subject but in relation to one another in the wider world mediated by meaning.

The next stage of meaning is interiority. It is the result of the emergence of three basic critical questions: "What am I doing when I am knowing? Why is doing that knowing? What do I know when I do it? With these questions one moves from the outer realms of common sense and theory to the appropriation of one's own interiority, one's subjectivity, one's operations."[48] The questions are no longer about the world one experiences, or how the data concerning such experiences are related to one another, but about one's own interior cognitional operations and their relationship to epistemology and metaphysics. This is a heightening of one's consciousness, as one is not only attending to objects and their relationship but to the intending subject. However, Lonergan warns, the "withdrawal to interiority is not an end in itself. From it one returns to the realms of common sense and theory."[49]

Lonergan scholar John Dadosky articulates another stage of meaning that is only latently present and unfortunately underdeveloped in Lonergan's work. To common sense, theory, and interiority, Dadosky develops Lonergan's transcendental exigency to speak about a "fourth stage of meaning [that] involves a turn to the Other: alterity. This alterity includes a vertical relation with a transcendent Other and the horizontal commitment to one's neighbour."[50] This clarifies Lonergan's position that one does not remain in one's own interiority but rather, precisely as a result of the stages of meaning coupled with the transcendental precepts, turns "from the subject's intentional consciousness to the subject's awareness of the Other."[51]

Bias and Decline

Another element in Lonergan's transcendental method that assists in clarifying Freire's critical consciousness has to do with the common good. Against any individualist interpretation of human knowledge, Lonergan posits that human knowledge itself is not an individual possession but a "common fund from which each may draw."[52] This common fund "may suffer blind spots, oversights, errors, bias, … [but] the critical and selfless stance … promote[s] progress and offset[s] decline."[53] Progress is promoted by being attentive, intelligent, reasonable, and responsible of one's conscious operations. It is the result of observing the transcendental precepts. Progress is a continuous flow of improvements. Such progress promotes the common good:

> The human good, then, is at once individual and social. Individuals do not just operate to meet their needs but cooperate to meet one another's needs. As the community develops its institutions to facilitate cooperation, so individuals develop skills to fulfil the roles and perform the tasks set by the institutional framework.[54]

But the common good comes under threat when the transcendental precepts are violated by "an egoistic disregard of others, by loyalty to one's group matched by hostility to other groups, by concentrating on short-term benefits and overlooking long-term costs. Moreover, such aberrations are easy to maintain and difficult to correct."[55]

While Lonergan has a basically positive human anthropology due to his theology of grace, he is not blind to the reality of sin or bias. Bias occurs when one does not follow the transcendental precepts. Instead of being attentive to relevant and new data, one opts to ignore them; instead of being intelligent in understanding such data, one opts to puts one's authentic intellectual faculties aside in favour of following an ideology; instead of being reasonable in making a judgment, one is irrational; instead of being responsible, one abdicates the responsibility of acting in accord with what one knows to be the case, all the while making justifications for doing so. Short-circuiting the dynamic of conscious intentionality results in individual and collective alienation. Lonergan enumerates four biases – dramatic, egoistic, group, and general biases – that threaten the common good.[56]

Dramatic bias is the result of an inattentiveness to data that results from an unhealed psychological trauma. Egoistic bias erodes the good of order by placing individual satisfactions before the needs of others. Beyond individual bias of the egoist there is the collective egoism of group bias, which "directs development to its own aggrandizement but also provides a market for opinions, doctrines, theories that will justify its ways and, at the same time, reveal the misfortunes of other groups to be due to their depravity."[57] Group bias divides society into "haves" and "have-nots," promoting the values of the "haves" and accepting their self-serving ideology to rationalize their behaviour, blinding people to the truth of reality and leaving "bewildered by the emergence of a contrary ideology that will call to consciousness an opposed group egoism."[58] General bias is the bias of common-sense thinking that places the "practical" above the "theoretical" and places them in opposition, seeking short-term and immediate solutions for what are actually deeper problems that require longer-term solutions. Such bias excludes deeper structural questioning.

As much as progress is possible, so is decline when "the basic form of ideology is a doctrine that justifies ... alienation," and that results from a disregard for the transcendental precepts: be attentive, be intelligent, be reasonable, be responsible.[59] Such ideologies corrupt minds, discredit authentic progress, and accept the "objectively absurd situation." It is a total distortion of progress and rationalization and a commitment to "inattention, obtuseness, unreasonableness, and irresponsibility" that "produce[s] objectively absurd situations."[60] The alienation that results is personal and subjective as much as it is social, economic, and political.

Conversion

A last point of connection between Freire and Lonergan's theories of consciousness explored in this chapter is conversion. Lonergan's positive theological anthropology would not leave us stranded in the grips of bias and decline. Instead, he affirms the possibility of addressing bias and reversing decline through what he terms "conversion." First, intellectual conversion is "a radical clarification and, consequently, the elimination of an exceedingly stubborn and misleading myth concerning reality, objectivity, and human knowledge."[61] The myth is that knowing is merely "taking a look," that the real is known by the experience of the data of sense alone.[62] Instead, knowing is a compound act that includes the acts of understanding and judgment.

Next, moral conversion is the shift in criterion for choosing and deciding between satisfaction and value.[63] Lonergan writes,

> we move to the existential moment when we discover for ourselves that our choosing affects ourselves no less than the chosen or rejected objects, and that is up to each of us to decide for himself [*sic*] what he is to make of himself.[64]

The criteria for choosing and deciding shifts from what is self-satisfying to what is valuable, from self-regard to regard for others (individuals and/or groups), from what may be immediately satisfying to what may take some time to bear fruit.

The highest form of conversion is religious. This entails "being grasped by ultimate concern ... It is revealed in retrospect as an undertow of existential consciousness, as a fated acceptance of a vocation to holiness."[65] The Christian theological tradition names this grace: it is the gift of the Holy Spirit, the gift of divine love that floods the human heart. The result "is a total being-in-love as the efficacious ground of all self-transcendence, whether in the pursuit of truth, or in the realization of human values, or in the orientation man [*sic*] adopts to the universe, its ground, and its goal."[66] Religious conversion colours all levels of consciousness. The power of love enables humans to "accept the suffering involved in undoing the effects of decline."[67] God's love transforms the human being into a being-in-love vis-à-vis others.

According to Lonergan interpreter James Marsh, intellectual and moral conversion implies a "radical political conversion" that transcends egoistic self-centredness, embraces principles of justice, and criticizes social and economic systems in solidarity with the "exploited, marginalized, and oppressed" in a praxis directed towards just systems.[68] Marsh further argues that moral conversion leads to "solidarity with the poor and oppressed. For insofar as people are exploited, dominated, and marginalized by an unjust racist, sexist, heterosexist, classist capitalism, then I have to respond to their cry and side with them against the oppressor."[69] Religious conversion overcomes individual and social sin (bias) when a subject is oriented by love. In reference to religious conversion in a Christian context, Marsh writes, "A Christianity that merely legitimates and reproduces the bourgeois, middle-class subject is incomplete and self-denying." Moreover, religious conversion includes the "orientation to community that is at odds with the individualistic, bourgeois subject, regarding others as obstacles or means on the way to affluent living."[70] The religiously converted subject loves lavishly in imitation of and in participation with God's own love. This is consistent with the preferential option for the poor gleaned from liberation theology, where God has a particular love for the poor, the oppressed, the vulnerable, the outcast, and the marginalized.

Conclusion

The heuristic proposed by Lonergan in *Method in Theology* complements the experiential-praxiological approach articulated by Freire in *Pedagogy of the Oppressed*. Both thinkers begin in the concrete experiences of the subject,[71] but while Freire remains rooted in the concrete and historical realms of the oppressed in Brazil, Lonergan develops a cross-cultural, heuristic account of human consciousness that begins with lived experience. Lonergan assists in clarifying Freire's thought by distinguishing consciousness from intentionality, horizons, realms of meaning, bias, and conversion. In Freire's levels of consciousness these distinct categories are conflated as he has a different set of commitments and concerns than Lonergan.

Lonergan's four levels of conscious intentionality shared by all human subjects underscore Freire's project linking education and humanization precisely because conscious intentionality is shared by all human operators and is constitutive of human development and flourishing. It is applicable to freedom-oriented learning. Restricting human development – whether this is imposed on subject by external social, religious, political, or economic forces, or whether the bias is insidiously internalized and self-imposed – alienates the knowing subject from him- or herself and from their world of meaning. This is what Freire calls "the distortion of the vocation of becoming more fully human."[72]

Self-awareness as conscious beings is, according to Freire, the defining feature of humankind, the quality that distinguishes us from other animals.[73] Further, this capacity for self-awareness through the objectification of one's own "activity" results in the freedom to overcome or to change one's situation. Lonergan offers a complex account of this "activity" at the level of human operations that are objectified in the dynamic process of conscious intentionality that leads to action. Like Lonergan, Freire argues that the achievement of self-transcendence is not completed once and for all, but is an ongoing process of constant self-examination.[74]

The constant re-examination of the self that Freire speaks of is both complicated and clarified by Lonergan's threefold conversion (intellectual, moral, and religious). Intellectual conversion results in one knowing the reality of a given situation; moral conversion transforms criteria for decision making into what is worthwhile rather than what is merely self-satisfying; and religious conversion enables one to love unrestrictedly and to place oneself at risk for the sake of the other. This radical change in consciousness is encapsulated in Freire's concept of the "Easter experience."[75] He writes, "Conversion to the people requires profound rebirth. Those who undergo it must take on a new form of existence; they cannot remain as they were."[76] The Easter experience moves us beyond the realms of common sense, theory, and interiority to include alterity, a commitment to the other. This loving commitment to the other, when coupled with the transcendental precepts, expands human knowing from a merely cognitional act to a performance of what is known to be good and true. This accounts for the possibility of personal and social transformation.

This chapter is but an initial attempt at a dialogue between two significant twentieth-century theorists of consciousness. I have focused primarily on the ways in which Lonergan complements, clarifies, and extends Freire's concept of conscientization through a thorough examination of Lonergan's helpful heuristic account of consciousness. While far from exhaustive, the chapter demonstrates that there is much to be gleaned from this dialogue between two great thinkers, who though different in so many ways that have not been treated here, share a fundamental belief in the capacity of the human person to come to know and do good, and to flourish individually and collectively as a result.

NOTES

1   According to Sandro Barros, Freire is the third most-cited education scholar; see Barros, "Paulo Freire in a Hall of Mirrors," *Educational Theory* 70, no. 2 (2020): 155.
2   Lonergan's collected works will eventually be published in twenty-one volumes as well an index by the University of Toronto Press. There are Lonergan centres at universities in Toronto, Boston, Los Angeles, Milwaukee, Rome, etc.

3   "Paulo Freire: A Brief Intellectual Biography," accessed 17 April 2021, https://
    cccwaproject.files.wordpress.com/2018/10/about_paulo_freire-1.pdf.

4   See Bernard Lonergan, *Lonergan's Early Economics Research*, ed. Michael Schute
    (Toronto: University of Toronto Press, 2010).

5   Frederick E. Crowe, "Bernard Lonergan and Liberation Theology," in *Appropriating
    the Lonergan Idea*, ed. Michael Vertin (Toronto: University of Toronto Press, 2006),
    116–27, 118–119. See Bernard Lonergan, *Collected Works of Bernard Lonergan*, vol. 3,
    Insight, ed. Frederick Crowe and Robert Doran (Toronto: University of Toronto Press,
    1992).

6   See James D. Kirylo and Drick Boyd, *Paulo Freire, His Faith Spirituality, and Theol-
    ogy* (Rotterdam: Sense Publishers, 2017), 77–104.

7   Bernard Lonergan, *Collected Works of Bernard Lonergan*, vol. 10, *Topics in Educa-
    tion*, ed. Robert M. Doran, SJ, and Frederick E. Crowe, SJ (Toronto: University of
    Toronto Press, 2005).

8   Paddy Walsh, "From Philosophy to Theology of Catholic Education, with Bernard
    Lonergan and Karl Rahner," *International Studies in Education* 10 (2018): 132–55,
    134–5.

9   Peter Roberts, *Paulo Freire in the 21st Century: Education, Dialogue, and Transfor-
    mation* (New York: Routledge, 2016), 15.

10 Stanley Aronowitz, "Paulo Freire's Radical Democratic Humanism," in *Paulo
    Freire: A Critical Encounter*, ed. Peter McLaren and Peter Leonard (London: Rout-
    ledge, 1993), 12.

11 Aronowitz, 23.

12 Paulo Freire, *Pedagogy of the Oppressed*, 50th ann. ed., trans. Myra Bergman
    Ramos (New York: Bloomsbury, 2017), 35.

13 "Conscientization," Freire Institute, accessed April 17, 2021, https://www.freire.org
    /paulo-freire/concepts-used-by-paulo-freire.

14 Although these are not found in *Pedagogy of the Oppressed*, it is important to have a
    clearer idea of what Freire means when he uses the term "consciousness" there. These
    levels are found in Paulo Freire, *Education for Critical Consciousness* (New York:
    Continuum, 1997). See also John L. Elias, "Paulo Freire: Religious Educator," *Religious
    Education* 71, no. 2 (1976): 40–56, 52.

15 Elias, "Religious Educator," 53.

16 Elias, 53.

17 Elias, 53.

18 Elias, 53. The authors discussed in this chapter often use the masculine
    third-person-singular pronoun, reflecting a usage that was dominant during
    the era in which they wrote; the author of this chapter does not endorse such
    non-inclusive language.

19 Elias, 52.

20 Alexis Jemal, "Critical Consciousness: A Critique and Critical Analysis of the Literature,"
    Urban Review 49 (2017): 602–26.

21   See Freire, *Pedagogy of the Oppressed*, 83.

22   Jemal, "Critical Consciousness," 612.

23   Jemal, 606.

24   Jemal, 606.

25   Jemal, 607.

26   Jemal, 619.

27   Jemal, 619.

28   Robert M. Doran, *Theology and the Dialectics of History* (Toronto: University of Toronto Press, 1990), 38.

29   Doran, 38.

30   Doran, 39.

31   Doran, 39.

32   Rohan M. Curnow, *The Preferential Option for the Poor: A Short History and Reading Based on the Thought of Bernard Lonergan* (Milwaukee, WI: Marquette University Press, 2012), 133.

33   Paulo Freire and Antonio Faundez, *Learning to Question: A Pedagogy of Liberation* (Geneva: World Council of Churches, 1989), 45.

34   Doran, *Dialectics of History*, 40.

35   Bernard Lonergan, *Collected Works of Bernard Lonergan*, vol. 14, *Method in Theology*, ed. Robert M. Doran and John Dadosky (Toronto: University of Toronto Press, 2017), 13.

36   Lonergan, 21.

37   Lonergan, 13.

38   Lonergan, 13.

39   Lonergan, 38.

40   Lonergan, 18.

41   Lonergan, 27.

42   Lonergan, 23.

43   Lonergan, 24.

44   Lonergan, 223.

45   Lonergan, 41.

46   Lonergan, 79.

47   Lonergan, 79.

48   Lonergan, 80.

49   Lonergan, 81.

50   John D. Dadosky, "Is There a Fourth Stage of Meaning," *Heythrop Journal* 51 (2010): 772. See also, John Dadosky, "Further Along in the Fourth Stage of Meaning: Lonergan, Alterity and Genuine Religion," *Irish Theological Quarterly* 85 (2020): 64–79.

51   Dadosky, "Fourth Stage of Meaning," 773.

52   Lonergan, *Collected Works*, 14:44.

53   Lonergan, 44.

54 Lonergan, 51.
55 Lonergan, 52.
56 These are found in volume 14 of the *Collected Works*, 50–8, but also in volume 3, 215–27, and most clearly in "Healing and Creating in History" and "Mission and the Spirit," both in *Collected Work of Bernard Lonergan*, vol. 16, *A Third Collection*, ed. Robert Doran and John Dadosky (Toronto: University of Toronto Press, 2017).
57 Lonergan, *Collected Works*, 14:53.
58 Lonergan, 53.
59 Lonergan, 53.
60 Lonergan, 53.
61 Lonergan, 223.
62 According to Lonergan, this would be the position on knowing of empiricists.
63 Lonergan, *Collected Works*, 14:225.
64 Lonergan, 225.
65 Lonergan, 226.
66 Lonergan, 227.
67 Lonergan, 228.
68 Lonergan, 213.
69 James L. Marsh, *Process, Praxis, Transcendence* (Albany: SUNY Press, 1999), 213.
70 Marsh, 225.
71 Freire, *Pedagogy of the Oppressed*, 95.
72 Freire, 44.
73 Freire, 99.
74 Freire, 60.
75 See Kirylo and Boyd, *Paulo Freire*, 13–18.
76 Freire, *Pedagogy of the Opressed*, 60.

5 "The Wolf Shall Dwell with the Lamb": Traces of Prophetic Judaism in the Concept of Love in *Pedagogy of the Oppressed*

GONZALO JOVER AND DAVID LUQUE

Introduction

The reasons why Paulo Freire has assumed a seemingly unmovable place in the history of education are many. To start with, his personality still sparks admiration as well as rejection to this day, and arouses interest either way. This is someone who grew up intellectually and spiritually in the folds of Marxism and a "subversive" Christianity, as Casaldáliga described the Eucharist in his poems; someone who decided to give up his career as a lawyer in order to help poor people learn to read and write, as a way to keep them from being manipulated; someone who, influenced by many readings, was able to articulate a pedagogy born of his own experience; someone who received the highest accolades in life for his theories and achievements; someone who continues to inspire the teaching practices of many today.[1]

Pedagogy of the Oppressed is considered the high point of Freire's bibliography.[2] The arguments in his previous works come into their own in this book; subsequent works delve into, develop, or add nuance to what was already present but often under-articulated in it. In the book, Freire draws on a variety of schools of thought such as existentialism, phenomenology, Marxism, and psychoanalysis, and from a host of influential authors such as Erich Fromm, Albert Memmi, and Frantz Fanon.[3]

The book was born from Freire's own experiences working in adult literacy campaigns in his native Brazil. The military coup d'etat in 1964 meant that he had to finish writing about those experiences from exile in Chile, where *Pedagogy of the Oppressed* was composed over the course of 1967 and 1968. Although incomplete copies were being circulated in those years, the first commercial publications in English and Spanish translation were released in 1970. The original Portuguese edition, however, took five more years to be published, by which time the volume had also been translated into Italian, French, and German.[4]

The text is a child of its time, but it also transcends it as well. It mirrors the controversies and aspirations of late-1960s politics as well as the subsequent search for alternatives to the traditional model of schooling. In Freire's discourse are ideas that have been a source of inspiration to many teachers. The concept of banking education, the very idea of the oppressed, and the dynamics of literacy as a practice of freedom all compose a distinctly Freireian pedagogy. But of all these elements, one seems to be the most characteristic of Freire's outlook: love.

For Freire's interpreter and collaborator Antonia Darder, if there is one expression that can best reinvent Freire, it is "a pedagogy of love."[5] She recalls an interview with Pepi Leisyna in which Freire expressed himself as follows:

> I understand the process of teaching as an act of love. I mean, it is not an act of love in the formal sense, and never in the bureaucratic sense. It is an act of love as an expression of good care, a need to love, first of all, what you do. Can you imagine how painful it is to do anything without passion, to do everything mechanically?[6]

Like Darder, there are many authors, such as the Spanish specialist Ramón Flecha, who hold that Freire will be remembered as the teacher of love.[7] However, beyond approaches that brandish it as the chief motto of his educational proposals, little hermeneutic attention has been given to the strict meaning of love in Freire's work. To Fraser, this absence has to do with a general tendency to sidestep the theological underpinnings of Freirean pedagogy. But as Fraser warns, "ignoring spirituality, ignoring Freire's own power as a 'spiritual guide,' is both a distortion of his work and an unnecessary impoverishment of our own understanding of the world."[8]

This chapter aims to reintroduce religious language into the analysis of the concept of love in *Pedagogy of the Oppressed*. Although we will mention other books by Freire, we confine our analysis to this particular work. Our interest originates in a few footnotes to *Pedagogy of the Oppressed* that can be used to trace the specific sources that Freire had in mind when he developed his notion of love. Freire spoke of love several times throughout the book, especially in chapter 1, where he relates the concept to necrophilia and biophilia as inherent forces in the processes of oppression and liberation, as well as in chapter 4, where he speaks of dialogue and anti-dialogue as matrices of opposing theories of cultural action. The footnotes in the book reveal the influence of two authors linked to Judaism in Freire's development of the concept: Erich Fromm and Martin Buber. These notes are dotted with discussions of other works of a more general nature, including references to Che Guevara to illustrate the revolutionary meaning of love. Before we analyse these two sources, we will succinctly outline the profile of love in *Pedagogy of the Oppressed*, which will then be expanded considering the sources.

Three Prior Notes on the Idea of Love in *Pedagogy of the Oppressed*

Freire wrote that love "is an act of courage, not of fear, love is commitment to others. No matter where the oppressed are found, the act of love is commitment to their cause – the cause of liberation. And this commitment, because it is loving, is dialogical."[9] This statement is the closest Freire ever comes to defining love in *Pedagogy of the Oppressed*. It contains the fundamental aspects of this concept. Love is, first and foremost, a courageous commitment to the oppressed yearning for freedom. It is a commitment to human growth, being, life, and biophilia, as opposed to the oppressor's fondness for annulment, death, and necrophilia. Thus, the commitment takes on an educational dimension insofar as it entails projecting into the future the decision to accompany the process of liberating the oppressed not as oppressors, or even as teachers, but as companions. This itself may mean being courageous: not falling into paternalism or tyranny.

The second aspect is derived from the previous one and states that love is a basic attribute in the relationship of liberation. The oppressed are the "unloved,"[10] those who have stopped being loved, and who may return to being fully human when they are loved. However, Freire refers not only to how the oppressors should relate to the oppressed, but also to how the oppressed should relate to their oppressors. As an act of love, revolution requires that the oppressed not use the same annulment of the other practised by the oppressors, since that would turn them into oppressors as well. In short, love encompasses a dynamic that can transform the relationship between the oppressors and the oppressed, thereby generating a new reality, which brings us to the third aspect.

Freire's interpretation of love has a Genesis-like undercurrent attributable to its dialogical dimension: uttering a new world means creating it. Love is a dialogical commitment that equalizes the relationships between the oppressors and the oppressed to the point of uttering/creating a new world actively aspired to as a horizon of possibility. In a decisive paragraph (one that Freire moved to different places in different editions of the book), he wrote, "From these pages I hope at least the following will endure: my trust in the people, and my faith in men and women, and in the creation of a world in which it will be easier to love."[11] With these words, Freire asserts that the main feature of a liberated world is the facility to love. Moreover, this facility is practically a consequence of the other two theological virtues: faith that men and women will be able to do it, which in and of itself implies an active disposition towards the third, hope. In sum, Freire's liberated world would emerge as an *ethos* according to which it would be relatively easy to perceive oppression and make use of love to carry out liberation.

Love of Death and Love of Life: The Mark of Erich Fromm

Freire's first reference in *Pedagogy of the Oppressed* in relation to love is the German writer Erich Fromm. Fromm was twenty-one years older than Freire. He was born in 1900 in Frankfurt, the only son of an Orthodox Jewish family related to several rabbis. From an early age, Fromm found refuge from a troubled family background in the study of the sacred texts of the Hebrew tradition, becoming fascinated with the prophetic writings of Isaiah, Amos, and Hosea and their visions of peace and harmony among nations. During the First World War, he became a leader of the Orthodox Jewish community in Frankfurt under the influence of Rabbi Nehemiah Nobel. From the circle of young people who gathered with Fromm around Nobel, the Freie Jüdische Lehrhaus (Free Jewish Teaching Institute) was founded, and it soon became a secular centre for the education of German Jews under the direction of Franz Rosenzweig. Another decisive influence on the young Fromm was Salman Rabinkow, a scholar of the Talmud. Rabinkow was most likely the one who introduced Fromm to Marxist theory and stimulated his appreciation for Hasidism, teaching him to interpret Jewish tradition in the spirit of radical humanism.[12] Although over time Fromm would come to reject religious ascription, he always held to the importance of spirituality in individual and social life, and the continuity of those teachings in his world view without the need to be a religious practitioner or believer.[13]

In the 1930s Fromm worked as a researcher at the Institut für Sozialforschung (Institute for Social Research) in Frankfurt and then in New York under the direction of Max Horkheimer, and in the 1940s, having resettled in the United States, as psychotherapist and lecturer at the New School for Social Research and other institutions. In 1950 Fromm moved to Mexico. He spent long periods in the country until 1973, promoting psychoanalysis clinically and academically, and helping to create the Instituto Mexicano de Psicoanálisis (Mexican Institute of Psychoanalysis), of which he was lifetime director. At first, Fromm lived in Mexico City, but in 1956 he moved to a house that he himself helped design in a private and quiet area in the town of Cuernavaca.[14]

Cuernavaca was also where Ivan Illich chose to establish the linguistic and intercultural training program for Catholic missionaries, which led to the founding of the Centre for Intercultural Documentation (Centro Intercultural de Documentación, CIDOC) in 1966.[15] Funk underscores the CIDOC's role in the relationship between Fromm, Illich, and Freire.[16] Fromm was a regular at this centre, where he became fast friends with Illich until his death in 1980.[17] In turn, Freire and Illich had met in Brazil in the early 1960s, through the mediation of Archbishop Helder Cámara, an eminent figure in liberation theology. When Freire was imprisoned by the military police, Illich interceded for him, and, later in exile, the Brazilian pedagogue visited the CIDOC several times. In 1968, the centre published Freire's first book outside Brazil, *Educaçao e Conscientizacao: Extensionismo Rural*,[18] and helped disseminate his works. Illich thought highly of Freire's work with Brazilian rural farmers, although he was critical of his proposal for conscientization, within the framework of his general criticism of schools and the institutionalization of education.[19]

The meeting between Fromm and Freire took place in 1966, during a CIDOC conference series on alienation in Marx. Freire would recall that first meeting fondly, which he says "left a deep impression on me, even today."[20] The relationship continued from that first moment on. Freire used to talk to Fromm by telephone, and he visited him when he went to Cuernavaca,[21] and Fromm counted on Freire's support in his project to advance socialist humanism internationally, about which they had some correspondence in the second half of the 1960s.[22]

Lake and Dagostino consider that of all the critical theorists who influenced Freire, the greatest convergence took place with Fromm, whose social and humanistic vision helped him outline the possibilities for individuals and collectives to liberate themselves from inward and outward oppression.[23] The presence of Fromm's work is detectable in Freire, even though he does not always cite it. Especially inspiring seems to have been *Escape from Freedom*, Fromm's main book, published in 1941 after several years of work. A copy of a 1957 Spanish edition, heavily underlined and annotated, is preserved in Freire's library.[24] In *Education, the Practice of Freedom*, Freire cites Fromm's book in relation to the modern individual's refusal to decide.[25] He also mentions a Spanish edition of *Marx's Concept of Man*, published by Fromm in 1961 as an edition of Marx's Economic-Philosophical Manuscripts,[26] in reference this time to the alienation of language.[27] *Education, the Practice of Freedom* was completed in Santiago de Chile in 1965, about a year after Freire's departure from Brazil. Although the book reworks some earlier pieces published by Freire between 1959 and 1963, including his dissertation for appointment to the Chair of History and Philosophy of Education in the Pernambuco School of Fine Arts, *Educação e Atualidade Brasileira*,[28] no references to Fromm are to be found in these works. Beisiegel notes that, from *Pedagogy of the Oppressed* onward, although Freire remained faithful to the central themes of his reflections, his authors of reference changed as he came to orient himself more closely to an ostensibly left-wing intellectual tradition committed to the problems of the time.[29]

In *Pedagogy of the Oppressed*, especially in relation to the construction of the concept of love, Freire draws on another famous book by Fromm, *The Heart of Man: Its Genius for Good and Evil*, published in 1964.[30] The book originated in an essay on the psychological causes of war that Fromm prepared for the American Friends Service Committee and that was subsequently submitted to six intellectuals for discussion: Jerome Frank, Paul Tillich, Hans Morgenthau, Roy Menninger, Pitirim Sorokin, and Thomas Merton.[31] *The Heart of Man* was one of his most popular books that decade, selling approximately two million copies and being translated into eighteen languages.[32] Freire probably read it at the time of his meeting with Fromm at the CIDOC, when he was preparing to write *Pedagogy of the Oppressed*.

In this book, Fromm takes a prophetic tone to propose a new humanism capable of standing as an alternative to an increasingly mechanical life. To this end, he interprets human nature from an Old Testament perspective, which serves to underscore his argument that human beings are not entirely good or bad. The text interweaves biblical references with Freudian theories to illustrate the two great forces that move the world: the love of death, which beats in the syndrome of decay, and the love of life, which nestles in the syndrome of growth; in other words, necrophilia and biophilia. These tendencies lead the human being either to destruction through a narcissistic act or to fullness through communion with other human beings. Historically, religions, especially the Catholic Church, have contributed to this polarization. But Fromm also sees in them signs of hope: "As a reaction to this threat to humanity, a renaissance of humanism can be observed today in all countries and among the representatives of diverse ideologies; there are radical humanists among Catholic and Protestant theologians, among socialist and non-socialist philosophers."[33]

Freire develops much of his notion of love on the basis of the confrontation between necrophilia and biophilia proposed by Fromm. The characteristic feature of the oppressor and the oppressed is necrophilia. This is a common feature among oppressors because to them, "being" and "having" are one and the same: "having more" equals "being more," at the cost of the oppressed "having less," which configures their "not being." However, necrophilia is also a feature of the oppressed, because they end up accepting oppression as their natural state of life, to the point that they do not even want to get out of it. As Freire himself noted, "the oppressed, who have been shaped by the death-affirming climate of oppression, must find through their struggle the way to life-affirming humanization, which does not lie simply in having more to eat (although it does involve having more to eat and cannot fail to include this aspect)."[34]

Freire cites the German social critic to underscore the fact that, without this sense of possession, of "having," the oppressor's conscience "would lose contact with the world."[35] Put differently, Fromm gives him a way to reveal how oppressors set up in the world and what kind of relationship they have with the oppressed, whom they treat as objects, whom they turn into a mere ledger entries, whom they use. This dynamic shows the necrophile tendency of "perverted love." Freire associates it with sadism, and once again quotes Fromm:

> The pleasure in complete domination over another person (or other animate creature) is the very essence of the sadistic drive. Another way of formulating the same

thought is to say that the aim of sadism is to transform a man into a thing, some-thing animate into something inanimate, since by complete and absolute control the living loses one essential quality of life- freedom.[36]

In contrast, biophilia marks the process of liberation. This requires getting the oppressed to experience and cultivate a "love of life,"[37] as a general attitude of affirmation of human beings. It goes far beyond mere improvement in the material conditions of existence, which Freire describes as "having more to eat." Love of life cannot mean that the oppressed aspire to a life similar to that of their oppressors; rather, it means a new state of things. Love of life is the desire for complete, almost eschatological liberation, one that activates the will for every human being to live a truly human life and to attain a time of brother-hood and committed struggle.

The Dialogical Meaning of Love: The Mark of Martin Buber

Along with affirmation of life, the other major motive of Freirean love in *Ped-agogy of the Oppressed* is dialogue, which equalizes human beings and pro-nounces a new world. Near the end of the book, Freire wrote that

> The antidialogical, dominating *I* transforms the dominated, conquered *thou* into a mere *it*. The dialogical *I*, however, knows that it is precisely the *thou* ("not-*I*") which has called forth his or her own existence. He also knows that the *thou* which calls forth his own existence in turn constitutes an *I* which has in his *I* its *thou*. The *I* and the *thou* thus become, in the dialectic of these relationships, two *thous* which become two *I*'s.[38]

Although no explicit reference need be given to find the philosopher Martin Buber behind this quote, a footnote in the US edition of *Pedagogy of the Op-pressed* identifies the source of that distinction as an English edition, from 1958, of *Ich und Du*, Buber's crowning achievement, first published in 1923.[39]

On a timeline extending from the last quarter of the nineteenth century to the first quarter of the twentieth, Buber and Freire represent the extremes, while Fromm, placed at the turn of the century, represents the middle. Between each point is a twenty-year span. Martin Buber was the eldest of the three. He was born in Vienna in 1878. After his parents' separation, he was raised by his paternal grandparents, Salomon and Adele Buber, in Lemberg, the capital of the Austrian crown land Galicia and Lodomeria (present-day Lviv, Ukraine). His grandfather was a wealthy philanthropist and one of the last great scholars of the *Haskalah* (Jewish enlightenment). The educated bourgeois environment in which he grew up opened doors for Buber when he began to show interest in Zionism and Hasidic literature. In his youth, he was one of the leaders of the

Zionist movement that advocated a Jewish cultural renaissance, as opposed to purely political Zionism. He studied philosophy and art history at the University of Vienna and the University of Berlin, receiving his PhD from the latter in 1904. From 1923 to 1933, he taught Jewish philosophy of religion and history of religions at the University of Frankfurt. In 1938, he left Germany to make his home in Palestine. From that year until 1951, he worked as a professor of social philosophy at the Hebrew University of Jerusalem, where he died in 1965.[40]

Löwy considers Buber to be the most important author of religious socialism in German Jewish culture. "His political and religious ideas left their mark on an entire generation of Jewish intellectuals, from Prague to Vienna and from Budapest to Berlin."[41] Although he was a prolific author, *I and Thou* brought him worldwide renown. As the leading Buber scholar, Maurice S. Friedman, comments, the work represents the moment at which Buber's thought reached its maturity. It is the result of a gradual movement "from an early period of mysticism through a middle period of existentialism to a final period of developing dialogical philosophy."[42] The most important influences in the development of *I and Thou* were Hasidism, Kierkegaard, Dilthey, Feuerbach, and Simmel.[43] Löwy, in turn, continuing an idea suggested by Levinas,[44] places *I and Thou* in the context of Buber's communitarian utopia, as a prelude to his proposal to move towards a new form of community in which the other counts as Thou. This was the point he would develop in his more eminently political works, such as *Paths in Utopia*.[45]

In *I and Thou*, Buber differentiates between two ways of relating with the world: the I-It relation and the I-Thou relation. Because words have the power to create, both relations are "primary words" – that is, they constitute reality depending on whether it is pronounced as It or as Thou. This opens onto the basic coordinates of Buber's philosophy. In the I-It relation, the pronoun "I" suggests differentiation from the other elements of reality, which appear endowed with qualities and limits that keep them from joining other objects. In contrast, the I-Thou relation is pure encounter, and entails the contemplation and acceptance of the other as something that is unique. In Buber's own words, "this does not mean that nothing exists except himself. But all else lives in his light."[46] Even so, the singleness of which Thou consists can break down into a multiplicity of traits, and in that process of decomposition, Thou becomes It. For Buber, this movement is inexorable: "This is the exalted melancholy of our fate, that every *Thou* in our world must become an *It*."[47]

Distinguishable within the I-Thou link are three spheres of relation: (1) with nature; (2) with other human beings; and (3) with intelligible forms. Of these three spheres, the relation with the human Thou is the special relationship par excellence. It is the only relation in which authentic dialogue is generated. "Here what confronts us has blossomed into the full reality of the *Thou*. Here alone, then, as reality that cannot be lost, are gazing and being gazed upon, knowing and being known, loving and being loved."[48]

Dialogue is not identified with love, because one cannot love everyone one encounters, but love without dialogue "is called Lucifer."[49] Love is the responsibility of an I facing a Thou. It is an equalizing factor because it is common to everyone, great or small. It is not a feeling. Feelings accompany love but do not constitute it. The feelings that occur in love may be different; they are not the same in the love for a mother or friend, whereas love is one. Love is beyond feelings. It is a universal metaphysical and meta-psychical act (*Wirken*) between an I and a Thou. In love, what is important is not what happens in one individual or the other, but what happens *between* the two, as something that involves them. Such a reality cannot always be directly present. Instead, like the I-Thou relation in which it is embodied, love alternates moments of actuality and moments of latency, in which the Thou becomes It; I can then abstract the qualities of the other, the colour of his or her hair, the nuance of his or her goodness, but I can only do so because he or she is no longer a Thou. Moreover, this change does not necessarily occur in a succession of identifiable moments, "but often there is a happening profoundly twofold, confusedly entangled."[50] In other words, in every dialogical relation, Buber seems to say, there is always some Thou and some It. The encounter with Thou is more an aspiration to carry out in the relation than it is an alternative to choose.

However fundamental it may be, human loving dialogue does not quite constitute a full relation. The culmination of every relationship with a particular Thou, in each of the spheres in which the encounter takes place, is the appeal to the ultimate relationship with the eternal Thou, which is the absolute relationship. "The inborn Thou is realized in each relation and consummated in none. It is consummated only in the direct relation with the Thou that by its nature cannot become It."[51]

As noted above, for Freire as well dialogue is consubstantial with love. Love is a commitment to the cause of liberation that acknowledges the other as an equal, a *Thou*. In Buberian terms, it may be said that it constitutes an almost linguistic act, which utters the world in order to create it and give it a new reality, as in Genesis. Without dialogue there is no love, but without love there can be no dialogue, for dialogue demands humility and cannot take place under the conditions established by the relation between oppressor and oppressed. This latter relation moves in the I-It relation schema, while dialogue demands a situation of equality closer to the I-Thou relationship mode. The force that generates this equality is love: "If I do not love the world – if I do not love life – if I do not love people – I cannot enter into dialogue."[52]

Freire does not clarify how love can make the conditions of dialogue horizontal. Instead, he ends up bestowing crucial importance on an ambiguous element, for which he finds himself forced to appeal to a kind of conversion in the last chapter of *Pedagogy of the Oppressed*. As the author himself recalled, he wrote that last chapter several months after having set aside the other chapters, considering the book finished. However, on returning to them, he recounted years later, "I did make the basic discovery that the text was unfinished. It needed one more chapter. And so it came about that I wrote the fourth and last chapter."[53] Written in the late-night hours or while he was travelling, this chapter outlines the characteristics of the world of liberation guided by the matrix of dialogics, which he juxtaposes with the world of oppression and anti-dialogics. This is the context in which the reference to the Buberian distinction of Thou and It appears. Love takes on an almost eschatological dimension, as a new act and state, an action between oppressors and oppressed leading to a state of peace and harmony. But what moves the gears to make It, every It, become Thou, and to propel anti-dialogue towards dialogue? Freire speaks here of love as the impetus for the conversion of revolutionary leadership. It seems as if the Brazilian pedagogue, imbued with Marxist theory, could not rely on the force of historical mechanics, and instead had to appeal to the salvific effect of love:

> Usually this leadership group is made up of men and women who in one way or another have belonged to the social strata of the dominators. At a certain point in their existential experience, under certain historical conditions, these leaders renounce the class to which they belong and join the oppressed, in an act of true solidarity (or so one would hope). Whether or not this adherence results from a scientific analysis of reality, it represents (when authentic) an act of love and true commitment.[54]

In short, Freire took from Buber the significance of loving dialogue in the mutual constitution of the I and the you (Thou) in the process of liberation. The Catholic liberation theology from which he drew probably helped him avoid a kind of Christianizing appropriation of the Jewish philosopher that, as Friedman notes, turns the I-Thou relationship into a Thou-I relationship. This type of reading is often found in "many neo-orthodox theologians, who wished to cling to the sundering of God and man through original sin and the total dependency of man on God's grace through faith in Christ."[55] Steering clear of this error, Freire's appropriation was more political, and it often led him to another type of biased reading whereby the distinction of the two modes of relationship "became a choice between I-Thou and I-It, rather than the alternation of the two, as Buber held."[56] This reading is possible by suppressing, as Freire did, the religious component in Buber's schema of union with an eternal "Thou," the only union in which that schema has room for full relation.

Buber, Fromm, and Freire in Conversation: The Hope of Prophetic Alternativism

The influence Fromm and Buber had on Freire cannot only be read separately from each other. Freire's joint conversation with the two Jewish intellectuals' ideas places the notion of love in *Pedagogy of the Oppressed* in the framework of a broader interpretation.

Buber and Fromm had many points in common. As Lundgren notes, both "were Jews with a secular German education, both were interested in mysticism, both were socialists, both worked for a binational solution in the Palestine conflict."[57] Both collaborated at the Freie Jüdische Lehrhaus in the 1920s, and Fromm used texts by Buber on Hasidism in his doctoral dissertation regarding the function of Jewish law in preserving social cohesion.[58] Later on, in 1948, Buber supported Fromm's letter to the *New York Times* in which he called for an end to violence between Jews and Muslims in Palestine.[59] However, as Lundgren points out, this does not mean there were no meaningful differences between them:

> Buber was more than twenty years older, already famous when Fromm was a young student. Buber came from a secularized family and approached Judaism through Zionism and Hasidism. His socialism was not as Marxist as Fromm's; he was closer to the anarchist tradition through his friend Gustav Landauer. He disliked Freud and psychoanalysis. And although Fromm and Buber agreed on the issue of the Israeli-Arab conflict, Buber was a Zionist and Fromm an anti-Zionist.[60]

What is striking is that Fromm denied having been influenced by Buber. Lundgren argues that this denial was due to a certain personal dislike and that "it is evident that Fromm was influenced by Buber in many respects."[61] According to Braune, Buber most likely exerted a great influence on Fromm's concept of alternativism and his distinction between prophetic and apocalyptic messianism, which Buber had outlined in *Paths in Utopia*.[62]

Buber and Fromm belong to the constellation of what Löwy has called early twentieth-century Central European Jewish libertarian messianism. Included under this heading is a wide range of intellectuals who in various ways combined Jewish restorative messianism and libertarian utopianism in a broad sense. "Theirs was a generation of dreamers and utopians: they aspired to a radically other world, to the kingdom of God on earth, to a kingdom of the spirit, a kingdom of freedom, a kingdom of peace. An egalitarian community, libertarian socialism, anti-authoritarian rebellion and a permanent revolution of the spirit were their ideals."[63] Within this constellation, Buber remained closer to the Jewish religious tradition and social utopia, in search of the regeneration of communal experience, while Fromm stood closer to Freud and Marx, and was interested in the anthropological and psychological sources of a new social and natural harmony. However, both shared the same biblical, prophetic, and messianic references.[64]

Perhaps somewhat unwittingly, Freire drew on this Jewish utopian messianism when he developed his concept of love, which in *Pedagogy of the Oppressed* he mixed with other sources related to liberation theology. Between the two configurations, there was a shared language, or as Löwy calls it, a kind of elective affinity.[65] Both focus on the dispossessed, and both articulate a religious tradition with a revolutionary social project, generally atheistic and materialistic.[66]

A major element in that affinity is the fact that all three authors discussed here wrote about utopia or hope. When Freire wanted to revisit *Pedagogy of the Oppressed* in the early 1990s, he called it *Pedagogy of Hope*, which he understood as the necessary correlation or extension of the former.[67] In this book, he recalled how affected he had been by his first meeting with Fromm at the CIDOC, when Fromm told him that the type of teaching he was doing was a kind of psychoanalysis inflected by historical, cultural, and political concerns.[68] A few years after that meeting, in another book dedicated to hope, *The Revolution of Hope*, Fromm mentioned Freire's experiences in adult literacy as a real example of the kind of participatory, humanistic, and less bureaucratic education to which one could hopefully aspire.[69]

Freire shared with Fromm and Buber a hope for a better world, a desire to build the kingdom of God on earth, a kingdom of equality and peace in which "the wolf shall live with the lamb" (Isa. 11:6). None of the three saw hope as a form of detached idealism,[70] or liberation as fatalism, a belief in "a liberation to come as a kind of gift or donation of history: the liberation that will come because it has been said that it will come."[71] The hope they had in mind was what Fromm called prophetic alternativism, which had remained in the Talmudic tradition and which he saw re-emerging in the radical wing of the Roman Catholic Church.[72] Although he did not cite it per se, one of these renewing movements was the nascent liberation theology then blossoming in Latin America. This entailed a hope based on an active commitment to the Promised Land, to the new world perceived as possible. Its driving force can no longer be entrusted to divine designs, but neither can it be entrusted to the impersonal forces of history. In *Pedagogy of the Oppressed*, their place is taken by love.

Last Words and Questions

The appeal to love runs throughout *Pedagogy of the Oppressed*, where it takes on different forms of argument to present itself not as a particular profile, but as a kind of ineffable force aimed at achieving liberation. In any case, to synthesize the analysis performed here, it can be claimed that in Freire love is a commitment between the oppressors and the oppressed. Because of this commitment, in a single act of uttering the world to create it, the oppressor and the oppressed attain a situation of fraternity that demonstrates they live in love.

Freire drew, either directly or indirectly, on Erich Fromm and Martin Buber when developing such a notion of love. This seems to place him, perhaps unwittingly, in the orbit of Jewish libertarian messianism, and we can uncover traces of prophetic Judaism in his construction of the concept in *Pedagogy of the Oppressed*. By that we are not alluding to the immediate presence of any Jewish prophets in Freire's text. Rather, we refer to the sense that the Jewish neo-Kantian thinker Hermann Cohen gave to this expression when equating it with the social Christianity of the Protestant philosopher Friedrich Albert Lange, his mentor and predecessor in the Chair of Philosophy at the University of Marburg. Franz Rosenweg recounted this dialogue between the two as reported by Cohen himself:

> Lange asked: "Are our views on Christianity different?" Cohen answered: "No, because what you call Christianity I call prophetic Judaism." The author of "Arbeiterfrage" [i.e., Friedrich Albert Lange] understood what he meant, and was able to indicate the passages in the Prophets he had underlined in his copy of the Bible. Cohen finished the story thus: So ethical socialism united us, in one blow, beyond the barriers of our religions.[73]

To Cohen, the style of the prophets is "unique to the Israelite people," although since that beginning, it "has become a timeless literary possession of all humankind."[74] Prophetism brings the proclamation of the social conscience of a universal ethics of love, founded not on science but on the relationship between human beings and God in monotheistic tradition.[75] What we have attempted to show here is that Freire shared this ethical prophetism of the kingdom of love, through which Buber and Fromm transited in direct conversation with Cohen's philosophy.[76] As noted at the beginning, in a decisive paragraph in *Pedagogy of the Oppressed*, Freire stated that the book was written with a faith in the creation of a world in which it will be easier to love. Therefore, the language used by Fromm and Buber would not have sounded unfamiliar to him.[77] Nevertheless, the mediation of the latter two authors poses two final questions. The first concerns the reading Freire made of them, and the second the reason behind his choice.

Regarding the first question, it has been noted that Freire was familiar with Fromm's work before he wrote *Pedagogy of the Oppressed*, and we know how affected he was by his encounter with the German author at the CIDOC in Cuernavaca, to which he would continue to refer many years later. In *Pedagogy of the Oppressed*, Freire based his treatment of love on *The Heart of Man*, one of Fromm's most popular books of the 1960s. As we saw, the book had its origin in the essay *The Psychological Causes of War*, which was proposed for discussion by six major critics. Most of them pointed out that the concept of necrophilia employed by Fromm was controversial and required further refinement. Psychiatrist and professor Jerome Frank, for example, called Fromm's thesis a powerful *sermon* on good and evil. In his view, "the delineation of necrophilic and biophilic personality types is essentially a literary exercise, with an honourable lineage tracing back at least to Theophrastus. The skill of the writer makes them convincing, but they are, after all, abstractions, and it would take a lot of research to test their validity."[78] Other commentators criticized the pretension of making war depend on psychological tendencies such as necrophilia, as the title of the essay announced. For the Protestant philosopher and theologian Paul Tillich, war is caused by the clash of power structures, and it is a mistake to try to explain it by resorting to a particular psychopathological perversion. "There are certainly suicidal and sadistic tendencies in men's estranged nature (Dr. Fromm rightly denies that they belong to men's essential nature) and such tendencies can use the war situation in order to be actualized. But it is a confusion of cause and occasion if they are made responsible for the outbreak of war."[79] Fromm agreed with many of these criticisms, and even changed the original title of the essay to *War within Man*. But this did not lead him to revise the biophilia-necrophilia distinction, which later formed the core of *The Heart of Man*.[80] Freire accepted this distinction without further questioning, within his attempt to make revolutionary Marxism compatible with Fromm's socialist humanism, the science of revolution with the deeper motive of the love of life.[81] According to Morrow, *Pedagogy of the Oppressed* constitutes a limited product of such an attempt, which Freire failed to articulate in a sufficiently compact way, despite the addition of a hastily written fourth chapter. Thus, the multiple readings to which it has been subject can be considered an effect of "the ambiguity, inconsistencies, and incompleteness of the argument of the book."[82]

As for Buber, there is an abundance of literature connecting his notion of dialogue with Freire,[83] and it has been suggested that "Freire's approach was certainly influenced by Buber."[84] However, the magnitude of that influence is questionable. Little information exists on the conditions that may have led Freire to cite Buber's ideas in *Pedagogy of the Oppressed*. The book makes no explicit reference to Buber as the author of these ideas; this is alluded to only in a footnote in some editions in English and Portuguese, but not in other editions. The original Portuguese manuscript just contains an asterisk with a note reading, "See Buber, Martín – 'I and You' – ."[85] Was this a note for himself? Was this a future footnote? Or did he want to improve the argument? How familiar was he with Buber? In his 1959 dissertation, Freire wrote extensively about dialogicity, but at that time he associated it with the concept of *parlamentarização* (parliamentarization) as described by the Brazilian sociologist and politician Alberto Guerreiro Ramos, with a few references to Zevedei Barbu's theory of government psychologies.[86] According to the bibliographical study of Freire's work by Pitano, Streck, and Moretti,[87] besides *Pedagogy of the Oppressed*, the only other place where Freire seems to mention the Buberian I-Thou and I-It distinction is in *Education, the Practice of Freedom*, although he does not cite its origin.[88] Nor does he seem to have been interested in Buber's extensive theoretical and practical background in the field of adult education.[89]

In fact, Jacobi suggests that Freire misunderstood Buber in his appropriation of the concepts of dialogue and the I-Thou/I-It relationship, which he approached from the Hegelian perspective of *Herr und Knecht* (master and servant). Among their respective formulations of these concepts, there are many differences in aspects such as the role of knowledge, reciprocity, or the very meaning of love, which Jacobi sees in Freire as being more anchored in a Christian conception that "does not necessarily include that of dialog."[90] Perhaps Jacobi's last observation is not entirely accurate, insofar as in *Pedagogy of the Oppressed* Freire intrinsically associated love with dialogue. His appropriation was, however, biased in another sense, to which Jacobi also refers when he states that "Freire's concept of dialog does not share Buber's existentialist connotation of the inner meaning of dialog."[91] Perhaps what was missing in Freire was the profound meaning that dialogical love has in Buber, given the theological implications Buber confers on it, as something that does not belong to one or the other member of the relation, to the oppressor or the oppressed, or to both. Nor is it just a "climate of mutual trust."[92] In Buber, love is a metaphysical and meta-physical reality that takes place in the space *between* an I and a Thou, as a form of encounter that takes on its full meaning in the relation with an eternal Thou.

The second question, which must necessarily remain open here, is why Freire turned to those two authors to articulate his concept of love rather than to Catholic sources, especially when such sources tried to overcome the outdated distinction of Christian love among *eros*, *ágape*, and *philia* with renewed approaches that placed the discourse in dialogue with historical events, as Freire himself did. The most evident source, and the closest to Freire, is liberation theology, which was emerging with force when he wrote the book. The least evident and most distant involves Europe and a spontaneous movement of books that sought to understand love as a vaticination or as a trembling disconcerted by the atrocities of the world. Hildebrand, Thibon, and Balthasar had written in the Catholic tradition; and Kierkegaard and Lewis in the Protestant tradition before them. In the Orthodox world, prior to his conversion, Soloviev had written, as did Tolstoy and Sorokin. However, here we begin to move in the world of imagination, since we have no data on Freire's motives for using those sources rather than others when writing about love. Perhaps the only claim that can be made in that regard is that Fromm's and Buber's proposals were consistent with Freire's own critical and Christian social perspective. Be that as it may, the only observable reality is that in *Pedagogy of the Oppressed*, Freire developed a notion of love whose most intensely explicit influence was Fromm, where there are recognizable echoes of Buber, seemingly sidestepping the Catholic developments on love that were underway in Latin America and Europe.

NOTES

1 We would like to thank Dr. Darren Dias, from the Toronto School of Theology, for the discussion of and insightful comments on a previous version of this chapter.

2 Jones Irwin, "Authority through Freedom: On Freire's Radicalisation of the Authority-Freedom Problem in Education," *Espacio, Tiempo y Educación* 5, no. 1 (2018): 64–5; Daniel Schugurensky, *Paulo Freire* (London: Bloomsbury, 2011), 68–9; Peter Roberts, *Education, Literacy, and Humanization: Exploring the Work of Paulo Freire* (Westport, CT: Bergin and Garvey, 2000), 23–33; Peter McLaren, *Che Guevara, Paulo Freire and the Pedagogy of Revolution* (Lanham, MD: Rowman and Littlefield, 2000), 148–60.

3 Schugurensky, *Paulo Freire*, 77.

4 Paulo Freire, *Pedagogy of Hope: Reliving Pedagogy of the Oppressed*, trans. Robert R. Barr (1992; reis., New York: Continuum, 1994) 61–2.

5 Antonia Darder, *Reinventing Paulo Freire: A Pedagogy of Love*, 2nd ed. (London: Routledge, 2017).

6 Pepi Leistyna, *Presence of Mind: Education and the Politics of Deception* (Boulder, CO: Westview Press, 1999), 57, quoted in Darder, *Reinventing Paulo Freire*, 80.

7 James D. Kirylo, "The Influence of Freire on Scholars: A Select List," in *Paulo Freire: The Man from Recife*, ed. James D. Kirylo (New York: Peter Lang Publishing, 2011), 249.

8 James W. Fraser, "Love and History in the Work of Paulo Freire," in *Mentoring the Mentor: A Critical Dialogue with Paulo Freire*, ed. Paulo Freire (New York: Peter Lang, 1997), 175.

9 Paulo Freire, *Pedagogy of the Oppressed*, trans. Myra Bergman Ramos (1968; reis., New York: Continuum, 2005), 89.

10 Freire, 89.

11 Freire, 40. This paragraph appears at the end of the preface to the English edition, whereas in the Spanish edition it is at the end of the book. See Paulo Freire, *Pedagogía del oprimido*, trans. Jorge Mellado (1968; reis., Montevideo: Tierra Nueva, 1972), 222.

12 Lawrence J. Friedman, assisted by Anke Schreiber, *The Lives of Erich Fromm: Love's Prophet* (New York: Columbia University Press, 2013), 3–18; Rainer Funk, *Fromm: Vida y obra* (1984; reis., Buenos Aires: Paidós, 1987), 16–58.

13 Erich Fromm, *You Shall Be as Gods: A Radical Interpretation of the Old Testament and Its Tradition* (1966; reis., New York: H. Holt, 1991), 15.

14 Friedman, *The Lives of Erich Fromm*, 156183; Jorge Silva García, "Erich Fromm en México: 1950-1973," in *El Humanismo de Erich Fromm*, ed. Jorge Silva García (Mexico City: Paidós, 2006), 63–74.

15 Rosa Bruno-Jofré and Jon Igelmo Zaldívar, "The Center for Intercultural Formation, Cuernavaca, Mexico, Its Reports (1962–1967) and Illich's Critical Understanding of Mission in Latin America," *Hispania Sacra* 66, no. extra 2 (2014): 457–87.

16 Funk, *Fromm. Vida y obra*, 163.

17 Friedman, *The Lives of Erich Fromm*, 335.

18 Paulo Freire, Raul Veloso, and Luís Fiori, *Educação e conscientização extensionismo rural* (Cuernavaca: Centro Intercultural de Documentación, 1968).

19 David Cayley, *Conversaciones con Iván Illich: Un arqueólogo de la modernidad* (Madrid: Enclave Libros, 2013), 166; Paulo Freire and Sérgio Guimarães, *Aprendendo com a própria história* (Rio de Janeiro: Paz e Terra, 2013), 135–9.

20 Freire and Guimarães, *Aprendendo com a própria história*, 136.

21 Freire and Guimarães, 138.

22 Friedman, *The Lives of Erich Fromm*, 240 and 379n5.

23 Robert Lake and Vicki Dagostino, "Converging Self / Other Awareness: Erich Fromm and Paulo Freire on Transcending the Fear of Freedom," in *Paulo Freire's Intellectual Roots: Toward Historicity in Praxis*, ed. Robert Lake and Tricia Kress (New York: Bloomsbury, 2013), 101–26.

24 Rodrigo da Silva Borgheti, "O problema da liberdade nas obras de Paulo Freire e Erich Fromm" (PhD diss., Universidade de São Paulo, 2013), 227; Rodrigo da Silva Borgheti, *Paulo Freire e a psicanálise humanista* (Curitiba: Editora Appris, 2015), chap. 6, e-book.

25 Paulo Freire, *Educação como prática da liberdade* (Rio de Janeiro: Paz e Terra, 1967), 43.

26 Erich Fromm, *Marx's Concept of Man* (New York: Frederick Ungar Publishing, 1961).

27 Freire, *Educação como prática da liberdade*, 94.

28 Paulo Freire, *Educação e Atualidade Brasileira. Tese de Concurso para a Cadeira de História e Filosofia da Educação na Escola de Belas Artes de Pernambuco* (Recife: Escola de Belas Artes de Pernambuco, 1959), http://www.acervo.paulofreire.org:8080/jspui/bitstream/7891/1976/1/FPF_OPF_14_001.pdf.

29 Celso de Rui Beisiegel, "Observaciones sobre la teoría y la práctica en Paulo Freire," *Mirandum* 3, no. 7 (1999): 35–48.

30 Erich Fromm, *The Heart of Man: Its Genius for Good and Evil* (New York: Harper and Row, 1964). In *Pedagogy of the Oppressed*, Freire also suggests a reading of Fromm's essay "The Application of Humanist Psychoanalysis to Marx's Theory," in relation to the distrust of the dominated consciousness. Freire, *Pedagogy of the Oppressed*, 166n41. The essay was included in the volume *Socialist Humanism: An International Symposium*, prepared by Fromm with contributions from thirty-five authors of different tendencies, including Marxists, socialists, Catholics, and independent liberals, who shared a common concern for humankind and a critical attitude towards political reality. See Erich Fromm, *Socialist Humanism: An International Symposium* (Garden City, NY: Doubleday and Co., 1965).

31 Erich Fromm, *War within Man: A Psychological Enquiry into the Roots of Destructiveness* (Philadelphia: American Friends Service Committee, 1963).

32 Friedman, *The Lives of Erich Fromm*, 255–8.

33 Fromm, *The Heart of Man*, 83.

34 Freire, *Pedagogy of the Oppressed*, 68.

35 Fromm, *The Heart of Man*, 41, quoted in Freire, *Pedagogy of the Oppressed*, 58.

36 Fromm, *The Heart of Man*, 32, quoted in Freire, *Pedagogy of the Oppressed*, 59.

37 Freire, *Pedagogy of the Oppressed*, 68.

38 Freire, 167.

39 Freire, 167n43. This note is not found in the Spanish version of the book. Several editions have been examined, including the initial one on which all the others were based, published in 1970 by Editorial Tierra Nueva in Montevideo, prepared by Marcelo Gajardo and José Luis Fiori and translated by Jorge Mellado from the original 1968 text. The third printing from July 1972 has been used. Also taken into account have been the reproduction published in Peru in 1971 (Lima: Retablo de Papel) and the subsequent editions published by Siglo XXI of Buenos Aires and Madrid, where the book was published in 1975. None of these editions contains any reference to Buber.

40 Maurice S. Friedman, *Martin Buber: The Life of Dialogue*, 4th ed. (London: Routledge, 2002), 9; Michael Zank and Braiterman Zachary, "Martin Buber," Stanford Encyclopedia of Philosophy Archive (Winter 2020 Edition), last modified 28 July 2020, https://plato.stanford.edu/archives/win2020/entries/buber.

41 Michael Löwy, *Redemption and Utopia: Jewish Libertarian Thought in Central Europe* (1988; reis., London: Verso, 2017), 48.

42 Friedman, *Martin Buber*, 29.

43 Friedman, 59.

44 Emmanuel Levinas, preface to *Utopie et Socialisme*, by Martin Buber (1977; reis., Paris: L'échappée, 2016), 27.

45 Michael Löwy, *Judíos heterodoxos. Romanticismo, mesianismo, utopía* (Barcelona: Anthropos, 2015), 119–31.

46 Martin Buber, *I and Thou*, trans. Ronald Gregor Smith (1923; reis., Edinburgh: T.&T. Clark, 1937), 8.

47 Buber, 16.

48 Buber, 103.

49 Martin Buber, "Dialogue," in *Between Man and Man*, trans. Ronald Gregor Smith (1929; reis., New York: Macmillan, 1967), 21.

50 Martin Buber, *I and Thou*, 17–18.

51 Buber, 75.

52 Freire, *Pedagogy of the Oppressed*, 90.

53 Freire, *Pedagogy of Hope*, 60.

54 Freire, *Pedagogy of the Oppressed*, 163.

55 Friedman, *Martin Buber*, xiii.

56 Friedman, xiii.

57 Svante Lundgren, *Fight against Idols: Erich Fromm on Religion, Judaism and the Bible* (Frankfurt am Main: Peter Lang, 1998), 103.

58 Lundgren, 91.

59 Friedman, *The Lives of Erich Fromm*, 11 and 269.

60 Lundgren, *Fight against Idols*, 103–4.

61 Lundgren, 104.

62 Joan Braune, *Erich Fromm's Revolutionary Hope: Prophetic Messianism as a Critical Theory of the Future* (Rotterdam: Sense, 2014), 67–71. In *Paths in Utopia* Buber wrote,

> There are two basic forms of eschatology: the prophetic, which at any given moment sees every person addressed by it as endowed, in a degree not to be determined beforehand, with the power to participate by his decisions and deeds in the preparing of Redemption: and the apocalyptic, in which the redemptive process in all its details, its very hour and course, has been fixed from everlasting and for whose accomplishment human beings are only used as tools, though what is immutably fixed may yet be "unveiled" to them, revealed, and they be assigned their function. The first of these forms derives from Israel, the second from ancient Persia. The differences and agreements between the two, their combinations and separations, play an important part in the inner history of Christianity. In the socialist secularization of eschatology, they work out separately: the prophetic form in some of the systems of the so-called Utopians, the apocalyptic one above all in Marxism (which is not to say that no prophetic element is operative here-it has only been overpowered by the apocalyptic).

See Martin Buber, *Paths in Utopia*, trans. R.F.C. Hull (1946; reis., Boston: Beacon Press, 1960), 10.

63 Löwy, *Redemption and Utopia*, 2.

64 Michael Löwy, "Messianismo e utopia no pensamento de Martin Buber e Erich Fromm," *WebMosaica* 1, no. 1 (2009): 72–81.

65 Löwy, *Redemption and Utopia*, 6–13.

66 Löwy, 14.

67 Freire, *Pedagogy of Hope*, 40.

68 Freire, 55 and 105.

69 Erich Fromm, *The Revolution of Hope: Toward a Humanized Technology* (New York: Harper and Row, 1968), 121.

70 Paulo Freire, *Letters to Cristina: Reflections on My Life and Work*, trans. Donaldo Macedo, Quilda Macedo, and Alexandre Oliveira (1994; reis., London: Routledge, 1996), 187.

71 Freire, *Pedagogy of Hope*, 101.

72 Fromm, *The Revolution of Hope*, 18–20.

73 Andrea Poma, "Hermann Cohen: Judaism and Critical Ideals," in *The Cambridge Companion to Modern Jewish Philosophy*, ed. Michael L. Morgan and Peter Eli Gordon (Cambridge: Cambridge University Press, 2007), 83.

74 Hermann Cohen, "The Style of the Prophets," in *Reason and Hope* (1901; reis., Cincinnati, OH: Hebrew Union College Press, 1993), 106.

75 Hermann Cohen, "The Social Ideal as Seen by Plato and by the Prophets," in *Reason and Hope* (1916; reis., Cincinnati, OH: Hebrew Union College Press, 1993).

76 On Buber and Fromm's relationship with Cohen, their convergences and divergences, see, for example, Jeffrey Andrew Barash, "Politics and Theology: The

Debate on Zionism between Hermann Cohen and Martin Buber," in *Dialogue as a Trans-disciplinary Concept: Martin Buber's Philosophy of Dialogue and Its Contemporary Reception*, ed. Paul Mendes-Flohr (Berlin: De Gruyter, 2015), 49–60; Nick Braune and Joan Braune, "Erich Fromm's Socialist Program and Prophetic Messianism, in Two Parts," *Radical Philosophy Review* 12, nos. 1–2 (2009): 355–89; Jonathan K. Crane, "Ethical Theories of Hermann Cohen, Franz Rosenzweig, and Martin Buber," in *The Oxford Handbook of Jewish Ethics and Morality*, ed. Elliot N. Dorff and Jonathan K. Crane (Oxford: Oxford University Press, 2013), 134–50; Ronen Pinkas, "Correlation and Orientation: Erich Fromm's Position on Religion in Light of Hermann Cohen and Franz Rosenzweig," *DAAT: A Journal of Jewish Philosophy & Kabbalah*, 85 (2018): 7–35; Ronen Pinkas, "Reason and the Future of Historical Consciousness: Examining a Possible Influence of Hermann Cohen on Erich Fromm," *Archivio di filosofia*, 88, no. 1 (2020): 149–64; William Plevan, "Holiness in Hermann Cohen, Franz Rosenzweig, and Martin Buber," in *Holiness in Jewish Thought*, ed. Alan L. Mittleman (Oxford: Oxford University Press, 2018), 181–204.

77   It has been suggested that Freire's ideas bear the mark of another of the main theorists of Jewish messianism, the critical Marxist philosopher Ernst Bloch, author of *The Principle of Hope*, written during his exile in the United States between 1938 and 1947. Freire, however, never cited Bloch, so in any case it would be an indirect mark, mediated, perhaps, by the latter's influence on liberation theology. See Nina Cemiloğlu, "'Flaschenpost' from the Past: The Critical Utopian Pedagogies of Ernst Bloch and Paulo Freire," *ETHOS: Dialogues in Philosophy and Social Sciences* 12, no. 2 (2019): 187–204. Fromm himself noted this affinity when he noted that no one had recaptured better than Bloch, in his *The Principle of Hope*, the prophetic principle of hope in Marxist thought, while seeing the resurgence of that principle in the radical movement of the Catholic Church. Fromm, *The Revolution of Hope*, 19 and 20n13.

78   Fromm, *War within Man*, 31.

79   Fromm, 33.

80   Friedman, *The Lives of Erich Fromm*, 257.

81   Freire, *Pedagogy of the Oppressed*, 89n4.

82   Raymond Morrow, "Rethinking Freire's 'Oppressed': A 'Southern' Route to Habermas's Communicative Turn and Theory of Deliberative Democracy," in *Paulo Freire's Intellectual Roots: Toward Historicity in Praxis*, ed. Robert Lake and Tricia Kress (New York: Bloomsbury, 2013), 77. On the many readings of *Pedagogy of the Oppressed*, see Gonzalo Jover and David Luque, "Relecturas de Paulo Freire en el siglo XXI. Cincuenta años de Pedagogía del Oprimido," *Educación XX1* 23, no. 2 (2020): 145–64.

83   See, for example, W. John Morgan and Alexandre Guilherme, *Buber and Education: Dialogue as Conflict Resolution* (London: Routledge, 2013), 111–13; Nel Noddings, "Freire, Buber, and Care Ethics on Dialogue in Teaching," in *Paulo Freire's Intellectual Roots: Toward Historicity in Praxis*, ed. Robert Lake and Tricia

Kress (New York: Bloomsbury, 2013) 89–100; Waldma Maíra Menezes de Oliveira, Ivanilde Apoluceno de Oliveira, and Lyandra Lareza da Silva Matos, "A teoria da dialogicidade em Martin Buber e Paulo Freire: Aproximações e divergências conceituais," *Periferia* 12, no. 1 (2020): 36–60; Alexandra Coelho Pena, Maria Fernanda Rezende Nunes, and Sonia Kramer, "Human Formation, World Vision, Dialogue and Education: The Present Relevance of Paulo Freire and Martin Buber," *Educação em Revista* 34 (2018): 1–18.

84   Yehuda Bar Shalom, Ruba Daas, and Zvi Bekerman, "Where Have All the Palestinians Gone?," *International Journal of Critical Pedagogy* 1, no. 2 (2008): 180.

85   Paulo Freire, *Pedagogia do Oprimido (O Manuscrito)*, ed. Jason Ferreira Mafra, José Eustáquio Romão, and Moacir Gadottis (1968; reis., São Paulo: Editora e Livraria Instituto Paulo Freire, 2018), 414.

86   Freire, *Educação e Atualidade Brasileira.*

87   Sandro de Castro Pitano, Danilo Romeu Streck, and Cheron Zanini Moretti, s.v. "Martin Buber (1878–1965)," in *Paulo Freire. Uma Arqueologia Bibliográfica*, ed. Sandro de Castro Pitano, Danilo Romeu Streck, and Cheron Zanini Moretti (Curitiba: Appris, 2019), e-book.

88   Freire, *Educação como prática da liberdade*, 114.

89   See, for example, Martha Friedenthal-Haase, "Educación de adultos y crisis en el pensamiento de Martin Buber," *Educación* 45 (1992): 21–38; Friedman, *Martin Buber*, 207–15; W. John Morgan and Ian White, "Revisiting Martin Buber and Adult Education," *Weiterbildung* 2 (2019): 28–30.

90   Juliane Jacobi, "Dialogue, Relatedness, and Community: Does Martin Buber Have a Lasting Influence on Educational Philosophy?" *Zeitschrift für Pädagogik* 63, no. 5 (2017): 668.

91   Jacobi, 667.

92   Freire, *Pedagogy of the Oppressed*, 91.

6 Sisters of Our Lady of the Missions and Paulo Freire: Weaving a Web of Life

VERONICA DUNNE

Introduction

Describing the cultural shifts brought about among the Sisters of Our Lady of the Missions (Religieuses de Notre Dame des Missions, or RNDM) through the influence of a seminal thinker such as Paulo Freire is challenging. Freire's insights are double-edged: liberating for those who are oppressed, and threatening to those who resist change in power arrangements. In reflecting on Freire's influence, which was not generally explicit in the "whole body" of the RNDMs in Canada, I turned to the possibilities of story as a way of better understanding the impact he had and indeed continues to have. A powerful story, enacted in public, can disrupt fixed understandings at a visceral level.

Such a story is told in a paper by Canadian theologian Ellen Leonard entitled "Feminist Voices in Theology." In that paper, Leonard recalls an experience she had that dramatically illustrates the possibilities and perils of "making visible" what is happening in a culture, and the threat or promise this presents to normative beliefs that may be conscious, and are more likely unconscious.[1] This is a rather lengthy story, for which I ask the reader's indulgence.

In 1991 Leonard attended the Seventh Assembly of the World Council of Churches in Canberra, Australia. The theme of the assembly was "Come Holy Spirit, Renew the Whole Creation."[2] The first address had been prepared by Parthenios, patriarch of Alexandria and all Africa, who was unable to be present because of the Gulf War going on at the time. Leonard notes that "his rather academic presentation on the Holy Spirit, read by an Orthodox priest, was followed immediately by a very different presentation by a young Korean theologian, Chung Hyung Kyung."[3]

Leonard says that Chung began by asking those present to remove their shoes because they were on holy ground. She had invited two Australian Aboriginal dancers and sixteen Korean dancers "to join with her in calling on the spirits present among us."[4]

Chung explained that in her Korean tradition, people who were killed or died unjustly became wandering spirits. "Without hearing the cries of these spirits we cannot hear the voice of the Holy Spirit."[5]

Chung successfully wove together ritual, music, dance, electronic slide projections, and her prepared text. Leonard says further that

> Chung's litany included the spirit of Hagar, Jephthah's daughter, Joan of Arc, the Amazon rain forest, the spirit of soldiers, civilians and sea creatures dying in the Gulf War, and the spirit of the liberator Jesus, tortured and killed on the cross. In a dramatic gesture she burned the list of names of persons who had died tragically, and let the ashes drift to the sky. She then presented a challenging call to *metanoia*: a change from anthropocentrism to life centrism, from dualism to interconnection, and from a culture of death to a culture of life.[6]

Chung ended the presentation by sharing an image of the Holy Spirit from her Korean background. Kwan In is venerated as goddess of compassion and wisdom in East Asian women's popular religiosity.[7] As an enlightened one Kwan In can go into nirvana, but she refuses to go in by herself. Her compassionate wisdom heals all forms of life. She waits until all creatures become enlightened and can go to Nirvana together. Gently Chung poses the question, "Perhaps this might also be a feminine image of the Christ who is the first born among us, one who goes before and brings others with her?[8]

I begin this chapter by sharing Leonard's memories of "that amazing Friday afternoon in the large tent at Canberra"[9] because Chung's invocation of spirit signalled what has happened and is happening in the social/cultural struggles and the corresponding actions for justice throughout the world. This particular event signalled the emergence of Asian perspectives in a largely Eurocentric religious body. The theological analysis and perspectives that she and other Asian theologians had been raising for some time were now given an ecumenical forum.

Like Paulo Freire, the principal focus of this chapter, Chung's presentation challenged the long-dominant Eurocentric approach, namely, by drawing on her own culture, inviting her hearers to listen, and also to draw on their cultures' ways of knowing, and accessing their insights/solutions to the challenges they face. The "frontier dwelling" and "border crossing" involved in the powerful metaphors and symbols of Chung's presentation are analogous to Freire's work. Both challenge the status quo, both evoke larger frontiers, and both turn to the margins for insight and hope. As Freire says,

> Revolutionary praxis must stand opposed to the praxis of the dominant elites, for they are by nature antithetical. Revolutionary praxis cannot tolerate an absurd dichotomy in which the praxis of the people is merely that of following the leaders'

decisions – a dichotomy reflecting the prescriptive methods of the dominant elites. Revolutionary praxis is a unity, and the leaders cannot treat the oppressed as their possession.[10]

In this chapter, I propose to do three things: 1. give a simplified overview of Paulo Friere's groundbreaking book *Pedagogy of the Oppressed* before describing in broad strokes something of the impact it had for RNDMs in Canada and Peru;[11] 2. further examine the ways Freire's work intersected with liberation theologians of the time, particularly Peruvian Gustavo Gutiérrez; and 3. explore how Freire's work, alongside the emergence of feminist liberation theories and theologies, led to a rising eco-feminist consciousness and a deepening sense of the "new cosmology" among Canadian RNDMs.[12]

I write this chapter not as a scholar of Paulo Freire, but as a white, middle-class, older Canadian woman who is part of an international group of women religious.[13] I have been an RNDM for over fifty years. My professional studies have been in education, psychology, and theology, and my "fields of engagement" have been in teaching and counselling. For the last forty years I have developed a great interest in the critical realm of cosmology and ecology.

As one who has benefited from Freire's insights, I undertake a retrospective search for his presence in my personal life, and in the history of the RNDM Canadian province. To be clear, I have no memory of any meeting where RNDMs directly cited Freire as a source for policy or directional change. My reflections are thus partial, and ordered from an appreciative retrospective glance, rather than a critical current analysis. However, it has been delightfully surprising for me while drafting this chapter to discover the many ways I have been shaped by Freire's thought, as have the Canadian RNDMs. In looking back at the choices the RNDMs have made over the past fifty years, it seems to me that Freire's principles seeped into my/our consciousness through a thousand fissures, in a Canadian culture that was in flux, and a Catholic Church experiencing a profound transition (and sometimes transformation). For me, taking this retrospective look has been illuminating.

I also drew on the reflections of two other RNDMs to "build" this reflection. Sister Susan Smith has been very active as a teacher, a scholar, and as a justice advocate, both in her homeland of Aotearoa, New Zealand, and internationally. Sister Patricia Orban is a teacher who served as a missionary in Peru for many years, and continues her mission with Indigenous persons in Saskatchewan, Canada. In addition, I draw on accounts of what might be called eco-pedagogy by three RNDM sisters who, in a rural context, were able to learn from the land, and invite others into their learning.[14] Sisters June Lenzen, Marie Finn, and Sheila Madden are educators who demonstrate some of Freire's insights in providing a place where visiting "city dwellers" could experience creation more immediately. The sisters saw it as a way of responding to the calls of the Earth

Charter by providing spaces where people could be close to the land, flora, and fauna of two particular Manitoba ecosystems, and learn from the processes and rhythms of the earth.

These earth initiatives were ways of remembering: remembering where we have come from and where we are going; remembering/rediscovering our place in the universe; remembering that every point in the human journey is linked to a particular piece of land. As a friend said to me recently, "To unite the present and the past is to make memory alive." It is that kind of evocative memory this reflection has awakened in me, much as Chung did in evoking the spirits of the ancestors and those whose lives have been cut short. It is an intersection at which the voices of the poor continuously echo down the corridors of history, and where Paulo Freire's voice continues to summon us with great urgency.

RNDMs in Canada and Paulo Freire: A Retrospective Glance

I will now turn to the RNDMs in Canada to consider some of the ways Paulo Freire's work has been influential on their evolutionary journey.

The RNDMs arrived in Canada from France in 1898. They initially went to a small French-Métis village in Manitoba called Grande Clairière. Over the next fifty years, they developed numerous primary and secondary schools in four Canadian provinces.[15] Following the Second Vatican Council, in 1968, they sent three sisters to Peru as part of an attempt to reclaim the missionary dynamism that had inspired their founder, Euphrasie Barbier.[16]

It was into this post–Vatican II world that Paulo Freire's *Pedagogy of the Oppressed* was published in English in 1970, and it fairly quickly made its way into my Canadian world.[17] I recall taking part in a University of Winnipeg symposium in 1972 at which we studied this book over six weeks of evening classes, finding insights for our lives and solidarity with our classmates. I was twenty-seven years old, a relatively new teacher, and Freire's insistence that the banking model of education was no longer helpful if education was to achieve radical change at a societal level had great personal resonance.

In addition, at about the same time that Freire's understanding of popular education and critical pedagogy was entering my life, in Peru Gustavo Gutiérrez published his catalysing work *A Theology of Liberation*.[18] This book, too, was disruptive, shaking my theological world in ways both delightful and dismaying. At the time, it seemed to me that the whole of South America was ablaze with the fire of justice, that creative and courageous thinkers like Freire, Gutiérrez, Leonardo Boff, and others were forging new ways to understand what it meant to be human, and creating a world that works for all.

In *Pedagogy of the Oppressed*, Freire lays out his understanding of how people can be awakened to the truth of their living situations, and to their true greatness, when they reflect and act together. This community-based approach to education and social change was revolutionary and transformative. Susan Smith, an RNDM sister from Aotearoa (the Māori word for New Zealand) has reflected on the impact of Freire's work in the community; she emphasizes "Freire's insistence that the banking model of education had had its day and that if education were to achieve radical change at a societal level, then education that had as its entry point the narration of stories from the so-called 'objects' of any educational exercise was the name of the game."[19]

An insightful and courageous aspect of Freire's approach was his point of departure. For Freire, the starting point is the impoverished, those made poor by the social structures within which they live. Freire himself knew what it was to lose everything, to be exiled, to be endangered. His deep and evolving faith was that "cultures of silence" in which oppression and inequity thrived could be met and overturned by a "critical pedagogy" that was liberating for all. He believed that anyone, no matter how poor or uneducated, given a kit of simple tools with which to see, to judge, and to act was capable of looking critically at the world s/he lived in.

In addition, Smith notes a "Catholic amplification" of Freire's work by way of Gustavo Gutiérrez's writing published about the same time:

> The 1973 publication in English of Gustavo Gutiérrez's *A Theology of Liberation* allowed many to see that history was where God was revealed. Exodus revealed a God who sees the misery of Israel in Egypt and resolves to liberate them. In hindsight, it can be seen that Vatican II still faithfully followed a banking model but it empowered Catholics, lay and clerical, to recognise that the world was the privileged arena of God's activity.[20]

Another important influence that was "in the air" at this time was the ongoing dissemination of the Vatican II documents.[21] One such document was *Gaudium et Spes*, which taught that "the joys and the hopes, the griefs and the anxieties of the men[22] of this age, especially those who are poor or in any way afflicted, these are the joys and hopes, the griefs and anxieties of the followers of Christ. Indeed, nothing genuinely human fails to raise an echo in their hearts."[23] These words encouraged Catholics to appreciate that salvation was a this-worldly activity and that we were to co-create with God through works of justice and peace.

Amplifying the ethos of this time, Canadian RNDM Patricia Orban writes that

> On October 4th, 1965, Pope Paul VI made a historic visit to the UN in New York. It was the eve of my departure for the Novitiate in Regina. Our family watched the news about it on TV. These were the times that were forming us. Pope Paul's talk spoke of Peace as respect for Human rights and development. The winds of change were happening.[24]

Alongside these visual reminders that change was happening in the staid Roman Catholic Church, individuals and families were engaging the world and its political organizations. A flux and ferment of creative and innovative ideas was rising "everywhere." To quote Orban further:

> In the Novitiate "*aggiornamento*" was present for us in the way Vatican II opened up space to embrace what was emerging in spirituality, theology and Biblical studies. One lecturer spoke of the Prophets of our time as singers Joan Baez, Bob Dylan and Simon and Garfunkel. We read Teilhard de Chardin's *Divine Milieu* and discovered an evolving, loving presence in every action building up the kin(g)dom of God. It moved us to live fully in the present moment as a "people of God." We were all on the journey together. We were evolving into "modern nuns" and citizens of our planet earth.[25]

For each of these "energy waves" the emphasis was on engaged living, on people reflecting critically on current events and being protagonists in their own lives. As a diverse array of countries became decolonized, many educators within those countries came to recognize that they needed to decolonize education too. Curricula, research, and authoritarian processes that preserved a Eurocentric focus needed to be challenged and largely abandoned. New educational methods and processes were emerging – Freire's being prime among them. This was a way of praxis, a way of "reflection and action upon the world in order to transform it."[26] Through praxis, oppressed people could acquire a critical awareness of their own conditions, and, within a trusted circle, and with an understanding that all were teachers and all were learners, everyone could struggle for liberation.

Impact of Freire on RNDMs in Canada and Peru

Canada

Freire's influence came to Canada as part of the general zeitgeist, the energetic swirl of change and renewal that accompanied the 1960s and '70s throughout the world. The Second Vatican Council (11 October 1962–8 December 1965) launched a wave of hope and expectancy that reverberated worldwide. The civil rights movements, so hopeful, so feared, and so bloody in the United States, gave rise to movements of solidarity and support in Canada. The shock of assassinations in the United States of John Kennedy (1963), Martin Luther King Jr. (1968), Robert Kennedy (1968); the ongoing war in Vietnam, which led to student protests and killings; worldwide solidarity with students in various countries; the emergence of "women's liberation" groups: these were all sweeping events of terror, tragedy, and transformation.[27] In South America, thinkers and theorists of deep consequence were emerging. Freire in Brazil was one of them. Thinking back on that period, I recognize it as the beginning of so many efforts I was involved with at the time and subsequently.[28] In some ways, this chapter has helped me "connect the dots."

In Brazil, Freire's literacy method grew out of circles/discussion groups within the Movement of Popular Culture in Recife in the late 1950s. Freire believed that in these "cultural circles" of illiterate people, the oppressed could learn to read "provided that reading was not imposed upon them in an authoritarian manner and that the process of reading validated their own lived experiences."[29] He did this by helping them to recognize and respect their own values and customs, their own languages, their own concerns – for all of which they needed literacy skills. Freire insisted that the function of education was to build on the language, experiences, and skills of the learners, rather than imposing on them the culture of the "educators." Learning would happen best in a community of learners.

Freire's work also had a significant influence on what became known as liberation theology. Gustavo Gutiérrez in Peru was another emergent thinker of the time, and a "founder" of liberation theology. Similar to Freire's work in Brazil, Gutiérrez's theologizing had arisen among the impoverished church parishioners with whom he worked in Peru. To Gutiérrez, the source of the problems of poverty and social inequity in Latin America manifested in unjust social structures. Alternately, he emphasized the dignity of the poor, their inherent worthiness as beings created in the image and likeness of God. He insisted that liberation meant becoming friends with those made poor, and sharing life together in what he called basic Christian communities (BCCs). In the solidarity of such communities, *campesinos* were discovering this "good news," and their emerging "new consciousness" became a further source of Gutiérrez's theologizing. As Freire succinctly puts it, "To speak a true word is to transform the world."[30]

Freire also challenged the normative assumptions of "equal opportunity" in a democratic society. For Freire, education is a political process that illustrates in word and action how schools become tools used by parents, businesses, churches, and schools to impose their values and beliefs. Part of this "imposition" is an understandable process of "handing on the heritage." But when one cultural/economic heritage diminishes that of others, it is not a worthy heritage. To distinguish this aberration, every person needs to develop a critical consciousness.[31]

While the insights of Freire, Gutiérrez, Boff et al. were coming from a Latin American context, they resonated in many Canadian hearts, as we, too, recognized our complicity in unjust social structures, and the clearly unjust ways poor people, Indigenous people, refugees, and women were treated in Canada and around the world. The interrelationship of "oppressed" and "oppressor" was coming into troubling focus.

Smith goes on to describe an awakening in Aotearoa that was also taking place in Canada:

> Initially RNDMs, who by this time were talking, and sometimes acting, about "making an option for the poor," were concerned with an economic analysis that revealed the structural and systemic nature of the poverty of those among whom they worked. But it moved beyond that as sisters applied the same tools to their experiences of being part of a hierarchical, patriarchal and sexist church. It moved even further when RNDMs began working with Maori suffering from the 19th century loss of land and culture. The reality of racism became an integral component of social analysis workshops.[32]

For us in Canada, the people of the land are the Indigenous people in their many tribes who live from coast to coast to coast. Canada has a long, often troubling, sometimes creative, too often violent history of relationship between those who came as settlers and the original inhabitants. Those who organized themselves to govern the "new land" were all European or of European descent.[33] It was at the request of this government that many Canadian religious became involved with the residential schools that subsequently emerged, with tragic consequences for all.[34] In the twenty-first century, reconciliation with Indigenous people is a key justice issue.

Similarly, the 1960s and '70s also saw some sisters question the very nature and meaning of mission – a kind of "crisis of conscience" for religious missionaries. The Vietnam War, and the widespread resistance to that war, the slow and steady crumbling of colonial power throughout the world, along with the realization of how missionaries often supported the colonial project, were eroding confidence and understanding of what it meant to be a "missionary religious." The process of becoming aware of this reality was a painful one. Some RNDMs studied liberation theologies. Others developed skills in social analysis and attended or offered workshops using these tools, which were largely based on Freire's work.[35]

Robert McAfee Brown asks, "Can a theology for the oppressed also become a theology for the oppressor."[36] In Freire's terms, the question is phrased as follows: "Can education for the oppressed also become education for the oppressor?" While that dynamic will not be deeply pursued in this paper, it, too, was part of the zeitgeist of the time, and the world into which Paulo Freire spoke his words of liberation.

Reflecting from the vantage of today on all the earlier work done through social analysis, Smith says,

> Today, older RNDMs who participated in social analysis workshops lament their virtual disappearance from their lives. There is still a lot of emphasis on storytelling

at both the personal and collective levels, but there is seldom any analysis which leads to action capable of resolving systemic issues in the congregation, church and society. This is a great loss.[37]

As I ponder Smith's assertion, I acknowledge a similar reality in Canada. I think social analysis per se was carried out more extensively in Aotearoa. I think in Canada, some of that analysis morphed into learning and practising "systems thinking," which formed the basis of how numerous provincial leadership meetings, and most of our annual assemblies, have been facilitated for many years.[38]

I see the choices that RNDMs made for "mission at the margins" as being influenced by Freire's insights. In particular, work with mentally challenged adults at Garrity House and Kramer Home in Regina, as well as work with refugees at Hospitality House in Winnipeg, initiated by insightful sisters, are clear examples of a Freirean care for those who are marginalized and often oppressed.[39] I will say more about ecological initiatives the sisters advanced later in this chapter.

Peru

The mid-sixties were a time when Pope Paul VI was urging North American religious to respond to the needs of the church in Latin America. Therefore, RNDMs in Canada made a decision to open a mission in Moquegua, Peru. The first three RNDM missionaries were selected from the many sisters who volunteered, and in 1968 the mission was opened.

Five years later, in 1972, Sister Patricia Orban was sent to join the RNDMs in Peru, bringing their number there to six. Of her arrival in Peru, Orban writes,

> Although the visible poverty of the country was overwhelming, the people that welcomed me to Peru were equally warm-hearted and friendly. Just days before there had been a violent coup in Chile. It was a manifestation of the complex political reality and unrest in most Latin American Countries.[40]

In 1968 Freire had written *Pedagogy of the Oppressed* while exiled in Chile. Through their courses and publications, CLAR (Confederacion Latinoamericana de Religiosas y Religiosos, a conference of women and men religious from South America, Central America, and the Caribbean) were educating religious and lay people. Orban particularly notes how CLAR tirelessly shared these ideas in diverse workshops, courses, and programs in Peru, and in the twenty-one other countries of Latin America. As Orban goes on to say,

> The CELAM (Latin American Episcopal Council) meeting took place in 1968, and the Bishops gathered there had adapted the Vatican II documents to the Latin

American reality resulting in its resounding "option for the poor" at Medellin. That same year Fr. Gustavo Gutiérrez had written his "Theology of Liberation." In the beginning, the Sisters' summers were often spent in Lima for courses with other missionaries, where we were being "conscientized."[41]

Assigned to the city of Ilo, Orban was getting to know and become friends with the diverse peoples in the five parishes she and her colleagues served from the Catechetical Centre. She states that the pastoral team's common purpose was to grow in friendship with the people, and to help Peruvians acquire additional skills so they could be evangelizers of their own population. In 1981, she and the pastoral team became aware of the Family Catechetics Program (known in Spanish as catequesis familiar, or CF) offered through the National Catechetical Office.[42] All agreed to take on the two-year project, the goal of which was to place the preparation for First Communion with parents in their local communities. The first year was the "time of conversion" and the second year was for forming BCCs. The method followed the "see, judge, act" process. Parent guides met with a coordinator to prepare the theme together. As Orban describes the process, along with weekly meetings at home, "Once a month we all got together, parents, children and youth animators ... This deepened the relationships on all levels and a spirit of joy and commitment to the gospel grew. We were celebrating our faith journey together. It was a 5 month, every week commitment to the process. We were all being conscientized through it all."[43]

Orban describes how, on the whole, people spoke of their increased dialogue among themselves and with their children. "It created a sense of solidarity and gave us confidence in the Spirit."[44] She goes on to muse how the whole experience seemed to mature everyone's skill for critical thinking and enabled them "to more deliberatively become agents/protagonists in [their] own lives. One thing is for sure, we became friends celebrating our faith in daily life and in the Eucharistic celebrations each Sunday and committed to the human society we lived in."[45]

As Freire, Gutiérrez, and others have noted, liberation requires an active participation of the oppressed. In Freire's words, "Liberation is a praxis: the action and reflection of men and women upon their world in order to transform it."[46] To Orban's delight, the little base communities of Ilo revealed the active participation of all. In the city neighbourhoods and barrios where Orban and her colleagues were meeting, they were actively engaging Freire's concepts of dialogue, praxis, and conscientization – and all within a communal context.[47]

A further example was in Candarave, a village in the Altiplano over fourteen thousand above sea level. Candarave had a pastoral team of three sisters and about ten pastoral agents who came from some of the seventeen villages in the area. Orban notes that

The first five years or so of our presence in that Mission gathered together men from the surrounding villages who wanted to be Pastoral agents in their Village. They would come from their villages once a month to a workshop in Candarave, study the documents from CELAM, and share on their ministry in their villages. We would visit the communities on biweekly schedules. In 1983, after study and much conversation they wanted to implement CF in Candarave and the villages surrounding.[48]

A team from the National Catechetical Office were invited to go to Candarave to coach the people in using the CF process. Ten couples and some youth from the Candarave area came to the formation program. A concern expressed by one couple was that their people would not listen to them, as they had only grade 3 schooling. Orban promised to go to their meetings for a while, and that if anyone had a question they couldn't find a way to deal with, she would help out. Having attended the first meetings, Orban says she admired how well this couple led their small group of neighbours. She states further that

The women particularly appreciated being a part of the whole process. They became more conscious of their dignity and took a place in their daily lives that was usually managed by the men of the village. It was a joy to see them coming as couples to the preparatory meetings ... They remarked how it helped them to pray with their families. They increased their ability to dialogue with each other as a couple and with their children about such themes as "La mujer Vale" (women have value). They were becoming BCCs. The relationships were forged in the common mission of evangelization they shared as Parent Guides.

While Orban et al. worked in an explicitly Catholic context, with families passing on a faith tradition, the larger agenda was liberation for all and the co-creation of a more just world. The summons to be protagonists in their own lives had been heard and responded to with growing courage. It is interesting to note that a greater valuing of women seems to have emerged. Following Freire's example, the leaders of these meetings rejected education as a means of domestication, and instead chose education as a means of liberation. In a dialogic process among engaged participants, with "gifts differing" for the good of the whole, new possibilities were born. To again cite Freire: "Leaders who do not act dialogically, but insist on imposing their decisions, do not organize the people – they manipulate them. They do not liberate, nor are they liberated: they oppress."[49] Orban's contention is that both she and the people experienced liberation.

Freire and Ecology

At the time of Freire's death on 2 May 1997, he was working on a book about eco-pedagogy. Freire, Francisco Gutiérrez, and Moacir Gadotti had apparently coined the term and the concept in the late 1990s. They had organized an international meeting under the title of "The Earth Charter in an Educational Perspective," and all three of them then set out to write books on the subject:

> Gadotti wrote *Pedagogy of the Earth*, Gutiérrez wrote *Ecopedagogy and Planetary Citizenship*, Freire however passed before he was able to write another book. Since then Leonardo Boff of the Liberation Theology movement and multiple others have joined them in Latin America to form what has become an Ecopedagogy movement, based out of the Paulo Freire Institute in Brazil.[50]

So it is encouraging to know that the work of addressing the current ecological crisis is being carried forward by some of the Freire Institutes and related associations around the world. Very significantly, these persons and organizations participants and practitioners in the development of the Earth Charter (Published 29 June 2000), to which they made significant contributions.[51] Publication of the Earth Charter was truly a watershed moment for the earth and all her inhabitants.[52]

Freire and *Laudato Si*

It is interesting to speculate on Freire's influence on Pope Francis's critical-ecological encyclical *Laudato Si*. As men of a "common-ish" age from Latin America who shared some similar sources of inspiration and struggle, the imagination is tempted. Furthermore, I am not alone in such speculation. In a recent movie review, Vincent Bevans of *The Atlantic* offers the following speculation:

> In *The Two Popes*, a recent feature film produced by Netflix, Father Jorge Bergoglio is sent into the wilderness, where he wanders alone in the Argentine mountains for two years. During an intense process of spiritual rebirth – crucial to his transformation into Pope Francis – he turns to radical books of the very kind he had cleared out of the Jesuit order in the late 1970s, during the military dictatorship in Argentina. In one scene, the camera pauses briefly on the cover of one volume: 1968's *Pedagogy of the Oppressed*, by Paulo Freire, the educator whose legacy the current Brazilian president, Jair Bolsonaro, spent the past year attacking.[53]

A more historical account is that given by James D. Kirylo, who sees the heart of Pope Francis's ministry in the "preferential option for the poor." This priority, articulated by Father Pedro Arupe, superior general of the Jesuits, in a 1968 letter to the Jesuits of Latin America, was picked up by CELAM at their historic conferences in Medellín and Puebla. Kirylo emphasizes that the core of Pope Francis's pontificate is having a heart for the poor. Kirylo says that shortly after he became pope,

> Francis invited Gustavo Gutiérrez to Rome, holding private conversations and concelebrating Mass … Indeed, in the 266th Pontiff, Gutiérrez sees a Church with a "change in atmosphere" … That change of atmosphere indeed caught the attention of Ana Maria (Nita) Araujo Freire. The widow of Paulo Freire, Nita requested a visit with Pope Francis, and he graciously obliged, receiving her at the Vatican in April 2015. Discussing Freire's work, which Francis has read, Nita not only sees Freire's writings as "more relevant today than 20 years ago," but also saw in Pope Francis one who is creating "a new face of the church" that has the plight of the poor in the forefront of his ministry.[54]

It is in this context that we can better understand Pope Francis's groundbreaking encyclical letter *Laudato Si*. In that encyclical, he speaks of a "splendid universal communion,"[55] and of an integral ecology that addresses all aspects of human life and culture – individual and corporate, economic and cultural, jurisprudential and governmental, political and religious, etc. He addresses the life of all creatures of land, sky, and sea, and makes concern for all of planet earth a central focus for decision making. The created world has an intrinsic value as well as an instrumental one, and requires a "conversion to earth," especially for Western cultures so heavily influenced by the "Great Chain of Being" arguments derived from Plato and Aristotle.[56] Instead, *Laudato Si* emphasizes that all created beings are bearers of God's presence. The community of creation, rather than any one species, must be the focus of our concern. In a beautiful section, Francis writes, "Even the fleeting life of the least of beings is the object of his love, and in its few seconds of existence, God enfolds it with his affection."[57]

Freire and RNDMs, Ecology, and *Laudato Si*

Over the years, the RNDMs in Canada have taken to heart the community of creation and the human-earth relationship. This care has involved personal study for numerous sisters, academic study for some, ecological action for others, and collective study at community meetings and provincial assemblies. It has also involved developing consistent and persistent ways of praying with and for earth – including laments amid songs of praise. These prayer rituals have developed over many years and are often aligned with the seasons and rhythms of the earth, involving sisters and often their friends and collaborators.

As Orban has already noted, in the 1960s, many sisters began to know about and study the work of Pierre Teilhard de Chardin, a twentieth-century palaeontologist and French Jesuit. Teilhard's sense of the evolutionary processes of the earth and the cosmos, and the sacredness of "matter" more broadly, opened worlds of meaning and possibility. He also wrote poetically about how spiritual energies – like compassion, generosity, humility, and love – were a significant planetary energy.

Many other insightful writers and practitioners soon became RNDM mentors as well.[58] Basically, those early "creation writers" like Thomas Berry, Mathew Fox, and Brian Swimme were saying in theological and mystical terms what scientists like Einstein and Hubble were discovering through their mathematical calculations and telescopes. The incredible energy that generated the cosmos could be understood as the divine love that permeated everything. The mysterious force of gravity could also be seen mystically, as an example of the earth holding all creatures to herself. We were all matter, and all matter was sacred.

I now turn to examples of two specific eco-pedagogical works in which the sisters engaged:

1. **Good Earth at Ste. Anne, Manitoba** – June Lenzen, RNDM, a founder and resident of Good Earth, describes this initiative as follows:

> The inspiration for Good Earth rose ... because we had a strong desire to honour the Good Earth, to live lightly on her; to foster care of her and of all the non-human inhabitants living on this small part of her and to grow in appreciation of her ourselves and let this happen to anyone else that came in contact with her though us.
>
> [Purchased in 1996] the property ... was a little over five acres ... There was a remarkable variety of vegetation: Poplar, scrub oak, ash and maple as well as some evergreens, which had been planted. There were willows, high bush cranberries, saskatoon and chokecherry bushes as well as innumerable grasses and shrubs. New discoveries of roses, tiger lilies and clumps of lady slippers showed up every spring. This abundance of vegetation made a great home for many species of animals, birds and all it takes to make up a living community.[59]

2. **Gurtishall – Place of Peace** – as described by Sheila Madden, RNDM, and Marie Finn, RNDM:

> Gurtishall is Gaelic for Place of Peace. In 2001, as "an integral part of Wiens Family Shared Farm," [w]ith an intuitive belief in the wisdom of earth, [we] committed [our]selves to deep listening to the earth's rhythms and gifts and to responding to all earth desires to teach us.[60]

Madden and Finn describe the many modes of outreach they made to a diverse slice of the human community who were drawn to Gurtishall, including Indigenous women, food co-ops, neighbourhood community groupings, food justice groups, climate change advocates, pilgrims passing through, friends, family, etc. They go on to say that

> A labyrinth and a hermitage now grace the land. Centering prayer sessions and days of prayer focused on the unfolding story of the Universe and the gifts of nature have been part of our shared life. Dogs and cats, sheep, goats, chickens, ducks, guinea hens and "Honker" (a stately goose), bees, birds and butterflies as well as much wildlife fill out the roll-call of our Earth Community at Lasko Road.[61]

Each of these projects provides an example of a way of living out an ecologically attuned life, and of inviting other persons into the learning and commitments required for such a life. In retrospect, similar to what I perceived in the work conducted by the RNDM in Peru, I recognize Freire's concepts of dialogue, praxis, and conscientization at work in these initiatives.[62]

By way of summary: I have long been inspired by a poem by Rubem Alves that speaks about planting dates. Until I wrote this chapter, I did not know that Alves is also considered a founder of liberation theology and was a collaborator with Paulo Freire. The whole poem is beautiful and evocative, and, to our point here, speaks to Freire's manner of acting in hope and love:

> Let us plant dates
> even though those who plant them will never eat them.
> We must live by the love of what we will never see.[63]

Conclusion

I began this chapter with a story about Chung Hyung Kyung's presentation in Canberra, which disrupted an academic conference accustomed to predictable ways of sharing knowledge. Similar to Freire, she unsettled a dominant way of thinking. To a predominantly Eurocentric crowd, with established ways of presenting to other academics within the discipline of theology, Chung anchored her presentation in the earth on which they all stood/sat. She drew on her own Korean cultural heritage, making memorable, through her courage, a conference in faraway Australia. It was a paradigmatic shift in the practice of theology. Many were deeply moved by her creative and challenging incarnation of the assembly's call of "Come Holy Spirit." Other delegates were upset. As Leonard notes, cries of heresy and syncretism arose, revealing the fear of those who felt that the Christian tradition was being threatened. Orthodox and evangelical delegates asked for an ecumenical study to develop criteria for determining the limits of theological diversity. A special plenary session was called to deal with the topic of the gospel and inculturation during which Chung identified the question of power behind the talk of syncretism. She reminded those who responded vehemently to her approach, "We have been listening to your intellectualism for 2,000 years," and she pleaded, "please listen to us." "Third-world theologies are the new paradigm, the new wine that can't be put in your wineskins ... Yes, we are dangerous, but it is through such danger that the Holy Spirit can renew the church." Not all the delegates were able to hear the Spirit speak in this way. Chung even received death threats. A few months later I met a bishop who had been at the Assembly. When I told him that I had been there his immediate response was, "I didn't like that little Korean girl."[64]

To kill or to demean – both are violent ways of eradicating prophetic voices. In every generation, humans are challenged to hear these voices, and to choose their response accordingly.

The prophetic voice of Paulo Freire has been the principal focus of this chapter. Hearing his voice retrospectively, in the communal life and mission of RNDMs in Canada, has been the task. May the danger and the promise of Freire's voice sound among RNDMs in new ways, and may we welcome the chaos of grace to which his voice continues to call.

NOTES

1   Ellen Leonard, private paper. Leonard gave this paper to me privately in 2001. I do not know if it was published elsewhere, and I am no longer able to speak with Leonard, who is in a nursing home in Toronto. Leonard did publish a paper about the Canberra conference in *The Way*, entitled "Come, Holy Spirit – Renew the Whole Creation: Theological Issues Arising at the Seventh Assembly of the World Council of Churches." That article is available at https://www.theway.org.uk/back/31Leonard1.pdf (accessed 4 January 2021).

2   For more, see Chung Hyun Kyung, "Come, Holy Spirit – Renew the Whole Creation," in *Signs of the Spirit Official Report, Seventh Assembly, Canberra, Australia, 7–20 February 1991*, ed. Michael Kinnamon (Geneva: World Council of Churches, 1991), 37–47.

3   Leonard, private paper.

4   Leonard.

5 Leonard.

6 Leonard.

7 Also known as Quan Yin, Kwan Yin, or Kuanyin, a name that means "One Who Sees and Hears the Cry from the Human World." For more, see "Guan Yin, Guan Yim, Kuan Yim, Kuan Yin," One World – Nations Online, accessed 16 January 2021, https://www.nationsonline.org/oneworld/Chinese_Customs/Guan _Yin.htm.

8 Leonard, private paper.

9 Leonard.

10 Paulo Freire, *Pedagogy of the Oppressed* (New York: Herder and Herder, 1972), 120.

11 In particular, I am thinking of Freire's emphasis on dialogue, on paying attention to all voices in a community. I believe this process has led to communal decisions that are liberating for women and for the earth.

12 By "new cosmology" I mean the scientific study of the origins of the universe, and our human place as the "consciousness" of the universe. I also mean to include the "stories of origins" of various cultures and religious traditions, many poetic texts in the Hebrew/Christian scriptures that speak to God's relationship with creation, the writings of mystics and poets of all cultures and various epochs, which are handed on from generation to generation.

13 For more about RNDMs and Paulo Freire, see Rosa Bruno-Jofré, *The Sisters of Our Lady of the Missions: From Ultramontane Origins to a New Cosmology* (Toronto: University of Toronto Press, 2020), 185, 210, 213, 218.

14 "Ecopedagogy: An Introduction," *Counterpoints* 359 (2010): 1–33.

15 Those provinces (in chronological order of foundation) are Manitoba, Saskatchewan, Ontario, and Quebec. For more, see Rosa Bruno-Jofré, *Sisters of Our Lady.*

16 I will say more about this "missionary dynamism" later in this chapter.

17 The first English translation was published by Seabury (New York) in 1970. The version I cite in this chapter was published by Herder and Herder (New York) in 1972.

18 Gutiérrez's work was published in 1971 in Spanish and in 1973 in English. Gutiérrez subsequently became known as "the father of liberation theology." See also James D. Kirylo, "Liberation Theology and Paulo Freire," *Counterpoints* 385 (2011): 167–93.

19 Susan Smith, RNDM, personal reflection sent to me in July 2020.

20 Smith.

21 The Second Vatican Council officially closed on 8 December 1965.

22 The authors discussed in this chapter often use the masculine third-person-singular pronoun, reflecting a usage that was dominant during the era in which they wrote; the author of this chapter does not endorse such non-inclusive language.

23 See article 1 of "Pastoral Constitution on the Church in the Modern World: *Gaudium Et Spes*, Promulgated by His Holiness, Pope Paul VI On December 7, 1965," Holy See, accessed 14 February 2021, https://www.vatican.va/archive

/hist_councils/ii_vatican_council/documents/vat-ii_const_19651207_gaudium
-et-spes_en.html.

24 Patricia Orban, RNDM, private paper shared in January 2021.

25 Orban.

26 Freire, *Pedagogy*, 36.

27 I am additionally thinking of the marvellous Training for Transformation
series based on Freire's method, about developing critical awareness and putting
insight into practice. First published in 1984, I discovered these books when I
went to Senegal in 1984, where they were "basic texts" for the sisters there.
For more, see the Training for Transformation website at http://www
.trainingfortransformation.ie/.

28 These range from principles of adult education (with the andragogy of Malcolm
Knowles, holistic education of Parker Palmer, and the *Fifth Discipline* approach
of organizational learning from Peter Senge), to doing social analysis (as per Joe
Holland and Peter Henriot), to facilitating group processes (as per Marge Denis
and Margaret Wheatley), to being involved with women's "consciousness raising"
groups in a variety of contexts.

29 Carmel Borg and Peter Mayo, "Reflections from a 'Third Age' Marriage: Paulo
Freire's Pedagogy of Reason, Hope and Passion: An Interview with Ana Maria
(Nita) Freire," *McGill Journal of Education* 3, no. 2 (Spring 2000): 107.

30 Freire, *Pedagogy*, 75.

31 Critical consciousness is Freire's theory/practice of "conscientization." As the
Freire Institute website notes, this is "the process of developing a critical awareness of one's social reality through reflection and action. Action is fundamental
because it is the process of changing the reality. Paulo Freire says that we all acquire social myths which have a dominant tendency, and so learning is a critical
process which depends upon uncovering real problems and actual needs." See
"Concepts Used by Paulo Freire," Freire Institute, accessed 23 April 2023, https://
www.freire.org/concepts-used-by-paulo-freire.

32 Smith, personal reflection.

33 With the possible exception of Loui Riel's key role in bringing Manitoba into
Confederation.

34 For more, see the online archives of the University of Winnipeg's National Centre
for Truth and Reconciliation at https://nctr.ca/map.php.

35 The social analysis of which I speak is that developed by Joe Holland and Peter
Henriot, *Social Analysis* (New York: Orbis Books, 1983).

36 Glenn R. Bucher, cited in the abstract of "Toward a Liberation Theology for the
'Oppressor,'" *Journal of the American Academy of Religion* 44, no. 3 (September
1976): 517–34.

37 Smith, personal reflection.

38 Systems thinking is a basis for examining any group constellated to carry forward a common task. RNDMs in Canada have been particularly influenced by

the work of Peter Senge, Otto Scharmer, and their associates at what became the Presencing Institute. They are concerned with "addressing the root causes of direct, structural and attentional violence." For more about the Presencing Institute, see https://www.presencing.org/.

39 For a list of RNDM works, see "Work Legacies," Sisters of Our Lady of the Missions, accessed 23 April 2023, https://rndmcanada.org/archive/.

40 Orban, private paper.

41 Orban.

42 In her private paper, Orban notes that by this time, their pastoral team had expanded to four sisters, two Franciscans, and a Jesuit. She says that they were all wholly involved in the program.

43 Orban.

44 Orban.

45 Orban.

46 Freire, *Pedagogy*, 66.

47 See Freire Institute, "Concepts Used by Paulo Freire."

48 Orban, private paper.

49 Freire, *Pedagogy*, 179.

50 See "Ecopedagogy," Partners for Collaborative Change, accessed 15 January 2021, https://static1.squarespace.com/static/5751c590746fb9c9be542bb3/t/5af9f4 b2352f53b1380f7713/1526330546619/Ecopedagogy+Handout+for+Web.pdf.

51 "The Earth Charter and Education for Social Change, the Paulo Freire Institute, Brazil," Earth Charter Initiative Secretariat, accessed 16 March 2021, https://earthcharter.org/wp-content/assets/virtual-library2/images /uploads/X-%20The%20Earth%20Charter%20and%20Education%20for %20Social%20Change.pdf.

52 More information about the Earth Charter is available at https://earthcharter .org/.

53 Vincent Bevans, "How *The Two Popes* Condemns Current-Day Authoritarianism," *The Atlantic*, January 24, 2020, https://www.theatlantic.com /culture/archive/2020/01/how-the-two-popes-condemns-current-day -authoritarianism/605398/.

54 James D. Kirylo, "Hate Won, but Love Will Have the Final Word: Critical Pedagogy, Liberation Theology, and the Moral Imperative of Resistance," *Policy Futures in Education* 15, no. 5 (2017): 590–601.

55 See article 220 in Pope Francis, "*Laudato Si*. Encyclical Letter on Care for Our Common Home," Holy See, accessed 19 December 2020, http://www.vatican.va /content/francesco/en/encyclicals/documents/papa-francesco_20150524_enciclic -laudato-si.html.

56 This chain begins with God and descends down through angels, humans, animals, plants, and minerals.

57 Pope Francis, "*Laudato Si*," article 77.

58   Each of the new eco-theologians engaged the implications and magnificence of the new cosmology that was emerging from the theories and discoveries of scientists like Albert Einstein and Edwin Hubble.

59   "Good Earth – St. Anne, MB," Sisters of Our Lady of the Missions, accessed 23 April 2023, https://rndmcanada.org/archive/#goodearth.

60   "Gurtishall – Place of Peace," Sisters of Our Lady of the Missions, accessed 23 April 2023, https://rndmcanada.org/archive/#goodearth.

61   "Gurtishall – Place of Peace."

62   See Freire Institute, "Concepts Used by Paulo Freire."

63   Rubem Alves, *The Poet, the Warrior, the Prophet* (Norwich, UK: SCM Press, 2002). The poem is also available at http://mpleroy-eng.blogspot.com/2004/10/rubem-alves-full-poem.html (accessed 12 December 2020).

64   Leonard, private paper.

PART THREE

Freire and Illich and Contemporary Critical Issues in Education

window marching alone

Alan Wilkinson

7 Ivan Illich, Gender, and Energy

R.W. SANDWELL

As concerns about climate change press people around the world to rethink their heavy dependence on fossil fuels and contemplate a post-carbon future, historians are showing renewed interest in industrialization as the starting point of the world's currently unfolding environmental crisis. Given the combination of fossil fuels' society-changing dominance around the world today and their catastrophic environmental consequences, the Industrial Revolution that ushered in the first massive use of hydrocarbons deserves, as J.R. McNeill recently opined, "to be elevated to the front of ranks among revolutions in the 250,000-year history of human society."[1] For as a result of more than a century and a half of ever-increasing fossil fuel burning, the earth is now witnessing a great acceleration in terms of humans' impact on the environment, and people are encountering for the first time "the possibility that our economy is transgressing the planetary boundaries that provide a safe operating space for humanity, threatening the functioning of our ecosystems and threatening rapid climate change."[2]

While Ivan Illich is not well known today as an energy activist, he was part of a broad spectrum of Euro-Americans in the 1970s and early 1980s who, mobilized by the 1973 "oil shock," collectively challenged for the first time a (still) stubbornly held "progressive" energy ideology: the belief that higher energy consumption always means a better world.[3] He was among the first to specifically identify the introduction of industrial energy, and the "progress" that supposedly followed from burning fossil fuels, as highly disruptive and even destructive forces in human and ecological history. Aware of some of the environmental devastation resulting from the burning of fossil fuels, he was particularly astute at describing and critically analysing the social and cultural damage that very high energy use has entailed. In *Energy and Equity*, *Shadow Work*, and *Gender* he articulated the very high cost that high-energy-consuming societies have long been paying in terms of inequality and cultural alienation.[4] While he did not explicitly discuss catastrophic climate change as one of the negative polluting effects of high energy use, this chapter argues that two aspects of Illich's work – his overall counter-narrative to Western "progress" through high energy use, and his particular insistence that changing gender roles have been among the most devastating results of the shift to fossil fuel use – demonstrate the importance of Illich's voice in urgent contemporary discussions about climate change. For as industrial societies today contemplate the drastic 80 per cent reduction in their fossil fuel consumption (which comprises about 90 per cent of the energy industrial societies consume) by 2050 needed to prevent catastrophic climate change, people desperately need a new and positive narrative about change, one in which less energy means a better, not a worse, future for humanity.[5]

Energy and Equity was published in 1974 shortly after the oil shock introduced to the oil-dependent world the spectre of massive and perhaps permanent oil shortages. While many writers of the time worried about how to maintain the "chain of ease" and the high economic growth provided to Euro-American societies by cheap fossil fuels,[6] Illich's *Energy and Equity* provided instead a sustained reflection on the many *disadvantages* of high-energy societies. Illich begins the book by challenging the nature of the so-called energy crisis that societies in the Global North were experiencing as fuel prices increased dramatically with limits in supply. The crisis was not, he argued, a result of the fact that energy supplies might be limited, but instead that "high quanta of energy degrade social relations just as inevitably as they destroy the physical milieu."[7] High energy consumption was not, as commonly assumed, a harbinger of progress or "the panacea for social ills," but rather a manifestation of society's unhealthy dependence on "energy slaves" to provide what was desired from life. He found a significant analogy between the damaging effects of industrial societies' overconsumption of energy and individuals' overconsumption of unhealthy foods, arguing that both reflected a kind of greed and lack of self-knowledge that inevitably led to an unhealthy and unsustainable situation. Even more important, he maintained that high levels of energy consumption were responsible for creating sustained inequality throughout society:

> While people have begun to accept ecological limits on maximum per capita energy use as a condition for physical survival, they do not yet think about the use of minimum feasible power as the foundation of any various social orders that would be both modern and desirable. Yet only a ceiling on energy use can lead to social relations that are characterized by high levels of equity.[8]

Illich was not completely opposed to what he refers to as "motors." But he argued that such innovations must be evaluated carefully to discover the right amount of energy required to create positive rather than negative effects for society: "below a threshold of per capita wattage, motors improve the conditions for social progress. Above that threshold, energy grows at the expense of equity."[9] Again, he draws on organic analogies to make his point: "if the ecologists are right to assert that non-metabolic power pollutes, it is in fact just as inevitable that, beyond a certain threshold, mechanical power corrupts."[10] The essays and reflections throughout the book explore just how a society should gauge the right amount of energy to avoid the corruption that excess consumption inevitably brings about.

Throughout *Energy and Equity*, Illich uses the example of traffic to explore his thesis. The automobile industry, he argues, successfully sold automobiles by appealing to people's desire for a kind of transportation that would be more comfortable and more efficient than walking. After a certain number of automobiles were on the road, however, these arteries became increasingly clogged, taxes for road infrastructure increased, travel slowed, pollution became worse, accidents proliferated, people's inconvenience and frustration grew, and earlier transportation alternatives became no longer practicable. Space and time were transformed by traffic, with the result that people have become "degraded by their dependence on transportation ... we have been industrially deformed."[11] Transportation had become a radical monopoly: "the passenger who agrees to live in a world monopolized by transport becomes a harassed, overburdened consumer of distances whose shape and length he can no longer control."[12]

These high-energy monopolies also, Illich argues, exacerbate inequality. Transportation infrastructures were designed for those who could afford the fastest cars, and the biggest automobiles and trucks. In the ensuing shortage of time and speed available to people in high-traffic areas, it was the wealthy who held substantial advantages over those who could not afford to live in low-traffic neighbourhoods, or to use low-capacity toll roads. The result was "extremes of privilege ... created at the cost of universal enslavement."[13] As Illich summarizes, "Traffic here serves as a paradigm of a general economic law: *Any industrial product that comes in per capita quanta beyond a given intensity exercises a radical monopoly over the satisfaction of a need.*"[14] He uses the counter-example of the highly efficient but very low-energy bicycle to explore how society might, by contrast, make better use of technology to improve the lives of all people, rich and poor alike, and with the expenditure of significantly less energy than that involved in building and maintaining automobiles and their massive and expensive infrastructure supports.[15]

Illich ends his essay "Energy Crisis" by noting the potential of the oil shock and the ensuing "crisis" to promote a social, cultural, and economic transformation of the industrialized world. It was a moment, he argued, that could possibly lead to a reconsideration and "search for [a] post-industrial, labour-intensive low energy and high equity economy." On the other hand, industrial societies' "hysterical concern with machine fodder can reinforce the present escalation of capital-intensive institutional growth, and carry us past the last turnoff from a hyper-industrial Armageddon."[16] The climate emergency confronting the world half a century later is one confirmation of Illich's fears. In contemplating their energy futures, he notes that most countries are "blinded to the fact that the threat of social breakdown is due neither to a shortage of fuel, nor to the wasteful polluting and irrational use of available wattage, but to the attempt of industries to gorge society with energy quanta that inevitably degrade, deprive and frustrate most people."[17] Looking back from our current vantage point amid crises of climate change and escalating inequality, Illich emerges not only as a prophet of doom, but also of the potential of a low-energy society to improve life in the future.

If Illich's work is unusual in challenging the more-is-better approach to energy consumption, he was even more unusual in identifying gender as a key component in the transition to fossil fuel use (a.k.a. industrialization). Indeed, while there are many histories of women and the family in the Industrial Revolution,[18] and a growing number of studies that look explicitly at the shift to fossil fuels that was responsible for that revolution,[19] few histories have looked at women or gender in the history of energy.[20] And notwithstanding the near total absence of women in histories of energy, gender is seldom discussed as a relevant factor in energy transitions. Most histories of energy have focused on the technological innovations that accompanied the Industrial Revolution, or on workplaces outside the home, and the larger structures of the formal market economy. My own research focuses on the ways that the nineteenth- and early twentieth-century household provides a focus and a scale of particular importance in understanding the last energy transition. I have argued that throughout most of human history, the household was the foundational centre around which people organized their social, cultural, political, and economic lives, and through which the energy that supported them flowed. The household, therefore, provides the historian with a significant vantage point from which to view the many overlapping and changing aspects of energy production and consumption that occurred within the spaces of the household in industrializing countries, and to observe their myriad links to the world outside its doors. The household, furthermore, has the advantage of being a place where women's roles in forging new relationships between people and their environment through energy use is central and therefore difficult to ignore.[21] But as I argued in a recent collection of essays, *In a New Light: Histories of Women and Energy*, women do not simply provide a new way of *looking at* energy transitions, but were also significant historical actors in the social, economic, and cultural changes associated with the transition to fossil fuels. Illich's work anticipated these arguments by almost half a century, and it speaks directly to the changing role of gender in the history of industrialization.

Drawing on a rich feminist literature about the household, the family, and the transition to capitalism, Illich identifies gender as central to the transition away from pre-industrial energy – what E.A. Wrigley has termed the organic energy regime – and towards today's modern industrial society.[22] In his 1981 essay "Shadow Work," Illich argues that women's unpaid labour as housewives and mothers within industrial capitalism cannot simply be seen as an extension of their earlier participation in largely non-waged pre-industrial and proto-industrial societies. He begins by providing an overview of the subsistence-oriented pre-industrial households that relied on the labour of all family members. As access to the commons was increasingly constrained by a variety of factors, including the enclosure of common lands for the benefit of wealthy landholders, he argues that people were forced to rely more and more on wages paid by employers. They became obliged to purchase the foods and other goods that they could no longer obtain through their own peasant-style labours. Illich emphasizes people's intense antipathy to the servitude of waged labour, and the difficulties that the new industrialists experienced in trying to attract workers at wages they wanted to pay.[23]

What finally coerced/persuaded people to accept waged labour, Illich argues, was "the economic division of labour into a productive and a non-productive kind, first pioneered through the domestic enclosure of women." This created an "unprecedented economic division of the sexes and an unprecedented conception of the family," which in turn created "an unprecedented antagonism between the domestic and public spheres [that] made wage work into a necessary adjunct of life. All this was accomplished by making working men into the wardens of their domestic women, one on one, and making their guardianship into a burdensome duty. The enclosure of women succeeded where the enclosure of sheep and beggars had failed."[24] Women's new labour within the home contributed directly to neither the subsistence nor the productive work that formerly characterized pre-industrial women's labour, Illich argues, and their relationship to the larger society and economy shifted. Illich argues that women's unpaid labour within industrial capitalism is "hidden by the industrial-age ideology ... it feeds the formal economy, not social subsistence ... Its unpaid performance is the condition for wages to be paid ... It is a form of bondage, not much closer to servitude than to either slavery or wage labour."[25]

In *Gender*, published in 1983, Illich elaborates on these arguments about the importance of gender in the transition to modern industrial capitalism. He argues that one of the most profound dislocations that industrial capitalism imposed on local communities, households, and economies was the transformation of gender and gender relations. Prior to capitalist industrialization, he posits the existence of a society characterized by what he terms "vernacular gender." As he discusses in "Shadow Work," within pre-industrial, household-focused societies, subsistence and use value dominated economic relations; households were dependent on their own labour on the land, and each individual member relied on other for their subsistence, and neither waged labour nor the exchange of commodities played a large role. Time-honoured "vernacular" gender relations provided the cultural and material foundation and support for all social and economic interactions. Vernacular gender was not egalitarian, Illich argues, but in a society where the individual was subordinate to both the community and the environment, and where people were culturally and materially well supported by strong, shared, and clearly defined social and economic values, individual equality was neither necessary nor, according to Illich, desired. He defines the old social roles and relations as "ambiguous complementarity." Gender was the foundation of what Illich calls a "vernacular culture" as a whole, a culture rooted in place, based on local peoples through time, and constantly reiterated in the gendered tools, kinship roles, and responsibilities that shaped daily life.

Illich's *Gender* emphasizes the contrast between living in a vernacular culture – where gender roles varied to some extent but everywhere shaped and supported people in their daily lives – and living in homogenous, characterless, and fundamentally unequal industrial capitalist societies. Waged labour and the necessary constant ("compulsory") purchase of commodities have, he argues, created a culture of possessive individualism that privileges uniform individual autonomy at the expense of collective health and well-being. The liberal economic theory used to explain how modern industrial societies work rests on a system of values that claims, Illich argues, to be gender neutral; everyone, man or woman, is equally pursuing their own self-interest in the common attempt to maximize it through the consumption of various commodities and commodified states. People have, as a result, become unhinged from the vernacular cultures that relied on gender to root them in time, place, and the activities of everyday life. With industrial capitalism, Illich maintains, gender has been downgraded to what he terms "economic sex." Without recognizing the complex roles and interactions that vernacular gender long provided, and in the context of a capitalist socio-economic system premised on individualism, shortage, and competition, individuals mistakenly identify the substantial differences between women and men, the female and the male, as *individual* hierarchical differences. On the contrary, Illich argues, these hierarchical, vernacular gender differences are the *essential* differences needed to create and support a stable economy, culture, and ecology.

Without the cultural support of vernacular gender, he argues, women are unfortunately but inevitably cast individually into a subordinate position in a series of systematic ways. He reiterates women's low wages relative to men in what he calls the "reported" or formal economy, and discusses their unpaid or badly paid labour in the unreported economy of tax evasion, crime, and other kinds of illegal work. Perhaps his most unusual "take" on women's inferiority is in women's unpaid labour within the household. As we have seen above, what others have called housework, or homemaking, or care work, or social reproduction, Illich calls "shadow work." He is emphatic that women's work in the home is not a continuation of traditional subsistence activities, such as storing and preparing food, or bearing and raising children. In severing the age-old relationship between households and their means of direct subsistence from the land, where all members of the household were interdependent with the others, capitalist industrialization drove a wedge between the roles of women and men for the first time: for the first time, men took on a "breadwinner" role for the entire household, whereby their wages became the sole means of economic support for landless families. Women, left in the now non-productive home, likewise took on a new economic role: "performing the unpaid toil that adds to a commodity an incremental value that is necessary to make this commodity useful to the consuming unit itself." Badly paid within the formal economy, women are "deprived of equal access to waged labour only to be bound with even greater inequality to work that did not exist before wage labour came into being."[26] Women have become, in effect, servants to the commodity form, their labour directed exclusively – and inherently meaninglessly – at making inert things more consumable for a passive, consumption-obsessed, de-culturated society.

Illich seemed unaware of just how offensive his description and analysis of gender roles might have been to women in the early 1980s; the response to the book was lukewarm at best. It was, after all, a time when women were locating their liberation precisely in their ability to throw off the kinds of domestic roles encouraged by "traditional" society, including the church. They were leaving their role as full-time homemakers to embrace full, active participation in the secular capitalist economy in their new roles as independent waged workers. The implications of Illich's arguments about gender and industrialization – that society should return to a world of "traditional" gendered identities and behaviours in order to create a healthier and more sustainable society – proved as unpalatable as his plea for a low-energy society. In the early 1980s women certainly were, however, getting the message that their work as housewives and mothers – their "shadow work" – could no longer be considered a venerable calling. Rather than going "back" to the social relations of the pre-industrial, pre-capitalist world, as Illich clearly would have preferred, women (including married women) of the 1980s decided instead to enter the waged workforce en masse for the first time, just as men had done two centuries earlier.

Unfortunately, it is now clear that, just as Illich might have predicted, women have not thereby achieved the desired equality with men. As economists have confirmed, and the COVID-19 pandemic has highlighted, women still tend to have a very different relationship to industrial society than men do. Around the world, most women continue to work outside their own homes for relatively poor wages at low-status jobs typically defined around women's traditional caring and home-based work, and to work as well "for free" performing most of the other labours needed to support and nurture their families at home.[27] Illich's concept of "shadow work," even though it does not give credit to the work that women have continued to perform under industrial capitalism, does provide some key insights into the gendered nature of the long transition to fossil fuels within industrializing countries, and the ongoing inequality of women within them. Like his thoughts on energy and equity, Illich's discussion of gender finds some disturbing connections between energy use and inequality in industrial and post-industrial societies more generally, reminding us how important it is to look back to the past as we consider how to negotiate the energy challenges lying ahead in the future.

NOTES

1 J.R. McNeill, "Cheap Energy and Ecological Teleconnections of the Industrial Revolution, 1780–1920," in "Forum: The Environmental History of Energy Transitions," special issue, *Environmental History* 24, no. 3, (July 2019): 31.

2 Astrid Kander, Paolo Malanima, and Paul Warde, *Power to the People: Energy in Europe over the Last Five Centuries* (Princeton, NJ: Princeton University Press, 2014), 2.

3 The Club of Rome published its first book, *The Limits to Growth*, in 1972, and its critique of both limitless economic growth and the increased populations that it spawned gained considerable purchase with the "oil shock" of 1973. The 1970s and early 1980s witnessed the growth of a large and varied literature about sustainability, from socio-economic and econometric treatises to do-it-yourself manuals for building hand-powered home machinery, and including some innovative discussions of energy in an oil-scarce world. Unfortunately, the warnings were disregarded in light of the neoliberal turn from the mid-1980s. Donella Meadows, Club of Rome, *The Limits to Growth: A Report for the Club of Rome's Project on the Predicament of Mankind* (New York: New American Library, 1972). Other important titles on the subject of sustainability included E.F. Shumacher, *Small Is Beautiful: Economics as if People Mattered* (New York: Perennial Library, 1973); Peter Chapman, *Fuel's Paradise: Energy Options for Britain* (Harmondsworth, UK: Penguin Books, 1975); Kimon Valaskakis, Peter S. Sindell, J. Graham Smith, and Iris Fitzpatrick-Martin, *The Conserver Society: A Workable Alternative for the Future* (New York: Harper and Row, 1979); Warren Johnson, *Muddling toward Frugality: A Blueprint for Survival in the 1980s* (Boulder, CO: Shambala Publishing, 1978). For an interesting overview of some of the engineering and design work, developed mostly in the 1970s, to reduce carbon use in the hope of creating a sustainable future, see "Pedal Powered Farms and Factories: The Forgotten Future of the Stationary Bicycle," *Low-Tech Magazine*, 25 May 2011, https://www.lowtechmagazine.com/2011/05/pedal-powered-farms-and-factories

.html. For a discussion of the failure of the oil shock to create lasting change, see, for example, Susan Krumdiek, *Transition Engineering: Building a Sustainable Future* (Boca Raton, FL: CRC Press, 2020).

4 Ivan Illich, *Energy and Equity* (London: Calder and Boyars, 1974), https://archive .org/details/energyequity00illi/mode/2up; Ivan Illich, "Shadow Work," in *Shadow Work* (London: Marion Boyers Publishers, 1981), 99–116; Ivan Illich, *Gender* (London: Marion Boyers Publishers, 1983).

5 An 80 per cent reduction in current fossil fuel consumption is needed if humanity is to "have a chance of avoiding run-away climate change," according to Susan Krumdiek, who cites the 2013 report of the International Panel on Climate Change. Krumkieck, *Transition Engineering*, 16. The need to create new *cultures* of low energy use is argued particularly persuasively by Elizabeth Shove, Heather Chappells, and Loren Lutzenhiser, eds. *Comfort in a Lower Carbon Society* (New York: Routledge, 2010).

6 Jennifer Wenzel, "Introduction," in *Fuelling Culture: 101 Words for Energy and Environment*, ed. Imre Szeman, Jennifer Wenzel, and Patricia Yaeger (New York: Fordham University Press, 2017), 1–16. This volume is representative of the work of scholars in the energy humanities who, like Illich, are deeply aware of the links between energy and society, and particularly the ongoing inequality so characteristic of modern industrial societies. See as well Matthew Huber, *Lifeblood: Oil, Freedom and the Forces of Capital* (Minneapolis: University of Minnesota Press, 2013); Bob Johnson, *Carbon Nation: Fossil Fuels in the Making of Modern Culture* (Lawrence: University of Kansas Press, 2014).

7 Illich, "The Energy Crisis," in *Energy and Equity*, 15.

8 Illich, 17.

9 Illich, 17.

10 Illich, 18.

11 Illich, "Speed-Stunned Imagination," in *Energy and Equity*, 36–7.

12 Illich, "The Radical Monopoly of Industry," in *Energy and Equity*, 57.

13 Illich, "The Industrialization of Traffic," in *Energy and Equity*, 29.

14 Illich, "Radical Monopoly of Industry," 58. Italics in the original.

15 Illich, "Degrees of Self-Powered Mobility," in *Energy and Equity*, 71–8.

16 Illich, "The Energy Crisis, 20.

17 Illich, 19.

18 For a recent overview of these, see R.W. Sandwell, "Changing the Plot: Finding Women in Energy History," in *In a New Light: Histories of Women and Energy*, ed. Abigail Harrison Moore and R.W. Sandwell (Montreal: McGill-Queen's University Press, 2021), 16–45.

19 See, for example, E.A. Wrigley, *The Path to Sustained Growth: England's Transition from an Organic Economy to an Industrial Revolution* (Cambridge: Cambridge University Press, 2016); Andreas Malm, *Fossil Capital: The Rise of Steam Power and*

the Roots of Global Warming (London: Verso Press, 2016). For the history of energy and energy transitions in Canada, see R.W. Sandwell, ed., *Powering Up Canada: A History of Power, Fuel and Energy from 1600* (Montreal: McGill-Queen's University Press, 2016).

20 For an overview of important exceptions to this, see the essays in Sandwell and Harrison Moore, eds., *In a New Light.*

21 For a larger discussion of the problem of women within environmental history more specifically, see Nancy C. Unger, "Women and Gender: Useful Categories of Analysis in Environmental History," in *The Oxford Handbook of Environmental History* ed. Andrew C. Isenberg (Oxford: Oxford University Press, 2014), https:// doi.org/10.1093/oxfordhb/9780195324907.013.0021, and Nancy Unger, *Beyond Nature's Housekeepers: American Women in Environmental History* (New York: Oxford University Press, 2012); Jennifer Bernstein, "On Mother Earth and Earth Mothers: Why Environmental History Has a Gender Problem," *Breakthrough Journal*, no. 7, (Summer 2017), https://thebreakthrough.org/journal/issue-7/on-mother -earth-and-earth-mothers (with thanks to Anna Antonova for this reference)

22 Wrigley, *Path to Sustained Growth.*

23 Illich's work on subsistence here is supported by the work of Ellen Meiksins Wood, "The Agrarian Origins of Capitalism," *Monthly Review* 50, no. 3 (July–August 1998), 14–31; and Ellen Meiksins Wood, *The Origin of Capitalism: A Longer View* (New York: Verso Books, 2002).

24 All quotes here are from Illich, "Shadow Work," 107.

25 Illich, 100.

26 Illich, *Gender*, 45.

27 See, for example, Nancy Fraser, "Behind Marx's Hidden Abode: For an Expanded Conception of Capitalism," *New Left Review*, no. 86 (March–April 2014): 55–72.

8 Building Convivial Educational Tools in the Twenty-First Century

ANA JOFRE, KRISTINA A. BOYLAN, AND IBRAHIM YUCEL

Introduction

This chapter describes the development and theoretical foundations of the Collaborative Interactive Tabletop for Education, which is a tangible interface that allows users to manipulate digital information using handheld tabletop objects. It is organized as follows: The first part provides our theoretical framework, which includes pedagogical theories informing our design, the theories on learning that inform our evaluation of the system, and an overview of other work done with tangible user interfaces. The second part describes the system itself, our design rationale, and our evaluation plans.

Theoretical Framework

Pedagogical Theories Informing Our Design

The Collaborative Interactive Tabletop for Education (CITE) project is motivated by the reminder to "reference service to educational objects," contributing towards undoing scenarios in which humans are pressured to adapt to digital devices and processes, rather than digital devices and processes being adaptable to their needs, desires, and creative impulses.[1] We are also inspired to create a tool that fosters conviviality, which Illich describes as something that "can be easily used, by anybody, as often or as seldom as desired, for the accomplishment of a purpose chosen by the user."[2]

The *necessity* of digital devices and learning through digital media is an all-too-common refrain in education, whether conventional or outside institutional school systems. We are told that the kids must learn to use these devices (whether they are computers, tablets, the Internet, coding, or some other tangible manifestation of digital communications technology), otherwise they won't be able to keep up, get ahead, or be successful. We identify limitations to this thinking that are both conceptual and tangible, and offer suggestions for using a digitally-based system in less limited ways.

CONCEPTUAL

Contemporary representations of education might have us believe that proof of competency in global affairs can be gained or manifested by googling the topic, finding the necessary information on Wikipedia, delivering the answer with the certitude of a game-show contestant, and – bam – there is the proof that one has worldly knowledge! Such pervasive attitudes perpetuate the notion that education is about regurgitating a succinct answer, that there is only one answer, that the answer is online, and thus that digital tools are for helping you find it. In this model, the individual is judged or graded on having the "correct" answer, rather than on problem solving or interpretive abilities, let alone critical thinking about the provenance of a given piece of information.[3] One consequence of such thinking is that there is little space for many of our digital tools to be utilized in open-ended and unique ways.

As Illich pointed out as early as 1983, using computing devices, particularly personal computing devices, has the potential to impoverish people's relationship with knowledge, just as enclosure impoverished people's relationship to the physical landscape. In his essay "Silence Is a Commons" he observes that access to the microphone would determine whose voice shall be magnified. Silence now ceased to be in the commons; it became a resource for which loudspeakers compete. Language itself was thereby transformed from a local commons into a national resource for communication. As enclosure by the lords increased national productivity by preventing the individual peasant from keeping a few sheep, so the encroachment of the loudspeaker has destroyed the silence that had hitherto given each man and woman his or her proper and equal voice. Unless you have access to a loudspeaker, you now are silenced.[4]

Many models of digital devices and learning replicate this problem. Pre-digested, searchable answers, and standardized, automated testing of them, drown out calls for other modes of enquiry and discussion of the results of the process of enquiry.[5]

In addition, the pressure one feels to locate "the answer" in the digital realm is magnified for persons with visual impairments, cognitive challenges, and strengths that lie outside of conventional metrics of verbal and mathematical ability. In other words, is that one answer, or the components that learners could use to formulate an answer, available in accessible formats? Far too commonly, learners with visual and cognitive impairments will not be able to obtain digital information directly or instantly, but instead will have to receive it through levels of interpretation. Regulations and recommendations notwithstanding, industry reviews of websites show that up to 70 per cent are inaccessible for persons with visual impairments.[6]

Technologies exist for making visual, digital interfaces more accessible, such as screen readers and refreshable Braille readers, but those interfaces must be designed to work with assistive technologies and the people who use them.[7] Such design also should include elements of democratization, that is, the ability for users to modify, re-envision, and redesign them, or use them as steps towards new designs.[8]

As Drick Boyd[9] and Michael Glassman[10] identify, Internet-based education has mimicked conventional classrooms' emphasis on the knowledge banking, uncritical sourcing, and repetition model of education, justified by purportedly insurmountable scarcity of resources, and brought to harmful extremes. This is evidenced by the crash of the wave of enthusiasm for massive open online courses (MOOCs) and concomitant claims that pre-recorded content and automated assignment grading could suffice for learning amid a scarcity of human and material resources.[11] This is not the only possible outcome of digital education platforms, however. As Richard Kahn and Douglas Kellner distinguish, learners are served better by an approach of "objective ambiguity" that is neither overly technophilic nor technophobic.[12] Poor designs and harmful uses of technologies can be remedied, and opportunities for learning facilitated, by critical design, engagement, and authentic exchanges among learners.[13]

As we will discuss below, functioning and well-maintained assistive technologies are of vital importance for creating multiple entry points to learning and other forms of engagement.[14] However, these must be accompanied by genuine "tools for conviviality,"[15] or ways in which learning is treated as a social act, recognized as having value in and of itself beyond assignment completion, and even, as Illich came to conclude later in his own explorations, moving beyond being a transformative tool towards educational or political ends.[16] Having the freedom to choose whom to associate with, in this case, includes greater freedom to participate without having to work through any, or at least as many, human and/or technological translators in order to participate in such processes as data visualization and communication.

TANGIBLE

Facile invitations to enhance learning by "going digital", in addition to being ahistorical, also tend to reinforce exclusion. Inclusive designers like Kat Holmes have noted that exclusion patterns emerge when computers, handheld devices, controllers, programs, and games have been designed by designers responding narrowly to their own abilities, habits, and preferences.[17] This not only replicates the exclusion of persons with varying abilities, but when devices do not welcome input from users, or allow only for low variability in device use, they impose new rigidities in thinking and behaviour.[18] In contrast, technologies that welcome (or can be made to welcome) user adaptation or modification have greater potential to mitigate deterministic design and usage.[19]

Too many digital interfaces, like a good deal of data visualization, exclude persons with differing abilities, as is the case, for example, in visual information intake and analysis. In far too many scenarios, visually impaired communities are put in the position of having to wait for pre-digested understandings of those learning processes: alt text, image descriptions, and mathematical renditions of work done by others. Thus, the members of these communities lose the opportunity to engage in the process of interpreting the necessary information.[20] Furthermore, many data visualizations exclude understandings of data relationships expressed in non-visual terms.

Data visualization that is conceptualized too narrowly privileges those able to work with abstract concepts projected visually onto two-dimensional planes, and replicates exclusion based on intelligence being measured through such actions, whether on paper or a screen. Such measures exclude possibilities of learning through movement and spatial relationships, an underrated but highly necessary intelligence. Overlooked by conventional measures of verbal and mathematical abilities, spatial ability also correlates to these less frequently than they do to each other, with the result that some stronger students are ranked as "less promising" for their relatively lower performance in other areas.[21] Though there are some "good news" stories of underrated students going on to earn Nobel Prizes, file patents, and gain similar achievements, many more such students come to see their strengths as disconnected from the worlds of intellectual and social exchange, or become completely alienated from formal education and professions demanding certification.[22] This is of special concern, as spatial intelligence can not only play "a unique role in assimilating and utilizing pre-existing knowledge, but also plays a unique role in developing new knowledge."[23] Creating adaptable learning environments that allow for learners to experience data spatially, and to use spatial relations to express their interpretations of data, could empower learners with stronger spatial abilities to participate and collaborate in more active ways in discussions and problem-solving exercises that involve mathematical, verbal, and two-dimensional visual representations of data.

CITE was intentionally designed to be highly adaptable to individual and group users' needs. CITE includes a set of objects (tokens, markers, table, software, computer), to be sure, but more completely understood, it is a set of instructions that users can build on to collect, comprehend, analyse, synthesize, and communicate data, utilizing those objects in individual and social processes. CITE is designed with multiple points of entry (sight, sound, position) and multiple modes of sharing output (diagram, sound), and invites users to engage with and modify the objects and their uses, adding to this list of possibilities and outcomes.

Theory on Learning and Educational Evaluation

CITE is intended to encourage active and critical learning in a number of contexts via a digital platform as it is defined by linguist, educator, and video game theorist James Paul Gee.[24] In part inspired by Freire's call to envision critical thinking and literacy as "reading the world" and not just "reading the word,"[25] Gee identifies learning principles and designs that are inherent in well-designed games and argues for their inclusion across learning, work, and social communities. For these reasons we have endeavoured to embed several of Gee's insights from his book *What Video Games Have to Teach Us about Learning and Literacy* into CITE's design. In particular, we draw inspiration from his "36 Learning Principles," included as an appendix to the book, in which he provides a list of the key principles that guide learning. Gee particularly highlights the ways in which players can probe, explore, identify with, and become contributing parts of "affinity groups" in order to share and expand on knowledge about them via digital platforms, showing their potential to be the sort of "tools of conviviality" sought by Illich rather than contributors to electronic enclosure and isolated, banking-model learning.

For these reasons we have endeavoured to embed several of Gee's many insights from years of scholarship, educational practice, and game play into CITE's design."[26] Here and below, we follow Gee's numbering convention for the principles. We expect learners will be aided by the CITE system's capacity for the "Material Intelligence Principle" (#21, i.e., its ability to store data and represent it so that learners are freed to engage in exploratory and questioning activities),[27] and we hope that learners using CITE will

- engage in practices that demonstrate the "Probing Principle" (#15, i.e., learning occurs in cycles of probing, hypothesizing, testing, and affirming or adjusting in new iterations);[28]
- demonstrate the "Amplification of Input Principle" (#10, i.e., obtaining and communicating much output with comparatively little input),[29] and the "Discovery Principle" (#28, i.e., that open-ended play and usage can begin and continue with overt "telling" of abstract information kept to a well-designed minimum);[30]
- reach levels of meaningful and rewarding Achievement (#11) commensurate with input, effort, and experience;
- be motivated to engage in iterative Practice (#12)[31] and more Committed Learning (#7);[32]
- engage in collaborative practices (e.g., the "Dispersed Principle" [#34] and the "Affinity Group Principle" [#35]),[33] and reflexivity regarding them (the "Self-Knowledge Principle" [#9][34] and the "Cultural Knowledge Principles" [#30–2]);[35] and
- demonstrate Transfer (#29) of knowledge among semiotic domains,[36] and so on.

These are in agreement with concepts and calls from Freire and Illich for meaningful learning that creates and strengthens community. All these are central to Gee's primary "Active, Critical Learning Principle" (#1),[37] and they are also consonant with Freire's and Illich's visions for learning. Therefore we want users of CITE to gain or increase their "active" capacity to work with concepts embodied in their experiences of system use. In other words, use of CITE should lead to a greater capacity to meaningfully find, dialogue about, represent, and communicate data, with learners moving from prescribed tasks with stricter parameters[38] towards more independent and sophisticated data visualization design (such as the more interpretive exercises offered by Le[39]) as well as experimentation and play.

Subsequently, we hope that extended use of CITE will allow learners to progress effectively towards genuine "critical" learning, in which they can compare experiences and the concepts embedded within them and apply them in more varied contexts. Also inspired by Freire and Illich, we realize that continuing to develop and test CITE will necessitate the formation of learning communities and longer-term relationships with educators and student users to observe whether such affinity groups form and the desired capacities emerge among them, particularly if, as we hope, some will work with its open-source programming and adaptable components to devise their own modifications.

It is also central to our goals that CITE genuinely incorporate the "Multimodal Learning Principle" (#20) promoted by Gee,[40] and in keeping with Holmes[41] and others' call for inclusive and adaptable design. Earlier work with tangible user interfaces (TUIs) indicates promise for increasing collaborative practices as well as enhancing performance in spatial cognition and problem solving,[42] and recent research points to the potential for TUIs to facilitate greater active participation, communication, and collaboration for visually impaired users.[43] CITE's design incorporates tactile experiences, movement and placement through space, and combinations of auditory, visual, and Brailled input and output. Our testing of the device, which we hope will be iterative and collaborative, will draw on similar methodologies to affirm and/or improve the implementation of these principles.

Overview of Tangible Interfaces

TUIs are broadly defined as graspable 3D physical objects that allow users to interact with digital data. Research in TUI for learning applications seeks to clarify which specific elements of tangible interface design support learning. While many TUI proponents in the learning environment assume a Piagetian model of children's development that benefits from tactile experiences, such claims have not been extensively tested.[44] However, evidence has mounted over more than a decade of observation to suggest that tangible interfaces augment student engagement with learning tasks, and that learning outcomes improve as engagement is increased. Students report more enjoyment while using tangibles in learning activities, compared to using a mouse.[45]

As learning tools, tangible interfaces have been shown to encourage activities and behaviours that augment learning and problem solving. One early study compared graphical user interfaces (GUI) with TUI in a collaborative design task, finding that the groups using TUI performed multiple cognitive actions in a shorter time, made more unexpected discoveries of spatial design features, and exhibited more problem-finding behaviours.[46] A 2015 study reinforced these findings; it also looked at how users approach a creative design task, and specifically found that application of a TUI reduces the user's cognitive load, compared to using GUI for an equivalent task.[47]

There is also significant evidence that TUIs improve learning outcomes. A 2019 study found significant improvements in students' test performances after they used a tangible interface to learn trigonometry.[48] In large college classes, the use of clickers (audience response devices) has become ubiquitous as a means to improve student outcomes, and the key factor explaining their success is physical interactivity, which promotes active collaborative learning and engagement.[49] Researchers also found a TUI 3D anatomical model to compare favourably to a virtual model of the heart for relieving cognitive load and enhancing student retention, cognition, and motivation.[50]

A 2011 study, which found that outcomes in solving logic puzzles are improved when interacting with a tangible interface compared to working on a touch screen, also noted that the participants using the tangible interface worked on the puzzles much more collaboratively than those using the multi-user touch screen.[51] This suggests that collaboration was the key factor that improved outcomes, and that using the tangible interface fostered such collaboration.

TUIs measurably increase collaborative behaviour. Studies using eye-tracking devices found that participants working in small groups on a problem-solving task experienced more moments of joint visual attention when working with graspable movable objects on a tabletop than when working with a screen-based interface.[52] Tangible interfaces have been designed specifically to support co-located collaboration in educational activities (see, for example, Active Pathways, which teaches biochemical modelling),[53] and in research activities (for example, to help users explore big data in genomics collaborations).[54] Again, a particularly interesting advantage of using tangibles is that they can be used to design collaborations that are inclusive of people with visual impairments.[55]

The Collaborative Interactive Tabletop for Education

Design Rationale

CITE allows users to create and interact with data visualizations using tabletop objects. The design harnesses human abilities to learn spatially and kinetically in an attempt to draw in more learners who otherwise might not be so inclined. Specifically, we target learners who doubt their own inherent aptitude to absorb information from or combine information in data visualizations.

CITE builds on Jofre et al.'s DataBlocks project,[56] which combines the benefits of tangible interactions with graphical representations to create an interactive learning environment. In this system, users create queries by placing and arranging clearly demarcated objects (small enough to be held in a person's hand) onto a tabletop, and the results of the query are displayed on an overhead screen placed at one end of the table. The visualizations that appear on the screen respond to the configuration of the objects on the table.

Participants in the CITE project identified a concern with the DataBlocks model: while the learning interface incorporates kinetics and spatial learning into its process, it ultimately creates intensely visual information outputs. Hence, one of our goals in building on and rethinking DataBlocks was to include learners with visual impairments as part of enhancing its kinetic and spatial attributes. We incorporated inclusive design principles throughout the planning stages in order to more thoroughly integrate spatial and auditory learning, the use of mutually legible text (Braille and print), and mutually accessible outputs (data visualizations with concomitant audio narration), so that learners otherwise excluded from visual learning interfaces could engage meaningfully and in an equivalent or analogous way along with sighted users.[57] In addition to inclusive design considerations for the visually impaired, CITE features new visualizations, new software that is robust and amenable to user edits, and digital models for tokens.

CITE, like DataBlocks, is designed to be a cost-effective, instructional device that is economically accessible across classrooms and other learning spaces such as libraries. We believe that the main impediment to widespread adoption of TUIs to date has been the fact that most designs require some kind of specialized hardware.[58] Our approach, instead, is to create a system, a set of verified instructions along with software packages, for adapting any combination of standard computer hardware into a highly customizable tangible interactive tabletop.

We strongly encourage our users to adapt the system in whatever way suits their needs. Even if users are not coders, we believe that the act of building the system and perhaps creating their own tokens can add meaning and personal expression to the tool. Engagement may be increased when learners are allowed to use their everyday physical play objects to interact with the digital information.[59] In this system, we intend for users to participate in the creation of their own learning tools, in keeping with the ideals expressed by Freire, Gee, and Illich, among others.

In the spirit of adaptably and economic accessibility, all our software has open licensing. Open source software ensures that it will reach users at no cost, and a non-proprietary model allows expert users to modify and build on the software as needed.

Description of Our System

CITE allows users to manipulate on-screen data visualizations through the manipulation of handheld tabletop tokens. The tokens are tracked by means of a camera placed beneath a transparent tabletop. The bottom of each object is marked with a fiducial marker specially designed to be identified by the (open source) reacTIVision software,[60] and the camera placed below the table captures the image of the fiducial markers in real time. The reacTIVision software outputs the ID of each identified marker and its x and y coordinates when they are in the field of view of the camera. This information is interpreted and processed by our software, which constructs the visualizations.

In order to maximize the system's accessibility and visibility, we have made it available on the web (see https://datablocks.org/). The website provides all the necessary resources to build CITE. We provide instructions on how to build a simple transparent tabletop, along with a list of parts needed with links to a vendor. We provide links for all the software downloads needed, and we provide 3D models of tokens as STL files that the user can download and 3D print. We also provide token labels for those who don't have access to 3D printing, or who want to either build the tokens by hand or use existing objects as tokens.

Our system offers multiple levels of use and affordances. Novice users can simply download all the software, 3D print our token models (or place our labels on their own tokens), and follow the instructions to directly use the system as is. Users interested in interface customization can create their own tokens, following our guidelines. Users seeking content customization can add different data sets to the system, and use CITE to explore other data. Finally, expert users can modify the software itself to adapt it to their needs.

CITE uses two software packages in tandem, which are both open source. We use reacTIVision software[61] to track the tokens, and we use our own software to interpret them and produce a visualization. Our software, written by Josh Rosenbaum, is freely available on Github (https://github.com/joshrosenbaum -dev/cite/), and our open licence allows users to modify and build onto it. We wrote the software in Python, which is a widely used language that many non-professional programmers are comfortable using.

In this initial prototype, we used data from the non-profit project Gap-minder[62] (https://www.gapminder.org/), which hosts a repository of data on the health and wealth of every nation in the world over more than a century. The data includes over four hundred socio-economic indicators, including GDP per capita, life expectancy, unemployment rates, energy consumption, and education level. While we hope to incorporate data sets in future iterations, and in principle expert-level users can already incorporate their own data, we chose to start with Gapminder data for several reasons. For one, we support Gapminder's vision and mission of educating citizens about their world, and we think this data is fundamentally of interest to everyone. Secondly, Gapmind-er's data, along with their proprietary visualization tools, has been used in the classroom to teach students about geography[63] and statistics.[64] Finally, the data is well organized and easily accessible.

While our visualizations follow the scheme of Gapminder's bubble chart, the way that users interact with the visualizations is our own contribution. Users control what they see on the screen using tabletop tokens. Gapminder's bubble chart plots two socio-economic indicators against one another on the x and y axes, with each point on the graph representing a country, and the size of the point being proportional to the population of the country. While Gapminder allows you to choose the countries to plot from a side menu, we offer a set of tokens that represent countries, and putting a country token on the table causes the country's data point to appear on the screen. Following Gapminder's model, the size of the country's data point is proportional to its population. We offer another set of tokens to allow the user to select the socio-economic indicators (hereafter referred to simply as "indicators") to be plotted along x and y. These indicators include income, life expectancy, CO_2 emissions, child mortality, gas prices, and population density. Note that the indicator tokens are shaped differently than the country tokens to avoid confusion.

Finally, there is a third, distinct set of tokens that represent the x and y axes, which each have a slot designed to fit an indicator token. To select what goes on the x and y axes, we use a system of constraints. To plot a given indicator along x, the selected indicator is placed into the slot in the x axis token. Like-wise, a different indicator can be placed into the slot in the y axis token. The x and y axis tokens are designed to fit only one indicator token into each of their slots. A country token will not fit into the slot. The illustration in figures 8.1a and 8.1b shows how the x axis token fits with an indicator token to plot the indicator along the x axis. Under the hood, the code is measuring the distance between either the x or y axis fiducial marker and the fiducial markers for in-dicators. If an indicator marker comes within a threshold distance of an axis marker, then that indicator will appear on that axis. The tokens are designed so that the only way to exceed the distance threshold is by fitting the indicator into the x or y axis slot.

Figures 8.1a and 8.1b. An illustration of an indicator token fitting into the *x* axis token to display it along the *x* axis. Left: top view. Right: bottom view. 3D designs by Nick Lejeune.

Our website offers STL files, which users can download and directly 3D print without any modifications. These tokens include the fiducial markers embossed on the bottom, and labels engraved on the top. To allow for active participation by visually impaired users, our labels include symbolic icons with names written in both letters and Braille.[65] We also offer our label designs on our website for those who do not have access to a 3D printer (see figures 8.2, 8.3, and 8.4).

Evaluation Plan

We regret that the onset of COVID-19 brought development of an initial testing phase to a halt in March 2020. Once we are able to resume in-person observation of use of shared objects in classroom-sized observational spaces, we hope to test and develop longer-term observational studies of CITE with educators and learners at our campus and in our local community. The methods explored by scholars and practitioners listed above will include close observation reading as well as analysis of user experiences and output, similar to methods used in other TUI studies.[66] Elements we will use to begin our system analysis can include tracking eye, hand, and device component movement; measuring and analysing time spent on tasks when compared to non-TUI interfaces; conversational analysis of collaborative processes; analysis of interpretations of data produced by users, and soliciting and analysing feedback on experiences of learning and collaboration from learners and instructors.

Having Brailled tokens with auditory indicators of position and information that interfaces with the digital visual display and that can connect to

Figure 8.2. Labels for country tokens. Designs by Kyle Frenette.

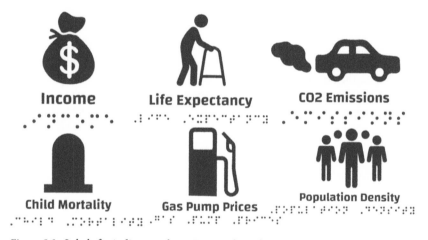

Figure 8.3. Labels for indicator tokens. Designs by Kyle Frenette.

Figure 8.4. Labels for *x* and *y* axis tokens. Designs by Kyle Frenette.

commercially available refreshable Braille displays should be indicative of effective inclusive design. In particular, we hope to work with the Center for the Advancement of the Blind and Visually Impaired (Utica, New York) as well as the SUNY Polytechnic Institute's Community and Behavioral Health and Psychology Programs to develop meaningful user testing with and for these user communities. Similarly, we hope to work with the SUNY Polytechnic Institute and community colleagues to gauge whether and how CITE system use affords users opportunities to enhance spatial cognition, relieve cognitive load, and facilitate communication of spatial, visual, and auditory concepts and insights among learners with different capacities and strengths.

As stated above, to evaluate the CITE project, we wish to engage with users to observe whether and how the system's use affords or enhances opportunities to engage in active, critical learning, such as those outlined and explored by Gee.[67] Users will be asked to collaboratively derive solutions to open-ended questions while we observe their interactions with one another as well as with the tool. We have designed the interface to be interactive and responsive to the user, allowing them to use the Probing Principal (#15) and explore pre-authored content such as Gapminder data, instead of being another medium that expects the user to more passively bank and reproduce data with little contextual understanding (indeed, seeking meaning as well as destabilizing stereotypes is consonant with Rosling's mission[68]). User testing and feedback solicitation will seek to identify and confirm consistent, active practices of information gathering, interpretation, and use. Usage of the system to engage in more open-ended exploration of the data also should demonstrate use of the Discovery Principle (#28).

Next, we designed the control tokens to be tangible and for their places and linkage to provide functionality to the user. This increases users' ability to see data in new ways, find novel correlations in the data sets, and communicate their findings, without the need to understand complex syntax commands. Consistent demonstrations of successful use of the CITE system should then demonstrate Gee's Amplification of Input (#10) and Material Intelligence (#21) Principles. Satisfaction with use among learners and educators should be demonstrated through the principles of Achievement (#11), Transfer (#29), Practice (#12), and Commitment to Learning (#7). CITE users will gain or increase their ability to communicate and collaborate in learning communities (principles #30–32 and #34 and #35) across various spectra of abilities (Multimodal Principle [#20]), and to reflect on these processes (Self-Knowledge Principle [#9]). We hope to observe and evaluate these practices in initial uses of the CITE system, and to develop age- and subject-appropriate puzzles and data-finding adventure "games" that allow for more open-ended use of Gapminder's data and to further test whether CITE indeed incorporates the strengths identified by Gee.

Conclusions and Future Outlook

Development of this system is ongoing. Specific components that are in development are (1) a method (a dial or a slider) to allow users to interactively explore the data across time (Gapminder, as we've mentioned, has over a century of data), and (2) adding haptic components within the tokens to augment interactivity for non-visual learners or for the visually impaired (for example, each token can vibrate in response to where the user has placed it).

CITE itself has been and will continue to be developed collaboratively, corresponding with the goals of educators like Freire and Illich, as well as other scholars and practitioners cited here. As we have detailed above, its participant researchers draw on design and educational theory and practice to create initial testing, to develop components, and to work through iterations of the prototypes in and for communities.

We believe, in ways also in agreement with Freire and Illich, not only that subsequent testing of the system will depend on learner and community interest and collaboration, but that increased user participation with CITE will develop greater degrees of meaning and complexity, as well as new variants and variables. These relationships will take commitment and time to develop (and widespread availability of COVID-19 vaccinations, community testing, and other health-care and social resources), but will be crucial to demonstrate CITE's capacities for enhancing data visualization and communication beyond a modest, initial scope. We hope to see learners return to and build on the CITE system as a means to explore, question, and challenge global and local resource allocation and access, and to continue to include ourselves within its active, critical, collaborative learning community.

ACKNOWLEDGMENTS

This work was funded by a SUNY Innovative Instruction Technology Grant, and made possible by our fellow team members: Josh Rosenbaum, who under Michael Reale's supervision wrote our software, Kyle Frenette, who designed our token labels, and Nick LeJeune, who created our 3D token designs. We also thank Angela Pietrobon for help with editing and formatting.

NOTES

1 Ivan Illich, *Deschooling Society* (New York: Harper and Row, 1971), 79.
2 Ivan Illich, *Tools for Conviviality* (New York: Harper and Row, 1973), 22.
3 Christine Counsell, "Historical Knowledge and Historical Skills: A Distracting Dichotomy," in *Issues in History Teaching*, ed. James Arthur and Robert Phillips

(London: RoutledgeFalmer, 2009), 54–71; Natalia Tognoli and Jose Augusto Chavez Gumaraes, "Provenance as a Knowledge Organization Principle," *Knowledge Organization* 46, no. 7 (2019): 558–68, https://doi.org/DOI:10.5771/0943-7444-2019-7-558.

4 Ivan Illich, "Silence Is a Commons" (1983), Digital Library of the Commons, Indiana University, accessed 3 March 2023, https://dlc.dlib.indiana.edu/dlc/bitstream/handle/10535/5962/Silence%20is%20a%20Commons.html?sequence=1&isAllowed=y.

5 Michael Glassman, "DeMOOCing Society: Convivial Tools to Systems and Back Again in the Information Age," *Educational Philosophy and Theory* 51, no. 14 (2018): 1418–19.

6 Rebecca Wetteman and Trevor White, "The Internet Is Unavailable," Research Note T103, Nucleus Research, 2019, https://accessibility.deque.com/nucleus-accessibility-research-2019.

7 Shawn Lawton Henry, "Essential Components of Web Accessibility," Web Accessibility Initiative, 27 February 2018, https://www.w3.org/WAI/fundamentals/components/.

8 Andrew Feenberg, *Transforming Technology: A Critical Theory Revisited*, rev. ed. (New York: Oxford University Press, 2002), 153–8, https://www.sfu.ca/~andrewf/Trans%20Tech%20Chapt%206.pdf.

9 Drick Boyd, "What Would Paulo Freire Think of Blackboard (TM): Critical Pedagogy in an Age of Online Learning," *International Journal of Critical Pedagogy* 7, no. 1 (2016): 166–86.

10 Glassman, "DeMOOCing Society," 1413–22.

11 Glassman, 1419–20; Boyd, "What Would Paulo Freire Think," 174.

12 Richard Kahn and Douglas Kellner, "Paulo Freire and Ivan Illich: Technology, Politics, and the Reconstruction of Education," *Policy Futures in Education* 5, no. 4 (2007): 431–48, https://doi.org/10.2304/pfie/2007.5.4.431.

13 Boyd, "What Would Paulo Freire Think," 177–80; Glassman, "DeMOOCing Society," 1420–1

14 Kat Holmes, *Mismatch: How Inclusion Shapes Design* (Cambridge, MA: MIT Press, 2018).

15 Rosa Bruno-Jofré and Jon Igelmo Zaldívar, "Ivan Illich's Late Critique of Deschooling Society: 'I Was Largely Barking Up the Wrong Tree,'" *Educational Theory* 62, no. 5 (2012): 573–92; Illich, *Tools for Conviviality,* 22.

16 Bruno-Jofré and Igelmo Zaldívar, "Ivan Illich's Late Critique of Deschooling Society," 586–90.

17 Holmes, *Mismatch*, 50.

18 Holmes, 100–1.

19 Holmes, 115–30; Feenberg, *Transforming Technology*, 126–7 and 184–8.

20 Braille Authority of North America, "Guidelines and Standards for Tactile Graphics," web version, February 2012, http://brailleauthority.org/tg/web-manual/.

21 Jonathan Wai, David Lubinski, and Camilla P. Benbow, "Spatial Ability for STEM Domains: Aligning over 50 Years of Cumulative Psychological Knowledge Solidifies Its Importance," *Journal of Educational Psychology* 101, no. 4 (2009): 817–35, https://doi.org/10.1037/a0016127.

22 Joni Lakin and Jonathan Wai, "Spatially Gifted, Academically Inconvenienced: Spatially Talented Students Experience Less Academic Engagement and More Behavioural Issues than Other Talented Students," *British Journal of Educational Psychology* 90, no. 4 (2020): 1015–38, https://doi.org/10.1111/bjep.12343.

23 Harrison J. Kell, David Lubinski, Camilla P. Benbow, and James H. Steiger, "Creativity and Technical Innovation: Spatial Ability's Unique Role," *Psychological Science* 24, no. 9 (2013): 1835, https://www.jstor.org/stable/23484685.

24 James Paul Gee, *What Video Games Have to Teach Us about Learning and Literacy*, 2nd ed. (New York: Palgrave Macmillan, 2007).

25 Gee, 43.

26 See "Appendix: 36 Learning Principles," in Gee, 221–7.

27 Gee, 106–10, 224.

28 Gee, 105, 223.

29 Gee, 64, 222.

30 Gee, 142, 226.

31 Gee, 68, 223.

32 Gee, 64, 222.

33 Gee, 211–12, 227.

34 Gee, 64, 222.

35 Gee, 176–7, 226.

36 Gee, 142, 226.

37 Gee, 41, 221.

38 Kenneth H. Keller, "Gapminder: An AP Human Geography Lab Assignment," *Geography Teacher* 9, no. 2 (2012): 60–3, https://doi.org/10.1080/19338341.2012.679893.

39 Dai-Trang Le, "Bringing Data to Life into an Introductory Statistics Course with Gapminder," *Teaching Statistics* 35, no. 3 (2013): 114–22, https://doi.org/10.1111/test.12015.

40 Gee, *What Video Games Have to Teach Us*, 110, 224.

41 Holmes, *Mismatch*, 81.

42 Mi Jeong Kim and Mary Lou Maher, "The Impact of Tangible User Interfaces on Spatial Cognition during Collaborative Design," *Design Studies* 29, no. 3 (2008): 222–53, https://doi.org/10.1016/j.destud.2007.12.006; Alexander Skulmowski, Simon Pradel, Tom Kuehnert, Guido Brunnett, and Guenter Daniel Rey, "Embodied Learning Using a Tangible User Interface: The Effects of Haptic Perception and Selective Pointing on a Spatial Learning Task," *Computers & Education*, nos. 92–3 (February 2016): 64–75, https://doi.org/10.1016/j.compedu.2015.10.011.

43 Quentin Chibaudel, Wafa Johal, Bernard Oriola, Marc J.-M. Macé, Pierre Dillenbourg, Valérie Tartas, and Christophe Jouffrais, "'If You've Gone Straight, Now, You Must Turn Left' – Exploring the Use of a Tangible Interface in a Collaborative Treasure Hunt for People with Visual Impairments," in *ASSETS '20: Proceedings of the 22nd International ACM SIGACCESS Conference on Computers and Accessibility*, article no. 19 (October 2020): 1–10, https://doi.org/10.1145/3373625.3417020.

44 Paul Marshall, "Do Tangible Interfaces Enhance Learning?," in *Proceedings of the 1st International Conference on Tangible and Embedded Interaction* (New York: ACM, 2007), 163–70, https://doi.org/10.1145/1226969.1227004.

45 Edward F. Melcer, Victoria Hollis, and Katherine Isbister, "Tangibles vs. Mouse in Educational Programming Games: Influences on Enjoyment and Self-Beliefs," in *Proceedings of the 2017 CHI Conference Extended Abstracts on Human Factors in Computing Systems* (New York: Association for Computing Machinery, 2017), 1901–8, https://doi.org/10.1145/3027063.3053115; Lesley Xie, Alissa N. Antle, and Nima Motamedi, "Are Tangibles More Fun? Comparing Children's Enjoyment and Engagement Using Physical, Graphical and Tangible User Interfaces," in *Proceedings of the 2nd International Conference on Tangible and Embedded Interaction* (New York: ACM, 2008), 191–8, https://doi.org/10.1145/1347390.1347433.

46 Kim and Maher, "Impact of Tangible User Interfaces," 222–53.

47 Tilanka Chandrasekera and So-Yeon Yoon, "The Effect of Tangible User Interfaces on Cognitive Load in the Creative Design Process," in *2015 IEEE International Symposium on Mixed and Augmented Reality – Media, Art, Social Science, Humanities and Design* (Fukuoka, Japan: IEEE, 2015), 6–8, https://doi.org/10.1109/ISMAR-MASHD.2015.18.

48 Francisco Zamorano Urrutia, Catalina Cortés Loyola, and Mauricio Herrera Marín, "A Tangible User Interface to Facilitate Learning of Trigonometry," *International Journal of Emerging Technologies in Learning (IJET)* 14, no. 23 (2019): 152–64, https://www.learntechlib.org/p/217244/.

49 Lorena Blasco-Arcas, Isabel Buil, Blanca Hernández-Ortega, and F. Javier Sese, "Using Clickers in Class. The Role of Interactivity, Active Collaborative Learning and Engagement in Learning Performance," *Computers & Education*, no. 62 (March 2013): 102–10, https://doi.org/10.1016/j.compedu.2012.10.019.

50 Skulmowski et al., "Embodied Learning Using a Tangible Interface," 64–75.

51 Bertrand Schneider, Patrick Jermann, Guillaume Zufferey, and Pierre Dillenbourg, "Benefits of a Tangible Interface for Collaborative Learning and Interaction," *IEEE Transactions on Learning Technologies* 4, no. 3 (July–September 2011), http://ieeexplore.ieee.org/stamp/stamp.jsp?arnumber=5654494.

52 Bertrand Schneider, K. Sharma, S. Cuendet, G. Zufferey, P. Dillenbourg, and A.D. Pea, "3D Tangibles Facilitate Joint Visual Attention in Dyads," in *International Conference on Computer Supported Collaborative Learning (CSCL)* (Gothenburg: International Society of the Learning Sciences, 2015), 158–65, https://repository

.isls.org//handle/1/403; Bertrand Schneider, Kshitij Sharma, Sébastien Cuendet, Guillaume Zufferey, Pierre Dillenbourg, and Roy Pea, "Using Mobile Eye-Trackers to Unpack the Perceptual Benefits of a Tangible User Interface for Collaborative Learning," *ACM Transactions on Computer-Human Interaction* 23, no. 6 (2016): article no. 39:1–23, https://doi.org/10.1145/3012009.

53   Meghna Mehta, Ahmed Sabbir Arif, Apurva Gupta, Sean DeLong, Roozbeh Manshaei, Graceline Williams, Manasvi Lalwani, Sanjay Chandrasekharan, and Ali Mazalek, "Active Pathways: Using Active Tangibles and Interactive Tabletops for Collaborative Modeling in Systems Biology," in *Proceedings of the 2016 ACM International Conference on Interactive Surfaces and Spaces* (New York: Association for Computing Machinery, 2016), 129–38, https://doi.org/10.1145/2992154.2992176.

54   Miriam K. Konkel, Brygg Ullmer, Orit Shaer, and Ali Mazalek, "Envisioning Tangibles and Display-Rich Interfaces for Co-located and Distributed Genomics Collaborations," in *Proceedings of the 8th ACM International Symposium on Pervasive Displays* (New York: Association for Computing Machinery, 2019), 1–8, https://doi.org/10.1145/3321335.3324953.

55   Chibaudel et al., "'If You've Gone Straight,'" 1–10

56   Ana Jofre, Steve Szigeti, Stephen Tiefenbach Keller, Lan-Xi Dong, David Czarnowski, Frederico Tomé, and Sara Diamond, "A Tangible User Interface for Interactive Data Visualization," in *Proceedings of the 25th Annual International Conference on Computer Science and Software Engineering* (Riverton, NJ: IBM Corp, 2015), 244–7, http://dl.acm.org/citation.cfm?id=2886444.2886484; Ana Jofre, Steve Szigeti, Stephen Tiefenbach-Keller, Lan-Xi Dong, and Sara Diamond, "Manipulating Tabletop Objects to Interactively Query a Database," in *Proceedings of the 2016 CHI Conference Extended Abstracts on Human Factors in Computing Systems* (San Jose, CA: Association for Computing Machinery, 2016), 3695–8, https://doi.org/10.1145/2851581.2890260.

57   Braille Authority of North America, "Guidelines and Standards for Tactile Graphics"; Shawn Lawton Henry, "Essential Components of Web Accessibility," Web Accessibility Initiative, 27 February 2018, https://www.w3.org/WAI/fundamentals/components/; Holmes, *Mismatch*; Chibaudel et al., "'If You've Gone Straight,'" 1–10.

58   Clifford De Raffaele, Serengul Smith, and Orhan Gemikonakli, "An Active Tangible User Interface Framework for Teaching and Learning Artificial Intelligence," in *23rd International Conference on Intelligent User Interfaces* (New York: Association for Computing Machinery, 2018), 535–46, https://doi.org/10.1145/3172944.3172976; Mehta et al., "Active Pathways"; Ricardo Langner, Anton Augsburg, and Raimund Dachselt, "CubeQuery: Tangible Interface for Creating and Manipulating Database Queries," in *Proceedings of the Ninth ACM International Conference on Interactive Tabletops and Surfaces* (New York: ACM, 2014), 423–6, https://doi.org/10.1145/2669485.2669526; Sean Follmer, Daniel Leithinger, Alex

Olwal, Akimitsu Hogge, and Hiroshi Ishii, "InFORM: Dynamic Physical Affordances and Constraints Through Shape and Object Actuation," in *Proceedings of the 26th Annual ACM Symposium on User Interface Software and Technology* (New York: ACM, 2013), 417–26, https://doi.org/10.1145/2501988.2502032; Stefanie Klum, Petra Isenberg, Ricardo Langner, Jean-Daniel Fekete, and Raimund Dachselt, "Stackables: Combining Tangibles for Faceted Browsing," in *Proceedings of the International Working Conference on Advanced Visual Interfaces* (New York: ACM, 2012), 241–8, https://doi.org/10.1145/2254556.2254600.

59 Xie, Antle, and Motamedi, "Are Tangibles More Fun?"; Orit Shaer and Eva Hornecker, "Tangible User Interfaces: Past, Present, and Future Directions," *Foundations and Trends®in Human–Computer Interaction* 3, nos. 1–2 (2010): 4–137, https://doi.org/10.1561/1100000026.

60 Martin Kaltenbrunner and Ross Bencina, "ReacTIVision: A Computer-Vision Framework for Table-Based Tangible Interaction," in *Proceedings of the 1st International Conference on Tangible and Embedded Interaction* (New York: ACM, 2007), 69–74, https://doi.org/10.1145/1226969.1226983.

61 Kaltenbrunner and Bencina, "ReacTIVision"; Martin Kaltenbrunner, Till Bovermann, Ross Bencina, and Enrico Costanza, "TUIO: A Protocol for Table-Top Tangible User Interfaces," in *Proceedings of the 6th International Workshop on Gesture in Human-Computer Interaction and Simulation* (May 2005), 1–5, https://www.researchgate.net/profile/Martin_Kaltenbrunner/publication/225075863 _TUIO_A_Protocol_for_Table-Top_Tangible_User_Interfaces/links /55adfa4708ae98e661a4510d.pdf.

62 See "About Gapminder," Gapminder, accessed 3 March 2023, https://www .gapminder.org/about/about-gapminder/.

63 Keller, "Gapminder," 60–3.

64 Le, "Bringing Data to Life," 114–22

65 Braille Authority of North America, "Guidelines and Standards for Tactile Graphics"; Chibaudel et al., "'If You've Gone Straight,'" 1–10

66 Kim and Maher, "Impact of Tangible User Interfaces," 222–53; Schneider et al., "Using Mobile Eye-Trackers," 1–23; Chibaudel et al., "'If You've Gone Straight,'" 1–10

67 Gee, *What Video Games Have to Teach Us*, 221–7.

68 "About Gapminder."

9 In Support of Critical Thinking Education: Praxis and Dialogue in Digital Learning

INA GHITA

Introduction

Freire saw critical thinking and dialogue as tools for self-determination and civic engagement, tools promoting a way of thinking that recognizes reality as a transformative and continuously changing process rather than a static, predefined construct. Critical pedagogy gives education the task of offering students the tools and habits of mind necessary for thinking critically and for actively and constantly questioning and negotiating between theory, practice, and the beliefs of the society they live in.

Today, many universities offer their students the option to learn digitally, but there is little research on how the instructional design and the user experience within a digital learning environment contribute to making learning in such an environment meaningful in order to make it transformative, and how they help drive critical thinking.

One of the crucial elements of critical thinking, and of critical pedagogy in general, is dialogue. For Freire, true dialogue cannot exist without critical thinking. It contrasts with naive thinking, which results in an accommodation with the normalized present without challenging it.

In this chapter, I will discuss the ways in which praxis, both active and reflective dimensions of the concept, can, along with dialogue, support critical thinking in digital learning environments.

The Right Context for Dialogue

Paulo Freire, particularly in his book *Pedagogy of the Oppressed*,[1] stressed the importance of the presence of true dialogue in education. Freire believed that education should reflect and promote the democratic ideals of participation, for both students and teachers.[2] Dialogue has a central role in an education aimed at liberation and not at oppression.

Moving away from the classic triad of modern dialectics, the Hegelian affirmation, negation, negation of negation, Freire takes up dialectics in its Greek origins and re-establishes the relationship between dialogue and dialectics. While the tendency of modern dialectics is to build the thesis (affirmation) in order to weaken the antithesis (negation), in the dialogue of Freire, none of the positions have a predominance over the others, because the value of the dialogue comes from the creation of new knowledge made possible only by authentically opening oneself to the other.[3] In an open dialogue, all points of view have equal chances of being heard and evaluated.

Freire's dialectical position is situated between modernity and postmodernity.[4] Freire rejected European modernity and its Eurocentric lens, which aimed to "emancipate" people from other continents. He saw colonization as deeply dehumanizing, destructive of cultures, and responsible for social exclusion.[5]

Freire believed that dialogue enables us to participate in the continuous construction and transformation of the world, to see society as a process instead of a given set of rules and static subjects. It offers us a way to show others the world we see. For Freire, human subjectivity is a central part of the socio-culturally structured world.

Freire promoted the dialogical exploration of lived experiences, experiences in which wisdom and truth are meticulously encased in a cultural black box that can only unlocked by dialogue. Both text and context, their social as well as their political dimensions, are to be taken into consideration in these explorations in order to drive positive social action. Similarly, student and teacher must meet in an environment of equality and mutual respect for all participants and for truth and learn from each other.

Dialogue, Freire believed, allows us to "apprehend the deeper meaning of facts and at the same time to strip them of their disguises."[6] It is through dialogue that we discover what we don't yet know.

For Freire, dialogue is not just a technique to be mechanically repeated or a classroom tactic – it is first and foremost a way of knowing. Dialogue is not a concession. As conquest, in principle, is anti-dialogical, dialogue cannot be a tactic for domination. It cannot be reduced to depositing ideas into someone's mind, nor can it be an exchange of ideas to be consumed by discussants. Dialogue is not an end in itself, but a means by which to gain a better understanding about the object of knowledge.

We engage in dialogue because we recognize the social and not merely the individual character of the process of knowing. We transform the world and ourselves through dialogue. Authentic thinking, believed Freire, takes place not in isolation but in communication with others. "Only through communication can human life hold meaning."[7]

Dialogue cannot be a method. It includes both action and reflection, and involves theorizing about the experiences shared in the process of dialogue.

Every such process is unique and unrepeatable in the same way that learning as a transformative process is unique for every person, and thus impossible to predict or shape in any strict sense.

For true dialogue to happen, Freire believed that dialogue needs an environment of acceptance and tolerance. He argued that dialogue cannot exist without humility, it cannot exist without hope and faith in humankind, and its power to create and recreate for positive social change. If life in society becomes a topic of discussion, we are then able to rethink who we are and what we do. Freire challenges us to interact with each other, to share our diverse points of view and knowledge of the world, and to create new knowledge as well as new, and better, societies.

Critical Thinking, a Requirement for Critical Pedagogy

The English word "pedagogy" comes from Greek via Latin. *Agogos* meant leader or guide in Greek, and *pais* or *paid* meant boy. A *paidagogos* was a slave who took boys to school and back and also taught them manners and tutored them after school. In time, the meaning of the word "pedagogue" became simply teacher.[8]

Freire believed that any human being, no matter how "ignorant," was capable of looking at the world critically, in a dialogical encounter with others. Through this process, the old paternalistic teacher-student relationship could be challenged. Through their education, as seen through the lens of critical pedagogy, students should be given the tools of the mind necessary for actively and constantly questioning and negotiating their beliefs and those of the society they live in.

Critical pedagogy contrasts with what Freire referred to as "banking education," in which students memorize mechanically what the teacher tells them; in this model, they become "containers" to be filled by the teacher. In banking education, communication is one-way only, from teacher to students, in a process that turns humans into automatons. Freire argued that in an education where the purpose is to domesticate rather than liberate, knowing means being able to receive information and to stock the "deposits made by others." In this conception of education, the educator, who is the sole source of knowledge and who possess complete knowledge, the one "who knows" transfers it to the students, "who do not know."

Freire defined critical thinking as the "manner of thinking which continually revises itself."[9] He saw critical thinking as a tool for self-determination and civic engagement, a way of thinking that recognizes reality as a transformative process, rather than a static construct.

Dialogue requires mutual trust and truth between those engaged in dialogue, and it cannot exist unless all participants engage in critical thinking – a way of thinking that perceives reality as a continuous process, as transformation.

In summary, Freire believed that the institution of the school is an instrument of social control and argued that education cannot be neutral. Education is the social praxis that can either domesticate or liberate men and women, and for this reason, in dependent societies, education is the expression and the instrument of the alienation of individuals.

Freire defined praxis as that human activity that consists of action and reflection. "Liberation is a praxis," he said. It is "the action of reflection of men and women upon their world in order to transform it."[10]

Is There Sufficient Dialogue in Digital Education Today?

In a society in which our time is always insufficient, and our patience short, in a society in which we aim to continuously optimize our efforts in order to increase productivity, dialogue is a luxury.

In the same way in which education cannot be neutral, neither can the use of digital technology in education be assumed to be so.

The technologization of higher education, similar to the corporatization of education, becomes a way to make students docile and easy to manage, in order to enable institutions to process their education faster. As Giroux argued, "As the market-driven logic of neoliberal capitalism continues to devalue all aspects of the public interest, one consequence is that the educational concern with excellence has been removed from matters of equity while higher education, once conceptualized as a public good, has been reduced to a private good."[11] To paraphrase Giroux, the consequence of higher education becoming a private good, of being subordinated by corporations and the education industry, is that critical pedagogy, education as civic, political, and moral practice, is being replaced by training for specific jobs.

The challenge with dialogue in digital education is that it cannot be standardized. Most digital learning environments, from business-focused tools like LinkedIn Learning (formerly Lynda.com), to companies like Coursera and EdX that specialize in massive open online courses (MOOCs), to the universities providing digital university-level education, include a version of a public forum, or a space of discussion, yet, from users' point of view, the forum is always situated by design outside the learning experience. One needs to leave the class to go to the forum, find the right thread, or create a new one and ask a question or share a personal opinion. In most cases, those pieces of content don't become conversations, much less the transformational form of social learning that Freire calls dialogue.

In MOOCs, peer review is often designed as a one-time and one-way interaction: the student submits work, which is then evaluated by a few individuals, randomly chosen from the classroom, where background knowledge, age, dedication, native tongue, and a host of other factors vary. No further interaction is required. That one-time interaction is usually where it starts, and also where the interaction that may lead to dialogue ends, before such dialogue can even be started.

Peer collaboration and feedback are crucial for learning, as social learning is inherently human. However, the subjective, superficial peer review of today's MOOCs is not a replacement for dialogue. Today, in these standardized digital learning environments, students need to behave, not like humans, but, as Freire would say, as "automatons."

Students cannot debate, explain, or decide together what the best direction or the best answer is, because dialogue is not part of the instructional design of MOOCs. As we saw in the first part of this chapter, dialogue requires an environment of acceptance and trust, it depends on participants engaging in a process of knowledge creation that is continuous and shared; it requires critical thinking, attention, dedication, and time.

Some universities with their own, standardized digital learning model, like the Open University of Catalonia, the first fully online university in Europe, have managed to go beyond the lecture/quiz/submission/peer review/certification model and include personalized feedback for each student. At every step of their learning journey, students receive feedback actively and proactively from instructors and tutors. This kind of personal and personalized attention to the individual, as well as the traditional model of following up closely throughout the term, allows both student and teacher to create human connections with each other.

Speaking with Digital Students about Critical Thinking

In my own research,[12] I found that many university students believed that their digital learning environment promoted neither dialogue nor critical thinking. They felt that their digital learning environment was limiting their ability to interact with their instructors and ask questions. As one student put it,

> It's a virtual communication environment, somewhat cold, but I miss the contact with the professor, the ability to make an appointment, to manifest my incompetence, to say, "I don't understand this" … It has created a lot of frustration in the beginning. At the same time it has helped me find my own answers, to search on YouTube, it has helped me, but sometimes I have been ashamed to not know [what to do]. (Anonymous, interview, February 2020)[13]

Talking about her virtual learning environment and sending in assignments, another student said,

> No, it limits me, because it gives me some steps to follow, do this and this, they give you some guidelines and if you don't do it like that, they suspend you because

they say you didn't follow the guidelines. Why do I have to follow the patterns that my professor has created and hasn't given me the opportunity to give it my own critical point of view? (Anonymous, interview, February 2020)[14]

Another student explained why he thought his digital learning environment was inhibiting him from engaging more with his peers and instructors:

Because it's not face to face, it's not synchronous … I think all the things, the vast majority of things should work smoothly, otherwise it's really complicated. Before this, my whole experience was in a face-to-face environment, as an instructor, and it's different, people send you an email, or call you, or talk to you in person. I used to teach face-to-face classes, and it's different. The student is there, I am there, and you can ask something at the same moment … This is complicated in online environments because they are asynchronous. Well in my university, for PhD students it's all asynchronous. Undergrads have synchronous meetings and so on. This is the main problem with the digital learning environment. Sometimes you have to wait, sometimes they don't answer, and you get a bit lost. Especially when you have problems with submissions and so on, you depend on the other person, but it's not like a face-to-face relationship … because it's not synchronous. (Anonymous, interview, February 2020)

Many students said that thinking critically was "not well seen," that their instructors did not like them asking questions or challenging an idea. One student said in an interview,

I tend to criticize a lot, and that actually gets me in trouble very often. For instance, when things don't work the way they should … I think, *Sorry,* [swear word] *you are not doing your job well* … I am a student, so this kind of criticism sometimes gets me in trouble … I gave you an example: in the forum and the emails sometimes I was maybe overcritical and people are not used to that, neither the teachers nor my colleagues, my fellow students. (Anonymous, interview, February 2020)

Another student said,

I have found that most professors, in the social world, they sell us everything as very beautiful, [they tell us that we are the] saviours of the world, [that] you have to use empathy … I work for the law of dependency, I am very critical, so it is difficult for me to [not] say, … "What you are saying is very nice, but I do not agree with you, I go to the [social] services, to the users['s homes], I know the poverty in which they live, so what you are giving me here is beautiful on the theoretical [level, but it] does not correspond to reality." But you have to be careful because it depends on which person … They don't like you to be critical. So because of this fear of facing the teacher, because you know that it will impact you negatively … you limit yourself … I am very critical … and I have had many disappointments in my life for perhaps not knowing how to say it and for giving my opinion about how I think things are, not what they want to sell me. (Anonymous, interview, February 2020)[15]

When asked how she imagined her ideal digital learning environment, one student said, "I think that for me [that would mean] improving the relationship between the teacher and students. There are many ways to do this, but sometimes students are afraid of the teachers, you know?"[16]

What May Happen if Our Digital Learning Environments Do Not Support Sufficient Dialogue?

Last summer, I was invited to deliver a guest lecture to undergraduate and master's students at a university in the Netherlands. My argument was that the business world needs the humanities, and I talked about the ways in which a knowledge of the humanities has helped me in my professional career in communications. The lecture was attended by around sixty student participants and was held on Blackboard, the digital platform that particular university used. While I waited for everyone to be "seated," I noticed something very peculiar: though it was a video conference, none of the students had their cameras on, and not only that: the majority did not have their microphones activated either. This meant that when they logged in and "prepared" for the lecture, they had already made the choice to not speak. They had decided that the lecture was only for listening.

How were we going to meet each other in dialogue, if speaking was not enabled for the students? I made it a point to ask questions and wait for answers, to which the students replied via the chat function, but the experience stuck with me.

In the creation and use of some contemporary digital learning environments, dialogue has been made obsolete by design. In the same way floppy disks and music CDs can no longer be plugged in to our devices because the interfaces that were once capable of reading them have been phased out, similarly dialogue is in danger of being completely phased out in digital learning environments that lack the space for dialogue. Yes, most online learning environments have a forum or a space for public discussion, but does genuine dialogue, as we have defined it here as a scholarly tool, happen in these forums? And is this type of forum the best place to create dialogue in digital learning?

If a learning experience is organized around a lecture or any other type of educational text, and there is an instructor and at least one student engaged in the learning experience, why does the student need to leave the learning space in order to engage in dialogue? Why is the ability to start a dialogue not embedded in the learning experience itself. Why is there a separate, secondary space for "talking"?

I argue that we must protect and make an effort to embed true dialogue in digital learning environments, specifically because such dialogue is difficult to achieve. We should perfect designs for those learning environments and experiences that are passive and identify when the environment itself suggests to students that they should behave as containers for information to be deposited and further processed.

NOTES

1 Paulo Freire, *Pedagogy of the Oppressed* (New York: Bloomsbury, 2018).

2 Kevin Kester and Ashley Booth, "Education, Peace and Freire: A Dialogue," *Development* 53, no. 4 (2010): 498–503.

3 Moacir Gadotti, *Pedagogy of Praxis: A Dialectical Philosophy of Education* (Albany, NY: SUNY Press, 1996).

4 Henry A Giroux, "Education Incorporated?," *Educational Leadership* 56, no. 2 (1998): 12–17.

5 Henry A Giroux, "Critical Pedagogy and the Postmodern/Modern Divide: Towards a Pedagogy of Democratization," *Teacher Education Quarterly* 31, no. 1 (2004): 31–47.

6 Paulo Freire, "Education: Domestication or Liberation?," *Prospects* 2, no. 2 (1972): 173–81.

7 Freire, *Pedagogy of the Oppressed*, 104.

8 *Merriam-Webster*, s.v. "pedagogue," accessed 7 March 2023, https://www.merriam-webster.com/dictionary/pedagogue.

9 Paulo Freire, "Unusual Ideas about Education," International Commission on the Development of Education, Series B: *Opinions*, no. 36 (1971): 2–12.

10 Freire, *Pedagogy of the Oppressed*, 105.

11 Henry A Giroux, "Rethinking Education as the Practice of Freedom: Paulo Freire and the Promise of Critical Pedagogy," *Policy Futures in Education* 8, no. 6 (2010): 715.

12 Ina Ghita, "Motivation and Engagement in Digital Learning Environments, at a Post-Secondary Level" (PhD diss., University of Barcelona, 2021).

13 This and the following quotes have been translated from the Spanish by me. The original reads as follows: "Es un medio de comunicación virtual, algo frío, pero echo de menos el contacto con el profesor, de poner una entrevista, de poder manifestar tu impotencia, no entiendo esto ... Me ha creado frustración al principio, pero a la vez me ha ayudado en buscarme la vida, buscar por YouTube, me ha ido ayudando pero a veces he tenido vergüenza por no tener esta habilidad, por no saber [que hacer]."

14 The original reads as follows: "No, me limita, porque te da unos pasos a seguir, has esto, y esto, te dan unas pautas y si no lo haces así, te suspenden porque te dicen que no has seguido estas pautas. Porque tengo que seguir unos patrones que el profesor ha creado y no me da la prioridad a mí dar este punto crítico bajo mi punto de vista."

15 The original reads as follows: "Me he encontrado con la mayoría de los profesores, en el mundo social, nos venden como todo muy bonito, salvadores del mundo, tienes que utilizar la empatía. Trabajo para la ley de la dependencia, soy muy crítica, entonces me cuesta decir … esto lo que estás diciendo es muy bonito, pero no estoy de acuerdo contigo, voy a los servicios, a los usuarios, sé la pobreza en que viven, entonces lo que me das tú dando aquí bonito de lo teórico no corresponde a la realidad. Pero hay que ir con ojo porque depende de que persona … no le gusta que seas crítica. Entonces por este miedo de enfrentarte al profesor, porque sabes que va a fastidiar … te limitas … yo soy muy crítica … y me he llevado en mi vida muchas desilusiones por quizás no saber decirlo y por dar mi opinión lo que yo pienso, no lo que tú me quieres vender."

16 The original reads as follows: "Creo que para mí mejorar la relación entre profesores y estudiante. ¿Es que hay muchas formas diferentes, pero en algunos momentos los estudiantes tiene miedo de los profesores, sabes?"

10 The Ideas of Ivan Illich in the History of the Homeschooling/Unschooling Movement and His Intellectual Relationship with John Holt

JON IGELMO ZALDÍVAR AND PATRICIA QUIROGA UCEDA

Introduction

Ivan Illich's writings on education have become essential reference material for those exploring the margins of the modern institutional imaginary. In particular, the theses in his book *Deschooling Society* opened a critical front that has continued in a wide variety of educational movements and teaching practices. Only a few short months after the book was released by Harper and Row in 1971, a notorious interest arose, especially in the United States, in developing Illich's ideas in practice. The opportunity of establishing teaching and learning spaces that would reveal the contradictions inherent to school systems led to projects such as the Learning Exchange, initially headquartered in Evanston, Illinois, but later opening schools all across North America.[1] There is even evidence of attempts by young computer programmers on the West Coast of the United States to develop a new generation of computers that responded to Illich's ideas. Key in this regard was Lee Felsenstein.[2]

This chapter analyses how Illich's ideas have been transferred to the homeschooling/unschooling movement.[3] From this perspective, the work encompasses the field of intellectual history in that it aims to trace how these ideas moved in transnational spaces.[4] This also leads us to delve into how educational ideas circulate in pedagogical movements that got their start in the second half of the twentieth century. Special attention is paid to how the criticism of educational institutions found in *Deschooling Society* ended up playing a major role in consolidating and deploying the homeschooling/unschooling movement around the world. It is important to bear in mind that in the years after his main book on education was published, Illich himself showed no interest in this pedagogic movement, and was in fact rather sceptical of it. The ideas put forth in *Deschooling Society* ended up contributing to the theoretical foundation of the anti-schooling movement thanks to the mediation of John Holt, who in the 1970s and '80s became one of the leading intellectuals for parents in different countries around the world who rejected schooling their children.[5]

This chapter aims to address a number of matters that have not yet been analysed diligently by those who have studied the history of the consolidation process of the homeschooling movement in the 1970s and early 1980s. To that end, our research looks at a variety of sources, mainly the works published by Illich and Holt, as well as letters written by Holt in the early 1970s. The research questions that guide this chapter are the following: What readings have been given to *Deschooling Society* over the last fifty years, and what are the main themes under which Illich's ideas have been received? What influence did Illich have on the development of Holt's ideas, and to what extent is their relationship key to the advent of the homeschooling/unschooling movement? To what extent did Illich choose to ignore how his ideas were circulating in key spaces and publications within this movement?

Multiple Frameworks for the Early Reception of Illich's Ideas

The strongest detractors of the school system since the 1970s converge in criticizing the monopoly that formal education systems have on teaching and learning processes. At the same time, they criticize the monopoly that communication systems exercise over the means of access to information and the increasingly limited power of education to transform specific social, economic, political, and cultural phenomena. As Petar Jandrić remarked, "contemporary society does not provide much room for critical action of individual educators against radical monopoly of information and communication technologies."[6] This monopoly hinders the possibility of exploring alternative educational experiences. Indeed, the educational system itself both monopolizes the official means for education and holds the legal power to certify the knowledge thus acquired.

Advocates of radical pedagogy, especially since the early 1970s, have denounced the implicit authoritarianism of educational systems, the bureaucratization of educational institutions, and the impact of the hidden curriculum as a means of discipline and control.[7] In this pedagogical school of thought, the ideas explored in *Deschooling Society* are vindicated insofar as they place great value on "Illich's insistence that sites of education remain open to the community, rather than rigidity institutionalized, in order to avoid monopolizations of informational/knowledge channels."[8]

According to one of the central theses developed in *Deschooling Society*, the urgent task would be "to liberate the critical and creative resources of people by returning to individual persons the ability to call and hold meetings – an ability now increasingly monopolized by institutions which claim to speak for the people."[9] Without this liberation, human beings are subject to the constant manipulation of a "pan-hygienic world," or in other words, "a world in which all contacts between men, and between men and their world, are the result of foresight and manipulation."[10] Moreover, its discourse contained an urgent call to action in a similar vein to that expressed by Paulo Freire in *Pedagogy of the*

Oppressed: "Those truly committed to the cause of liberation can accept neither the mechanistic concept of consciousness as an empty vessel to be filled, nor the use of banking methods of domination (propaganda, slogans – deposits) in the name of liberation."[11] In their advocacy for institutional transformation and in their respective visions of the role of education, Freire and Illich partici- pated in the linguistic conventions of progressive ideology in the so-called long 1960s.[12] In Daniel Schugurensky's estimation, "Together with Illich's *Deschool- ing Society* (1971), *Pedagogy of the Oppressed* was one of the most widely read books on education during the 1970s. The two books challenged deeply held assumptions about the role of education in society."[13]

In addition to his theses of monopoly and manipulation, Illich harshly criti- cized the reformist attempts that had cropped up around the "free school" move- ment since the end of the Second World War, especially in the United States. In *Deschooling Society* he argued that "Only disenchantment with and detachment from the central social ritual and reform of that ritual can bring about radical change."[14] More explicitly, he went so far as to draw an analogy between the Catholic reformist bishops who had participated in the Second Vatican Council and the reformist educators involved in the free school movement: "The mood among some educators is much like the mood among Catholic bishops after the Vatican Council. The curricula of so-called 'free schools' resemble the liturgies of folk and rock masses."[15] The quest for radical transformation and the rejection of any and all attempts at reform found in Illich's work are key influences on how his ideas were first received. Within this framework Illich is featured as a "repre- sentative libertarian educator"[16] of the 1960s and '70s, a "radical liberal human- ist,"[17] and according to one scholar, it is even "possible to position him [Illich] in anarchic theory … Deschoolers confront, attack, and sabotage the hidden curriculum."[18] This framework of reception opened at a key time in the history of education, especially in North America, in that, as Josh Cole points out, "some progressive ideas rebounded in the late 1950s and 1960s, taking new forms."[19]

A second frame of reception is constituted by the ongoing debate during the second half of the twentieth century on the purpose of educational institutions in the technological environment that was then emerging on a global scale. Practically from its publication, *Deschooling Society* had an important impact on those who studied the development of tools of information and communi- cation technology in education; in particular, the book attended to the chal- lenge these technologies represented in institutionalized teaching and learning processes. Particularly inspiring in this respect was the chapter on "learning webs" included in the first edition of the book in 1971. Lee Felsenstein, who designed the first mass-produced portable computer (the so-called Osborne Computer) in 1981, was one of the most prominent of Illich's acolytes. Accord- ing to his own testimony, "The learning process should be built into the design of the equipment. I have personally followed this principle in designing per- sonal computer equipment with some success. I call the quality of the design which includes the user in the learning process the conviviality of the design, a term concept taken from Ivan Illich."[20] In the last three decades, with the development of the Internet, new approaches to Illich's work have been put forward by advocates of such theories as connectivism[21] and edupunk.[22] As Kirsten Olson observes, "As Illich might have predicted, new *tools* have changed the paradigm. With the advent of the Internet, the usual assumptions about who gets access to knowledge – who owns it, how it is produced, who is authorized to 'legitimate' it, what 'it' actually is – are radically altering."[23]

The third framework for the early reception of *Deschooling Society* was formed among those involved in the homeschooling/unschooling movement. It is important to point out that Illich's theses were mainly embraced by the unschooling side, which in recent years has backed away from the conservative, puritanical ebb of the wider homeschooling movement, which contributed to the disfiguration of the pedagogical foundation that underpinned the rejection of schooling, especially in the United States. And all despite the fact that Illich himself, as will be analysed later in this chapter, was critical of the way in which some of the central theses of his book were developed, even to the point of regret: "[in *Deschooling Society*] I called for the disestablishment of schools for the sake of improving education and here, I noticed, made my mistake. Much more important than the disestablishment of schools, I began to see, was the reversal of those trends that make of education a pressing need."[24]

The intellectual figure who introduced and did the most to uphold Illich's ideas within the homeschooling/unschooling movement, especially in its beginnings, was John Holt, who met Illich personally on his first trip to Cuernavaca, Mexico, in early 1970.[25] Holt became one of the most prominent figures in educational debates in the United States in the late 1970s and early 1980s. He was an intellectual and activist in educational matters and was highly relevant to the movement that organized parents who rejected compulsory schooling.[26] Suffice to say that by the late 1970s and early 1980s, the movement enjoyed notable recognition within the American educational imaginary. In December 1978, Holt's article "Teaching Children at Home" was published in the prestigious magazine *Time*.[27] In addition, at the early 1980s Holt participated regularly in televised debates, most notably on the *Phil Donahue Show*. The homeschooling movement was subsequently recognized in the pages of the popular publication *Phi Delta Kappan*, which noted that while homeschooling had been "a subversive activity until a very few years ago," it was by the late 1970s "quickly becoming a national movement with its own gurus, publications, and support networks."[28] Undoubtedly, Holt was one of the main gurus in that he was the founder and first editor of the magazine *Growing without Schooling*.[29] This periodical became highly influential in many countries and helped significantly to spread the movement throughout the world. It was also a space where families that homeschooled could also discuss Illich's ideas. References to Illich were numerous.

John Holt's Trip to CIDOC in Cuernavaca

Holt first received an invitation from Illich and the Centro Intercultural de Documentación (CIDOC) in Cuernavaca in 1969. As Holt himself recounted, "One day in the fall of 1969 Jonathan Kozol called me up to say that someone named Ivan Illich whom I probably had not heard of (I had in fact seen one newspaper story about him), was going to invite me to teach some sort of seminar in Cuernavaca … Not long after, Illich did call and invite me."[30] In the months leading up to his first trip to meet Illich personally, Holt became familiar with Illich's ideas. Illich's first texts in which he announced his criticism of schools had appeared between 1968 and 1970 in major American publications to which Holt had easy access. Such was the case with "The Futility of Schooling in Latin America" (1968)[31] and "The False Ideology of Schooling" (1970),[32] which were published in *Saturday Review*, and "Why We Must Abolish Schooling" (1970)[33] and "Schooling: The Ritual of Progress" (1970),[34] which both appeared in the prestigious magazine the *New York Review of Books*. The first evidence of Holt's initiation in Illich's ideas is in a letter he wrote to James Herndon, author of the book *The Way It Spozed to Be*,[35] on 25 November 1969. In it, Holt mentions that along with the letter, "I'm also sending along some very important articles by Ivan Illich."[36]

In January and February 1970 Holt travelled for the first time to Cuernavaca to take part in the activities at CIDOC, the think tank then led by Ivan Illich in Mexico.[37] The visit lasted two weeks. This was the first of a series of trips Holt made annually between 1970 and 1975 to participate in the seminars CIDOC held at the Rancho Tetela facilities for the purpose of thinking critically about modern educational institutions.[38] A few days before starting this first trip, on 6 January 1970, he wrote a letter to Illich in which he informed him of his imminent arrival: "the time for my visit with you is coming closer, and I await it eagerly. I wish I could say that my Spanish would be better, but it won't be."[39]

About his first visit to Cuernavaca, in a letter to CIDOC students on 19 February 1970, he wrote, "the two weeks I spent among you and with you were among the most interesting, pleasant, and valuable of my live."[40] In the same letter, Holt added information about the kind of discussions he had had in the seminars he had taken part in:

> My short visit to CIDOC made me feel much more strongly than before that our worldwide system of schooling is far more harmful, and far more deeply and integrally connected with many of the other great evils of our time, than I had supposed. I have been very critical of what we might call "schoolism," but I had not thought of it as being anywhere near as harmful as, say, militarism or modern nationalism, and would have considered such comparisons overdrawn. They now seem altogether apt and exact.

This raises a kind of ethical dilemma. You are of course free to disagree with what I or Ivan Illich and his colleagues have been saying about schooling. But if you agree in any large measure, it seems to me that you have a kind of duty to begin some form of what we might call school resistance, or credential or diploma resistance, just as those who strongly disapprove of war in general or our war against Viet Nam in particular ought to express their disapproval in some form of war resistance.[41]

Holt was satisfied about his first participation in the CIDOC seminars. Illich the intellectual did not disappoint. In another letter written on 27 February 1970, just a few days after his first trip to Cuernavaca, this time to students of Boston University, Holt alluded to what he considered one of Illich's fundamental contributions in his studies of educational institutions: "One of the things Illich talked about in Mexico ... was the degree to which our imaginations have been captured, not just by schools but even more largely by institutions and the idea of institutions."[42] The American pedagogue's writing at this time reflected many of the doubts expressed by people all around the world who were then opting for home education, given that Holt did not settle the dilemma of determining to what extent schools could serve as centres of genuine learning and whether it was viable to reject formal schooling, taking into account that it had solid roots for the organization of life in society in the modern world.

Particularly relevant is the letter Holt sent on 1 April 1971, addressed again to the CIDOC. In it he questions some of the central ideas that were being developed in his work. Regarding his second trip to Cuernavaca, he stated,

Once again I find myself back in Boston after two of the most pleasant, stimulating, and though-stretching weeks of my life. I can't thank you enough for having helped make this stay in Cuernavaca what it was for me ...

One way of saying what has happened is that I have been helped to resolve, or at least reformulate, what had been for me a very difficult tension. For the last year I have been completely convinced for the necessity for de-schooling society, for all the tensions that you very well know. On the other hand, I was very much involved in and committed to the whole notion of school reform, partly because this was something that I was very much interested in, partly because I have made a great many close friendships and connections with people who are working hard to reform the schools. My problem was how to resolve this apparent contradiction; how could reforming schools, making them more interesting, less punitive, less coercive, less inhuman, be reconciled with the larger problem of de-schooling society.[43]

Cuernavaca and specifically CIDOC witnessed the meeting of two intellectuals who explored the possible margins for the critique of educational institutions in the early 1970s. Although Illich and Holt came from different backgrounds (Illich had devoted a good part of his intellectual development to being a Catholic priest in Europe and the United States, whereas Holt accumulated major experience as much in pacifist movements as teaching at free schools), their critical ideas of the educational institutions converged to a considerable extent. In Holt's case, his trips to Mexico proved key to investigating fundamental theoretical concepts that would eventually allow him to delve not only into the endeavours of educational institutions, but also into the dominant discourse that sustained them. Likewise, his time in Cuernavaca gave him a glimpse of the complexity of criticizing the institution of school head-on in the late twentieth century, especially since schools by then had come to play a strategic role in people's hopes of having education solve the main political, social, cultural, and even spiritual problems of the time.

Illich's Ideas in Holt's Radicalization

John Holt was born in 1923 and began his career as a teacher at private schools on the East Coast of the United States. It was as a result of this teaching experience that he wrote his first book, *How Children Fail* (1964). The book went on to sell a million copies. Holt used clear language and strove to understand children from their own perspective, which gained him the attention of teachers and parents who were disappointed with the American school system. Holt's ideas twisted and turned significantly over time, although the way he presented his ideas was set out in his early works. As Adam Dickerson has pointed out, "He wrote for an audience of 'ordinary people,' not educational theorists, and aimed to remind that audience of their own capacity to act with courage and imagination."[44]

His postulates about education contained an optimistic conceptualization of the capacities of subjects immersed in a teaching-learning process. At the same time, he asserted that the best learning environment was one that did not require constant adult intervention. Holt's main point of reference was A.S. Neill, who was headmaster of Summerhill School and whom he came to know personally in 1965.[45] In a letter to Neill written on 30 September, Holt expressed his admiration for the British educator's work, especially his recently published book: "I have been reading *Talking of Summerhill* [1968]. It is wonderful, much better, in fact, that I am recommending to my students at Harvard that they order it from England."[46]

The first school Holt taught at was the Rocky Mountain School near Aspen, Colorado. It had just been founded and was striving to put into practice a model of food self-management. Holt volunteered at the school for a few months before taking over for one of the teachers for four years between 1953 and 1957.[47] He then began to write letters to his friends in which he systematically presented his observations and ideas about teaching and learning. After four years at the Aspen school, Holt moved to Boston. A friend lent him his apartment for the year. Holt liked the city, to the point that he ended up settling in Boston for the rest of his life. In short order, he also managed to get a school in Boston to hire him. However, in his first year there as a teacher, his educational ideas clashed with the school management, and he had to quit his job there.

After several bad experiences at different private schools in Boston, Holt managed to get his first book published in 1964, *How Children Fail*. This successful first book reads like a teacher's diary. As Adam Dickerson, observed, in this book, "through the use of ethnographic-like techniques of close observations, and the detail recording of children's conversations, Holt is able to move away from the all-too-familiar teacher's perspective on a class, and let us come closer to seeing educational activities from the students' perspective."[48] What Holt tried to convey with this book was the change that he himself was internalizing between 1958 and 1961 in terms of how he perceived life in the classroom. This proved key to his name becoming more widely known within key education circles in the United States. Two years later, the general public took note of his second book *How Children Learn*, which sold close to a million copies in the United States alone.[49] Nineteen sixty-eight was the last year Holt worked at free schools, at which point "he left teaching … to lecture at the Harvard Graduate School of Education and the University of California at Berkeley, still believing that schools could be transformed into positive resource centers."[50]

It is interesting to note how Holt's thinking evolved from a commitment to reforming the school structure, latent in his participation in the free school movement, to a more radical stance that led him to directly approach homeschooling practices. His dissatisfaction, a consequence of his reformist experiences, was the result of the relationship he began in 1970 with the group of thinkers at the CIDOC in Cuernavaca. He is known to have corresponded throughout the 1970s with Illich, who invited him to participate in the pedagogical seminars being held at the centre in Mexico. Patrick Farenga argues that

> it was Ivan Illich's *Deschooling Society* (1971) that most influenced Holt. After *Deschooling Society* appeared, Holt studied and corresponded with Illich at length, and was deeply influenced by Illich's analysis, particularly with his analysis that school serves a deep social function by firmly maintaining the status quo of social class for the majority of students.[51]

Along the same lines, in the recent work published by James G. Dwyer and Shawn F. Peters, special emphasis is placed on the influence that Illich's ideas had on Holt's intellectual path:

> Initially, Holt was more of an educational reformer than an outright revolutionary. He clung to belief that schools could and should be overhauled and transformed

into sites of authentic learning. However, his perspective changed over time, in part because of the influence of Ivan Illich, who in the 1971 book *Deschooling Society* questions the entire idea of institutionalized education.[52]

Holt's radicalization deepened after his visit to the CIDOC and his personal encounter with Illich. In the years following his trip to Cuernavaca, Holt experienced a shift in his educational conception that was soon to be reflected in his writings. The most obvious case, as already noted, was his book published in 1972, *Freedom and Beyond*. In the first few pages, Holt makes an interesting statement of the new turn in his way of thinking: "It no longer seems to me that any imaginable sum of school reforms would be enough to provide good education for everyone or even for all children. People, even children, are educated much more by the whole society around them and the general quality of life in it than they are by what happens in schools."[53] This was an idea around which his best-known books published in the seventies would also revolve, such as *Escape from Childhood* (1974), *Instead of Education* (1976), and *Never Too Late* (1979). In the words of Adam Dickerson, "by the time of *Instead of Education* ... Holt has largely given up on the idea that the 'best learning' can be achieved in any real way within the context of compulsory schooling. The strategies he proposes in this work thus shift to what might be termed, with a nod to anarchist thought, 'mutual aid solutions.'"[54]

But the key to Holt's head-on critique of compulsory schooling in the 1970s and '80s was Illich's *Deschooling Society*. Illich's book emphasized that schooling could be analysed as one of the most contradictory and counterproductive rituals in the modern industrialized world. Many years later, in a text widely considered his intellectual testament, Illich clarified that he came to articulate his criticism of school institutions after examining schooling: "I proposed that it be analysed as a ritual because only then did it become evident that the major effect of these institutions was to make people believe in the necessity and goodness of what they were supposed to achieve."[55] It was a hollow promise in the form of ritual, and one that Holt believed could and should be confronted.

Hence, any organized movement that could result from his critique should aim "not to improve 'education' but to do away with it, to end the ugly and anti-human business of people-shaping and let people shape themselves."[56] Holt's discourse was a continuation of the ideas that Illich himself had intuitively formulated in *Deschooling Society* when he pointed out that "an educational revolution depends on a twofold investment: a new orientation for research and a new understanding of the educational style of an emerging counterculture."[57] After Cuernavaca, Holt was convinced that it was time to go beyond school reform, since the institutional structure itself had to stop being seen as a means, and instead be studied as an obstacle to free learning. In his book *Freedom and Beyond*, Holt made his point perfectly clear in this regard:

We certainly have schools, and we are likely to have quite a few of them for some time, so it makes sense to try to improve them. But the fact that we have an institution or condition, be it schools, jails, poverty, cancer, or war, ought not to bar us from asking ourselves, "Should we have it? Do we want to have it? If not, how might we get rid of it, and what else might we have in its place?" And even in the here and now it seems to me foolish to put all our hopes for a truly educative society or enlightened way of rearing children into the basket of school reform. To ask or expect the schools, given their present functions, given our present understanding of education, to be innovative and imaginative as a whole, consistently, and in the long run seems to me to be asking for the impossible. People have been working at reforming schools for years. Not many of the ideas of today's school reformers are new. This is not the first time people have talked as if we were at the dawn of a new age of humane schooling. Why have we still so far to go?[58]

After his time at the CIDOC, Holt went so far as to state bluntly that he envisioned a society without schools or institutions to administer education, in which learning was not separate from the rest of life. Back in the 1970s Holt launched the Beacon Hill Free School in Boston. This project "in its first years has attracted a hundred or more pupils, and on a budget of practically nothing – a good example of the kind of open educational network that Ivan Illich has written about."[59] Regarding such initiatives, it has been observed that "Holt echoes the distinction made by Illich when he distinguishes between coercive institutions based on compulsion, and convivial ones based on choice."[60] Moreover, one of the arguments on which he based his approach to theories of unschooling was the social injustice promoted by schools. This was indeed a new critique of American pedagogy, since Holt, together with Illich, denounced the fact that financial resources dedicated to public instruction benefited well-to-do children because they were the ones who could stay in school the longest.

Illich and His Lack of Interest in Homeschooling/Unschooling

Ivan Illich set a clear theoretical distance from the schooling debate shortly after the publication of *Deschooling Society*. By 1971, in an article published in the magazine *Social Policy* in which he analysed certain readings that were being made of his main theses against educational institutions, he noted that

Since the crisis in schooling is symptomatic of a deeper crisis of modern industrial society, it is important that the critics of schooling avoid superficial solutions. Inadequate analysis of the nature of schooling only postpones the facing of deeper issues. But most criticism of the schools is pedagogical, political, or technological ...
I believe all these critics miss the point, because they fail to attend to what I have elsewhere called the ritual aspects of schooling ... [I] refer to the structure of

schooling as opposed to what happens in school, in the same way that linguists distinguish between the structure of a language and the use the speaker makes of it … Of course schools are by no means the only institutions that pretend to translate knowledge, understanding, and wisdom into behavioral traits, the measurement of which is the key to prestige and power. Nor are schools the first institution used to convert knowledge to power.[61]

As he acknowledged in a text published in 1990, a few months after his book was released, "Much more important than the disestablishment of schools, I began to see, was the reversal of those trends that make of education a pressing need rather than a gift of gratuitous leisure."[62] Hence, in the following years, on the few occasions in which he participated in meetings with educators or educational researchers, he presented a critical approach to alternatives to schooling that failed to challenge the ideological constructs of what he called the "educational sphere." In a lecture given at the Teacher's College of New York in 1979 he noted that "I am under the impression that the educational debate, no matter how radical, is still only concerned with a rearrangement of social spheres."[63] He further noted, in allusion to those who were exploring forms of education outside formal educational institutions, that "the construct of the educational sphere is zealously guarded by the various bodies of educators who identify educational needs in terms of problems for which they alone possess the social mission to find institutional solutions in and out of schools."[64]

Illich was in fact very critical of homeschooling, feeling that, in practice, it meant integrating the educational sphere into the familial sphere. This he said in a lecture delivered in 1978 at the Central Institute of Indian Languages in Mysore, India. To show his scepticism towards certain radical pedagogical discourses, he ended his presentation with an anecdote that clearly illustrates the distance he felt vis-à-vis practices such as homeschooling:

A short while ago I was back in New York in an area that two decades ago I had known quite well: the South Bronx. I was there at the request of a young college teacher who is married to a colleague … In the evening, at dinner in my colleague's home, I suddenly understood … [that] this was no longer a man but a total teacher. In front of their own children, this couple stood *in loco magistri*. Their children had to grow up without parents – because these two adults, in every word which they addressed to their two sons and one daughter, were "educating" them. And since they considered themselves very radical, off and on they made attempts at "raising the consciousness" of their children.[65]

In conversations he recorded with David Cayley, and that were published in the 1990s, when reviewing his position on schooling, Illich did not hesitate to point out that "the alternative to schooling, entrusted within the domestic walls to the parents, could be even more terrible than schooling."[66] Hence, his studies from the 1980s and '90s underwent a clear turn. As he himself admitted, "from criticism of schooling I moved on to criticism of what *education* does to society: foster the belief that people need help to understand reality, to live or uphold their lives."[67]

All in all, Illich's view of Holt as an intellectual figure was positive. After their meetings in Cuernavaca he felt a particular fondness for him. He went so far as to admit that "thanks to his bulletin and his association" he had been able to "discuss and confront ideas with him."[68] Illich once described Holt as follows "This was a beautiful monomaniacal guy, someone you occasionally went to see, just to touch him, to make certain that he did exist! And there he was with his paperclip on his shirt, strengthening his fingers for playing the cello."[69] What was clear was that in the study of the educational spheres that Illich had undertaken since the 1970s, Holt's ideas had little to contribute to his work. From then on he looked to others such as Milman Parry, Eric Havelock, Walter Ong, and Karl Polanyi.

For his part, Holt turned to Illich's ideas in many of the books that he published until his death in 1985. In 1976, in his book *Instead of Education*, he looked back on his experience at the CIDOC to deepen the theoretical underpinnings of his radicalized pedagogical position:

> When I first went to CIDOC and met Illich … I was surprised at how strongly he resisted the idea of what was then called informal teaching, and defended the old-fashioned schoolmaster. Later I was surprised again by the passion with which he argued against free schools. Most puzzling of all was his fear that what people were beginning to call the deschooling society might simply produce a society that was itself a universal or perpetual school, or his remark that a global schoolhouse would be like a global madhouse or a global prison.[70]

In 1978, in a book entitled *Never Too Late*, Holt made an interesting portrait of CIDOC:

> CIDOC was a kind of established permanent floating seminar. It began with a discussion of schools and education. Illich himself was a very traditionally schooled man. As a result of his life and work in Puerto Rico and other poor Latin American countries, he had come to feel that, useful though they might be in rich countries, schools and schooling were a disaster for poor countries, and could only lock them deeper into poverty, ignorance, dependency, and helplessness. From this beginning he began to be interested in the whole question of educational reform in rich countries. He invited a number of people who had spoken or written, in the U.S. or elsewhere, to come to Cuernavaca. In theory, they were there to teach seminars. A more important reason for their being there was that Illich wanted to pick their

brains – and wanted them to pick his. It was a thing often spoken of, but which too seldom happens, a meeting of minds. We were there to put our heads together, and all of us including Illich were much changed by doing it. In time we came to see that what was most wrong with modern people and modern societies spread much wider, and went much deeper, than schools.[71]

Conclusions

In this chapter, we began by analysing the early reception of Ivan Illich's ideas after his book *Deschooling Society* was published in 1971. We identified three frames of reference: people who worked on technological developments from an educational perspective, people who sought radical ideas to confront the expansion of educational institutions, and organized groups of parents who rejected schooling for their children. With these three groups as our reference, we turned our attention to how Illich's ideas became a key intellectual influence on John Holt, arguably the most prominent leader of the homeschooling/unschooling movement in the United States in the 1970s and '80s.

The attention has mainly been given to analysing Holt's encounter with Illich at the CIDOC in Cuernavaca in the early 1970s. Holt himself defined that time as being of great significance in his intellectual career; it was also the beginning of a shift in the line of criticism of educational institutions that he had been developing up until this meeting. From then on, Holt, under Illich's influence, would seek to explore the possibility of opening new spaces that would challenge the hegemonic relations of teaching and learning in the Western world.

This is substantiated based on both primary and secondary sources, mainly the texts that Holt himself published in the CIDOC series and the letters he wrote to students at the centre as well as to Illich himself. All together, these sources affirm that Holt's trips to Mexico were fundamental to his researching the key theoretical aspects that would allow him to delve deeper into the endeavours of educational institutions as well as the dominant discourse that upheld them. Likewise, his time in Cuernavaca gave him a glimpse into the complexity of head-on criticism of school institutions in the second half of the twentieth century, since by then schools had become strategic places where hopes were laid that education would solve the main political, social, cultural, and even spiritual problems of the time. Meanwhile, after the 1970s, Illich himself showed no particular interest in how his ideas were circulating within the homeschooling/unschooling movement. Rather, he became quite sceptical of any alternatives to schooling that, instead of challenging the educational spheres of industrial modernity, only integrated those constructs into other spaces such as the home.

NOTES

1   See G. Robert Lewis and Diane Reiko Kinishi, *The Learning Exchange: What It Is, How It Works, How You Can Set Up a Similar Program for Your Community* (Evanston, IL: Learning Exchange, 1977).

2   Marcelo Sabbatini, "Em Busca da Folkconvivialidade: Aproximações entre a Teoria da Folkcomunicação e o Pensamento Filosófico-Educacional de Ivan Illich," *Revista Internacional de Folkcomunicação* 10, no. 19 (2012): 55.

3   Our conceptualization of homeschooling/unschooling as an educational movement draws from the work of Ed Collom and Douglas E. Mitchell, "Home Schooling as a Social Movement: Identifying the Determinants of Homeschoolers' Perception," *Sociological Spectrum* 25, no. 3 (2005): 273–305, https://doi.org /10.1080/027321790518807.

4   David Armitage, "The International Turn in Intellectual History," in *Rethinking Modern European Intellectual History*, ed. Darrin M. McMahon and Samuel Moyn (New York: Oxford University Press. 2014), 232–52.

5   Joseph F. Murphy, "The Organizational Development of Homeschooling in the U.S.," *American Educational History Journal* 40, no. 2 (2013): 335–54.

6   Petar Jandrić, "In and Against Radical Monopoly: Critical Education and Information and Communication Technologies," *Problems of Education in the 21st Century* 35, no. 1 (2011): 70–84.

7   Daniel T. Rodgers, *Age of Fracture* (Cambridge, MA: Harvard University Press, 2011), 215.

8   Justin Mueller, "Anarchism, the State, and the Role of Education," in *Anarchist Pedagogies: Collective Actions, Theories, and Critical Reflections on Education*, ed. Robert H. Haworth (Oakland, CA: PM Press, 2012), 26.

9   Ivan Illich, *Deschooling Society* (New York: Harper and Row, 1972), 146.

10 Illich, 158–9.

11 Paulo Freire, *Pedagogy of the Oppressed* (New York: Continuum, 2005), 79.

12 Rosa Bruno-Jofré, "The 'Long 1960s' in a Global Arena of Contention: Re-defining Assumptions of Self, Morality, Race, Gender and Justice, and Questioning Education," *Espacio, Tiempo y Educación* 6, no. 1 (2019): 5–27, http://dx.doi.org/10.14516/ete.256.

13 Daniel Schugurensky, *Paulo Freire* (London: Bloomsbury, 2011), 69.

14 Illich, *Deschooling Society*, 54.

15 Illich, 71.

16 Emily Comer, "A Libertarian Approach to Teaching Reading" (master's thesis, University of Illinois at Urbana-Champaign, 2016), ii.

17 Peter M. Lichtenstein, "Radical Liberalism and Radical Education: A Synthesis and Critical Evaluation of Illich, Freire, and Dewey," *American Journal of Economics and Sociology* 44, no. 1 (1985): 51.

18 Joseph Todd, "From Deschooling to Unschooling: Rethinking Anarchopedagogy after Ivan Illich," in Haworth, ed., *Anarchist Pedagogies*, 74.

19 Josh Cole, *Hall-Dannis and the Road to Utopia. Education and Modernity in Ontario* (Montreal: McGill-Queen's University Press, 2021), 98.

20 Lee Felsenstein, "The Golemic Approach," accessed 4 September 2020, http://www .leefelsenstein.com/wp-content/uploads/2013/01/Golemic_Approach_MS.pdf.

21 Marc Clarà and Elena Barberà, "Three Problems with the Connectivist Conception of Learning," *Journal of Computer Assisted Learning* 30, no. 3 (2014): 197–206, https://doi.org/10.1111/jcal.12040.

22 Anya Kamenetz, *Edupunk, Edupreneurs, and the Coming Transformation of Higher Education* (White River Junction, VT: Chelsea Green Publishing, 2010).

23 Kirsten Olson, "Everywhere All the Time: A New Deschooling Reader," review of *Everywhere All the Time: A New Deschooling Reader*, by Matt Hern, *International Journal of Illich Studies* 1, no. 1 (2010): 50–2.

24 Ivan Illich, "Foreword," in *Deschooling Our Lives*, ed. Matt Hern (Gabriola Island, BC: New Society Publishers, 1995), viii.

25 Patricia Quiroga and Jon Igelmo Zaldívar, "El Viaje a Cuernavaca, México, de John Holt y su Relevancia para la Historia del Movimiento Global de la Educación en Casa," *Práxis Educativa*, no. 15 (2020): 1–15, https://doi.org/10.5212/PraxEduc .v.15.14772.033.

26 Roland Meighan, *John Holt* (London: Bloomsbury, 2007).

27 John Holt, "Teaching Children at Home," *Time*, 4 December 1978, 78.

28 Diane Divoky "The New Pioneers of the Homeschooling Movement," *Phi Delta Kappan* 64, no. 6 (February 1983): 395–7.

29 See Patrick Farenga and Carlo Ricci, eds., *Growing without Schooling: The Complete Collection*, vol. 1, *1977 to 1981* (Medford, MA: HoltGWS, 2016), and Patrick Farenga and Carlo Ricci, eds., *Growing without Schooling: The Complete Collection*, vol. 2, *1981 to 1982* (Medford, MA: HoltGWS, 2018).

30 John Holt, *Never Too Late: My Musical Life Story* (New York: Da Capo Press, 1991), 183.

31 Ivan Illich, "The Futility of Schooling in Latin America," *Saturday Review*, 20 April 1968, 57–9.

32 Ivan Illich, "The False Ideology of Schooling," *Saturday Review*, 17 October 1970, 42, 56–8, 68.

33 Ivan Illich, "Why We Must Abolish Schooling," *New York Review of Books*, 2 July 1970, 9–15.

34 Ivan Illich, "Schooling: The Ritual of Progress," *New York Review of Books*, 3 December 1970, 10, 20–6.

35 James Herndon, *The Way It Spozed to Be* (New York: Simon and Schuster, 1968).

36 Susannah Sheffer, ed., *A Life Worth Living: Selected Letters of John Holt* (Columbus: Ohio State University Press, 1990), 54.

37 About CIDOC, see Rosa Bruno-Jofré and Jon Igelmo Zaldívar, "The Center for Intercultural Formation, Cuernavaca, Mexico, Its Reports (1962–1967) and Illich's Critical Understanding of Mission in Latin America," *Hispania Sacra* 66, extra

2 (July–December 2014): 457–87, http://doi.org/10.3989/hs.2014.096, and Todd Hartch, *The Prophet of Cuernavaca: Ivan Illich and the Crisis of the West* (New York: Oxford University Press, 2015).

38 On the CIDOC seminars, see Jon Igelmo Zaldívar, "La Ciudad Mexicana de Cuernavaca. Punto de Encuentro de la Pedagogía Mundial en los Años Setenta del Siglo XX," *Sembrando ideas*, no. 4 (2009): 27–36.

39 John Holt, "A Commentary about 'The Magnitude of the American Educational Establishment, 1960–1970'" (6 February 1970), in CIDOC (1972, pp. 274/1–274/2) *Alternatives in Education* (July 1970–June 1971, v. 2), Cuernavaca: CIDOC Document no. 76, quote: 274/1.

40 John Holt, "A Letter Advocating School Resistance, Addressed to Participants in the Author's Seminar Course Held at CIDOC in February 1970," Folder: 370.4D637, p. 1–5, 1970, p. 1, Biblioteca Daniel Cossío Villegas del Colegio de México.

41 Holt, 1–2.

42 Sheffer, ed., *A Life Worth Living*, 61.

43 John Holt, "Reformulations: A Letter Written after Two Weeks in Cuernavaca" (1 April 1971), in CIDOC (1972, pp. 307/1–307/4) *Alternatives in Education* (July 1970–June 1971, v. 2), Cuernavaca: CIDOC Document no. 76, quote: 307/1.

44 Adam Dickerson, "John Holt (1923–85)," in *The Routledge Encyclopedia of Educational Thinkers*, ed. Joy A. Palmer Cooper (New York: Routledge, 2016), 433–8.

45 Meighan, *John Holt*, 5.

46 Sheffer, ed., *A Life Worth Living*, 29.

47 Meighan, *John Holt*, 4.

48 Adam Dickerson, *John Holt: The Philosophy of Unschooling* (London: Springer. 2019), 40.

49 Meighan, *John Holt*, 4.

50 Milton Gaither, "John Holt (1923–1985)," in *Encyclopedia of Educational Reform and Dissent*, ed. Thomas C. Hunt, James C. Carper, Thomas J. Lasley, and C. Daniel Raisch (Thousand Oaks, CA: SAGE, 2010), 447.

51 Patrick Farenga, "John Holt and the Origins of Contemporary Homeschooling," *Paths of Learning: Options for Families & Communities* 1, no. 1 (Spring 1999): 8–13.

52 James G. Dwyer and Shawn F. Peters, *Homeschooling: The History and Philosophy of a Controversial Practice* (Chicago: University of Chicago Press, 2019), 44.

53 John Holt, *Freedom and Beyond* (Portsmouth, NH: Boynton/Cook, 1995), 4.

54 Dickerson, *John Holt*, 80.

55 David Cayley, *The Rivers North of the Future: The Testament of Ivan Illich as Told to David Cayley* (Toronto: Anansi, 2005), 141.

56 Cayley, 4.

57 Illich, *Deschooling Society*, 101.

58 Holt, *Freedom and Beyond*, 213.

59 Holt, 68.

60 Meighan, *John Holt*, 120.

61 Ivan Illich, "After Deschooling What?," *Social Policy* 2, no. 3 (September–October 1971): 5–6.

62 Ivan Illich, "Foreword," in Hern, ed., *Deschooling Our Lives*, viii.

63 Ivan Illich, "The Educational Sphere," in *In the Mirror of the Past: Lectures and Addresses, 1978–1990* (New York: Marion Boyards, 1993), 110.

64 Illich, 111.

65 Illich, 142.

66 David Cayley, *Ivan Illich in Conversation* (Toronto: Anansi, 1992), 169.

67 Cayley, 167.

68 Cayley, 170.

69 Cayley, 208–9.

70 John Holt, *Instead of Education: Ways to Help People Do Things Better* (New York: Penguin Books, 1977), 110–11.

71 Holt, *Never Too Late*, 183–4.

11 "The Time Has Come to Make the World Safe from Lifelong Education": John Ohliger, Ivan Illich, and Mandatory Continuing Education

JOSH COLE

In a collection featuring so many luminaries of recent educational thought – Illich, Freire, Holt – the name John Ohliger might fall upon deaf ears. Unlike the others, he was never famous, and he worked in adult education, a field often left out of serious intellectual consideration. And yet, his most important contribution – identifying and critiquing what he called mandatory continuing education (hereafter, MCE) – has enormous historical and contemporary value, particularly in our own time, in which the line separating education and the economy is blurring out of recognition. This chapter seeks to situate Ohliger in his time, and in relation to Ivan Illich, who was an indispensable influence upon him. Without Illich, Ohliger never could have developed his razer-sharp analysis of MCE, and yet through it, he moved into areas undreamed of by Illich, which are of the utmost importance for scholars and practitioners of education today.

John Ohliger, who would become adult education's consummate outsider by the 1970s, began working through the ideas and techniques associated with adult education in his teenage years. He was born in 1926 in Cleveland, Ohio. After a brief sojourn in Toronto, Canada, his family settled in Detroit in search of new opportunities that never materialized. Ohliger's childhood was marked by poverty, and a sense of capitalism's corrosive social effects never left him. To supplement his family's income, he began working at the Detroit Public Library at age thirteen, which gave him an insatiable, lifelong appetite for the written word. In addition to this, he began writing for his high school's newspaper and working at its radio station. Long after Ohliger passed through, and then left academia, these public fora – the library, the newspaper, and the radio station – would sustain him financially while keeping him in touch with the foundations of modern adult education, which for him entailed "knowledge building, exchange, and distribution," in small-group settings, through the printed word, and via mass mediated pedagogy.[1]

After graduating from high school, he was drafted into the military, serving for three years in Austria and Germany as a newspaper reporter, writer, and information specialist. He also began teaching adults during the war, instructing soldiers in Morse code.[2] Later, he was put in charge of his company's Troop Information and Education Program, in which he guided discussions on current affairs. It was here that he began to have misgivings about a version of adult education in which people – in this case, soldiers – were required to participate. This, as he recalled to a university audience in 1982, was his first brush with MCE, which he would come to associate with a gamut of ills afflicting adult education since the war, including "professionalism; competence; accountability; the compulsory education of adults ... science, scientism, and technology ... graduate programs; and the meaning of knowledge."[3]

After the war, Ohliger, like so many returning veterans, entered the post-war university through the Servicemen's Readjustment Act of 1944, commonly known as the GI Bill. The university he entered in 1948 was a radically new institution, wrenching itself into a new era. As Paul Mattingly notes, universities, to a degree unique among modern institutions, "embody singular assumptions about their social environment at any given moment of time."[4] This is certainly the case with the post-war "multiversity," though as the name suggests, it was designed to corral *multiple* assumptions about the post-war world and the place of learning within it. As the 1947 President's Commission on Higher Education for Democracy proclaimed, "the social role of education in a democratic society is at once to insure equal liberty and equal opportunity to differing individuals and groups, and to enable the citizens to understand, appraise, and redirect forces, men, and events as these tend to strengthen or to weaken their liberties."[5] Once a bastion of elite privilege, tertiary education would now be open to all. Clark Kerr waxed eloquently about the new institution's omnivorous nature, which forged "fragments" of educational tradition – Platonic humanism, British undergraduate culture, German graduate education and research, and American vocational education – into "a new type of institution in the world ... not really private and it is not public ... neither entirely of the world nor entirely apart from it." What held this "unlikely consensus" together was the conviction that "the university's invisible product, knowledge, may be the most powerful single element in our culture, affecting the rise and fall of professions and even of social classes, of regions and even of nations."[6]

Ohliger quickly took a bachelor's degree in social sciences and speech at Wayne State University as one of the last veterans able to trade military service for academic credit. He spent much of his extra-curricular time on Democratic Party politics, which left him deeply unsatisfied due to the hierarchical nature of the party. As he later recalled, "In the Army I had lived with many persons – ordinary GIs not officers – who were not considered 'leadership' materials. Yet they were just as capable of running their own affairs and making decisions as the officers who commanded them. I was slowly reaching the belief that real small-d democracy was possible." Thereafter, he would begin to formulate a different form of politics, one that recognized that change in the hyper-complex post-war world would be a long time coming." Aside from participation in marches and other peaceful demonstrations, Ohliger would now focus his political energies on adult education, which, as he argued, "offered one modest path" towards those democratic ideals.[7]

He then spent much of the 1950s practically engaged in adult education. He worked for the University of California's Extension Department in Los Angeles, as well as the Labor Education Department of the Michigan Congress of Industrial Organizations, where he ran a portable bookstore and taught union members speaking techniques. In these classes, he was dismayed that he was expected to fall back on corporate formulas for effective communication. This was his "first brush as a teacher with the use of snappy techniques" that favoured efficiency over enlightenment – an attitude that would fundamentally inform his critique of MCE in the late 1960s and early 1970s. In 1957, after years of itinerant teaching and factory work, he won a grant from the Ford Foundation Fund for Adult Education. This would enable him to return to the university as a master's student at the University of California's Department of Education under the tutelage of adult education scholars Paul Sheats and Abbott Kaplan.[8]

But Ohliger would soon discover that the kind of informal and non-utilitarian education he inclined towards was not favoured by the multiversity-based adult educators he began encountering in graduate school. By the 1950s, adult educators began to split into two groups: one "institutionalized and professionalized," housed in the post-war multiversity; and a smaller residue of adult educators who remained dedicated to adult education as a movement "which is of the people and an instrument of spiritual, cultural, social and political change," on the outside of it.[9] The first group, who would come to dominate academic adult education in the post-war period, sought to make adult education a certified profession, based upon scientific research, and geared towards utilitarian ends. This led to the development of "andragogy" as "the art and science of helping adults learn," in the words of its most famous exponent, Malcolm Knowles. This would prove to be, according to Ralf St. Clair and Bernd Käpplinger, "the most durable intellectual project of adult education in the 20th century" due to its success in tying together professional identity, scientistic (psychological, anthropological, gerontological) discourse, and practical aims – a formula that would ensure, in Knowles's words, that in the era of "knowledge explosion," adult citizens would become "competent people … able to apply their knowledge under changing conditions."[10] The proponents of andragogy were able to carve out minor spaces in the multiversity, primarily in departments of education and social work. More significant was andragogy's success in becoming the post-war standard in adult education theory and practice – leading to decades of research limited to "programme planning and administration, instructional material and [andragogical] methods."[11] The result saw the "vast, effulgent, and colourful landscape of adult learning screened out."[12]

Although Ohliger would master these andragogical ideas and techniques during his graduate education, his heart clearly lay in the humanistic and socially meliorist impulses of the earlier era. Ohliger's developing sense of what adult education is and what it might possibly do, had a great deal more to do with educators sidelined with the advent of andragogy, such as R.W. Tawney and Eduard Lindeman.

From Tawney, an eloquent British advocate of adult education whose socialism disqualified him from serious consideration in post-war America, Ohliger drew the idea that adult education could serve as kind of bulwark against the most corrosive effects of capitalism. In a strange irony, Ohliger, the most American of post-war adult educators, hewed to Tawney's Victorian critique of what Thomas Carlyle, another thinker disgruntled with modernity, called the "cash nexus." For Tawney, intellectuals should critique and oppose that concatenation of money and power, not support it. His critique of capitalism was, as Tim Rogan points out, a moral one: capitalism puts "the pursuit of pecuniary gain over all other human motivations in envisaging social order, reducing society to a matrix of economic transactions."[13]

Neither Tawney nor Ohliger could stomach a society built upon these foundations. But how to combat it? Tawney saw the adult education extension classes he taught through Oxford University as a possible solution – a nascent counter–public sphere. For Tawney, the tutorial class was "an example of the good society … a functioning example of fellowship, equality and democracy" in an era that seemed to value such things less and less. Eduard Lindeman, an American, added a crucial element: the idea that adult education should be free and disinterested. But this was hardly the case, as he wrote in his 1926 book *The Meaning of Adult Education*:

> Once the belief was current that if only education were free to all intelligence it would become the proper tool for managing the affairs of the world. We have gone even further and have made certain levels of education compulsory. But the result has been disappointing; we have succeeded merely in formalizing, and mechanizing, educational processes. The spirit and meaning of education cannot be enhanced by addition, by the easy method of giving the same dose to more individuals.[14]

Ohliger's UCLA dissertation was completed in 1966 and published in 1967 as *Listening Groups: Mass Media in Adult Education*. This was a short yet intensely detailed history of the use of radio and television programs to stimulate group discussion among adults, "usually under the leadership of a lay person and sometimes with the assistance of supplemental printed materials and with arraignments for two-way communication (feedback) between listeners and the broadcasters."[15] The document is unlike anything else Ohliger would write on adult education. In almost clinical prose, he attempts to squeeze the unruly energies of pre-war adult education into the "becalmed and technicized" framework of Knowlesian andragogy.[16] And yet, he himself could barely maintain this high-wire act. Though the vast bulk of the book is purpose-built out of stock phrases ("Educational researchers credit the listening group approach with the ability to spread the learning of factual material efficiently on a mass basis"), Ohliger's dissatisfaction with the post-war consensus is also apparent in his subtle endorsement of adult education as the province of "unprofitable troublemakers," and his treatment of Canada's Farm Radio Forum listening group project, which he lauds for its fulsome "political" approach to adult education, in contrast with the narrowly technical, "educational" interpretation of learning across the lifespan advanced by the United Nations Educational, Scientific and Cultural Organization (UNESCO).[17] After *Listening Groups*, Ohliger would almost entirely forsake the Apollonian approach of Knowles (and UNESCO) for a more Dionysian slant on adult education's place in the post-war world.

While he was finishing up his graduate work, Ohliger came across an advertisement in the popular magazine *Saturday Review* calling for a continuing education director in the newly minted Selkirk College in British Columbia, Canada. He was attracted to the position because it seemed to offer a more humanistic, community-oriented alternative to the andragogy staking its claim on the 1960s North American multiversity.[18] This was indeed the case, but only for a short period of time. Soon after opening, the college was enrolling more adults than young people. Principal Gordon Campbell insisted that every faculty member consider themselves adult educators, in the classroom and the community – promotion and tenure being explicitly tied to such activities. The college would act, as Ohliger later reflected, "as a leaven in the community," providing "an opportunity for continuing education among interested citizens in a changing society."[19] Campbell's vision for Selkirk displeased the college's Board of Directors, however, and he left within a year, along with those he initially recruited, including Ohliger, whose assessment of the experiment was a harsh one: Selkirk was to be "a college built on the dream of true community involvement," but was forced, through external pressures, to regress into "an extension of high school," which confirmed adult education's "essential marginality" in the post-war tertiary educational system.[20]

Ever the optimist, Ohliger accepted a position in the adult education program at Ohio State University in 1966, where he remained until he retired from academia in 1973. As he explained, in this program, "Adults did not have to enroll in classes. They were also free to leave them if they didn't like them. I justified my participation … on that basis – at least people were not forced to take all those courses."[21] Ohliger, alongside a small coterie of like-minded colleagues, did their best to keep a version of Tawneyian humanism alive at Ohio State for seven years. For instance, in 1970, Ohliger and his wife organized a major Workshop in Adult Basic Education, featuring scholars and practitioners from across North America. The workshop was designed to oppose andragogical scientism, a fact made clear in the text documenting the workshop, which opened with a quote from Martin Luther King Jr.: "Education without social action is a one-sided value because it has no true power potential. Social action without education is a weak expression of pure energy. Deeds uninformed by educated thought can take false directions." Ohliger's own contribution to the workshop displayed both his belief in liberal adult education, as realized in discussion groups (immediate or mass-mediated), as well as his growing exasperation over the disinterest, if not subtle contempt, with which such ideas were held in the age of andragogy.

In "Adult Basic Education and the Liberal Arts Approach," Ohliger proclaimed that in an age of Cold War atomic militarism and one-dimensional capitalist reductionism, liberal arts education for adults was more, not less, imperative than it was in the early twentieth century. "Men and women" could not live "in decency and dignity" in the post-war world unless they were "free." There were but "two routes to freedom" for Ohliger: "action and education, inextricably intertwined." Action, including "civil rights and civil liberties," was "the responsibility of us all." Education, however, was the "special concern" of those gathered at the workshop. Even if, as the governments of the post-war period had promised, an individual's "conditions of life are adequate, even if he has a good job and a good place to live," without education, that person would be lost, their essential freedom stunted, for they would not know how to exercise that freedom and why they should do so. The "right kind of education ... a liberal arts education," realized among adults participating voluntarily, would help them to discover for themselves how to "play a significant part in society."[22]

Ohliger's efforts did little to move the needle at Ohio State, and he began to become increasingly alarmed at the spread of andragogical solutions to social problems – what scholars would later come to call "educationalization" – outside of the academy.[23] As he later recalled, though adult students at Ohio State were free to enter and exit classes as they saw fit, "I soon learned that this was not true for many millions of adults and becoming less true every day. Sad to say, without the opposition of most leaders of adult education. More and more adults were being pressured into or required to enrol in courses, to get involved in a group that provided 'educational therapy,' or to unwillingly learn in factory or office jobs to do things that were contrary to all human values."[24] It was at this time that Ohliger encountered the writings of Ivan Illich, who, he immediately recognized, offered him the critical tools he required to identify and disarm what he would soon call mandatory continuing education, perhaps once and for all. After reading Illich, the words of his fellow adult education scholars "seemed just that – words." The Austrian polymath's utterly unique ideas gave him so much more: a "new-found consciousness" of "the oppressive direction" that adult education was moving in.[25]

Ohliger quickly began crafting an adult education–oriented response to Illich's provocations. In *Lifelong Learning or Lifelong Schooling? A Tentative View of the Ideas of Ivan Illich with a Quotational Bibliography* (1971), which Ohliger co-wrote with Colleen McCarthy, they argued that although Illich had paid little attention to adult education, his ideas where uniquely suited to contextualizing and critiquing that distinct corner of the educational system. An Illichian perspective on post-war adult education recognizes that adult education, by the later 1960s, was thoroughly "geared into the mechanism of the school system," meaning that it perpetuates "the myth that a human being is not ready for full recognition as a person until he has undergone a lengthy period of [educational] treatment" subject to the whims of an "authoritarian teacher" who instils "bits" of often useless "information" into the heads of students. More importantly than this, the educationalizing logic of the system itself was the true content of post-war education, whether it takes place in the schoolhouse or in the andragogical seminar. Like Illich, Ohliger and McCarthy were eager to separate "education" from "learning," as the former short-circuits the latter. They also saw a clear and fruitful connection between what Illich famously called "learning webs" and pre-war modes of adult education, both characterized by "self-motivated" individuals freely participating in informal "learning networks." They did not agree with Illich on everything, however. They took exception to Illich's contention that education should be divested from the state and handed over to the marketplace. They opposed "the bureaucratic vampire," but argued that "the commercial vampire" would bring with it an entirely new set of anti-intellectual forces.[26]

But this was a dry run for Ohliger's Illichian breakthrough, which occurred, appropriately enough, at Illich's Center of Intercultural Formation (CIF) in Cuernavaca, Mexico, in late 1971. There he entered into intense conversations about the nature of schooling and adult education with Illich. At CIF, Ohliger also presented his first major statement of his own ideas. The paper he presented was entitled "Adult Education: 1984," and took the form of a vicious and inspired parable of andragogical educationalization. This was the first appearance of MCE, though he would not call it that until the mid-1970s.

"Adult Education: 1984" opens with this statement: "A child is born in the year 1984. He can never look forward to getting out of school." Ohliger's narrator then explains this was also the year that the United States of America became a "permanent school district," "because by 1984, it was recognized that all people must go to school all their lives – permanently." The district was organized by a "board of lifelong education," featuring former school trustees and members of the former draft board – both now part of the new district structure. Colleges and universities were also folded into the permanent school district, "because few rich people or corporations would contribute money to such 'disruptive' and 'permissive' institutions." Those faculty members deemed responsible for such disruption would be educationalized out of existence, "sent to 'retraining camps,' or to mental institutions for 'the good of society.'" The state would now fund and exert total control over education, from cradle to grave.[27]

This was, Ohliger's surrogate proclaims, terrific news for the child. He would now pass through "infant school" to elementary school to junior high school, where he would be subjected to a battery of tests to determine his "mental abilities, social adjustment potential, and motivation." After this, he will enter high school (as preparation for still "higher schooling"), or "vocational school which will prepare him for life as a worker." The narrator explains that the child under consideration was to follow the second path, which would lead to more, not less education. "After graduation perhaps he is placed in a job, or perhaps he is sent to technical school to prepare him as a paraprofessional." More likely, however, due to "great strides of automation," he will end up briefly employed before moving in and out of "job bank schools" for the rest of his "career." There, he will learn "some skills that experts think he might just possibly use a few years later." More tangibly, he will also learn some "worthwhile hobbies" to keep him out of trouble in between jobs and job training.[28]

And if he breaks out of this precarious cycle and finds steady work? Then he can put down roots, get married, and perhaps start a family. Before he does that, he will be required to attend a "School for Marital Adjustment," and after that, a "School for Home Ownership Responsibilities." Should the happy couple have a child, they would attend a "School for Child Care" to ensure that they can manage the responsibilities involved to the government's satisfaction – squeezing all of these in between mandatory recurring lessons at the "Citizenship Institute," in which adults are taught to keep "up-to-date on current political issues," so they "can vote intelligently, which is now compulsory." At age forty, the still young man would attend a "geriatric preparation academy" so that he would learn how to retire, "which he must now do at the age of 55." After retirement, he will be taught arts and crafts, which will keep him "'happy' and out of 'mischief'" until he dies."[29] Ohliger concludes with one last twist of the knife:

> When he does die, a minister eulogizes him over his grave. By the way, the minister has gone through a "higher school" and has been required to go back to the "higher school" every two years for refresher courses in order to keep his licence to preach. The minister delivers a beautiful eulogy. He points out that this man was very lucky, for he was born in 1984, the first year that the national "Permanent School Law" was in effect. The minister extols the wisdom of the late Spiro Agnew, who in the last year of his second term of office was able to get that great law passed. "And so, we bid goodbye to this lucky man," the minister chants, "firm in the conviction that he will go to heaven where he will attend a 'school for angels' into infinity."[30]

This unusual and caustic work won Ohliger the first Ivan Illich Dystopia Award at Cuernavaca, which he considered "the best honor I have ever received."[31]

In 1973, Ohliger quit Ohio State, and aside from a short-lived part-time position at the University of Wisconsin's Extension Department, he never returned to the multiversity system. Instead, he struck out as an independent researcher, writer, and activist, leaving behind once and for all any notion of being a "professional" intellectual who spends their time "between the hours of nine and five with one eye on the clock, and another cocked at what is considered to be proper, professional behavior," in favour of a radical amateurism, which harkened back to the days of pre-war adult education. He became an intellectual in the sense later favoured by Edward Said, displaying a consistent "vocation, an energy, a stubborn force engaging as a committed and recognizable voice in language and in society," promoting "a combination of enlightenment and emancipation or freedom."[32] While he continued to speak at universities and publish in academic journals, he was ultimately much more interested in popular communication. To this end, he co-founded a listener-supported, non-commercial radio station in Madison, Wisconsin, called WORT in 1975. The next year, he spearheaded the creation of a think tank called Basic Choices as a "Midwest Center for Clarifying Political and Social Options." And from 1978 to 1984, he published two newsletters on adult education entitled Second Thoughts and the Basic Choices Newsletter. Through these, Ohliger gained a small but dedicated audience inside and outside of North America. Through correspondence (first on paper, and later through email) with like-minded adult education practitioners and scholars he was able to keep a bead on developments within the profession while remaining firmly outside of its grip; in this way he occupied a liminal space in which he was finally able to bring his ideas on MCE to fruition. He remained active through these unorthodox means until his death in 2004, at age seventy-seven.

MCE is a complex and even contradictory concept, befitting the phenomena it describes. Nonetheless, it can be discerned through Ohliger's many statements on the matter over the course of a thirty-year period. After the triumph of "Adult Education: 1984," Ohliger sought a more analytic interpretation of the subject that had consumed him since the 1960s.

In a 1974 piece entitled "Is Lifelong Education a Guarantee of Permanent Inadequacy?," published in the journal Convergence, Ohliger proclaimed that adult education was more prevalent than ever before. But this was an adult education bereft of its democratic potential. Instead, MCE held a narrow, stultifying view of human nature and the possibilities for human improvement. "Schools, other educational institutions, and now more adult educational institutions define people as inadequate, insufficient, lacking, incomplete. You don't know something so you have to go to school for the temporary relief of your inadequacies," a phenomenon endemic to a "technologically complex, crisis ridden" era.[33]

"Adult education as we know it," Ohliger wrote in 1980, "is a product of industrial society, which made mass education at once possible and necessary." Thereafter, it extended its reach from "technical training for workers [and] culturally deprived farmers," eventually evolving into "vocational and professional education." The post-war period marked another evolutionary stage, in which modern life, wrapped up in technological innovation, bent the education of adults to its ends. Liberal education, non-utilitarian and politically troublesome, was out of favour. In its place? An "emerging form of technocratic liberalism," drawn from "the natural sciences, the social sciences and engineering." This technocratic liberalism retained an "unbounded confidence in the liberal idea of transforming society through education," without the humanistic curb that liberal education placed upon those transformations.[34]

Technocratic liberalism, as a founding principle of MCE, was not just an American, or even a North American, phenomenon, according to Ohliger. It was worldwide. In 1974, Ohliger targeted one of the most feted international andragogical projects of the post-war period: UNESCO's 1972 report *Learning to Be: The World of Education Today and Tomorrow*. The report, which featured a smattering of Illichian contributors and more than a few advocates of the Brazilian educator and philosopher Paulo Freire, was met with particular scorn from Ohliger. As he wrote, "If it is bad enough to promote technocratic control ... in the false name of equal chances to one nation, it is even worse to propose it for the whole world." Though the report evinced a "cosmetic" commitment to the humanist tradition of adult education, Ohliger argued that its true substance pointed in the opposite direction – that of global technocratic control of "developed" and "developing" peoples through adult education. It was built upon the "rigidity and extremism of moderates," in this case, educators working with politicians and big business "to provide continuously trained manpower" for an economy centred on "spiralling technological complexity." The possibility that "a person *is* and is capable of self-motivated and self-disciplined learning" was ruled out of court. Instead, this manifestation of MCE proceeded through "structured knowledge, modules of instruction, interchangeable blocks of information, and units of learning," which would be put through a kind of feedback loop – "a complex cybernetic system" in which the learner's progress would be continually surveilled, "evaluated and modified," in order to produce the desired result: a politically docile subject, continually retooled to suit emerging economic demands – a dynamic worker for a dynamic post-industrial society.[35]

Channelling Illich, Ohliger maintained that what one learned through MCE above all else was an attitude: that one's social and economic security and standing required deference to MCE as a process, without questioning its obvious shortcomings and contradictions. Adult educators of the andragogical mould aided in this ideological procedure by portraying MCE as a "non-ideological, all-purpose approach" to the educationalization of social problems, severed from the "historical context" in which those problems arose. Instead, MCE was offered up as an ahistorical and even natural solution to them. MCE encouraged people to accept "the contemporary context as a given," an ideal that they should "adjust to" and "prosper within," rather than "rebel against." The "concepts of wisdom and learning are then converted into knowledge as information gathering, increasingly conceived not as a process of self-initiated discovery in conjunction with other learners, but as the transfer of information from technical experts (adult educators) to learners viewed as passive receptacles for such information."[36] Ohliger had no doubt that MCE would be good for business – for why wouldn't capitalists desire workers eager to learn more to earn more? – but he was also convinced that the end for adult education as a humanistic, democratic set of ideas and practices was nigh, and that this process would only deepen and accelerate in the twenty-first century.

Was Ohliger on to something big, or was he a spirited yet eccentric critic crying in the wilderness? With the benefit of hindsight, we see clearly that he was right about MCE, and how it would grow in political-economic importance over time. *Learning to Be*'s novel mix of humanist rhetoric and MCE made a major, albeit brief, impact on educational and economic policy. What came after, however, put MCE over all other concerns. Now, other international organizations, including the Organisation for Economic Co-operation and Development (OECD) and the World Bank took the lead in MCE, jettisoning most of the idealism of *Learning to Be* in favour of a direct focus on MCE's potential contributions to human capital theory and practice in an increasingly volatile, neoliberal global economy. The very term "adult education" was squeezed out of MCE, in favour of "recurrent education," and later "lifelong learning," the latter having far fewer democratic connotations than "adult education," making it easier to instrumentalize as policy.[37]

By the 1980s and into the 1990s, governments, including in the United Kingdom and the United States, began to look at MCE as a way to stabilize neoliberal capitalism as an economic system, while spreading its spoils more evenly. As Bill Clinton proclaimed to the Democratic National Congress in 1996, lifelong learning would be central to the twenty-first-century American economy, proposing continual retraining opportunities for those out of work so they would be able to transition to "good high-skill jobs for a good future."[38] In the United Kingdom, Tony Blair and Gordon Brown's "New Labour" governments, in power from 1997 to 2010, went further, announcing that "Education is now the centre of economic policy making for the future," and that countries like theirs will "succeed or fail on the basis of how it changes itself and gears up to this new economy, based on knowledge."[39] New Labour declared the redistribution of wealth outmoded in the new global economy, choosing instead to focus on the "redistribution of possibilities" through lifelong education, or MCE.[40] According to the *Leitch Review of Skills* (2004), "in the new global economy, people's economic security will not depend on trying to protect particular jobs." Instead, "the best form of welfare will be to ensure people can find their next job," which will be done by guaranteeing that they are given a suite of "basic skills" that they can build upon "flexibly ... as the economy changes."[41]

Yet, it was with the 2008 global financial crash that reality truly caught up with Ohliger's critique. Now neoliberal capitalism was in genuine trouble, staring down a deep-seated legitimation crisis. Even the OECD, the world's premier champion of the free market, recognized that things had to change, for "conventional" economic models were revealed as "insufficient to address the complexity of the modern global economy." Trust, they argued, had to be restored through long-term economic growth that would be "inclusive" so that "prosperity is fairly shared and economic and technological progress [can] benefit all."[42] Western states now began studying countries like Hong Kong and Singapore, which had small populations and few natural resources, but which proved able to generate significant growth – particularly in the high-tech sector – through unprecedented systems of lifelong learning, in which citizens were expected to continually upgrade their skills to match the requirements of the market. Economics and education were no longer two policy areas, but one synthetic whole. Just as importantly, and as Ohliger had predicted, Hong Kong, Singapore, and countries like Canada have discarded notions of targeted vocational training in favour of a more generalized attitude towards lifelong learning, in which the worker is to demonstrate an ability, and just as importantly a *desire*, to make themselves "employable" through continuous learning.

As Phebe Moore explains, this "employability mindset" "requires the productive woman/man to become a citizen/worker," but also a "learner worker" with a "flexible personality," someone who is "self-managed/directed," innovative," and "adaptable," all qualities realized through the worker's most important trait: that of being an "incurable learner."[43] As a recent Canadian government document insists, our "world is in a time of unprecedented transformation, moving at a pace and scale that has never been experienced before ... Canadians must be equipped with the right competencies and provided the flexibility to meet the evolving demands of the workplace [and all] ... Canadians, including youth, women, Indigenous people, and other underrepresented groups, must continually train and upskill, and have more opportunities to develop key skills."[44] Following Ohliger's lead, we can easily see the ideological machinations at work in contemporary MCE. These new programs are clearly a way to generate more human capital, and while shoring up a demonstrably dysfunctional economic system, they are sold to learner-workers and the general public as a boon for human freedom, creativity, and democratic unity. In this, they resemble the program of "Adult Education: 1984," in which workers move from job to job bank and back, learning skills that will keep them productive and "happy," so that they don't ask questions and "keep out of mischief."[45]

In one of his earliest statements on compulsory schooling, Ivan Illich wrote that it serves to inaugurate children and young people into "the membership of disciplined consumers of the technocracy."[46] John Ohliger, as a scholar and practitioner of adult education, took Illich's idea to its logical conclusion: in a liberal-capitalist society, in which knowledge and "data" drive economic growth, school was just the beginning. According to Ohliger, by the later twentieth century, adult learning, as a freely chosen, self-directed activity, was being systematically eradicated in favour of the technocratically planned and administered "lifelong learning" of utilitarian economic and social "skills" – the two being increasingly entangled. Adding insult to injury, what Ohliger called "mandatory continuing education" would be presented as a mark of individual improvement, rather than the result of compulsion, if not coercion. Though he was considered eccentric by his conservative contemporaries, history has vindicated John Ohliger. In the twenty-first century, his dystopic vision has become all too real, even commonsensical. From neoliberalism's assault on public and tertiary education, to elite enthusiasm for imposing STEM education upon students, to the OECD's post-COVID efforts to make social and economic "resilience" training a basic part of educational policy,[47] Ohliger's insights are essential to a critical understanding our contemporary socio-educational environment. Just as important, Ohliger refused to lose hope in the face of these daunting pressures, and he implored his readers to do the same. As one of his favourite maxims has it, "Learning is a delicate but durable plant. It should be nurtured respectfully, tenderly, and with a warm sense of humor."[48] For Ohliger, MCE was essentially inhumane. To beat back these powerful forces, we must respond with an educational politics that has a radical warmth and humanism at its centre.

NOTES

1 Jeff Zacharakis, "Icons and Pariahs: Mentorship and the Archeology of Adult Education," in *Challenging the Professionalization of Adult Education: John Ohliger and Contradictions in Modern Practice*, ed. André P. Grace, Tonette S. Rocco, and associates (San Francisco: Jossey-Bass, 2009), 187–8; André P. Grace and Tonette S. Rocco, "Mediating Challenges in Adult Education and Culture: John Ohliger's Radical Social Project," in Grace et al., eds., *Challenging the Professionalization of Adult Education*, 20.

2   Zacharakis, "Icons and Pariahs," 188; André P. Grace and Tonette S. Rocco, "John Funnell Ohliger: A Brief Biography of His Life and Vocations," in Grace et al., eds., *Challenging the Professionalization of Adult Education*, 8.

3   John Ohliger, "Adult Education in a World of Excessive Riches/Excessive Poverty," JohnOhliger.org, accessed 2 September 2020, http://www.johnohliger.org /adultedworld.pdf.

4   Paul Mattingly, *American Academic Cultures: A History of Higher Education* (Chicago: University of Chicago Press, 2017), 2.

5   President's Commission on Higher Education, *Higher Education for American Democracy*, vol. 1, *Establishing the Goals* (New York: Harper and Brothers, 1947), 972.

6   Clark Kerr, *The Uses of the University*, 5th ed. (Cambridge, MA: Harvard University Press, 2001), 13–14, xii.

7   Ohliger, "Adult Education in a World of Excessive Riches."

8   Ohliger.

9   Gordon Selman, *Invisible Giant: A History of Adult Education in BC* (Vancouver: Centre for Continuing Education, University of British Columbia, 1988), 43.

10 Ralf St. Clair and Bernd Käpplinger, "Alley or Autobahn? Assessing 50 Years of the Andragogical Project," in *Adult Education Quarterly* 71, no. 3 (2021): 274; Malcom Knowles, *The Modern Practice of Adult Education: From Pedagogy to Andragogy*, revised and updated (New York: Adult Education Company, 1980), 18–19.

11 Andreas Fejes and Erik Nylander, "Introduction: Mapping the Research Field on Adult Education and Learning," in *Mapping Out the Research Field of Adult Education and Learning*, ed. Andreas Fejes and Erik Nylander (Cham: Springer Nature Switzerland, 2019), 6.

12 Michael Welton, *Unearthing Canada's Hidden Past: A Short History of Adult Education* (Toronto: Thompson Publishing, 2013), 197.

13 Tim Rogan, *The Moral Economists: R.H. Tawney, Karl Polanyi, E.P. Thompson, and the Critique of Capitalism* (Princeton, NJ: Princeton University Press, 2018), 3.

14 Eduard Christian Lindeman, *The Meaning of Adult Education* (New York: New Republic, 1926), 5.

15 John Ohliger, *Listening Groups: Mass Media in Adult Education* (Brookline, MA: Center for the Study of Liberal Education for Adults, 1967), 1.

16 Welton, *Unearthing Canada's Hidden Past*, 201.

17 Ohliger, *Listening Groups*, 1, 3, 45.

18 Ohliger, "Adult Education in a World of Excessive Riches."

19 John Ohliger "The Integration of Continuing Education in Community Colleges" (1968), Institute of Education Studies, accessed 18 September 2020, https://files .eric.ed.gov/fulltext/ED029188.pdf. Quotes at 2, 4, and 3.

20 Ohliger, "Adult Education in a World of Excessive Riches"; Ohliger "The Integration of Continuing Education."

21 Ohliger, "Adult Education in a World of Excessive Riches."

22 John Ohliger, "Adult Basic Education and the Liberal Arts Approach," in *Workshop in Adult Basic Education* (Columbus: Center for Adult Education, College of Education, Ohio State University, 1970), 73.

23 Paul Smeyers and Marc Depaepe, eds., *Educational Research: The Educationalization of Social Problems* (Gent: Springer Netherlands, 2008); Rosa Bruno-Jofré, ed., *Educationalization and Its Complexities: Religion, Politics, and Technology* (Toronto: University of Toronto Press, 2019).

24 Ohliger, "Adult Education in a World of Excessive Riches," 12.

25 Quoted in Zacharakis, "Icons and Pariahs," 190.

26 John Ohliger and Colleen McCarthy, *Lifelong Learning or Lifelong Schooling? A Tentative View of the Ideas of Ivan Illich with a Quotational Bibliography* (Syracuse, NY: Publications in Continuing Education, 1971), 16, 17–18, 18–19.

27 John Ohliger, "Adult Education: 1984," in Grace et al., eds., *Challenging the Professionalization of Adult Education*, 43–4.

28 Ohliger, 44.

29 Ohliger, 44–5, 45–6.

30 Ohliger, 46.

31 Zacharakis, "Icons and Pariahs," 191.

32 Edward Said, *Representations of the Intellectual* (New York: Vintage, 1996), 44, 43.

33 John Ohliger, "Is Lifelong Education a Guarantee of Permanent Inadequacy?," in Grace et al., eds., *Challenging the Professionalization of Adult Education*, 48.

34 Ohliger, 67.

35 Ohliger, 55, 56, 56–7, 57, 58–9, 57–8.

36 John Ohliger, "The Social Uses of Theorizing in Adult Education," in Grace et al., eds., *Challenging the Professionalization of Adult Education*, 66–9.

37 Colin Griffin, "National Policies and Lifelong Learning," in *The Routledge International Handbook of Lifelong Learning*, ed. Peter Jarvis (Oxon, UK: Routledge, 2009), 265–7.

38 Bill Clinton, "Clinton's Speech Accepting the Democratic Nomination for President," *New York Times*, 30 August 1996, https://www.nytimes.com/1996/08/30/us/clinton-s-speech-accepting-the-democratic-nomination-for-president.html.

39 Quoted in Richard Hatcher, "Academies and Diplomas: Two Strategies for Shaping the Future Workforce," *Oxford Review of Education* 34, no. 6 (2008): 665.

40 Anthony Giddens, *The Third Way: The Renewal of Social Democracy* (London: Polity, 1998), 101.

41 Leitch Review of Skills, *Prosperity for All in the Global Economy – World Class Skills* (Norwich, UK: Her Majesty's Stationery Office, 2006), 9.

42 "What Have We Learnt from the 2008 Crisis?," Organisation for Economic Co-operation and Development, accessed 13 February 2021, https://www.oecd.org/naec/lessons-from-the-crisis/#lessons-from-the-financial-crisis.

43 Phebe Moore, *The International Political Economy of Work and Employability* (Hampshire, UK: Palgrave Macmillan, 2010), 71–2, 103, 40.

44 Innovation, Science and Economic Development Canada, *Building a Nation of Innovators* (Ottawa: Innovation, Science and Economic Development Canada, 2019), 25, https://ised-isde.canada.ca/site/innovation-better-canada/sites/default /files/attachments/New_ISEDC_19-044_INNOVATION-SKILLS_E_web.pdf.

45 Ohliger, "Adult Education: 1984," 46.

46 Ivan Illich, *Celebration of Awareness: A Call for Institutional Revolution* (Harmondsworth, UK: Pelican, 1980), 106.

47 Organisation for Economic Co-operation and Development, *An Assessment of the Impact of COVID-19 on Job and Skills Demand Using Online Job Vacancy Data* (Paris: OECD, 2021), 2.

48 T.S. Eliot, quoted in John Ohliger, "Forum: You Shall Know the Truth and the Truth Shall Make You Laugh," in Grace et al., eds., *Challenging the Professionalization of Adult Education*, 90.

PART FOUR

Freire and Illich and Indigeneity

dichroic yet clear

Alan Wilkinson

12 From *Nutrix Educat* to *Ju-jum Dakim:* A Possible Resolution for Ivan Illich's Forsaken Ritual

CHRIS BEEMAN

Educare and *Nutrix Educat*

The Rivers North of the Future: The Testament of Ivan Illich as Told to David Cayley holds a curious passage. In it, Ivan Illich gives an account of the etymological journey he made in consulting ancient Latin dictionaries while trying to establish the original use of the term *educare*, the infinite form of the Latin verb that is the root of the English "educate." That he made an examination of the roots of central terms is not at all curious, but where the journey ended is something of a riddle.

Recall that *The Rivers North of the Future* comprises some of the last interviews David Cayley conducted with Ivan Illich, at the very end of the 1990s, not long before Illich's death in 2002. Cayley reports that the conversations from which the first chapters of the book were derived were not conventional interviews, but rather consisted, on Illich's request, of Illich riffing, with Cayley attending and occasionally prompting. Because these conversations happened later in his life, Illich was in a position to reflect back on his previously held ideas and theories, which he often revised. The conversations are especially useful because Illich is able to contextualize some thought or other, while giving the "back story" to his deeply personal philosophical journey. At least in the first phase of his life as a public intellectual, each new theoretical leap is revealed to have been inspired by particular events.

A case in point is how Illich's interest in public education derived from his time in Puerto Rico. In 1956, when he became vice-rector of the Catholic University of Puerto Rico, Illich encountered a stark contrast between the inflated claims regarding the value of public education and what actually went on. In Puerto Rico and other countries of the Global South, there appeared to be a universal commitment to public education, accompanied by proclamations of its key role in development.[1]When Illich was confronted with the evidence, though, the contradiction between education's claimed value and its actual benefit baffled him. Illich later explored these ideas in more detail in *Deschooling Society* (1971), in which his critique of universal public schooling was extended to all places, including the developed world. I will explore the bigger intellectual story behind Illich's views in this chapter. But in the etymological journey I began with – the origins of the word "educate" – Illich notes that, since the mid-nineteenth century, *educare* was understood to derive from *ex* (out) and *ducere* (to lead): literally, then, it meant to lead outward.[2] To lead outward from what and to what, we do not know. The Online Etymology Dictionary traces this meaning of *educare* further back than this, to the mid-fifteenth century. It notes some cognates in various languages, with the "to bring up" meaning predominating in some. Schooling is first mentioned as part of its meaning in the 1580s. This dictionary cautions against a figurative interpretation of the phrase "to lead outward."[3]

But Illich looked further, this time at the really, really big, ancient Latin dictionaries. And on this consultation, finding a passage from Cicero, he came across the phrase *nutrix educat*. This phrase couples the noun for wet nurse (a person who breastfeeds), *nutrix*, with the third-person singular form of the verb, *educare*. Prima facie, this looks like "the wet nurse educates." But Illich finds that the phrase actually means "the wet nurse suckles." He is confident in this interpretation because, in literary passages contemporary with the earlier meanings described above, he finds that other verbs, such as *docere* and *instruire*, rather than *educare*, are used to refer to teaching. In fact, Illich notes that in the first two centuries of the Common Era, the verb *educare* was only used in the sense of breastfeeding. So, at least according to Illich, we can assume that this earlier meaning was commonly used (at least in the recorded canon) as the primary meaning at the time to which Illich refers. I have not had access to very, very large Latin dictionaries during the pandemic, so I am happy to assume that Illich is correct.[4]

Illich deduces from this, then, that at an earlier time, the verb *educare* meant to breastfeed a baby. Or, perhaps more broadly, with a view to where my argument is going, *to nourish* an infant. What might be the connection between the two meanings, earlier and later? Is it that in the earlier use, the infant is nourished by milk, then later, by knowledge? Or is it that it is milk, from the breast, that is first "led outward," and then, in its more modern sense, that something else is led outward from (or fed to) the learner?

Then, in the passage in *The Rivers North of the Future*, the etymological investigation abruptly stops. Illich goes elsewhere. This may be as a result of the above-mentioned, riffing-not-being-interviewed format. Maybe Illich had just found another thought that interested him more. Or, maybe – in the next breath, it seems – in reverting to talking again about public education in Puerto Rico, Illich assumes that the point implicit in the etymological journey he has just made has been understood and needs no further explanation. But the recollection of the word's etymology sustains, resonating a little like the muttered word "Rosebud" at the beginning of Orson Wells's film *Citizen Kane.*[5] It tints the rest of the discussion.

The curious jump in Illich's talk leaves the reader to make sense of it, and, on first blush, it appears that its purpose may be to simply lead up to the point that I will make in more detail later: that the ritual of education is linked to the ritual of the church. But I see more than that. In this chapter, I will go on a kind of quest as well, but the nourishing font I come to is of quite a different kind than Illich's. To make this quest, I have to return to Illich's own intellectual journey in considering and encountering schooling and education. His conceptualization of education happens in three phases.

Tracing Illich's Three Intellectual Encounters with Schooling and Education

Illich's early theorizing appears to derive from practical contexts and particular, traceable events in his life, but it often does so in complex ways. In addition to the detailed critique of universal public schooling included in *Deschooling Society*, the account of the progression of Illich's theorizing around education that I use here comes from Illich's foreword to Matt Hern's *Deschooling Our Lives* (1996); from David Cayley's *Ivan Illich in Conversation* (1992); and from David Cayley's *The Rivers North of the Future* (2005). Rosa Bruno-Jofré and Jon Igelmo Zaldívar's excellent summary, "Ivan Illich's Late Critique of *Deschooling Society*" (2012), helped to guide the process.

Cayley's works give very clear descriptions of Illich's early life. These include his Catholic devotion and dedication to the downtrodden. There is not space to give a full account of Illich's life here, but a few things need to be said. Ivan Illich was a Catholic priest, from an old, aristocratic European family, his mother's side coming from the region around Vienna and his father's side from the Dalmatian coast. His encounters with issues of social justice come from the perspective of a devout Catholic dedicated to living in the world in an ethical manner as defined by Catholic Christianity. His origins thus both define and limit his critique. But given his origins and context, the solutions he proposes may be considered uncomfortably progressive for a conservative church. For example, in 1960, he was forced to leave Puerto Rico after criticizing the Catholic Church for intervening on the issue of birth control there.[6]

It occurs to me that, in a less historically focused way and without using the terms "genealogy" and "archaeology,"[7] Illich's projects overlapped and sometimes anticipated Foucault's. Or perhaps it is simply that, fifty years ago, our planet, which was then so much larger, permitted separate spheres of operation. For a brief time in the 1970s, Illich was an intellectual and popular star in North America. Foucault was better known in Europe. Foucault's most recognized contributions occurred over a longer period of time, and his ideas initially appealed more to an academic audience. In the 1970s, fame did not extend globally as readily as it does in a Web-based world. Thus, it was possible for both Illich and Foucault to be working on parallel tracks in related areas of thought, without much interaction or apparent intellectual engagement. In terms of the similarities of their projects, among other things, both Foucault and Illich were concerned with institutions and social performances that were commonly so taken for granted as to almost go unnoticed. Both were aware, in differing ways, of power relations being played out through public institutions. Both had an interest in re-examining the unquestioned value of some public institutions. Both in particular addressed social institutions that had come to be beyond doubt. Regarding their differences, the social institutions Illich examined appeared to be regarded as needing radical resuscitation. Foucault's enduring quest is considered the relationship between power and knowledge. While such themes are implicit in Illich's work as well, Illich appeared to be more focused on the societal institutions in which these played out. And, as Charles Taylor points out in the Forward to *The Rivers North of the Future*, Illich's recurrent thesis is that the modern world can only ever be truly understood as a corruption and mutation of Christianity.[8]

Illich's insights and critiques were radical enough that, within the context of the conservative Catholic Church, he is rightly called an iconoclast. But as noted above, he is an iconoclast who also happened to be a devout Catholic, and from a wealthy and old European aristocratic family. As refreshing as many of his insights were, the reference point for change was rooted in the stability of Catholic Christianity. Illich would never be one of the downtrodden he tried to help through his work. That said, he was still one of the citizens of the modern West, and so he suffered, even if only superficially, some of the ill effects of what he viewed as the blundering and predicable way in which various aspects of organized modern culture became the mutated offspring of Christianity.

In several of the sources listed at the beginning of this chapter, Illich gives a retrospective account of the three major phases in his own orientation to schooling and education. Illich is able to reflect on the difference between what he was doing in his earlier life (and sometimes what he thought he was doing) and his later recognition of where these ideas led. I think, in part, because the sudden changes in the direction of Illich's life were based on what might be called instinct – or perhaps, in Christian terms, the response to a call – hindsight provided him a clearer orientation to his overall intellectual direction than he may have been aware of at the time he was actually engaged in new areas of thought. In this section, I will refer to these sources because they are the places Illich eventually came to, but I will also refer to his *Deschooling Society* to look at what Illich initially said about schooling and education. In particular, I wish to note the contributions of Rosa Bruno-Jofré and Jon Igelmo Zaldívar's earlier analysis of the three phases in Illich's intellectualizing. They point out that these phases actually represented different epistemological orientations.[9]

The first phase consisted in what Illich initially attempted in *Deschooling Society*.[10] As noted above, this work emerged from Illich's real-world experience with the contradictory nature of public education, which he learned through his role as vice-rector at the Catholic University at Ponce, in Puerto Rico, from 1956 to 1960. This position automatically made him a member of the board that governed education for the country. Illich learned from this work that, in stark opposition to what was said about it, public schooling did not decrease social inequality, but increased it; did not benefit the poor, but degraded them; did not create opportunity, but curtailed it; did not open possibility, but restricted it further for those already disadvantaged – in short, it did the opposite of everything it promised. And yet, schooling was seen by all, but most emphatically by poor societies like Puerto Rico, to be of unquestionable benefit to all its citizens.[11]

The abiding faith in the virtue of schooling that Illich witnessed, despite its manifest failings, was in part responsible for Illich's seeing a connection between schools and the Catholic Church. For Illich, the only way to understand such devotion to a failed social entity was to see schooling as based on faith and as a kind of ritual. Returning, finally, to the etymological quest I began this chapter with, Illich's encounter with the phrase *nutrix educat* appeared to prompt a conceptual understanding. It is not clear from his story if the phrase precipitated it. In my account of this etymological journey, I left out a small part of Illich's discovery. It was that, after *educare*'s initial meaning of breastfeeding, which Illich traced from Cicero through to the second century of the Common Era, there came a new passage with a changed orientation, from Tertullian. At this time, the use of the verb was associated with priests giving knowledge to the faithful. In a literal reading, priests were breastfeeding the flock. Thus, the meaning of *educare* came to be moved from breastfeeding an infant to the nourishment that presumably came from the scriptures, through the offices of the priest. In this way, *educare* became linked with faith. For Illich, the realization made him feel sick to his stomach.[12] From the perspective of a priest who was suddenly drawn into trying to understand the Puerto Rican government's devotion to universal public education despite its evident failure, Illich began to see the symbolic connection of public education to the kind of ritual that occurred in organized religion. The same faith was required to make it work. Through the idea of ritual, Illich began to make sense of the otherwise inexplicable hold that universal public education had on developed and developing societies. And this is why, in a moment of recognition, Illich felt sick. The myth-creating ritual of education assured its continuance as much as it ensured its failure.

This passage might help to explain why, in Cayley's interview, Illich abruptly moves on, Rosebud-like, to other things. Perhaps the malaise brought on by his earlier recognition of the emptiness of the project of public education persisted. But this idea ultimately led, through Illich's interest in ecclesiology, to the thought that modern society as whole, in the West and its colonies, could best be explained as forms of secularized, Christian ritual, or, as David Cayley puts it, "as a mutation of Christianity."[13] Schooling's ritualistic nature would help to explain the broad acceptance of contradictory expectations, outcomes, and prescriptions: every failed outcome could be met with the answer that more schooling (and faith in it) was what was lacking. Illich used the term "mythopoesis," a myth-generating ritual, to describe schooling.[14]

Illich is especially well known for an intensive period of writing from 1971 to 1976, when he was director of CIDOC, the Centre for Intercultural Documentation, in Cuernavaca. CIDOC examined various aspects of modernity that were generally considered to be above question, including education, medicine, transportation, and tool use. Illich wrote four books during this time, all of which engaged societal institutions whose broad societal value was unquestioned. These included *Deschooling Society* (1971) and *Tools for Conviviality* (1973). Consideration of the role of ritual extended from the church to the social institutions that, in Illich's conceptualization, replaced the church.

In his earlier work in Puerto Rico, Illich had met Edward Reimer, and it was through their engagement that the two men began to ask the following, and to their mind novel, question: What is schooling?[15] Or, as Illich later would ask, "what do schools do when I put into parenthesis their claim to educate?"[16] This question is similar to Foucault's interest in "what what [people] do does."[17]

The correspondence between Reimer and Illich went on for many years until, in 1971, CIDOC provided the right context for the latter's seminal book. Illich tells the story in *Deschooling Society* of how it was brought to life. In the spring and summer months of 1970, Illich would present a chapter each Wednesday to interested CIDOC discussants, including John Goodman, Paulo Freire, and Gustavo Esteva, who had gathered there and who critiqued his work.

As Illich notes in his foreword to *Deschooling Our Lives* and elsewhere,[18] it was the president of Harper and Row, which published the book, who was responsible for the misleading title. One can understand the appeal of a simpler title to a popular press. But as Illich established in his conversations with Cayley, the book was not about eradicating schools altogether – "deschooling" – but changing the nature of schooling by "disestablishing" it.

Illich uses "disestablish" in a technical sense. He means by it the same process by which the United States disestablishes churches. As Cayley notes, the First Amendment of the Constitution of the United States of America reads, "The State shall make no law with respect to the establishment of religion."[19] Illich makes a parallel case for how schools should be treated. Schools can still exist, but they should not be given any particular support by the state.

According to Illich, removing public support through this process of disestablishment would achieve at least two things. First, it would undercut the expectation of that formal schooling should be universal, and so would not contribute to the growing phenomenon, both in the developed and the underdeveloped world, of formal education being perceived as – and thus, in a self-fulfilling way, becoming – a necessity. Second, no special privileges would be given to those people who attended schools. For instance, the requiring of credentials would be made illegal. The argument went that to protect what was valuable in education, schools needed to be disestablished. In other words, the greater good of education was being threatened by the destructive effect of schooling.[20] The book had not yet been published when Illich began to question this idea.

In the second phase, which, by Illich's account, began just before *Deschooling Society* was to come out, Illich recognized a theme that was latent in the book, but that had not yet clearly emerged: that rather than schools, it was the Western preoccupation with education itself that ought to be the focus of concern. He was becoming aware that there was already underway a kind of migration of education into non-formal settings. Or, as he later put it, "This talk of 'lifelong learning' and 'learning needs' has thoroughly polluted society, and not just schools, with the stench of education."[21] If schools were to be disestablished, the alternative ought not to be a new kind of education, or the seeping of education into every aspect of life. Nor would the solution be to get rid of schools altogether, because schools could sometimes serve a useful function. And the greater good would not be achieved by allowing education to flourish in new ways, a many-headed Gorgon that would find expression in a neoliberal context as just another personal item to be consumed. Illich's and CIDOC's proposed solution was to encourage a different kind of relationship between people and tools. This statement might seem abstruse until it is understood that, in Illich's phrasing, "tool" is a simpler word for "technology," and that he and CIDOC regarded education as a kind of technology. The idea that simply eliminating schools would not solve the underlying problem of education was the substance of the essay published in *Saturday Review* during the same the week that *Deschooling Society* was published. Once again, this new insight hid another.

In the third phase, which Illich traces to the cusp of the 1980s, he recognized a flaw in his own theorizing: until this time, the question had been whether education in its current form was a suitable means for an accepted end. In the third, historical phase of his investigations, Illich began to question the nature and value of education itself. In these investigations, he came to realize that the underlying difference between education and learning was perceived scarcity.

Thus, education became societally justified when the possibility of learning was, either through artificial means or real limitations, perceived as being scarce.[22] Of course, a central principle of neoliberalism is creating perceived scarcity to increase value. Perhaps in this way Illich's initial conundrum over what education claimed it could do for the Puerto Rican people versus what it actually did came to be resolved: education, the publicly condoned form of learning, is intended to order and separate not ideas but people, and to be consumed by those who can afford it. It is also there to promulgate the notion of scarcity, thus ensuring its own continuance in a particular context. Through ritual of the kind Illich saw in the phrase *nutrix educat*, the institution continued without being seriously challenged.

Ju-jum Dakim (Djoo-djoo N'dakim) and Another Way of Educating

At this point, I want to ask about the opposite of scarcity – specifically, a kind of learning that Illich points to but does not spend much time on: learning in a context of abundance. Of course, David Jardine has a book with a similar title. Here, I am not considering a phenomenological approach, which makes all curricula continually re-encountered, reinvented, and therefore perpetually abundant. I am thinking of the more-than-human world around us, always open to our learning. I want to ask, what if there were a kind of *educare* that could include the sense of nourishing an infant as well as nourishing an adult, such that the threat of scarcity is never experienced? Would this permit the two ideas that are obliged to be opposed in Illich's thought – education and learning – to be actually allied?

For me, a bell rang when I read Illich's passage on education being predicated on scarcity. It was the bell of two different things spoken to me by Elders,[23] spaced decades apart, that I happened to remember at this moment. The first was from Alex Mathias, an Elder with whom I have worked for about two decades now. It was his explanation of the phrase (in Teme Augama Anishinabemowin) that I transliterated then as *ju-jum dakim*.

A brief note of linguistic explanation is needed here. Throughout our conversations, when I was writing things down, Alex reminded me that the language he speaks derives in part from the place in which it his spoken: his family (Misa'bi) territory, within unceded Teme Augama Anishinaabe (also written as Timeaugama Anishinaabe) territory. He requested several times that when I wrote the words that he spoke in his own language, I "just write them down like they sound." I like this idea (despite the limitations and confusions of English) because Alex is resisting the regularization of representation of sounds. Alex is also one of the approximately three living speakers of his dialect. Speakers, not writers. Alex is less interested in writing than in speaking a language that is living and thus in constant flux.

Standardization has benefits for communication between diverse speakers of a language like Anishinabemowin, with diverse pronunciations. But such regularization also leads to precisely the same kind of exclusion that Alex (and Illich, through the formalization of education) feared. And it could be argued that, despite this being a language of resistance, formalizing it through writing can be viewed as an aspect of the same kind of abstraction and standardization of thinking that underlies the project of colonization. Imagine the trauma for an Elder if a new linguistic standardization – that was written down, and therefor appeared reliable – came to dominate or replace the still-living knowledge contained in the being of persons. Or, perhaps more accurately, that was expressed in the co-being between people and place.

On the other hand, English letters do not reproduce sounds reliably. Yet I wanted to avoid technical phonetic spelling because this excludes many readers. But I also wanted to ensure that I did not unduly obfuscate meaning for interested future scholars, particularly those interested in local dialect. We agreed to check my spelling with people in the local area, if possible.[24]

In many cases, after consulting standard Anishinabemowin orthography, the sounds Alex spoke simply did not sound like any standard written expression. Nuances of sound were missing. I am not a linguist. But what I heard Alex say on my many requests for repetition seemed different than the standardized spellings. So, if I wrote the words the way they were *supposed* to be written by those determining standard speech, I would be ignoring Alex's pronunciation. And we would potentially be losing something of value contained in that difference.

There is one more thing: the above views on standardized orthography perhaps place the *comprehension* of language above the complex differences contained in its *expression*, which is perhaps especially true in the context of a dialect or language that is still not standardized. By this I mean that standardization makes it easier for a person looking up a word to find a standard spelling. But from the point of view of the speaker, this permits less range in variation in sound and expression. To some extent, this is understandable. But there is another view, which is that, as much as possible, accuracy within the land and territory that the language is spoken, whether or not this can be synchronized with that of other areas, might be of even greater significance. What I have decided to do here is to meet Alex's request: to write things down the way they sound. This is not as straightforward as it may sound, for the reasons given above. But I have used letters that most frequently make the sounds Alex spoke. I include in parentheses after the word or phrase the standardized spelling, if I have been able to find it.

Alex gave the meaning of *ju-jum dakim* (*djoo-djoo N'dakim*) as "mother earth." But, he also noted the etymology, connecting *ju-jum* to a mother's breast. I knew *aki* (earth) from the term he used, *Daki Menan* (*N'dakimenan*), meaning "land of ours." So, *ju-jum dakim* brings together the land with the idea of nourishment gained from the mother: with sustenance. It was the place that nourished, or that sustained in the way that a mother would. It is the place of the original food, of the most nourishing kind. It is the comforting relationship that contains it.

There is another story from another Elder that goes with this one, that I will mention in a moment. But there is also this detail to the first story. Alex Mathias is the hereditary head of his family territory. Indigenous hereditary governance has recently gained in public profile. For example, the Wet'suwet'en protest against the Coastal GasLink pipeline is based on a position taken by heredi-tary chiefs, not representatives elected through the band council system. The latter was a system of governance designed and approved by the Government of Canada through the Indian Act (1876). Many have criticized this system of governance because representatives elected under it are ultimately responsible to the Crown. Thus, it has been criticized for sometimes functioning to control First Nations, rather than represent them. Hereditary systems of governance have frequently been associated with resistance to neoliberal development that threatens the important relationship with *ju-jum dakim*. The point of noting this is that Alex holds his hereditary position because his father passed the territory down to him. The reason his father did so is because, as he told Alex, Alex was the only person who knew how to live there.

To the mind of *homo mobilis* – the state of being of the modern West – this makes no sense. How could only one person know how to live in a place? But to a person who understands the depth of intimate connection with a place that is needed for something like mutual understanding between people and place to unfold, the relationship looks quite different. Alex has been taught about this particular land by the person who best understood it, his father, who himself learned this through his family's long history there. And the land itself was co-teacher. Alex has been taught how to find food, and shelter, and a livelihood, in this particular place. This is not just a case of picking up a few tips on how to trap and hunt. This is a case of understanding specific information that has to do with human-place interaction in a unique location. This information and interpretation has been tested and proved, and then has evolved through centu-ries of inhabiting. Or better, co-habiting between humans and place.

But it is also about a reciprocal love of a place based on careful and conscious being, such that the well-being of both the place and the human participants are assured. This kind of learning is explicitly not a form of *education* in the way in which it is understood in the modern West. It is certainly not schooling. In fact, one might claim that the reason Alex was able to learn this unique knowledge, and to stabilize and honour his kinship relations through enacting this knowl-edge, is because his progressively minded and prudent father was able to nego-tiate Alex's legal requirement to attend conventional schooling by substituting correspondence courses at a time when this was rarely done. Many Indigenous people felt obliged to relinquish the possibility of their way of life continuing, succumbing to the overwhelming force of public education. Just as in Illich's experiences in Puerto Rico, the ill effects of public schooling become most visible at the margins. A tragic outcome of this was that many students in residential schools lost their connection to their families and to the land. What Alex's story reveals is that even when schools did not take the form of distant residential schools, and were actually located within First Nations, the cycle of public education prevented families from being on their family territory for most of the year. The only time when school was not in session was during summer, when relatively little trapping and hunting tended to be done.[25] The obligation for children to be in school served to break people's connection with the land, by breaking the cycle of land-based living. Most families opted to live with their children, who were attending school on the First Nation. So seasonal patterns of hunting, trapping, guiding, and finding a living on the land were lost. Alex's family managed to counter this trend. They lived for almost the whole year on their family territory, with Alex doing lessons by correspondence.

The cult of education that would separate whole nations from their traditional patterns of living is similar to what Illich saw in Puerto Rico and in Central America in the third quarter of the twentieth century, with the move from subsistence poverty to "modernized poverty," which Illich deemed among the most cruel aspects of development's "war on subsistence."[26] Alex's family managed to maintain the nurturing part of the idea of "education," which is the opposite of what Illich saw enacted in other parts of the Global South. This occurred through Alex's parents' recalling, reaffirming, and enacting the necessary located-ness of knowing and learning. Formal schooling and education could not provide the kind of learning that emerged in this kinship relationship. And there was no scarcity here of the kind Illich identifies, which makes formal education seem necessary: less human-controlled places, with few other humans, meant that the natural world was always present in the nourishing it provided, to both the spirit and the body.

A Place That Can Feed You

The bell also rang when I recalled the words spoken to me about two decades ago by another Elder, Michael Paul. On Alex and his partner's request, I was making a documentary film to help protect a spirit place from clear-cut forestry. Alex had arranged for several Elders to come and speak with me, so that their voices could be heard in the film. Michael was one of them. At one point in our conversation, recalling his own upbringing, which for part of the year was in the bush, Michael paused, looked around, made a broad sweep of his arm to gesture at the world surrounding us, and said, "This! This was my education." In this moment, Michael was referring to the world as a teacher in the more conventional sense, the way we generally use "education" now. But he also meant that it freely gave relevant lessons to his own survival. So, for him to be *educated* was also for him to be raised in such a way that he was taken care of, and, as above, nourished. If he paid attention, he was rewarded, on balance, with having his needs met, being in relatively good health, and experiencing himself as deeply interconnected with an ecosystem. His reciprocal responsibility, in this position, was to take care of the land. This is a quality that Alex Mathias has extended and to which he has devoted the past several decades of his life: a duty to protect the spaces in the natural world for which he is responsible. In this case, that responsibility entails his family territories, the traditional Misa'bi lands.

Just now I wrote "duty," but as soon as I did, I was aware that it was not quite the right word. There is certainly an aspect of duty in this, but it is not everything. As Illich reminds Cayley, it is not duty that motivates the Samaritan, but a response to an internal call. I am not suggesting that humans are the Samaritans in a human-nature relationship, despite the ravaged state in which the natural world now finds itself. I mean, rather, that the nature of connection with the land goes much deeper than simply a sense of responsibility for something that is apart from oneself. It is more a sense of feeling actual kinship with another being. This is something that is difficult to understand from the perspective of the modern West. It is not simply love, entertainment, fascination, or appeal; it is a way of being in the world in which human-place interconnection makes simple, individualized, selfish, human-oriented thought much more difficult to effect. This is not because of the force of some abstract ethical standard. Rather, as kinship comes to be understood, one recognizes selfishly that the well-being of an ecosystem is also the well-being of oneself. The border of the skin stops being the limitation of the person. And the recognition is not an intellectual awareness, but an affective experience of an enacted relationship.

The responsibility I am getting at here, if there is one, is based on a felt and experienced shared kinship, rather than the "stewardship" model that is still so common in Western conceptions of human responsibility for the natural world. In this relationship, human well-being and ecosystem well-being are ensured through shared being.

Michael also said, "This place ... well it feeds me ... and it'll feed you." Around this point in our conversation, I was aware that Michael, who seemed to me very articulate, was nonetheless struggling to find words (or concepts) with which to express this idea. But the core of what Michael was getting at was agency in the natural world, something that has recently gained new momentum with the work in new materialisms. After all, he didn't say, "You can find food here." He said, "this place ... [w]ill feed you."[27]

In my interpretation of Michael's words, I see the coupling of two notions of education that have come up in this chapter already. The first, which is relevant to more conventional ideas of "educating," is that it is the place that teaches, but with the result of a mutually beneficial relationship of care. With this idea, if you pay attention, you are given the lessons in how to survive, and you come to belong. The second idea of education corresponds with the meaning of nourishment, and, following Michael's words, it is clearly the *place* that nourishes. With this idea, the place gives you not only the knowledge of how to live there, but also sustains you while you are gaining such knowledge. It is like a full scholarship. Your only responsibility is to care for the place that cares for you in this way. Both ideas begin with agency of the place. The one who is taught – or who is nourished – is the learning recipient.

In this way of educating, we learn in conjunction with place, the place that is not only nourishing us and imparting knowledge but also giving us belonging. It is more the soul or spirit than the mind, if these could ever be conceptualized separately, that learns. And, what is learned is not "education" in Illich's sense. What is learned occurs through interaction with a loving, agential other, with infinite capacity to accommodate all forms of learners.

Another Teacher

I want to turn here to one other teacher who has helped me along the way, some of whose ideas are in mind as I write this. In Robyn Wall Kimmerer's *Braiding Sweetgrass* (2013), what is most evident is not what she manages to say so clearly about Indigenous orientations to the world. Rather, she both describes them and enacts them in the same moment. She is a botanist trained in the Western scientific tradition: an academic tradition of scarcity, competition, and want. But she has also learned by observing the land and its participants, and she has stayed in the company of Elders. Her interactions with the land are not those of an objective observer, but an active participant in the world. In her chapter entitled "Allegiance to Gratitude," she writes,

> You can't listen to the [Haudenosaunee] Thanksgiving Address without feeling wealthy. And, while experiencing gratitude seems innocent enough, it is a revolutionary idea. In a consumer society, contentment is a radical proposition. Recognizing abundance rather than scarcity undermines an economy that thrives by creating unmet desires. Gratitude cultivates an ethic of fullness, but the economy needs emptiness. The Thanksgiving Address reminds you that you already have everything you need.[28]

In attempting to understand this idea, one could do worse than to substitute, as per Illich, the word "education" for every mention of "economy" and "consumer society." Thus, the revised statement would read, "In education, contentment is a radical proposition. Recognizing abundance rather than scarcity undermines an education that thrives by creating unmet desires ... education needs emptiness."

And this is not a coincidence. Illich's critique of education was based on a broader understanding of how industrial-scale consumer capitalism works.[29] Illich was not successful in deschooling society, nor did he have a solution to the scarcity of schooling and education. His contribution was perhaps more the formulating of an original critique, and this deepened with his later explorations of the origins of education.[30] Illich, like many scholars, was not able to see all the evidence. In Illich's context, it was the Catholic Church, his training as a priest in it, and his devotion to it, that both provided the context for his deeply radical critique to emerge, but that also constrained what other possibilities he was able to see.

Perhaps we ought not to look for a solution to the scarcity implied by the term "education," as Illich uses it, in the conventional contexts of education. Rather, we might seek out learning in contexts in which a new kind of thinking and being occurs. Perhaps Illich does have something like this in mind, in passages as far back as *Deschooling Society*, when he speaks of protecting education from schooling. What might not have occurred to him was just how abundant the world of learning is, when it extends not just into the more-than-human world, but to the relational epistemology that derives from and is understood to derive from knowing that is inseparable from a person's enacted relationship with the more-than-human. When it is the world that is co-learner (and co-teacher), learning itself is changed to a state of being that is incompatible with the state of scarcity investigated in Illich's ideas on education and schooling. It is a place of abundance and awareness. But a fuller exploration of this must remain the subject of another work.

NOTES

1   David Cayley, *The Rivers North of the Future: The Testament of Ivan Illich*. (Toronto: House of Anansi Press, 2005), 3.
2   Cayley, 143.
3   Online Etymology Dictionary, s.v. "educate," accessed 26 March 2021, https://www.etymonline.com/search?q=educate.
4   Cayley, *The Rivers North of the Future*, 143–4.
5   The film *Citizen Kane* is based in part on the real-life character of William Randolph Hearst, the newspaper tycoon. "Rosebud," is the first word uttered in the film, and the dying words of the ruthlessly successful Kane. The film's flashbacks parallel the news reporter's quest to find the meaning of Kane's last words.

The reporter is our way in. But Rosebud is never explained to the reporter. Only the audience understands the meaning of the first word murmured at the beginning of the film, through the visual evidence provided in its last frames – and, come to think of it, last *flames*. This same feeling persists in this passage of Cayley's. The meaning, if there is one in Illich's diversion, figures like a mystery. I come back to this later in this chapter.

6 David Cayley, *Ivan Illich in Conversation* (Toronto: House of Anansi Press, 1992), 12.

7 In *The Rivers North of the Future*, Cayley does use the term "archeology" when he writes that "he wanted to undertake an archeology of modern 'certainties,' those ideas and feelings that seem to obvious and too 'natural' ever to be put into question" (19). I am speculating here, but it seems that Illich was dismantling in order to put back together again, under a known, supervening structure (Christianity). For most of his intellectual life, Foucault's dismantling held the (to some) terrifying, relativistic-seeming prospect of there being no known standard by which to judge competing theories.

8 Cayley, *The Rivers North of the Future*, x.

9 Rosa Bruno-Jofré and Jon Igelmo Zaldívar, "Ivan Illich's Late Critique of *Deschooling Society*: 'I Was Largely Barking Up the Wrong Tree,'" *Educational Theory* 62, no. 5 (2012): 573–92, https://doi.org/10.1111/j.1741-5446.2012.00464.x.

10 Ivan Illich, *Deschooling Society* (1971). I consulted the digital edition at https://archive.org/details/DeschoolingSociety.

11 Cayley *The Rivers North of the Future*, 140.

12 Cayley, 140–3.

13 Cayley, 1.

14 Matt Hern, *Deschooling Our Lives* (Gabriola Island, BC: New Society Publishers, 1996). Foreword by Ivan Illich.

15 Cayley, *The Rivers North of the Future*, 139.

16 Cayley, *Ivan Illich in Conversation*, 62.

17 The line from Foucault is as follows: "*People know* what *they do*; frequently *they know* why *they do* what *they do*; *but* what *they don't know* is what what *they do does*." Quoted in Hubert L. Dreyfus and Paul Rabinow, *Michel Foucault: Beyond Structuralism and Hermeneutics* (Chicago: University of Chicago Press, 1982), 187.

18 Hern, *Deschooling Our Lives*, vii

19 Cayley, *The Rivers North of the Future*, 13.

20 Illich, *Deschooling Society*, 1–23.

21 Hern, *Deschooling Our Lives*, viii.

22 Hern, ix.

23 I wish to recognize and thank the Elders with whom I have worked in the Temagami region, some of whom I have known for over two decades now. In this chapter are the words of Michael Paul, whom I met while responding to Alex

Mathias's request to make a documentary film to help protect the spirit place of Chiskon-Abikong in late 2000. Alex's stories emerged though participatory and collaborative research that has been ongoing in various forms for the past two decades.

24 As of the time of writing, I had tried on several occasions to check if there are standard spellings for Teme Augama Anishinaabe sounds, but I have not yet received a response.

25 Alex notes that fur quality improves late in the fall – usually November or December – as the animal adds a warmer coat. Quality diminishes with warmer weather. Many large animals like moose were best hunted in cold weather, when low surrounding temperatures simplified the work of preserving the flesh.

26 Cayley, *The Rivers North of the Future*, 7.

27 The new materialisms make a case for the agency and vibrancy of the more-than-human world. See Karen Barad, *Meeting the Universe Halfwa: Quantum Physics and the Entanglement of Matter and Meaning* (Durham, NC: Duke University Press, 2007); Jane Bennett, *Vibrant Matter: A Political Ecology of Things* (Durham, NC: Duke University Press, 2010).

28 Robin Wall Kimmerer, *Braiding Sweetgrass: Indigenous Wisdom, Scientific Knowledge and the Teachings of Plants* (Minneapolis: Milkweed Editions, 2013), 111.

29 Illich, *Deschooling Society*, 34–64.

30 See Rosa Bruno-Jofré and Jon Igelmo Zaldívar, "Ivan Illich's Late Critique of *Deschooling Society*," for an excellent examination of the epistemic changes in Illich's three phases of exploring education.

13 Reading *Pedagogy of the Oppressed* through the Lens of Indigenous Education: Reflections on Overlaps, Departures, and Social Developments

LINDSAY A. MORCOM

Introduction

Paulo Freire's *Pedagogy of the Oppressed* changed the way educators and social activists viewed the potential for anti-oppressive action through education. Interestingly, however, the work is not as widely cited in the field of Indigenous education as one might think. In some ways, it parallels the efforts and goals of Indigenous education as a tool for decolonization very closely. For example, in this text Freire calls attention to the need for conscientization for both the oppressed and the oppressor. He points out quite rightly that oppression cannot be overcome, and the full humanity of both groups cannot be realized, unless both are aware of the systems at play that reinforce and perpetuate oppression, and work to dismantle those systems. While the mechanisms of conscientization may differ for the oppressed and oppressor, for both, it is necessary to underscore the humanity of all members of society and question the societal mythologies that keep oppressive systems in place. It is also necessary to disrupt a "banking" model of education, whereby content is simply fed to learners, thus reinforcing existing oppressive systems.

However, Freire focuses largely on class-based oppression rather than colonial oppression, and so there are significant departures between Indigenous approaches and Freire's approach to conscientization as described in *Pedagogy of the Oppressed*. Freire's position is perhaps based in his cultural and geographic context, in which the oppressed are the disempowered majority and the oppressor the powerful minority. While such contexts are important to examine, the situation is different for Indigenous populations in Settler colonial contexts. There are also differences between this specific text and Indigenous philosophies regarding awareness of oppression; perspectives on leadership; resistance to assimilation that may be viewed as sectarianism; the relationship of humans to the natural world; the nature of progress; and the nature of dialogue as it relates to Indigenous and colonial language use. The goal of Indigenous education is not assimilation with the oppressor, but decolonization through conscientization to create education systems that critique colonialism, centre Indigenous ways of knowing, are guided by Indigenous languages, cultures, and philosophies, respect Indigenous concepts of relationship, and promote sovereignty and self-determination.[1]

Approach, Positionality, and Methodology

In writing this chapter, I acknowledge that my reflection is not representative of the entire cannon of Freire's work. I understand that Freire's thought developed as his lengthy career unfolded, but it is beyond the scope of a single chapter to critically encounter the entirety of his work. I therefore focus only on *Pedagogy of the Oppressed* as a seminal text. Moreover, I am not attempting to critique Freire as a person. Indeed, as Michael W. Apple points out in his reflection on his personal relationship with Freire, Freire himself was open and responded thoughtfully to critique, and he encouraged dialogue as a way to move forward in identifying commonalities between peoples. [2] While his focus remained on class inequality, Freire had a "constant struggle to expand his understanding of – and action against – the relations of dominance and subordination that are so deeply cemented into all of our societies."[3] Apple goes on to write that this included both gender and race, and that "when he spoke about the murderous histories of the treatment of Indigenous people in Brazil and throughout the world, this sense (that in many ways oppression was 'colour-coded') became even stronger."[4] I very much respect Freire's career-long fight to use education as a tool to dismantle oppressive systems, and I think there is much to be learned from his work in all areas of social justice education.

Still, the roots of *Pedagogy of the Oppressed* are firmly planted in the context of mid-twentieth-century Latin America, in which issues and philosophies surrounding land reform and classism were at the fore, and it is also informed by primarily European philosophies. These include post-Enlightenment principles such as progressivism, individualism, and democratization of society,[5] as well as Marxist and Christian philosophies.[6] The text does not address in detail the realities of colonial oppression as a cause of class inequality (and other forms of oppression) in Brazil as a Settler colonial state, or the need to adapt Freire's approach based on differences in cultural philosophies, values, and goals. As Apple writes, "a person can be fully committed to an emancipatory pedagogy in terms of class oppression and at the same time participate in the reproduction of racially oppressive categories and relations."[7] The text also fails to recognize what Crenshaw terms "intersectionality": that there are multiple forms of oppression, and that these intersect to impact people depending on their occupation of various oppressor/oppressed roles in society.[8]

Since it is not possible to critique the whole of Freire's body of work in a single chapter, I have approached *Pedagogy of the Oppressed* essentially as a qualitative data set. I have coded it for salient themes, and then compared those themes to the reflections of other authors on Freire's work, particularly *Pedagogy of the Oppressed*, as well on as critical pedagogy more broadly, both in philosophical and historical terms. I have done my best to enrich my perspective and ensure accuracy of Indigenous and critical philosophy by viewing this subject primarily with reference to Indigenous scholars and scholars of colour.[9] I will also be focusing largely on decolonization and Indigenous education in Settler colonial contexts outside of Latin America or the developing world. This is based on my own lived experience and expertise in the Canadian context. As such, the majority of works cited focus on decolonization in Western (and formerly British) Settler colonial states: Canada, the United States, Hawaii,[10] New Zealand, and Australia. I acknowledge that, like Freire, I have divided society via a false dichotomy of oppressor and oppressed, equated here as Settler (non-Indigenous) and Indigenous.[11] I am acutely aware as a person of mixed heritage that this dichotomy does not make space for the nuances of mixed identities. It also does not take into account the historical complexities of communities of colour, particularly communities within the African diaspora who are the descendants of enslaved people. These communities exist outside of this dichotomy as neither Indigenous to the lands where they live nor willing Settlers who have relocated by choice, instead having been removed from their lands through colonization and relocated by force through enslavement. I am also aware that by referring to "Indigenous people," I run the risk of pan-Indigenizing rather than respecting the diversity of Indigenous Nations. I have used literature from authors representing multiple Indigenous heritages, and it is my intent to address Indigenous conscientization broadly, without speaking either for any single community or for all Indigenous communities as a totality. Addressing these complexities is again not within the scope of a single chapter, but I believe they need to be acknowledged and kept in mind throughout this work.

I feel it is also necessary to clarify my relationship to this work. I am a researcher in critical education with a focus on Indigenous education. As I mentioned, I come to this work as a person of mixed heritage. I carry Anishinaabe heritage and am a member of Ardoch Algonquin First Nation and the urban Indigenous community in Kingston, Ontario. I also carry Settler heritage, particularly French and German. So, I feel a responsibility to my Indigenous ancestors to contribute to decolonization with the hope of serving the Anishinaabe Nation and other Indigenous Nations. I also feel a responsibility as someone who has benefited from colonization through my Settler ancestry to dismantle systems that are inherently oppressive, White supremist, and Eurocentric. I am exceedingly grateful to the Knowledge Keepers who have shared their teachings and philosophies with me. However, as I write, I fully acknowledge that I speak only for myself, and any misunderstandings of Indigenous ways of knowing are my responsibility; I am growing in my knowledge, and I recognize as well as hope that my understanding as it is now will change and deepen as I learn.

Conscientization in the Context of Settler Colonialism

Since most Indigenous and Settler people in Western Settler colonial states are already literate (generally in the colonial language[s]), the most obvious contribution of *Pedagogy of the Oppressed* to anti-colonial resistance is conscientization.[12] This is a clear necessity in decolonization; indeed, Smith points out that conscientization and decolonization are essentially the same, except that decolonization continues to centre the colonizer, while conscientization does not.[13] Societal conscientization requires the (re)education of both Indigenous and Settler communities. Colonialism and White supremacy are endemic to Settler colonial states, and they infiltrate every aspect of society, including education.[14] In the current education system, Eurocentric education and Whiteness are centred such that they are simultaneously positioned as the norm and also rendered invisible.[15] In other words, the vast majority of the content and pedagogy offered in schools in Settler colonial states present European or Settler perspectives, but at the same time there is little discussion of the implications of that fact for learners. There is also little recognition that Settler culture even exists, and even less that it exists alongside "other" cultures that are equally valid.[16] As Battiste writes,

> Whiteness is hidden in this system, because it never looks at itself, only the perceived "different other." Norms surrounding whiteness then are the measure for success or failure, and rewards for whiteness are not critiqued for the benefit and rewards it gives to a few and the kinds of punishment and low outcomes it gives to those who are different in terms of skin colour, religion or non-religion, sexual orientation, abilities, age, or class status.[17]

This is particularly the case in a system where the banking model of education is employed; this approach to education, as Freire points out, is mechanistic and static, and positions students as recipients of knowledge rather than participants in a process of mutual education through praxis, dialogue, and reflection.[18] The banking model, then, enforces the social order, reinforcing in oppressors their own superiority and convincing the oppressed that oppressive norms are a natural state of reality.[19] In fact, the banking model has been used to purposely inculcate Indigenous children with the norms of Whiteness through aggressive assimilation, most notably through the residential school and Indian day school systems in Canada and Indian boarding schools in the United States.[20]

The normalization of systemic inequality needs to be disrupted and trans-formed, and because it is so insidious, the only way to do that is through overt, purposeful conscientization.[21] Through this process, those who are oppressed develop the tools to critique their own oppression and to see it as an imposed system that can be changed rather than an objective reality or necessity.[22] At the same time, those in the oppressor class must engage in a process of decon-structing their own power and understanding their role in creating and main-taining oppressive systems. In this process, the perspectives of the oppressed need to be centred since their voices have been previously silenced through the oppressive system, and because the oppressors are unlikely to instigate the pro-cess of conscientization since the oppressive system benefits them.[23] For both, conscientization requires a process of reflecting on the world, taking action, and reflecting again, with oppressed and oppressor co-constructing knowledge to dismantle asymmetrical power relations.[24]

Dehumanization is at the heart of Settler colonialism. To justify the taking of Indigenous lands and the killing of Indigenous peoples and cultures, Indige-nous people had to be "other", "less than," and "threatening to" Settlers and the Settler state.[25] That dehumanization is present throughout history, starting with the issuing of papal bulls in the fifteenth and sixteenth centuries that set global colonialism in motion through evangelization and the Doctrine of Discovery, particularly the *Inter Caetera*, issued by Pope Alexander VI in 1493. It was pres-ent in the creation of arbitrary categories of race that divided society and offered distorted views based in contempt and pity for those categorized as "other."[26] It was present in the creation of the Indian Act and other racist legislation aimed at aggressive assimilation through both physical and cultural force.[27] And it is present today across our society and clearly visible in our Euro-normative school system and curricula, which all but ignore Indigenous knowledges and perspectives prior to and after colonization, and which continue to serve In-digenous learners extremely poorly.[28] The process of societal conscientization in Settler colonial contexts, then, begins with acknowledgment that the dehu-manization of Indigenous people, and the processes of genocide and aggressive assimilation that this dehumanization enables, are pillars of the Settler colonial state.

Indigenous dehumanization also reinforces other mythologies that form the basis of the Settler colonial state, and that need to be disrupted to achieve mean-ingful decolonization. These include the idea that Indigenous societies were hierarchical in the same way as European ones prior to colonization, and so the process of conscientization as Freire describes represents progress from both colonization and Indigenous traditional lifeways;[29] that race is a biological re-ality rather than a social construct;[30] that Indigenous knowledge is less sophis-ticated than its Western counterpart and that Indigenous history is less rich;[31] that the colonized possess intrinsic weaknesses such as laziness, ingratitude, or lesser intelligence, thereby placing them in a naturally disadvantaged position;[32] that "we" are a nation of immigrants with equal rights to the land and to power;[33] that the creation of a more egalitarian society places White people in a position of disadvantage with respect to other groups;[34] or that those in power have an inherent right to that power.[35]

While the mechanisms of conscientization are different for the oppressed and the oppressor, they are intertwined and are both necessary, since both participate in the same society.[36] Commonly, oppressor and oppressed need to understand that while Indigenous dehumanization has been at the heart of colonialism and colonial mythologies, the resulting oppressive systems negatively impact everyone.[37] While on the surface, these system would seem to benefit Settlers, participating in them is still harmful to them, both pragmatically, because inequality produces drains on social systems, and morally, because inequality robs us all of our collective humanity.[38]

Indigenous Conscientization

For Indigenous peoples, conscientization requires recognition of the oppression inherent in colonialism, and of how Settler colonial states seek to marginalize and assimilate Indigenous people. It also requires the creation of systems of education that are proactive rather than reactive, based on community consensus and collaboration, aimed at alleviating the deleterious impacts of colonization on Indigenous communities, and determined to achieve a culturally informed vision of the future. Throughout, Indigenous perspectives must be centred such that they replace colonialism, Eurocentrism, and Whiteness as dominant norms.[39] Furthermore, Indigenous conscientization requires deep self-reflection on internalized colonialism for both individuals and communities. Freire insightfully writes, "during the initial stages of the struggle the oppressed, instead of striving for liberation, tend themselves to become oppressors, or 'sub-oppressors.'"[40] The lateral violence that is sometimes experienced by Indigenous people can be understood within this context, as can the abandonment of Indigenous knowledges and practices,[41] as Indigenous people internalize the hegemony of the dominant society. As Smith points out,

> Hegemony is a way of thinking – it occurs when oppressed groups take on dominant group thinking and ideas uncritically and as "common-sense," even though those ideas may in fact be contributing to forming their own oppression. It is the ultimate way to colonize a people; you have the colonized colonizing themselves![42]

This internalized colonialism is exacerbated by colonial techniques such as "divide and conquer," in which Indigenous communities are pitted against one another in competition for colonizer-controlled resources and recognition,[43] and what Smith describes as the "politics of distraction," in which Indigenous people are kept busy through colonial processes, which distracts from the identification and pursuit of communities' ultimate visions and goals.[44]

Settler Conscientization

Critical pedagogy can also be a tool for Settler conscientization, which is arguably a more difficult type of emotional work than Indigenous conscientization. As Freire writes,

> Discovering himself to be an oppressor may cause considerable anguish [to the Settler], but it does not necessarily lead to solidarity with the oppressed. Rationalizing his guilt through paternalistic treatment of the oppressed, all the while holding them fast in a position of dependence, will not do. Solidarity requires that one enter into the situation of those with whom one is in solidary; it is a radical posture.[45]

The adoption of this radical posture is made all the more difficult by the fact that in Settler colonial states, the oppressors form the majority in the context of Settler-Indigenous relations, in contrast to the oppressed majority that Freire describes.[46] As a majority and as holders of power, Settlers are not compelled to engage in conscientization; they can simply opt out of the process and continue on as normal with little social pressure.[47]

To engage in conscientization, Settlers must undergo a difficult process in which they question Whiteness and Eurocentrism as the norm and relinquish their perceived entitlement to power and dominion in all its forms, since "the oppressor consciousness tends to transform everything surrounding it into an object of its domination. The earth, property, production, the creations of people, people themselves, time – everything is reduced to the status of objects at its disposal."[48] They must also engage in meaningful dialogue with Indigenous people, without the pretence of "saving" them, the tendency to exotify and romanticize them, or the expectation that Indigenous people have the sole responsibility for educating their Settler counterparts.[49] Furthermore, they must take meaningful action to dismantle the colonial systems that harm both Indigenous and Settler people. [50] In this work, Freire cautions against what he calls "false generosity,"[51] which Austin describes as "the [hallmark] of such attempts to soften the exploitative colonial relationship without actually addressing the structural framework of this relationship."[52] This sentiment is supported by Indigenous scholars; in the words of Gangulu Elder Lilla Watson, "if you have come here to help me, you are wasting your time. If you have come here because your liberation is bound up with mine, then let us work together."[53]

Incongruences between Freirean and Indigenous Education for Conscientization and Decolonization

While much can be learned from *Pedagogy of the Oppressed* that can enrich processes of conscientization in Settler colonial contexts, there are nonetheless some significant gaps between this text and decolonizing or Indigenous education approaches. This is because rather than localizing it within a Brazilian context or examining its focus on critical class consciousness as compared to other areas of critical study, Freirean education as described in *Pedagogy of the Oppressed* is presented as an approach that can be applied across cultural and global contexts.[54] By not taking cultural and geographic context or multiple forms of oppression into account, educators risk essentializing the concept of liberation as the achievement of class equality, and also essentializing processes of education and critical thought. That approach does not take into account the fact that oppressed people, and Indigenous people in particular, may have other philosophies, strategies, and goals for critical education and self-liberation.[55] As Kee and Carr-Chellman write,

> Freire's strictly dialectical construction of knowledge as a critical and reflective process reinforces a troubling essentialism and an approach to empowerment that can be more like a disguised form of colonization. The tie to class consciousness also implicates the Freirean dialectic in further misreading culture as an either/or construction, a false dichotomy that again ignores complicated realities, producing curriculums that reflect colonial condescension more than Indigenous sovereignty.[56]

For this reason, it is vital to examine the incongruences between Indigenous education and *Pedagogy of the Oppressed* to ensure that work towards conscientization serves the goals of Indigenous communities.

Critical Class Consciousness and Critical Colonial Consciousness

As mentioned previously, *Pedagogy of the Oppressed* neglects the fact that there are many ways in which oppression is made manifest, and that these differ across cultures and global contexts, tending instead to focus on class as the great divider. This is in spite of the fact that Brazil is also a Settler colonial state that gravely oppresses Indigenous people. While Indigenous people in Settler colonial societies are more likely to experience class inequality, this is a by-product of colonization, which oppresses all Indigenous people in multiple ways regardless of their socio-economic status.[57] That is not to say that all Indigenous societies were/are without inequality outside of colonization;[58] however, it is clear that colonization has been so damaging to Indigenous people that all forms of oppression they experience within Settler colonial states can be traced back to it to at least some degree. The failure to recognize this fact on the part of those engaging in the process of conscientization, whether oppressor or oppressed, poses the risk of recolonizing Indigenous peoples by imposing external and supposedly superior ways of thinking and understanding that do not reflect the actual reality of their oppression. [59] While colonization is a common experience, Indigenous conceptions of it, reactions to it, and resilience in the face of it are different across the hundreds of Indigenous Nations that persist within Settler colonial states. Instead of meaningfully acknowledging the root of oppression as colonialism, as well as the diverse reactions to and ways of resisting colonialism, it can be assumed that a liberation model based on critical class consciousness "is universally applicable and unquestionably justifiable, a kind of absolute good, regardless of the cultural or religious context of the population that is perceived to be oppressed."[60] While the approach outlined in *Pedagogy of the Oppressed* risks perpetuating colonialism when applied in diverse contexts because it does not attach any aspects of its approach to the specifically Brazilian context in which it was developed, Freire acknowledges this risk, writing, "One cannot expect positive results from an educational or political action program which fails to respect the particular view of the world held by the people. Such a program constitutes a cultural invasion, good intentions notwithstanding."[61]

The Inherent Power of Indigenous Knowledge

The risk of perpetuating colonization is exacerbated by the assumption that oppressed Indigenous populations lack critical consciousness or power. For example, Freire writes, "were it not possible to dialogue with the people before power is taken, because they have no experience with dialogue, neither would it be possible for the people to come to power, for they are equally inexperienced in the use of power."[62] However, in the case of Indigenous peoples, nothing could be further from the truth. First, Indigenous ways of educating seldom take the form of banking models, focusing instead on learner growth and transformation.[63] Furthermore, Indigenous people, while certainly oppressed by colonialism, are not now, nor have they ever been, powerless or ignorant of how power works. The conception of the powerless oppressed is problematic because it "erases Indigenous forms of power and knowledge while seeking to induct the oppressed into a class awareness based in European Leftist constructions of political power."[64] Indigenous forms of power and knowledge are different from Western leftist conceptions. The imposition of Western views of power and hierarchy without consideration of existing Indigenous views is colonial in itself.[65] The conception of power in this text positions economic and state authority as real power, and seeks to impress upon the oppressed that that power is within everyone's reach. However, not all oppressed or colonized peoples necessarily seek modes of power that are the hallmark of the Settler colonial state.[66] Furthermore, while the oppressed may not possess power as conceived in the Western sense, Indigenous power, as expressed in different ways, remains vital within Indigenous communities and within the colonial society and enables real and ongoing resistance to oppression and assimilation.[67] In addition, lack of colonial power also does not inherently rob Indigenous people of the inner freedom they possess, which enables personal resistance and contributions to an Indigenous culture of resistance.[68]

Perspectives on Leadership

Since Indigenous conceptions of power and the inherent power of Indigenous knowledge are not considered in the text, the conception of leadership in revolution laid out in *Pedagogy of the Oppressed* is problematic in a Settler colonial context. Freire consistently assumes that the oppressed are incapable of seeing their own oppression, and therefore await the enlightenment of outside educators to spark revolution. He writes,

> The oppressor elaborates his theory of action without the people, for he stands against them. Nor can the people – as long as they are crushed and oppressed, internalizing the image of the oppressor – construct by themselves the theory of their liberating action. Only in the encounter of the people with the revolutionary leaders – in their communion, in their praxis – can this theory be built.[69]

However, Indigenous people have always understood colonization as oppression and offered resistance to it, which is why Indigenous peoples and cultures continue to exist in the face of centuries of genocide and aggressive assimilation. Since Indigenous people are aware of colonial oppression, and since they possess power within and outside of their own communities, it is only appropriate that leadership in anti-colonial resistance come from within Indigenous communities, for Indigenous communities.[70] Indeed, Indigenous leadership in resistance, both formal and informal, has been a force across political, social, and educational domains; a few of the many examples include the plethora of Indigenous educators who have designed culturally restorative education for their communities and for other educational institutions; the Knowledge Keepers who have, often at great personal risk, maintained cultures, traditions, languages, knowledges, and sacred items; and grassroots, community, and political activists who continue to fight for Indigenous sovereignty, rights, and land. Held up against these examples, "assigning outsider(s), who have committed 'class suicide,' to the role of critical educator seems patronizing and paternalistic."[71] Freire is not wrong that Indigenous leaders may have something in common with the colonizer in the form of post-secondary or other Western education, which can offer tools for resistance. He is also correct that when

Indigenous people in possession of those tools, who can then integrate more easily into the settler colonial society and gain Western power, choose instead to fight against colonial oppression for their own and other Indigenous communities, it "represents … an act of love and true commitment."[72]

Non-Indigenous leadership poses a risk of recolonization to Indigenous communities. It is essential that Indigenous people, in working against colonial oppression, "choose models that are not those of the oppressors. Obviously the best-placed people for making that choice are indigenous people themselves who are familiar with the context and committed to the aboriginal culture's fundamental values."[73] While Freire discusses the conscientization of the oppressor, and indeed appears to be primarily addressing people of the "oppressor class" who wish to aid the oppressed in achieving liberation, this text is vague about what that conscientization must entail.[74] That lack of guidance can result in individuals of the oppressor class, in this case Settlers, who believe they are working for liberation but who are unable to see the colonial mentality inherent in their assumption, thinking that it is they who must lead. That has been the case in Indigenous communities where Freirean education has been unsuccessfully applied.[75]

As previously discussed, conscientization of the oppressor is much more difficult than conscientization of the oppressed, particularly in a Settler colonial context where Eurocentrism convinces Settlers that their knowledge is superior, and that their role is to bring good to Indigenous people and other oppressed populations. This mentality "is part of the West's messianic tradition that has its roots both in messianic Christianity and in liberating ideologies,"[76] and it has been present throughout the colonial process in the concepts of manifest destiny and global evangelization through colonization. Freire is very much correct, however, in pointing out the need for Settler leadership in whole-of-society conscientization. By engaging in a constant, iterative process of self-reflection and decolonization, Settlers may act as allies by contributing to the conscientization of other Settlers, thereby relieving Indigenous people of the emotional and time-intensive labour of contributing to Indigenous resistance while also conscientizing Settlers. They can also take action to centre Indigenous voices and leverage their power to support Indigenous efforts against colonialism.[77]

Sectarianism versus Sovereignty

A further incongruence between Pedagogy of the Oppressed and Indigenous conceptions of conscientization relates to how each considers difference and division within society. Freire cautions against what he terms "sectarianism," which, in his opinion, "mythicizes and thereby alienates."[78] For him, the goal of revolution is societal conscientization that removes divisions between oppressor and oppressed to achieve equality and dismantle oppressive systems. Freire has a valid point here, since the mythologizing of Indigenous people has contributed to their dehumanization and oppression. However, here con-scientization requires acknowledging the diversity of Indigenous peoples such that we do not "subsume the oppressed into one undifferentiated category."[79] That means recognizing how vital it is to maintain distinction, since distinction is necessary for sovereignty and self-determination.[80] Indigenous conscientiza-tion involves the assertion that Indigenous Nations still exist and are sovereign nations within colonial states. It also involves self-direction in conscientization and education such that culture and language are passed on to the next genera-tion. Because each Indigenous Nation is distinct, and each Indigenous commu-nity is distinct, Indigenous conscientization involves not only differentiation from the Settler colonial state, but also resistance to pan-Indigenizing solutions that assume all communities have identical goals for decolonization and iden-tical needs in terms of culture, language, and education.[81] Distinction is also necessary because community belonging is central to Indigenous identity, and service to community is central to Indigenous conscientization.[82]

Humans and the Environment

The approach in *Pedagogy of the Oppressed* is further incongruous with In-digenous conscientization because it is anthropocentric.[83] In this text, Freire frequently critiques the fact that the oppressed, "usually submerged in a colo-nial context, are almost umbilically linked to the world of nature, in relation to which they feel themselves to be component parts rather than shapers."[84] He writes that they see themselves as equal to animals; he also argues at length that fully realized humanity is completely distinct from animals, such that "men who are bound to nature and to the oppressor in this way must come to discern themselves as *persons* prevented from *being*."[85] The assumption that reciprocal, equal connection with the land and the other-than-human is limiting and reflective of low self-worth misunderstands Indigenous ways of seeing human relationships with nature. Humans are part of and innately connected to nature, and are not in a position of dominion with respect to other beings; this perspective by no means prevents Indigenous people from being fully human. Really, it can be argued in contrast that failing to recognize oneself as a being connected to everything in the land and environment is a failure to recognize the fullness of one's humanity. The goal of undermining Indigenous connection with the natural world is based in assumptions of Eu-rocentric intellectual and philosophical superiority and is a form of cognitive imperialism.[86]

Reclamation of Indigenous relationships to the land and the natural world is central to Indigenous conscientization – not just because of assertion of territorial sovereignty,[87] but also because global Western colonialism, which assumes human dominion over the earth, has been an environmental catastrophe. *Pedagogy of the Oppressed* ignores the environmental desecration brought about by colonialism and industrialization in its focus on achieving material and class equality.[88] Indigenous ways of being recognize responsibility to the land and our other-than-human relations, and Indigenous liberation and cultural reclamation is tied to reconciliation with them.[89] As Trinidad writes, "reinhabitation (and reconciliation with land) is the process of reconnecting through collective memory and recovering the historic truths that were erased as a result of colonialism."[90] Freire's text does not recognize the cognitive imperialism implicit in assumptions about humans and the natural world. Correspondingly, Freire does not recognize that here Indigenous knowledges would positively contribute to the Western knowledge and education he seeks to share. Indeed, to achieve a sustainable future, Western society needs to change according to Indigenous philosophies.[91]

Progress

The environmental neglect inherent in *Pedagogy of the Oppressed* is characteristic of "progressive" thinking. "Progressiveness" is often based on an assumption of a fairly linear path towards a better future, guided by leaders with knowledge of the process.[92] However, this is not representative of Indigenous goals for conscientization, or Indigenous conceptions of the process of conscientization. In terms of cultural progress, Indigenous conscientization does not just involve moving forward to create a new, better society; it also involves returning to past knowledges to reclaim Indigenous ways of knowing, understanding, doing, and honouring that have been disrupted by colonization.[93] Similarly, the process of conscientization is not linear. Reconciliation, which results from the conscientization of both the oppressor and the oppressed, requires a cyclical, iterative, synergistic process.[94] As Smith states, "There is a significant critique of much of the writing on these concepts that tend to portray a lineal progression through the stages of 'conscientization, resistance, and transformative action.' Maori experience tends to suggest that these elements may occur in any order and indeed all may occur simultaneously."[95]

Dialogue and Language

The final incongruence between the approach proposed in *Pedagogy of the Oppressed* and Indigenous conscientization has to do with language. The text emphasizes not only the importance of literacy education (in the dominant language), but also the need for dialogue. Dialogue is central to the conscientization of both oppressor and oppressed because it allows each to know the other, and it allows for the collaborative naming and thereby collaborative creation of a new way of being. It must be bilateral and equal. Freire writes,

> Because dialogue is an encounter among women and men who name the world, it must not be a situation where some name on behalf of others. It is an act of creation; it must not serve as a crafty instrument for the domination of one person by another. The domination implicit in dialogue is that of the world by the dialoguers; it is the conquest of the world for the liberation of humankind.[96]

Freire is correct that dialogue between oppressor and oppressed is absolutely necessary for mutual understanding and the realization of the other's equal humanity. However, dialogue, based as it is in language, takes on new connotations in the context of colonialism. Colonialism and the imposition of colonial languages have seriously threatened Indigenous languages around the globe. Western education has been a significant factor in Indigenous language loss because it is nearly always carried out in the colonial language. Freire's approach is no different; his assumption that a revolution would be led by members of the dominant class implicitly assumes that it would also be done in the dominant language.[97] Since language influences how we see the world, it is impossible to create dialogue in the colonial language that accurately communicates Indigenous perspectives, and therefore colonial norms and perspectives are once again reinforced. Already, Indigenous people have little choice about which language they use on a daily basis in Settler colonial states, and Indigenous knowledges and connections to the land are undermined by colonial renaming and consequent claiming.[98] Language revitalization is a part of Indigenous conscientization and reclamation of Indigenous knowledges; an approach that is rooted in colonial languages runs counter to that.[99]

It must also be acknowledged that ways of using language, including ways of engaging in dialogue, differ across cultures. Many Indigenous people in Settler colonial societies, and particularly Indigenous learners in colonial education, are acutely aware of the need to adapt to dominant ways of communicating, even when they are fluent in the dominant language. For real, mutual conscientization to occur, dialogue would need to happen not only according to Western norms, but also according to Indigenous cultural ways of communicating; that requires Settlers to gain awareness of Indigenous cultures on a deep level, since norms of communication are seldom obvious at the surface. Without that, the interaction is but another experience of colonial domination in which colonial ways of sharing knowledge are implicitly assumed to be both normal and superior, and dominant voices are once again centred.[100] To avoid that, both oppressor and oppressed must acquire "the language necessary for exercising the communicative competence required in the democratic process of deciding what needs to be resisted, fundamentally changed or conserved and intergenerationally renewed."[101]

Conclusion: The Need for Critical Indigenous Pedagogy

Through *Pedagogy of the Oppressed*, Freire provides necessary insights about processes of conscientization that can inform efforts towards decolonization in Settler colonial contexts. However, in applying these, it is necessary to focus on the specific context of Settler colonialism, and to centre Indigenous approaches to conscientization and decolonization. Unless education is reflective of Indigenous knowledges, norms, languages, and goals, it is another tool for colonization. For that reason, it is important to synthesize critical Indigenous pedagogies (CIPs).[102] CIPs take into account the approaches of critical scholars like Freire, but they also maintain at their core Indigenous ways of knowing, understanding, doing, and honouring, and Indigenous visions and goals for the future, with the ultimate aim of replacing colonial norms.[103] There are two elements to this: conscientization/decolonization, which involves the critique of colonial systems that oppress Indigenous people;[104] and Indigenization, which involves the (re)construction of a *sui generis* system of Indigenous education.[105] As Garcia and Shirley write,

> For indigenous peoples, education is not simply about the process of acquiring Western knowledge within the walls of schooling structures. Rather, we suggest Indigenous schools be encouraged to reconsider themselves as a *sacred landscape* where Indigenous knowledge is recognized and offers a re-newed beginning for revitalizing Indigenous epistemologies and ontologies in contemporary contexts.[106]

CIPs must by nature differ from colonial pedagogies because they are a tool for engaging in a process of conscientization and claiming Indigenous ways that were undermined by colonialism.[107] The ongoing development of Indigenous pedagogy is therefore in itself an act of defiance vis-à-vis historical and ongoing colonization.[108] CIPs also need to be reflective of local cultures and relationships, including relationships to the land and other-than-human relations.[109] They will therefore naturally differ across communities, although Smith has identified a set of governing principles to guide their development that make sense in diverse Indigenous contexts: "self-determination or relative autonomy ... validating and legitimating cultural aspirations and identity ... incorporating culturally preferred pedagogy ... mediating socio-economic and home difficulties ... incorporating cultural structures which emphasise the collective rather than the individual ... [and] a shared and collective vision/ philosophy."[110]

Beyond these, conscientization in Indigenous communities must be led by Indigenous people, through the centring and normalizing of Indigenous knowledges, the overt critique of colonial oppressive systems, and engagement in iterative processes for further decolonization and educational improvement.[111] Indigenous education can then be a tool for Indigenous conscientization by affirming the validity of Indigenous ways of knowing, and asserting Indigenous sovereignty and self-determination over education and all aspects of Indigenous life.[112]

It is vital to remember that decolonization through conscientization is not the sole responsibility of Indigenous people, nor should it be left entirely to Indigenous education systems and communities.[113] Freire rightly points out in *Pedagogy of the Oppressed* that both oppressed and oppressor are in need of conscientization if we are to dismantle oppressive systems. This informs what can be done in Settler and mixed education contexts, such as public schools, to promote a new relationship between Settlers and Indigenous people. That requires the even harder work of conscientizing the Settler majority; here, too, it is necessary to not only question colonial mythologies, but also to question colonial educational norms that promote Eurocentric ways of thinking. That can only be done by creating an environment characterized by constant dialogue, where both Indigenous and Settler knowledges are present and are treated with equal esteem, and by creating curriculum for critical thought in which students are taught to examine all unequal power relations within their societies, with a focus on their own roles in systems of oppression and their own positionality-informed responsibilities for dismantling them.[114] This will create "programs that allow students to switch between Indigenous and Western modes of thinking without deeming one culturally inferior or inappropriate for the classroom environment."[115]

While Freire's contribution to critical pedagogy cannot be overstated, his work is not a panacea, nor it is wholly appropriate for all contexts, and particularly contexts of Indigenous and decolonizing education; here, if it were to be applied carte blanche without consideration of context, it has serious pitfalls that could lead to ongoing colonization. As with all such seminal texts, and in the spirit of Freire's commitment to dismantling oppression in all its forms,[116] readers must understand that the approach needs to be contextualized before it is applied. In so doing, we will create educational opportunities that dismantle Settler colonial oppression in a spirit of reconciliation, that normalize and dignify Indigenous ways of knowing, understanding, doing, and honouring, and that support Indigenous self-determination. This work will be long and difficult, but it has already commenced. Now that we have begun as a society to engage in decolonization, we have no choice but to move together in the iterative process of collective conscientization, resistance, and transformative action that will enable us to regain our collective humanity.[117]

NOTES

1 Graham Hingangaroa Smith, "Mai te Maramatanga, ki te Putanga Mai o te Tahuritanga: From Conscientization to Transformation," *Educational Perspectives: Journal of the College of Education/University of Hawai'i at Mānoa: Indigenous Education* 37, no. 1 (2004): 46–52.

2 Michael W. Apple, "Freire and the Politics of Race in Education," *International Journal of Leadership in Education* 6, no. 2 (2003): 107–18.

3 Apple, 107.

4 Apple, 108.

5 Andrew P. Hodgkins, "A Critical Analysis of Freirean Pedagogy: The Case of Development in Northern Canada," *Journal of Transformative Education* 6, no. 4 (2008): 302–16.

6 James Blackburn, "Understanding Paulo Freire: Reflections on the Origins, Concepts, and Possible Pitfalls of His Educational Approach," *Community Development Journal* 35, no. 1 (2000): 3–15.; C.A. Bowers, "Why a Critical Pedagogy of Place Is an Oxymoron," *Environmental Education Research* 14, no. 3 (2008): 325–35.; Elizabeth A. Lange, "Is Freirean Transformational Learning the Trojan Horse of Globalization and Enemy of Sustainability Education? A Response to C.A. Bowers," *Journal of Transformative Education* 10, no.1 (2012): 3–21.

7 Apple, "Freire and the Politics of Race in Education," 110.

8 Kimberlé Crenshaw, "Mapping the Margins: Intersectionality, Identity Politics, and Violence against Women of Colour," *Stanford Law Review* 43, no. 6 (1991): 1241–300.

9 Approximately half of the articles I consulted were written by Indigenous authors, and another 20 per cent are by authors of colour.

10 The Hawaiian Kingdom was recognized as an independent state in 1842 by the United States of America, and declared itself to be a neutral state in 1854. Since 1898 it has been illegally occupied by the United States, but it nonetheless remains sovereign. I therefore list it separately out of respect for Hawaiian people who maintain their commitment to asserting sovereignty and self-determination. See David Keanu Sai, *Ua Mau ke Ea – Sovereignty Endures: An Overview of the Political and Legal History of the Hawaiian Islands* (Honolulu: Pū'ā Foundation, 2011).

11 Céleste Kee and Davin J. Carr-Chellman, "Paulo Freire, Critical Literacy, and Indigenous Resistance," *Educational Studies* 55, no. 1 (2019): 89–103, https://doi.org/10.1080/00131946.2018.1562926.

12 Paulo Freire, *Pedagogy of the Oppressed*, 30th anniv. ed. (New York: Bloomsbury, 2015).

13 Graham Hingangaroa Smith, "Indigenous Struggle for the Transformation of Education and Schooling" (keynote address, Alaskan Federation of Native Convention, Anchorage, AK, October 2003), 2.

14   Brian McKinley Jones Brayboy, "Toward a Tribal Critical Race Theory in Educa-
     tion," *Urban Review* 37, no. 5 (2005): 425–36.

15   Apple, "Freire and the Politics of Race in Education", 114–15; Marie Battiste,
     Lynne Bell, and L.M. Findlay, "Decolonizing Education in Canadian Universi-
     ties: An Interdisciplinary, International, Indigenous Research Project," *Canadian
     Journal of Native Education* 26, no. 2 (2002): 82–95; Felipe de S. Ferreira, "Critical
     Sustainability Studies: A Holistic and Visionary Conception of Socio-ecological
     Conscientization," *Journal of Sustainability Education*, no. 13 (March 2017): 7;
     Marc Higgins, Brooke Madden, and Lisa Korteweg, "Witnessing (Halted) Decon-
     struction: White Teachers' 'Perfect Stranger' Position within Urban Indigenous
     Education," *Race Ethnicity and Education* 18, no. 2 (2015): 251–76, http://dx.doi
     .org/10.1080/13613324.2012.759932.

16   Higgins, Madden, and Korteweg, "Witnessing (Halted) Deconstruction," 257–61.

17   Marie Battiste, *Decolonizing Education: Nourishing the Learning Spirit* (Saskatoon:
     Purich, 2013), 106.

18   Freire, *Pedagogy of the Oppressed*, 77.

19   Apple, "Freire and the Politics of Race in Education," 115; Freire, *Pedagogy of the
     Oppressed*, 74.

20   Kee and Carr-Chellman, "Paulo Freire, Critical Literacy, and Indigenous Resist-
     ance," 99; Jackson Pind, "Indian Day Schools in Michi Saagiig Anishinaabeg Ter-
     ritory, 1899–1978" (PhD diss., Queen's University, 2021).

21   Freire, *Pedagogy of the Oppressed*.

22   Apple, "Freire and the Politics of Race in Education," 7; Freire, *Pedagogy of the
     Oppressed*.

23   Freire, *Pedagogy of the Oppressed*, 136.

24   Freire, *Pedagogy of the Oppressed*; Rubén A. Gaztambide-Fernandez, "Decolo-
     nization and the Pedagogy of Solidarity," *Decolonization: Indigeneity, Education
     & Society* 1, no. 1 (2012): 41–67; Rita Kohli, "Racial Pedagogy of the Oppressed:
     Critical Interracial Dialogue for Teachers of Color," *Equity & Excellence in Educa-
     tion* 45, no. 1 (2012): 181–96; Nina Wallerstein, Leandro L. Giatti, Cláudia Maria
     Bógus, Marco Akerman, Pedro Roberto Jacobi, Renata Ferraz de Toledo, Rosilda
     Mendes, Sonia Acioli, Margaret Bluehorse-Anderson, Shelley Frazier, and Marita
     Jones, "Shared Participatory Research Principles and Methodologies: Perspectives
     from the USA and Brazil – 45 Years after Paulo Freire's 'Pedagogy of the
     Oppressed,'" *Societies* 7, no. 2 (2017): 6, https://doi.org/10.3390/soc7020006.

25   Fereira, "Critical Susatinability Studies," 6; Sweeney Windchief and Darold H.
     Joseph, "The Act of Claiming Higher Education as Indigenous Space: American
     Indian/Alaska Native Examples," *Diaspora, Indigenous, and Minority Education* 9,
     no. 4 (2015): 267–83, https://doi.org/10.1080/15595692.2015.1048853.

26   Jon Austin, "Decolonizing Ways of Knowing: Communion, Conversion, and
     Conscientization," in *Paulo Freire: The Global Legacy*, ed. Michael A. Peters and
     Tina Besley (New York: Peter Lang, 2015), 489–501.

27 Battiste, Bell, and Findlay, "Decolonizing Education in Canadian Universities," 89.

28 Apple, "Freire and the Politics of Race in Education," 112; Battiste, Bell, and Findlay, "Decolonizing Education in Canadian Universities," 91–2.

29 Cf. Lange, "Is Freirean Transformational Learning the Trojan Horse of Globalization?," 12.

30 Austin, "Decolonizing Ways of Knowing," 497.

31 Wallerstein et al., "Shared Participatory Research Principles," 13.

32 Freire, *Pedagogy of the Oppressed*, 155.

33 Apple, "Freire and the Politics of Race in Education," 113.

34 Apple, 113.

35 Freire, *Pedagogy of the Oppressed*, 58.

36 Freire.

37 Freire, 47–50. My thanks to Adam Morcom and the students in the Queen's Indigenous Teacher Education Program for helping me reflect on the necessity of decolonization for Settler people.

38 Freire, *Pedagogy of the Oppressed*, 47–50.

39 Austin, "Decolonizing Ways of Knowing," 499; Kohli, "Racial Pedagogy of the Oppressed," 193–4; Battiste, Bell, and Findlay, "Decolonizing Education in Canadian Universities," 82–95; Gregory A. Cajete, "Contemporary Indigenous Education: A Nature-Centred American Indian Philosophy for a 21st Century World," *Futures*, no. 42 (2010): 1126–32; David Corson, "Community-Based Education for Indigenous Cultures," *Language, Culture and Curriculum* 11, no. 3 (1998): 238–49, https://doi.org/10.1080/07908319808666555; Garcia and Shirley, "Performing Decolonization," 80; Marie M. Marchand, "Application of Paulo Freire's *Pedagogy of the Oppressed* to Human Services Education," *Journal of Human Services: A Journal of the National Organization for Human Services* 30, no. 1 (2010): 43–53; Kiara Rahman, "Belonging and Learning to Belong in School: The Implications of the Hidden Curriculum for Indigenous Students," *Discourse: Studies in the Cultural Politics of Education* 34, no. 5 (2013): 660–72, http://dx.doi.org/10.1080/01596306.2013.728362/; Siemens, "Education for Reconcilation," 132; Smith, "Mai te Maramatanga"; Alma M.O. Trinidad, "Sociopolitical Development through Critical Indigenous Pedagogy of Place: Preparing Native Hawaiian Young Adults to Become Change Agents," *Hūlili: Multidisciplinary Research on Hawaiian Well-Being* 7 (2011): 185–221.

40 Freire, *Pedagogy of the Oppressed*, 45.

41 Jeremy Garcia and Valerie Shirley, "Performing Decolonization: Lessons Learned from Indigenous Youth, Teachers, and Leaders' Engagement with Critical Indigenous Pedagogy," *Journal of Curriculum Theorizing* 28, no. 2 (2012): 76–91; Kee and Carr-Chellman, "Paulo Freire, Critical Literacy, and Indigenous Resistance," 99; Teresa L. McCarty and Tiffany S. Lee, "Critical Culturally Sustaining /Revitalizing Pedagogy and Indigenous Education Sovereignty," *Harvard Educational Review* 84, no. 1 (Spring 2014): 101–27.

42   Smith, "Indigenous Struggle," 2.

43   Hodgkins, "A Critical Analysis of Freirean Pedagogy," 307.

44   Smith, "Indigenous Struggle."

45   Freire, *Pedagogy of the Oppressed*, 49.

46   Freire, 57.

47   Higgins, Madden, and Korteweg, "Witnessing (Halted) Deconstruction," 268.

48   Freire, *Pedagogy of the Oppressed*, 58.

49   Apple, "Freire and the Politics of Race in Education,"114–15; Blackburn, "Understanding Paulo Freire," 10–11; Marchand, "Application of Paulo Freire," 49.

50   Vanessa Anthony-Stevens, "Cultivating Alliances: Reflections on the Role of Non-Indigenous Collaborators in Indigenous Educational Sovereignty," *Journal of American Indian Education* 56, no.1 (2017): 81–104; Austin, "Decolonizing Ways of Knowing," 500; Gazambide-Fernandez, "Decolonization and the Pedagogy of Solidarity"; Majid Rahnema, "Participation," in *The Development Dictionary: A Guide to Knowledge and Power*, 2nd ed., ed. Wolfgang Sachs (London: Zed Books, 1992), 127–45. Jeremy D.N. Siemens, "Education for Reconciliation: Pedagogy for a Canadian Context," *Canadian Journal for New Scholars in Education* 8, no. 1 (2017): 127–35.

51   Dawn Darlaston-Jones, Jill Harris, Kelleigh Ryan, and Pat Dudgeon, "Are We Asking the Right Questions? Why We Should Have a Decolonizing Discourse Based on Conscientization Rather than Indigenizing the Curriculum," *Canadian Journal of Native Education* 37, no. 1 (2014): 86–104; Freire, *Pedagogy of the Oppressed*, 45.

52   Austin, "Decolonizing Ways of Knowing," 500.

53   Marchand, "Application of Paulo Freire," 50; Lilla Watson, "About," Lilla: International Women's Network, accessed 19 March 2021, http://lillanetwork.wordpress.com/about/.

54   Blackburn, "Understanding Paulo Freire," 10; Kee and Carr-Chellman, "Paulo Freire, Critical Literacy, and Indigenous Resistance," 91–2.

55   Hodgkins, "A Critical Analysis of Freirean Pedagogy," 304.

56   Kee and Carr-Chellman, "Paulo Freire, Critical Literacy, and Indigenous Resistance," 101.

57   Apple, "Freire and the Politics of Race in Education," 112; Battiste, *Decolonizing Education*, 106; Blackburn "Understanding Paulo Freire," 7; Corson, "Community-Based Education," 238–9.

58   Lange, "Is Freirean Learning the Trojan Horse of Globalization?," 13.

59   Rahnema, "Participation," 136.

60   Blackburn, "Understanding Paulo Freire," 10.

61   Freire, *Pedagogy of the Oppressed*, 95.

62   Freire, 137.

63   Battiste, *Decolonizing Education*, 136; Cajete, "Contemporary Indigenous Education," 1129; Hampton, "Towards a Redefinition of Indian Education."

64 Kee and Carr-Chellman, "Paulo Freire, Critical Literacy, and Indigenous Resistance," 91–2.

65 Blackburn, "Understanding Paulo Freire," 10; Kee and Carr-Chellman, "Paulo Freire, Critical Literacy, and Indigenous Resistance"; Bowers, "Why a Critical Pedagogy of Place Is an Oxymoron," 89.

66 Blackburn, "Why a Critical Pedagogy of Place Is an Oxymoron," 10; Rahnema, "Participation," 135.

67 Blackburn, "Why a Critical Pedagogy of Place Is an Oxymoron," 10; Rahnema, "Participation," 135.

68 Blackburn, "Why a Critical Pedagogy of Place Is an Oxymoron," 10; Rahnema, "Participation," 140–1.

69 Freire, *Pedagogy of the Oppressed*, 183.

70 Corson, "Community-Based Education," 244; Hodgkins, "A Critical Analysis of Freirean Pedagogy," 313; Kee and Carr-Chellman, "Paulo Freire, Critical Literacy, and Indigenous Resistance," 98–9; Marchand, "Application of Paulo Freire," 49; Rahnema, "Participation."

71 Hodgkins, "A Critical Analysis of Freirean Pedagogy," 313.

72 Freire, *Pedagogy of the Oppressed*, 163.

73 Corson, "Community-Based Education," 244.

74 Austin, "Decolonizing Ways of Knowing," 499; Blackburn, "Understanding Paulo Freire," 8; Rahnema, "Participation," 137–8.

75 Blackburn, "Understanding Paulo Freire," 11–12.

76 Bowers, "Why a Critical Pedagogy of Place Is an Oxymoron," 331.

77 Anthony-Stevens, "Cultivating Alliances," 101.

78 Freire, *Pedagogy of the Oppressed*, 37.

79 Hodgkins, "A Critical Analysis of Freirean Pedagogy," 313.

80 Tiffany S. Lee, "'I Came Here to Learn How to Be a Leader': An Intersection of Critical Pedagogy and Indigenous Education," *InterActions: UCLA Journal of Education and Information Studies* 2, no. 1 (2006), http://escholarship.org/uc/item/92m798m0; McCarty and Lee, "Critical Culturally Sustaining/Revitalizing Pedagogy," 7.

81 Lee, "I Came Here to Learn," 9; McCarty and Lee, "Critical Culturally Sustaining/Revitalizing Pedagogy."

82 Lee, "I Came Here to Learn," 9.

83 Lange, "Is Freirean Learning the Trojan Horse of Globalization?," 13.

84 Freire, *Pedagogy of the Oppressed*, 94.

85 Freire, 174. Emphasis in the original.

86 Battiste, *Decolonizing Education*.

87 Ferreira, "Critical Sustainability Studies," 10.

88 Bowers, "Why a Critical Pedagogy of Place Is an Oxymoron," 331.

89 Bowers, "Why Critical Pedagogy of Place Is an Oxymoron," 326–31; Siemens, " Education for Reconciliation," 132–3; Trinidad, "Sociopolitical Development," 191.

90   Trinidad, "Sociopolitical Development," 192.

91   "Bowers, "Why Critical Pedagogy of Place Is an Oxymoron," 331; Cajete, "Contemporary Indigenous Education," 1128–9; Siemens, "Education for Reconciliation," 132–3; Trinidad, "Sociopolitical Development," 199.

92   Bowers, "Why a Critical Pedagogy of Place Is an Oxymoron," 325; Hodgkins, "A Critical Analysis of Freirean Pedagogy," 313.

93   Bowers, "Why a Critical Pedagogy of Place Is an Oxymoron," 330–1; Hampton, "Toward a Redefinition of Indian Education"; "Siemens, "Education for Reconciliation," 132–3.

94   Darlaston-Jones et al., "Are We Asking the Right Questions?," 11; Hodgkins, "A Critical Analysis of Freirean Pedagogy," 315; Kee and Carr-Chellman, "Paulo Freire, Critical Literacy, and Indigenous Resistance," 94; Siemens, "Education for Reconciliation," 132; "Smith, "Indigenous Struggle"; Smith, "Mai te Maramatanga," 51.

95   Smith, "Indigenous Struggle," 16. Emphasis in the original.

96   Freire, *Pedagogy of the Oppressed*, 89.

97   Kee and Carr-Chellman, "Paulo Freire, Critical Literacy, and Indigenous Resistance," 93–5.

98   Linda Tuhiwai Smith, *Decolonizing Methodologies: Research and Indigenous Peoples* (Dunedin. NZ: University of Otago Press 2012); McCarty and Lee, "Critical Culturally Sustaining/Revitalizing Pedagogy," 107, 150.

99   Kee and Carr-Chellman, "Paulo Freire, Critical Literacy, and Indigenous Resistance," 93–5.

100 Apple, "Freire and the Politics of Race in Education," 115; Bowers, "Why a Critical Pedagogy of Place Is an Oxymoron," 329; Kee and Carr-Chellman, "Paulo Freire, Critical Literacy, and Indigenous Resistance"; Marchand, "Application of Paulo Freire," 49.

101 Bowers, "Why a Critical Pedagogy of Place Is an Oxymoron," 331.

102 CIP has generally been used to refer to critical Indigenous pedagogy (singular). However, I use it here in the plural because it must vary across diverse Indigenous Nations and communities in order to meet the needs and goals of those communities.

103 Lee, "I Came Here to Learn," 20–1; Smith "Mai te Maramatanga"; Sweeney Windchief and Timothy San Pedro, *Applying Indigenous Research Methods: Storying with Peoples and Communities* (New York: Routledge 2019).

104 Garcia and Shirley, "Performing Decolonization."

105 Hampton, "Towards a Redefinition of Indian Education."

106 Garcia and Shirley, "Performing Decolonization," 80.

107 Bowers, "Why a Critical Pedagogy of Place Is an Oxymoron," 331; Corson, "Community-Based Education," 245–7; Siemens, "Education for Reconciliation," 133.

108 Siemens, "Education for Reconciliation," 133; Smith, "Indigenous Struggle."

109 Cajete, "Contemporary Indigenous Education," 1131.

110 Smith, "Indigenous Struggle," 10–14; Smith, "Mai te Maramatanga," quote at 49–50.

111 Cajete, "Contemporary Indigenous Education," 1127; Garcia and Shirley, "Performing Decolonization"; Lee, "I Came Here to Learn," 3–8.

112 Lee, "I Came Here to Learn," 3–8.

113 Corson, "Community-Based Education," 247.

114 Corson, 245–7; Siemens, "Education for Reconciliation," 131.

115 Kee and Carr-Chellman, "Paulo Freire, Critical Literacy, and Indigenous Resistance," 110.

116 Apple, "Freire and the Politics of Race in Education."

117 Smith, "Indigenous Struggle," 94.

PART FIVE

Freire in Attempts at Transformation in Asia in the Last Decades

navigation reversals invert

Alan Wilkinson

14 A Historical Analysis of the Application of Paulo Freire's Critical Literacy in the Design of the Bangladesh Rural Advancement Committee's Functional Education Curriculum from 1972 to 1981

MOHAMMAD ABUL FATEH

Introduction

Brazilian pedagogue Paulo Freire's work was known in Bangladesh in the 1970s, and several organizations applied his adult literacy methods and principles. The Bangladesh Rural Advancement Committee (BRAC, or ব্র্যাক in Bengali) was one of the NGOs in which Freire's discourse was made explicit in terms of theory, policy, pedagogy, and practice. BRAC's key founder, Fazle Hasan Abed, brought Freirean principles to the organization's initiatives after 1973, with the objective of alleviating poverty by developing human resources through education.[1] BRAC's literacy program in the early 1970s had been unsuccessful, but it had better outcomes in the mid-1970s after adapting and contextualizing Freirean principles in its functional education curriculum. Therefore, I will focus on BRAC's education initiatives from 1972 to 1981. In this analysis, I will provide a brief history of Bangladesh, its socio-economic conditions, the establishment of BRAC, and its adoption of adult education as a development tool. Then I will look at Abed's interpretation of Freire in the context of his political intentionality and his perception of BRAC's needs. In this way I will uncover how Freire's adult literacy theory was incorporated into the design and practice of BRAC's functional education curriculum.

My analysis examines internal pedagogical sources such as discussion topics, themes, context, teachers' training, teachers' roles, and in-class activities related to BRAC's literacy programs that made use of Freirean pedagogy. I also investigate some of BRAC's documents and publications, such as annual reports and project proposals. Quentin Skinner's theory of interpretation provides a theoretical and methodological framework through which to examine Abed's statements and documents. Skinner's approaches illuminate the intentionality behind his utterances, and I embrace his claim that "historical differences over fundamental issues may reflect differences of intention and convention" rather than differences in values.[2] Skinner's theory thus throws light on Abed's intentionality in designing BRAC's curriculum in the socio-political context of Bangladesh. I also rely on Martyn Thompson's reception and interpretation theory to analyse the uptake of Freire's philosophy by Abed and BRAC. Thompson suggested that both the meanings perceived or understood by readers and the views proposed by authors are important in the process of reception.[3] In my analysis of the documentation, I use Glenn A. Bowen's approach to examine the reception of Freire "within an interpretative paradigm," and in this case across cultures.[4] Bowen argued that the researcher-analyst needs to take "into account the original purpose of each document, the context in which it was produced, and the intended audience."[5]

There is literature, in some cases laudatory, referring to BRAC's development strategy involving education and microcredit.[6] Others are critical of the way BRAC dealt with Freire's modified version of conscientization within a functional approach.[7] This chapter tries to cover a gap in the analysis, mainly in terms of how Freire's adult literacy methods were integrated into BRAC's curriculum and practice, and how the notion of conscientization was transformed. I will take a critical approach to explain BRAC's reception of Freire's ideas and praxis.

Historical Background of Bangladesh: Decolonization and Continuity of Poverty and Oppression

Before its independence in 1971, Bangladesh was an integral part of the history of the Indian subcontinent, particularly of British India from 1757 to 1947, and then of Pakistan from 1947 to 1971. When the British departed in 1947, the subcontinent was partitioned between India and Pakistan. Until 14 August 1947, Bangladesh was known as East Bengal, then as East Pakistan from 1947 to 1971. It is critical to mention here that, although Pakistan (East and West together) achieved independence from the British colonizers in 1947, it was still in the shadow of British rule due to its colonial mechanisms and aspects of its the government and society. Independent Pakistan did not make any significant changes in its new constitution. Therefore, all forms of oppression, discrimination, and exploitation continued to mount soon after 1947. The country, having fallen victim to military dictatorship, poverty, inequality, political subjugation, language discrimination, insecurity, and diminished civil and citizenship rights, saw massive resistance under the leadership of political activist Sheikh Mujibur Rahman and his associates in East Pakistan at the end of the 1960s. These protests and demonstrations against oppressive social, political, and economic mandates led to a war of liberation in East Pakistan in 1971. After this nine-month-long conflict, at the cost of three million lives, the sovereign country of Bangladesh was born on 16 December 1971.

At the time of independence, Bangladesh was one of the poorest countries in the world on almost every socio-economic indicator. It had an international debt of US$500 million, and the 1971 war resulted in more than US$1.2 billion in damages.[8] Only a small amount of infrastructure had been developed between 1947 and 1971 in East Pakistan, and the transportation, communication, housing, power transmission, public utilities, bridges, railways, and academic and hospital infrastructures were all seriously damaged during the war.[9] Education and health services were basic or absent, and 80 per cent of the population was illiterate. Most people lived in mud, bamboo, or thatch houses in rural areas where water and sanitation facilities were poor.

In independent Bangladesh, overpopulation and food scarcity were the two biggest challenges throughout the 1970s. Most of the rural poor experienced food insecurity and struggled to provide for their families. Referring to these conditions, Smillie states that "in the rural areas, almost three fourths of the income of a rural family was devoted to food, and the poorer the family, the greater the level of effort required to obtain it."[10] In 1974, more than three-quarters of Bangladeshis lived in poverty, and almost half lived in conditions of extreme poverty.[11] Though these numbers reflected the dire circumstances of the population, behind this poverty, there existed social, political, and economic factors that were invisible or missed in interpretations of the real crisis. There were also international and regional political influences on rural poverty and deprivation, as well as structural oppression.

Creation of BRAC and Its Journey to Functional Education

It is important to note that after Bangladesh achieved independence in 1971, NGOs were differentiated by their functions and activities. NGOs were considered distinct entities and were often referred to as institutional spaces. NGOs' participatory and collective style of work in communities, as well as their ownership structures, made them different from traditional governmental and private organizations.[12] However, the characteristics of NGOs evolved over time, and they could no longer be regarded as discrete functional spaces. This history helped shape the context for the development of BRAC and its later functional education curriculum.

Fazle Hasan Abed and colleagues established BRAC in 1972 as an independent relief organization to help the rural poor and those affected by the war in Sulla, a remote area in the country's Sylhet District. In the beginning, BRAC's "early objective was to provide relief and rehabilitation assistance to the refugees returning from India to resettle in Bangladesh."[13] However, after working with returning refugees to rebuild their houses, BRAC shifted its focus to long-term rural community development. Because Abed believed that long-term relief programs would promote dependency and weaken the morale of the rural poor,[14] he broadened BRAC's efforts to include economic and social development projects that would promote sustainable poverty reduction.

Abed understood that poverty was the result of the oppressive social structure of the rural elites, and he recognized that, unless deprived people became aware of their betterment options, all economic supports provided to assist them would be wasted. He was also aware of the value of education and its correlation with sustainable socio-economic growth. The critical ideas of Ivan Illich, Frantz Fanon, Andre Gunder Frank, and Paulo Freire inspired Abed to consider education from a more diverse perspective, as an integral part of development.[15] In the context of BRAC, he recognized illiteracy as a barrier to socio-economic development.

Abed consequently introduced an education campaign for adults in Sulla in 1973, where he had started BRAC's relief and rehabilitation project in 1972. Sulla was a remote and largely underdeveloped Hindu-populated area where 90 per cent of the population was illiterate.[16] In the Sulla proposal to Oxfam, the donor agency, Abed stated, "We believe that an adult literacy program is critical to the success of all development efforts and that it must be functionally related to the improvement of the occupational skill of the people so that literacy can directly contribute to higher productivity."[17]

BRAC launched its first adult literacy program through the Sulla Project: Phase II (1 November 1972–30 June 1974) in the "Sulla Project area to cover the entire illiterate population, male and female, of the 15–50 age group in three years."[18] However, BRAC's first literacy drive was unsuccessful despite the allocation of resources and the best efforts of those involved in the program. It is important to note that BRAC did not use Freire's critical literacy approach in this first literacy drive, but after analysing "the poor performance,"[19] BRAC decided to initiate an informal functional education program. Regarding the development of a new functional education course, Abed stated that "we therefore put into practice Brazilian educator Paulo Freire's principles on conscientization, enunciated in his *Pedagogy of the Oppressed*."[20]

Freire's Critical Literacy Approach

Freire's critical literacy is an instructional approach that has essential features for its learners to bring about structural changes, or a "model of an alternative society."[21] The approach refers to an emancipatory process through which a person is empowered to uncover and decode social and political aspects of texts, organizations, the social status quo, and cultural practices to expose concerns relevant to their immediate environment.[22] Freire's critical literacy attempts to incite consciousness among learners and to drive them to undertake critical interventions to deal with exploitation and oppression in their social contexts. According to Mayo "cultural action for freedom" and "cultural revolution" are the key concepts of Freire's critical literacy.[23]

The Freirean terms "critical literacy," "conscientization" (*conscientização*), and "praxis" are inseparably intertwined. The concept of praxis, as reflected in Freire's critical pedagogy, speaks to the dialectical connection between consciousness and the real world. Freire also drew on Marx and Engels for "conscientization,"[24] which refers to a psycho-social process in which people constantly learn, unlearn, and relearn about the contradictions of their society. Therefore, conscientization is an important aspect of a praxis that is evolving continually. Freire's *conscientização* stands for the awakening of critical awareness, and praxis is the reflection and action directed towards structural transformation.[25]

In the critical literacy approach, Freire opposes education that has an ideological intent of indoctrination in order to make learners adjust to their world of structural oppression.[26] In his pedagogical model, individuals learn to cultivate their own growth through situations from daily life that provide useful learning experiences. Freire believed in the liberating potential of education, and therefore viewed politics and pedagogy as inseparable. He stated that education and politics are connected, and teaching and learning are thereby profoundly political.[27] Freire described this relationship between education and politics as the key principle of his critical pedagogy and emphasized that teachers and students should be made aware of the politics that surround education. He also argued that political force is required to liberate education and that oppressors are against any humanizing or liberating education. Therefore, the oppressed should not expect the oppressor to liberate them. Because freedom will not be bestowed on the oppressed by the oppressor automatically, Freire urged the oppressed to take responsibility for their own struggle, to liberate themselves and their oppressors as well.[28]

BRAC's Early Literacy Program and Why It Failed

As mentioned above, BRAC's first initiative to educate adults in Sulla was unsuccessful. For that project, BRAC had developed an adult literacy curriculum that consisted of three textbooks (including one on numeracy skills designed as an accounts book), constructed 255 literacy centres in 220 villages, and trained 293 local men and women to be teachers to provide free lessons. BRAC planned to deliver lessons to 84,000 illiterate people in the evenings, to complete two courses per year, and to eradicate adult illiteracy from the region within three years. After eighteen months, only 5 per cent of participants were still attending, even though 5,000 villagers had signed up for the program. BRAC wrote a report to Oxfam and explaining that the initiative had failed as a result of poor law and order in the country, inflation (at a rate of 70 per cent in over the eighteen months of the project), and the fact that its field assistants were "wanting in leadership qualities and mental discipline."[29] BRAC also pointed out that the teachers they had hired to run the program were disappointing, as most of them "were unable to impart functional education to the learners as they concentrated more on alphabetization."[30] BRAC reported that the teaching materials and methodology failed to retain learners' interest because they were designed to teach only literacy and numeracy, which had no immediate benefit for this audience. However, Nobusue[31] has stated that technical errors and the social power structure were the two main reasons for the project's failure. The first was caused by boring textbooks and vocational training unsuitable to the rural economy; the second was due to BRAC's services being passed into the hands of wealthy farmers.

In an interview, Abed reflected on the project's failure and noted how the community centres unfortunately disregarded the learners' needs in the initial program design. Abed commented on BRAC's failure, asking, "after a hard day's work who wants to go to a community centre to read and write? Something that will never come to any use for them."[32] Regarding situations like this, Freire said, "authentic education is not carried on by 'A' *for* 'B' or by 'A' *about* 'B,' but rather by 'A' *with* 'B,' mediated by the world – a world which impresses and challenges both parties, giving rise to views or opinions about it."[33] Clearly, these aspects were absent in BRAC's first education initiative in the Sulla project area. In response to these unsatisfactory outcomes, BRAC discarded its traditional approach to adult literacy, and in 1974 adopted and adapted the Freirean literacy method.

Reception of Critical Pedagogy: BRAC's Development of a Functional Curriculum

Having learned from the failure of its first literacy drive in Sulla, BRAC wanted to design a curriculum that was related to the practical improvement of the people's occupational skills and directly contributed to increased productivity. To this end, BRAC took steps to develop "a non-formal functional education program suitable to adult learners and compatible to BRAC's development strategy."[34] BRAC's new approach aimed at changing learners' attitudes and behaviours and to push them towards newer ideas on health, family planning, and agricultural practices. It was also expected to teach learners to read and understand simple texts that were likely to be of use and to write legibly. Lastly, it aimed to enhance learners' awareness of their ability to think, plan, and act on their own for a better life. According to BRAC's documents,[35] the methodology to teach illiterate adults was completely redesigned to match the principle that the course should seek to draw the participants into an investigative activity.

To achieve these new objectives, BRAC defined fifteen types of activities connected to the problems and interests of the potential learners. The activities were then divided into components "to be carried out in three cycles over a period of 21 months from May 1974 to January 1976."[36] BRAC set up a material development team in its head office in Dhaka in May 1974. A survey was conducted of landless villagers in the program area to figure out themes connected to their life and skills that could be discussed in classes. Later, to improve its curriculum, BRAC also enlisted the help of international consultants like World Education Inc., based in New York.[37]

Although BRAC undertook consultations when it developed the functional education curriculum and materials, these primarily involved the local people and analysts from the target group. BRAC's material development team conducted surveys and supported the process with institutional and logistical assistance. According to Imam, BRAC's functional education "approach has always been one of allowing felt needs to emerge from the target population's own analysis of its situation within the overall socio-economic environment."[38] Therefore, BRAC's functional education curriculum was designed based on learners' participation through dialogue facilitated by the teachers, with the goal of creating a curriculum that was relevant to the people's real-life problems and that offered practical solutions. According to BRAC's *Functional Education: An Overview*, the learning process of a functional education class was composed of the following steps:

1. Large group discussions of stimulus (e.g., illustrations, stories, role plays, games), and analysis of this stimulus developed through the following questioning sequence:
   a. questions to elicit simple descriptions and observations dealing with obvious facts
   b. questions that call for analysis to uncover cause-effect relationships
   c. questions that deal with attitudes, feelings, and values
2. Small group discussion for consolidation of ideas for action
3. Reports from small groups
4. Large group discussion about the reports for generalization of the group decision[39]

In an overview of the development of its functional education curriculum, the same report stated that "much of the inspiration for this course was derived from the ideas of the famous Brazilian educationist Paulo Freire."[40]

How Freirean Concepts Were Incorporated into BRAC's Literacy Curriculum

Although Freire's ideas had a profound impact on BRAC's curriculum design and practice, I will discuss Freire's major concepts as they were adapted and adopted in BRAC's literacy curriculum in relation to its needs and development initiatives. I will then focus on how BRAC dealt with vernacular issues in the Bangladeshi context in relation to critical literacy, and what people perceived about Freire's critical consciousness in BRAC's initiatives.

Conscientization

"Conscientization," or raising critical consciousness (বিশ্লেষণাত্মক/ সমালোচনামূলকসচেতনতা বৃদ্ধি), is one of the most important aspects of Freire's critical literacy. Freire's notion of conscientization refers to the ways in which learners develop a sense of investigation into and critical understanding of their immediate social reality and the root causes of their oppression. Such understanding or conscientization (বিশ্লেষণাত্মক/সমালোচনামূলক সচেতনতা) makes students realize that their suffering is not caused by God's will or "organized disorder,"[41] which in turn leads them to challenge the oppressive social structures in which they live. For Freire, conscientization is the essence of education, the integral part required to shape a person and society. Interestingly, although BRAC adopted a few tenets of Freirean pedagogy, conscientization was not one of the key objectives of their new curriculum. BRAC's version of conscientization was largely guided by the learning experiences of its adults "for deepening their self-perception" in order to alleviate their material poverty.[42] Thus, BRAC's adult learners did not perceive or understand the revolutionary and politically radical essence of Freire's conscientization. To them, conscientization was largely about coming together to enhance learning about health and agriculture and to take loans to initiate activities that might allow them to improve their economic conditions.

To maintain students' interest and to deal with absenteeism and dropout rates, BRAC focused on designing engaging activities related to the lived experiences of the learners. BRAC intended "to modify students' attitudes and behaviour towards family planning, nutrition, health care and agricultural practices."[43] Although Abed knew about the revolutionary work of Paulo Freire by 1973, as stated by BRAC's number two employee, Khushi Kabir,[44] BRAC's new curriculum did not reflect Freire's radical conscientization, or indeed any radical ideology.

BRAC launched the new curriculum based on Freirean principles in Sulla Project: Phase II, in May 1974. However, the outcome was not as satisfactory as expected. While there were some positive outcomes in terms of class attendance, retaining learners' interest, communication among the learners, and reduced dropout rates, more than 50 per cent of the participants did not complete the course.[45] Nevertheless, BRAC continued with its education initiative and launched new adult literacy programs in other districts, including Jamalpur and Manikganj.

In 1978, BRAC adopted a target-group development approach along with its own form of conscientization.[46] The organization now targeted households with less than half an acre of land and at least one household member who did manual labour for more than a hundred days per year. Following the new policy, BRAC started to systematically conscientize all its Village Organization (VO) members through functional education starting in 1978. BRAC used VOs as the main vehicle for following Freire's principle that if the oppressed are to be conscientized, they need to be unified through a shared cultural synthesis.[47] Through VOs, BRAC's intention was to create a space in which adult learners could learn, meet, and discuss issues relevant to their problems and to organize "cultural circles," such as Freire had done. However, although the literacy sessions included topics such as money, land, interest, social status, and famine,[48] there was nothing in the process that could bring political consciousness to the participants.

In the new curriculum, BRAC did not engage its teachers to act as political agents in the process of conscientization to mediate discussions and promote praxis in and outside the classroom, as Freire suggested. BRAC did not equip teachers to be committed to political actions on the side of the learners, or to take action with them, although Freire considered such acts by teachers as "pedagogical action in the authentic sense of the word."[49] Rather, BRAC's teaching materials and guidelines were highly prescriptive. Teachers were trained to stick to the guidelines provided by BRAC, and there was little scope for them to act and reflect freely. It is also important to note that although BRAC conducted surveys in its project areas before designing its revised curriculum, the resulting reports do not specify how much teachers' voices were reflected in the new curriculum. Rather, in the second cycle of curriculum development, BRAC's field staff, instead of teachers, were asked to fill out forms while observing classes regularly, and field managers were asked to write weekly observation reports.

BRAC's actions show that it did not trust its teachers and had no faith in the ability of its own people. Following the frameworks of interpretation of historical documents and analysis proposed by Skinner, Thompson, and Bowen, it can be seen that BRAC's attempts to conscientize its own functional education learners and teachers were not radical or political in the way we see in Freirean pedagogy. Rather, BRAC used its curriculum, teacher training, teaching materials, and guidelines to maintain the learners and teachers in a position of dependence.[50] This reflects the concreteness of BRAC's domination and implies that BRAC's use of learner-teacher dependence was an oppressive tactic, one that obstructed the growth of radical conscientization in and among the learners and teachers.

Negation of Banking Education

The negation of banking education is another key element of Freire's critical literacy. Freire stated that, in banking education, the all-knowing teacher sees students as empty objects that know nothing, and hence pours knowledge into them. This approach limits the thinking and action of learners, making them compliant and adaptable to oppressive social structures and the world as it is. Freire argued that banking education resists dialogue mythologizes reality "to conceal certain facts which explain the way human beings exist in the world."[51] Freire also considered banking education dehumanizing as it obstructs the learner's autonomy and ability to justify and conceptualize knowledge at a personal level. For Freire, banking education serves the interests of the oppressors, who do not want to expose the oppressed to their real-world conditions.

BRAC also opposed banking education – at least in theory. The organization viewed teachers as facilitators with mutual respect for learners, not as dispensers of knowledge. BRAC used dialogic education facilitated by different student-centred formats of teaching, such as demonstrations, role playing, discussions, drama, story, brainstorming, and debates. It also used unconventional seating arrangements in the classrooms, similar to Freire's "cultural circles,"[52] where learners freely take part in dialogue and generate discussion to understand their immediate social reality. In terms of selecting topics and engaging learners in class discussions, BRAC surveyed and consulted villagers, and trained its teachers to be dialogical to avoid boring lessons where words are used without facts, emotions, or feelings. To break with the mechanistic, static, and vertical pattern of banking education, BRAC also introduced problem-posing education to avoid teacher-owned lessons, and it maintained room for reciprocal teaching and learning in the new curriculum.

However, BRAC did not negate banking education in the radical way Freire did. Abed had a different intention within the framework of BRAC's needs in the critical socio-political context of Bangladesh. BRAC's rejection of banking education was not aimed at liberating learners from oppression along with its teachers, the way Freire had intended. Rather, learning from its early failure in Sulla, BRAC rejected banking education in order to retain students' interest and reduce absenteeism.

Despite criticizing the banking model of education, BRAC largely followed it in the design of its curriculum. A consultant from the United States was hired to design the curriculum in BRAC's "laboratory" in Dhaka, where classroom teachers were not directly involved in the decision- or lesson-making processes. Although a baseline survey was conducted and some field work was done, BRAC's staff designed the complete curriculum with the goal of a "possible eventual implementation throughout Bangladesh."[53] Essentially, regional teachers and teacher-trainers were not "called upon to know,"[54] but instead were expected to follow the guidelines prescribed by BRAC. After examining documents and testimonies based on Skinner, Thompson, and Bowen's theoretical frameworks,[55] it is evident that mimicking the pedagogical prescriptions provided by BRAC resulted in no less a banking education than that provided by any other similar model. In BRAC's eyes, teachers were viewed as empty vessels who were expected to follow an authoritative, top-down approach, just like the oppressed learners in the classroom described by Freire.

Although BRAC adopted Freirean principles in its teacher-training module in keeping with the needs of the trainees, the objective was to familiarize them with BRAC's methods. In its reports and materials, BRAC did not make it clear to what extent facilitators were able to avoid banking education in their initiatives. It is important to consider this, because BRAC's early literacy program in Sulla was largely unsuccessful because it followed the conventional banking model.

With the new curriculum, there was about a 50 per cent dropout rate because banking education was still an issue. In a study of BRAC's early functional education program in Sulla Project: Phase II, Montgomery and colleagues found that some adult learners could remember only a few lessons or bits of content, and could not explain the relevance of the topics they studied to their lives.[56] The authors criticized BRAC's promotion of rote learning (the banking model) in its functional education program, noting that VO members had to memorize seventeen promises related to credit rules as prescribed by BRAC. They stated: "Once a VO is formed, members begin to save Tk. 2 per week, learn seventeen 'promises' which have to be ritualistically repeated in chorus at every weekly meeting, and are instructed on credit rule."[57] Here we see that BRAC was pushing the credit rule of monetary activities as part of their functional education program, while promoting banking education.

In my own analysis of BRAC's report,[58] I also noticed that BRAC used all-knowing authoritative and prescriptive approaches to train its teachers and teacher-trainers, a method very much aligned with the banking model of education that Freire harshly criticized. Unfortunately, BRAC did not realize that it was dehumanizing its teachers and that, paradoxically, it was using the same alienating instrument of banking education, in what it considered an effort to help.

Problem-Posing Education

Freire's problem-posing method of education is the basis of modern critical pedagogy. Problem-posing education resolves student-teacher conflict, and teachers and learners share their knowledge mutually and respectfully. In this process, teachers are ready to accept solutions from their students, unlike in traditional banking education. Freire believed that through problem-posing education, learners improve their ability to perceive and judge critically, while coming to understand the world as something transformable.[59]

After analysing its poor performance in Sulla, BRAC understood the impact of traditional banking education, and hence adopted problem-posing education in its curriculum. BRAC stated that the "problem-posing method was used to teach literacy and numeracy around a problem perceived by the people but [was] codified to focus attention and stimulate discussion."[60] BRAC used problem-posing education to help learners understand their existing financial conditions, how their economic activities could be improved, and how they could alleviate their poverty level in a real world that is not static but dynamic. BRAC focused on learners' understanding of income-generating activities as a solution to the poverty or economic oppression they faced. To make classroom activities more engaging, BRAC included lessons on sentence structure, phonemes, and pronunciation of combined letters and vowel sounds, all of which were structured around problem-posing themes and topics.[61] Numeracy activities were also integrated to support these problem-posing lessons. Freire focused on the essence of freedom through problem-posing education, in which arguments are not constructed on authority. BRAC, by contrast, did not direct its problem-posing approach towards liberation from oppression, but rather to maintain its own dominance. BRAC did not intend to stimulate praxis – that is, reflection and action towards structural oppression and social transformation. Thus, BRAC acted as an authority in posing the curriculum, rather than standing "*on the side* of the freedom."[62]

In its problem-posing approach, BRAC intentionally depoliticized the discontent or frustration of learners and directed them towards a more passive path of microcredit, investment opportunities, and health-related activities. While the educator acts as a co-creator in problem-posing education to unveil reality and strive for the materialization of critical intervention, BRAC did not intend to engage its teachers and students authentically in creative enquiry and transformation. BRAC increased the number of lessons to address rural issues in the third cycle of material development (the project was extended then ended in December 1976), but it put less emphasis on regional-specific problems and local context.[63]

Based on Skinner's theory of interpretation,[64] my analysis suggests that BRAC did not design functional curriculum to mobilize its adult learners to become complete beings with the ultimate goal of liberating them from oppression or helping them to question their circumstances, as Freire had advocated. BRAC instead organized its clients or participants mostly to understand the social problems that hindered their income-generating opportunities and prevented them from enjoying basic social services. It did this despite Abed's awareness of the multidimensional aspects of poverty, and how all kinds of deprivation constituted the complex nature of poverty in rural Bangladesh.[65] While Freire's "pedagogy of the oppressed" is a radical humanist pedagogy accomplished with – not for – the people to engage them in the struggle for their own liberation,[66] BRAC's problem-posing approach did not affirm its learners "as beings in the process of *becoming* – as unfinished, uncompleted beings in and with a likewise unfinished reality."[67]

Dialogue

Dialogue is another important element of Freire's critical literacy that was adapted in the design of BRAC's functional education curriculum. For Freire, dialogue is a human phenomenon, and "the essence of dialogue itself: *the word.*"[68] Freire stated that dialogue is a cognitive act of innovation that unveils reality, an "encounter between men, mediated by the world" and a fundamental precondition for people for their true humanization.[69] He viewed dialogue as a process of learning and knowing, and stated that it should not be perceived simply as a technique for engaging students in any specific task. He stated that communication is not possible without dialogue, and that there is no education without communication.[70] He further said that authentic dialogue that requires critical thinking generates more critical thinking, and that preoccupation with the subject of dialogue is like "preoccupation with the content of education."[71] Thus, his methodology is dependent on dialogue, which results in the "open[ing] and extend[ing of] the conversation without necessarily coming to closure with the final word coming from the more powerful person."[72] Freire argued that dialogue cannot exist without humility and profound love for people and the world, and that dialogical education starts with thematic investigation. For Freire, the goal of dialogic education is to expose reality through communication and collaboration with others and the world.[73]

Following Freire, BRAC designed a curriculum and set of materials that rejected narrative lecturing by its teachers and that adopted a participatory format to promote teacher-student learning in a collaborative process to act on reality. After 1974, BRAC adapted the dialogic method in its functional education curriculum, which engaged the students in problem-solving activities with real-life considerations that allowed them to discuss or come up with multiple and adaptable solutions to the problems they faced. In classroom activities, learners sat in circles, worked in small groups, and took part in discussions where both "teacher and learners became actors in a process of mutual communication."[74] Students and teachers identified problems and solutions together, after which open-ended questions and answers resulting from collaborative efforts were presented to analyse the situation and possible alternatives.[75] Teachers were to act as facilitators and initiate discussions through various classroom activities.

BRAC expected that in using such lessons and classroom activities, people would talk about their concerns and interests. In this way, village institutions would grow as people realized the need to come together "to deal with various problems of credit, health, family planning, nutrition, education, agriculture, economic activities etc."[76] BRAC did not expect to foment cultural revolution or radical action along the lines advocated by Freire. However, BRAC claimed that through functional education, it provided opportunities for teachers and learners to become more aware of social issues and situations compared to rural residents who did not participate in the functional education program.[77]

Generative Theme

The generative theme is another major concept of Freire's critical literacy. Freire suggested that a methodology of thematic investigation should be dialogical and stimulate both teachers and learners to be consciously connected to their social reality.[78] A generative theme should be consistent with its liberating intention, and relevant to teachers' and learners' language and ability to understand the real world. Freire stated that if generative themes are perceived and comprehended in existing reality, it will encourage critical thinking in the minds of the people as they encounter and view the world "fatalistically, dynamically or statically."[79] He believed that to stimulate community action, people must recognize issues about which they have a passion and show a willingness to initiate action for transformation. Freire said that "the concept of a generative theme is neither an arbitrary invention nor a working hypothesis to be proved."[80] For him, a generative theme was a cultural or political topic particularly relevant to the learners, one that allowed them to stimulate a didactic class discussion. BRAC also considered generative words and sentences centring on the themes identified as the main concerns of rural people. BRAC recognized that lesson themes needed to connect learners to the issues that had an impact on their daily existence.

In May 1974, BRAC's functional material development unit was formed, and in June 1974, BRAC's field workers conducted a survey in nineteen villages in the Sulla project area to determine the content of the functional education curriculum.[81] As a result, the first batch of lessons included generative words and suggestive short sentences. Large charts with drawings were used to stimulate discussion during lessons. In its report on searching for generative themes and topics, BRAC stated that "the search for relevant topics, generative words and preparation of effective formats for each lesson was done through repeated surveys, discussions, pretesting, and revisions for about 21 months."[82] BRAC's lesson plans included questions designed to elicit descriptions and observations about learners' social reality. The questions also contained prompts related to learners' emotions, feelings, values, and attitudes. By incorporating these generative themes, the lessons included diverse topics related to villagers' concerns, including "agriculture, pisciculture, horticulture, animal husbandry, poultry raising, health, hygiene, nutrition, family planning, mother and child-care, cooperatives, exploitations, social prejudices and vices and so on."[83]

BRAC claimed that all lessons included generative words and phrases that sprang from the central concerns covered in the lessons and that were particularly evocative of the issues being discussed. Examples include "house," "hunger," "money," "co-operative," "germ carrier," "vegetable cooking," "multiple cropping," and "self-interest versus community development."[84] In the classes, these words and phrases were introduced in written and visual forms, so learners could grasp the meanings for later recognition in written contexts. A diverse array of formats, such as illustrations, stories, letters, demonstrations, discussions, role playing, debates, and workshops, were used to introduce topics and initiate discussions.

With the new curriculum, BRAC tried to provide learners with the opportunity to be aware of their social reality, to feel competent about their ability to act, and to bring them together.[85] However, I argue that BRAC did not clearly define this in its functional curriculum materials, nor did it indicate what type of praxis it wanted to generate among the learners so as to enable them to demand, act, and react in the service of structural transformation. BRAC did not include any expected or visible outcomes of thematic investigations in its reports, or information on how and to what extent the learners were able to decode the systemic social oppression and thereby generate a radical struggle against it.

BRAC wanted to include generative themes relevant to its adult learners' immediate concerns in order to retain their interest in attending the lessons and to understand the social issues they faced. However, based on Skinner's theory of interpretation, and placing BRAC's documents in their historical contexts, it can be assumed that BRAC did not aim to use this method as a tool of conscientization, humanization, and liberation in the way Freire did. I argue that the generative themes used in BRAC's functional education curriculum did not contribute to any ongoing political debate, and were instead intended to focus the attention of the rural poor on social adaptation rather than genuine transformation.

According to Freire,[86] educators' language should be familiar to the learners they communicate with. If the language used by educators is not aligned with the real situation of the learners they address, their talk becomes "alienated or alienating rhetoric."[87] Freire asserted that the language and thought of an educator or politician should be like the thought and language of the world at large. He said, "To communicate effectively, educator and politician must understand the structural conditions in which the thought and language of the people are dialectically framed."[88] However, in my assessment of BRAC's report, based on

Bowen's document analysis framework,[89] I found that BRAC placed more emphasis on a national or standard practice of language than on regional language.

It is important to note that people of different regions in Bangladesh speak different dialects, and many standard words are quite unknown to rural people. For example, the Bengali word for quarrel (ঝগড়া) can be spoken or written as বিবাদ, কলহ, ঝগড়াঝাঁটি, or ঠেস্সাঠেস্সি, depending on the region. Although Freire advocated for contextualizing language, it is not clear in BRAC's literature how the organization dealt with this issue. In terms of including problem-posing topics in the curriculum, I also noticed that BRAC covered more topics with national implications than regionally specific ones. BRAC stated that "there are fewer regional-specific problems covered but more with national implications."[90] Therefore, it can be argued that BRAC designed a common curriculum for all people, regardless of their different dialects and region-specific problems, in a one-size-fits-all approach to education, which was of course contrary to the one suggested by Freire.

Conclusion

BRAC's functional education curriculum is rooted in a community development approach based on a co-opted version of Freire's critical pedagogy. Although BRAC recognized that the landless poor were victims of exploitative social structures established by rural elites, its curriculum guided the rural poor to engage with single, micro, personal, and community issues, rather than the underlying root issues of poverty, corruption, exploitation, and social injustice. Although no evaluation or empirical study was conducted, BRAC claimed there were visible changes among the participants after Sulla Project: Phase II, and that they were able to better their lives in the long run. They indicated that the education campaign went well as part of the development strategy, although there was no initiation of any cultural revolution by its participants against the structures of oppression in which they were alienated.[91] BRAC did not provide any specific evidence in its reports on functional education around what political and structural transformation resulted from this literacy program.[92]

In my analysis, I found that while Abed facilitated the fight of the poor against poverty, he was nonetheless politically passive. Abed's plan of betterment for the poor was not in line with Freire's notion of liberation and the subject as political agent. Although he acknowledged that Freire wanted to raise the critical consciousness of the oppressed through critical pedagogy that aimed to balance the power structure, Abed only intended to raise a naive consciousness among the participants. Abed understood the complex nature of rural poverty and acknowledged the existence of class conflict and struggle, but BRAC's deliberate "cultural circles" and systematic actions did not aim to challenge these issues.

Abed talked about the influence and reception of Freirean principles in BRAC's development strategy, project proposals, reports, and adult education curriculum.[93] However, BRAC's field activities did not reflect these principles in any genuine sense. While Freirean principles were highly radical and promoted political freedom, Abed intentionally depoliticized and de-radicalized Freirean concepts to suit BRAC's needs in the socio-political context of Bangladesh. Abed's intention and BRAC's documents suggest that neither the organization nor its founder wanted to be politically involved with the struggle of the participants. Abed did not act as the leader of BRAC's movement to mobilize the villagers in their struggle for freedom, but rather manipulated them towards small income-generating activities and microfinance projects, which in turn weakened villagers' struggle for freedom. It is also important to note here that some of BRAC's staff left the organization because they thought its microfinance activities did not serve the poor in their struggle for better conditions.[94]

Although Freire suggested that the leader must act dialogically with the people in their struggle for freedom and "say it *with* the people,"[95] I argue that Abed imposed his decisions as an outsider and from a superior and safe position. He developed programs to alleviate poverty but did not take part as one of the oppressed in these struggles. Of such leaders, Freire said, "they do not liberate, nor are they liberated: they oppress."[96] Thus, I argue that, for BRAC, alleviating the harshest aspects of poverty was equivalent to liberating the poor. Freire, by contrast, argued that authentic liberation entails a process of humanization, and that the praxis of all the oppressed is "to transform the world."[97] However, BRAC did not intend to initiate any humanization process in its functional education curriculum for adult learners, who were in turn dehumanized by rural elites. BRAC did not instil any radical component of praxis that would allow program participants to act and reflect on Freire's call to challenge oppressive social structure.

As such, BRAC's functional education curriculum was flattened and conformist. Freire demanded complete freedom for the poor and challenged the established social status quo, whereas BRAC limited its scope to economic opportunities and took a redemptionist approach to change within the system of oppression. BRAC's struggle for the poor was largely limited to material gain in a capitalistic structure and the support of the production system of the rural people. BRAC's functional literacy program was more successful than its first program in Sulla, after it adopted and adapted Freirean ideas. However, it lacked the broader Freirean view of freedom and the humanizing process of education.

While BRAC's literacy program probably addressed some of the needs of the villagers in terms of numeracy, literacy, and vocational skills, it did not lead them to become radical subjects capable of leaving behind their status as alienated objects.[98] I argue that although BRAC's functional education curriculum created a platform for rural people to move towards limited and personal economic improvement vis-à-vis material poverty, it did not help them move away from systemic poverty and oppression. As such, I suggest that BRAC's literacy curriculum was devoid of true liberating praxis. Instead, it manipulated its learners and made them dependent on BRAC. It also limited the learners' capacity and opportunity to fight for structural change, social reform, and justice, in contrast to the call for genuine social transformation that Freire wrote of in his *Pedagogy of the Oppressed*.[99] Clearly, Freire's goal of enabling learners to read the world, to challenge it, change it, and humanize it[100] did not align with Abed's vision for BRAC's functional education curriculum.

NOTES

1 BRAC, *Report on Development of Innovative Methodologies in Functional Education for Bangladesh* (Dhaka: BRAC, 1977).

2 Quentin Skinner, "Meaning and Understanding in the History of Ideas," *History and Theory* 8, no. 1 (1969): 3–53.

3 Martyn P. Thompson, "Reception Theory and the Interpretation of Historical Meaning," *History and Theory* 32, no. 3 (1993): 248–72.

4 Glenn A. Bowen, "Document Analysis as a Qualitative Research Method," *Qualitative Research Journal* 9, no. 2 (2009): 27–40.

5 Bowen, 38.

6 Ian Smillie, *Freedom from Want: The Remarkable Success Story of BRAC, the Global Grassroots Organization That's Winning the Fight against Poverty* (Sterling, VA: Kumarian Press, 2009).

7 Mohammad Fateh, "A Historical Analysis on Bangladesh Rural Advancement Committee (BRAC) and Abed's Reception of Paulo Freire's Critical Literacy in Designing BRAC's Functional Education Curriculum in Bangladesh from 1972 to 1981" (master's thesis, Queen's University, 2020); Mohammad Rafi, "Freire and Experiments in Conscientisation in a Bangladesh Village," *Economic and Political Weekly* 38, no. 37 (13–19 September 2003): 3908–14.

8 Smillie, *Freedom from Want*.

9 Just Faaland and J.R. Parkinson, *Bangladesh: The Test Case of Development* (London: Hurst & Co., 1976).

10 Smillie, *Freedom from Want*, 37.

11 Abdul Hye Hasnat, *Below the Line: Rural Poverty in Bangladesh* (Dhaka: University Press, 1996).

12 Sajjad Zohir, "NGO Sector in Bangladesh: An Overview," *Economic and Political Weekly* 39, no. 36 (January 2004): 4–10.

13 BRAC, *BRAC Annual Report* (Dhaka: BRAC, 2004), 9.

14 BRAC, *BRAC's Functional Education: An Overview* (Dhaka: BRAC, 1980).

15 Smillie, *Freedom from Want*.

16 BRAC, *BRAC's Functional Education*.

17 BRAC, *Sulla Project: An Integrated Programme for Development* (Dhaka: BRAC, 1972), 13.

18 BRAC, 13.

19 BRAC, *BRAC's Functional Education*, 3.

20 Fazle Hasan Abed, "Education Reform," WISE Summit, Doha, Qatar, 2011, https://blog.brac.net/wise-prize-for-education-laureate-speech-by -sir-fazle-hasan-abed/.

21 Peter Mayo, "Praxis in Paulo Freire's Emancipatory Politics," *International Critical Thought* 10, no. 3 (2020): 363.

22 Peter McLaren and Colin Lankshear, *Politics of Liberation: Paths from Freire* (London: Routledge, 1994).

23 Peter Mayo, "Critical Literacy and Emancipatory Politics: The Work of Paulo Freire," *International Journal of Educational Development*, no. 15 (1995): 1.

24 Mayo, "Praxis in Paulo Freire's Emancipatory Politics," 363.

25 Paulo Freire, *Pedagogy of the Oppressed*, 30th anniv. ed. (New York: Continuum, 2000).

26 Freire.

27 Freire.

28 Freire.

29 Smillie, *Freedom from Want*, 30.

30 Smillie, 30.

31 Ken'ichi Nobusue, "Bangladesh: A Large NGO Sector Supported by Foreign Donors," in *The State and NGOs: Perspective from Asia*, ed. Shinichi Shigetomi (Singapore: ISEAS, 2002), 34–56.

32 Scott Macmillan, "Glorious Failure: The Joy of Learning from Your Mistakes," *The Guardian*, 30 March 2015, https://www.theguardian.com/global-development -professionals-network/2015/mar/30/glorious-failure-joy-learning-from -your-mistakes.

33 Freire, *Pedagogy of the Oppressed*, 93.

34 BRAC, *BRAC's Functional Education*, 3.

35 BRAC, *Manikganj Project Report: April 1976 to March 1977* (Dhaka: BRAC, 1977).

36 BRAC.

37 BRAC.

38 Izzedin Imam, "Functional Education: A Development Structure of Learning in Bangladesh," *International Review of Education* 28, no. 2 (1982): 267.

39 BRAC, *BRAC's Functional Education*, 6–7.

40 BRAC, 6–7.

41 Freire, *Pedagogy of the Oppressed*.

42 BRAC, *Manikganj Project Report*, 7.

43 BRAC, 2.

44 Smillie, *Freedom from Want*.

45 BRAC, *Manikganj Project Report*.

46 Rafi, "Freire and Experiments in Conscientisation in a Bangladesh Village," 3908–14.

47 Freire, *Pedagogy of the Oppressed*.

48 BRAC, *Manikganj Project Report*.

49 Freire, *Pedagogy of the Oppressed*, 66.

50 BRAC, *Manikganj Project Report*.

51 Freire, *Pedagogy of the Oppressed*, 81.

52 BRAC, *Manikganj Project Report*.

53 BRAC, *Report on Development of Innovative Methodologies in Functional Education for Bangladesh* (Dhaka: BRAC, 1977).

54 Freire, *Pedagogy of the Oppressed*, 78.

55 Skinner, "Meaning and Understanding in the History of Ideas"; Thompson, "Reception Theory and the Interpretation of Historical Meaning"; Bowen, "Document Analysis as a Qualitative Research Method."

56 Richard Montgomery, Debapriya Bhattacharya, and David Hulme, "Credit for the Poor in Bangladesh. The BRAC Rural Development Programme and the Government Thana Resource Development and Employment Programme," in *Finance Against* Poverty, ed. H. David and P. Mosley (London: Routledge, 1996), 94–176.

57 Montgomery, Battacharya, and Hulme, 104.

58 BRAC, *BRAC's Functional Education*.

59 Freire, *Pedagogy of the Oppressed*.

60 BRAC, *Report on Development of Innovative Methodologies in Functional Education for Bangladesh*, 7.

61 BRAC, *Manikganj Project Report*.

62 Freire, *Pedagogy of the Oppressed*, 80. Emphasis added.

63 BRAC, *Manikganj Project Report*.

64 Skinner, "Meaning and Understanding in the History of Ideas."

65 Kyle Poplin, "Sir Fazle Hasan Abed of BRAC: Poverty's About Deprivation, and It's Fixable," *Next Billion*, 13 April 2016, https://nextbillion.net/sir-fazle -hasan-abed-of-brac-povertys-about-deprivation-and-its-fixable-video/.

66 Freire, *Pedagogy of the Oppressed*.

67 Freire, 37. Emphasis in the original.

68 Freire, 87. Emphasis in original.

69 Freire, 40.

70 Freire.

71 Freire, 43.

72 Beverley Moriarty, P.A. Danaher, and Geoff Danaher, "Freire and Dialogical Pedagogy: A Means for Interrogating Opportunities and Challenges in Australian Postgraduate Supervision," *International Journal of Lifelong Education* 27, no. 4 (2008): 432.

73 Freire, *Pedagogy of the Oppressed*.

74 BRAC, *Manikganj Project Report*.

75 BRAC.

76 BRAC.

77 BRAC, *BRAC's Functional Education*.

78 Freire, *Pedagogy of the Oppressed*.

79 Freire, 106.

80 Freire, 97.

81 BRAC, *Report on Development of Innovative Methodologies in Functional Education for Bangladesh*.

82 BRAC, *BRAC's Functional Education*, 5.

83 BRAC, *Report on Development of Innovative Methodologies in Functional Education for Bangladesh*, 8.

84 BRAC.

85 BRAC, *BRAC's Functional Education*.

86 Freire, *Pedagogy of the Oppressed*.

87 Freire, 45.

88 Freire, 45.

89 Bowen, "Document Analysis as a Qualitative Research Method."

90 BRAC, *Manikganj Project Report*, 6.

91 BRAC, *Report on Development of Innovative Methodologies in Functional Education for Bangladesh*.

92 BRAC, *BRAC's Functional Education*.

93 BRAC, *Manikganj Project Report*; BRAC, *BRAC's Functional Education*; Smillie, *Freedom from Want*.

94 Smillie, *Freedom from Want*.

95 Freire, *Pedagogy of the Oppressed*, 178. Emphasis in the original.

96 Freire, 178.

97 Freire, 79.

98 Freire, 79.

99 Freire, 79.

100 Donaldo Macedo, "Introduction to the 30th Anniversary Edition," in *Pedagogy of the Oppressed*, by Paolo Freire, trans. M.B. Ramos (New York: Continuum, 2005).

15 The Influence and Legacy of Freire's Ideas on Adult Literacy in Post–New War Timor-Leste

TOM O'DONOGHUE

Introduction

Adult literacy campaigns in many countries are often bound up with social and political movements. Such has been the case in Timor-Leste since 1974. From then to the present that nation went through a process of decolonization from Portugal, to colonization by Indonesia, to national independence as a post–new war society in 2004. In all three phases its adult literacy projects were influenced to different degrees by a Freirean approach. That is hardly surprising given the country's long period under the rule of Portugal and the impact of the Portuguese language in many quarters there.

To some extent, the roots of the thinking behind Freirean-influenced literacy movements in Timor-Leste as a whole are in the Cuban effort of 1961, when thousands of high school students, teachers, and literate urban workers were mobilized to teach adults in the countryside.[1] That campaign predated the early work of Freire, who not long after commenced his literacy practices in Brazil.[2] In 1974, he visited Australia,[3] where many became advocates of his emancipatory model of literacy work, yet they had little impact. On that nation's doorstep, though, his ideas began to have an influence on a literacy campaign on the eastern portion of the island of Timor, within Portuguese Timor, a few hundred kilometres north-west of Darwin.[4]

Examining subsequent developments in Timor-Leste in relation to Freire's influence on adult literacy campaigns in the nation is valuable for a number of reasons. For one thing, providing an understanding of the particular ways in which they unfolded is of interest as a historical phenomenon in its own right. Furthermore, detailing how they were not only accepted but also modified in order to fit the political and economic context of the host nation illustrates how advocates of particular positions often need to compromise their fidelity to associated theoretical ideas in order to try to ensure that they be considered useful by those working in other settings.

Much of the remainder of this chapter is taken up with providing an exposition of the adult literacy campaigns in Timor-Leste during each of the three periods detailed already. In doing so emphasis, following what has been stated above, is placed not only on the adoption but also on the adaptation of Freirean ideas. First, however, it is necessary to outline some related general points regarding studies on adult literacy in general.

Freire and Studies on Adult Literacy

This short section is a summary of an extensive exposition by Cabral[5] on the development of studies on adult literacies in countries in the Global South that have experienced major social and political change. In particular, it focuses on the attention he draws to research on the relationship between such change and literacy practices and discourses. On that, Lankshear[6] and Freeland[7] come in for special mention, especially in relation to their work on debates about literacy and the campaign with adults launched in Nicaragua immediately after the Sandinista Revolution. Cabral also highlights the historical work of Kerfoot[8] on how adult basic education projects conducted in South Africa played a part in commencing and supporting action there geared towards promoting social justice and participatory democracy. In similar vein, Stroud and Wee[9] illustrated how local political and ideological settings in parts of South-East Asia influenced and were influenced by particular emancipatory approaches to adult literacy.

Developments in other parts of the world have also come in for academic analysis. In Nepal, for example, an emphasis on the new literacies as part of a pro-democracy campaign influenced various groups of women there. In particular, attention has been drawn to how such semiotic objects as writings, maps, and songs were valuable for learning during engagement in literacy activities.

Distilling generalizations from considerations like those noted above, Cabral concluded that the study of literacy in social movements can have three major foci: the contribution of literacy activities to the formation and dissemination of ideologies, the ways in which literacy serves as a means of imagining or evoking "liberated" worlds, and the processes of inclusion or exclusion set in motion by the introduction of new literacy practices among particular groups of historical actors. In line with Freirean thinking, he also expressed agreement with Barton and Hamilton's[10] view that literacy is a social practice. Thus, the argument went, the everyday lives of people and their participation or otherwise in politics need to be related to the development of adult literacy through reading and writing.

Barton and Hamilton[11] also argued that there are multiple literacies, and that these are linked with different domains of life; have hierarchies of power relationships; are embedded in specific cultural practices and historical contexts; and continue to change and evolve. This is quite a different notion to that promoted by those who advocate functional literacy. Stated in abstract terms, the focus is on the cultural practices within which written and spoken words and numbers are embedded – the ways in which texts are socially regulated and used and the historical contexts from which these practices have developed. In concrete terms, what is stressed is the importance of taking account of what people do with literacy, numeracy, and language, with whom they do it, where they do it, and how they do it.

A possible outcome of implementing practices in line with the latter position, Street[12] argued, is that literacy could set illiterate adults free from oppressive power relations. He also argued that instead of focusing on literacy, one has to understand multiple literacies, understood differently in different social contexts as people absorb literacy practices in their own oral conventions, languages, and ways of making sense of the new literacies. Thinking like that informed developments in Timor-Leste in the recent past, and it is still relevant for today in what is a post-conflict, post–new war society, as it is for similarly situated nations.

Timor-Leste: Education Background

Timor-Leste is the Portuguese name of the nation state in South-East Asia sometimes referred to in English as East Timor. It is also known as the Democratic Republic of Timor-Leste, and it became the first new nation of the twenty-first century when it became independent on 20 May 2002. Prior to that, the Timorese education system operated under three distinct foreign administrations, starting with Portuguese colonization from approximately 1515 to 1975, followed by the Indonesian military occupation from 1975 to 1999, and then by the United Nations Transitional Administration in East Timor (UNTAET) from 1999 to 2002. Each regime attempted to implement its own education ideology and strategies. At the same time, each adopted a similar approach insofar as the Portuguese, Indonesians, and UNTAET each had a clear intention of ensuring domination.[13]

During the long period of Portuguese colonial administration, the education system was severely neglected. However, in the 1950s and '60s, the final decades of foreign rule, some efforts were made by the Catholic Church and by the Portuguese state to provide education for the Indigenous population. Even then, however, access to the most basic education was still limited in comparison to what was available in other Portuguese colonies, including Angola, Cape Verde, Guinea-Bissau, Mozambique, and São Tomé e Príncipe.

Both the Portuguese and the Indonesian administrations saw education as an effective strategy to oppress the local population and to gain political, social, and cultural control. In the case of Portugal, educating a small elite enabled its members, the *assimilados*, to assist it in administering the colony effectively. In the case of Indonesia, the school system promoted *pancasila*, an ideology based on the notion of a singular Indonesia with a shared history and set of values and beliefs, despite the marked diversity in cultures that exists within the archipelago. Furthermore, while there was greater access to primary-level education during the Indonesian military occupation than there was under the Portuguese, it still tended to be the "brightest" Timorese students and the high achievers who received well-paid jobs.

Education was also used by both the Portuguese and the Indonesian administrations to segregate the local society. In the case of the former, a perception that one could not be a civilized person without being schooled in the Portuguese language and literature was promoted. In the case of Indonesia, schooling under tightly regulated and centralized Indonesian control was a mechanism for the development of nationalistic loyalties. Despite such attempts to subjugate the local population, not all students accepted passively every aspect of what they were taught. Thus, under Indonesian rule, two distinct and opposing social groups gradually emerged – namely, those Timorese who were outwardly pro-Indonesia, and those who were quietly pro-independence and partaking in the resistance movement.

Education under both administrations was also promoted to oppress the unique and distinctive cultures of the local population. Under Portugal's rule, the speaking of Tetum, the Austronesian language spoken throughout much of the island, was strictly forbidden in classrooms. Under Indonesian rule, the curriculum conveyed the message to local students that Timorese culture was inferior. Concurrently, Indigenous knowledge, including that relating to traditional foods, medicinal plants, and fishing skills, was downgraded and devalued, and Bahasa Indonesia was the sole language of instruction.

On 30 August 1999, 78.5 per cent of the eligible adult population voted to begin the process that led to formal recognition of an independent nation. The outcome was the birth of the Democratic Republic of Timor-Leste, which became the first new nation of the twenty-first century on 20 May 2002. Violence, however, had gripped the country when Indonesia withdrew three years previously. Pro-Indonesia, anti-independence militias subsequently wrecked most schools. Additionally, 20 per cent of primary school teachers, many of them Indonesian, departed.

During the UNTAET period, the focus in education was on emergency reconstruction. With the help of international donors, the education sector was completely rebuilt. However, even after independence early curricular interventions remained dependent on foreign assistance and were only minimally adapted to Timorese culture and conditions. Hence, in a sense what took place was yet another attempt by a foreign power to disparage the unique Indigenous cultures and history of the local Timorese population.

Problems with infrastructure also continued. Many buildings were reconstructed in haste, and soon were in disrepair. In many schools there were no windows that could be closed to prevent rain from sweeping across the room, making the classrooms unusable during the monsoon season. Most classrooms were dark, as few schools had electricity. In addition, the rush to fill schools led to many teachers being recruited without appropriate pedagogical or educational preparation. Under the Portuguese and Indonesian administrations, people with limited academic backgrounds had been able to enter the profession. Furthermore, due to historical under-investment in education, the pool of well-educated people in the country as a whole was extremely small.

Since 2002, the challenges of nation building in Timor-Leste have remained extensive. Currently, it is a post–new war society in transition to "development." New wars contrast with old wars. Old wars are wars that took place between states in Europe from the late eighteenth until the middle of the twentieth century.[14] These wars, Kaldor has argued, were related to state building, with states protecting their own people to obtain legitimacy.[15] Also, in old wars, the distinction between combatants and non-combatants was, at least in theory, prioritized to minimize civilian casualties.

The situation that emerged in Timor-Leste in the period immediately after the official withdrawal of Indonesia qualifies as a new war. That is because new wars tend to take place in the context of the collapse of authoritarian states under the impact of globalization. They emerged after 1945 and increased in number at the end of the Cold War.[16] They result in significant civilian causalities, and sometimes ethnic cleansing, as conditions laid down by the Geneva and Hague Conventions are often ignored.

As the overwhelming majority of new wars are fought within countries, as opposed to between sovereign states, the education systems in these countries can become debilitated and face a number of challenges. In general, these challenges are related to a lack of domestic revenue to run pre-crisis educational programs, the destruction of education infrastructure, a lack of qualified teachers, poor record keeping, corruption, lack of transparency, poor coordination and planning, and a substantial number of war-affected children and youth.[17]

Freire-Inspired Adult Literacy Programs in Timor-Leste after 1974

Most of the circumstances mentioned above apply in the case of post–new war Timor-Leste. The government, still drawing on assistance from international donors, continues to rebuild the education sector in line with its larger aim of achieving a middle-income economy by 2030. In line with that aim, the national Ministry of Education (MoE) has taken action to address the ongoing challenges faced by the primary education sector, known officially as "basic education." Capacity for policymaking, planning, program development, and teacher management are elements of the development support provided. At the same time, adult education programs continue to be offered, some still influenced by Freirean ideas going back to the early 1970s. An overview of the fortunes of such programs up to the present will now be presented in three phases.

Phase 1

When the Carnation Revolution took place in Portugal in April 1974, political parties were established in Timor-Leste, but the Revolutionary Front for an Independent East Timor (Frente Revolucionária de Timor-Leste Independente, or FRETILIN) was the only one that sought immediate independence. It also made improving literacy, including among adults, a priority. A small group of its leaders had been university students in Lisbon, where they studied Freire's activity in Brazil and the take-up of his ideas in adult literacy classes in Guinea-Bissau and Mozambique during the colonial wars there. On returning home in September 1974, some of them initiated similar work in Timor-Leste.

The *Campanha de Alfabetização* (Literacy Campaign) became part of the political program of FRETILIN. It was undertaken through the use of oral history, texts, and photographs. Because the vast majority of the adult population had had no education in Portuguese, Tetum was used for promoting the campaign and for writing an adult literacy handbook based on Freirean principles and used by volunteers, who were referred to as *brigadistas*.

The training of *brigadistas* aimed to instil in these volunteers an ability to engage in dialogue about political struggle, strive for emancipation, and work for self-determination. The newly formed National Union of Timorese Students (União Nacional dos Estudantes Sahe) provided many of the literacy workers in the field.[18] Most were secondary school students as no university existed. Also, female volunteers far outnumbered men up until a coup was undertaken in 1975 that led to a three-month civil war by the Democratic Union of Timor (União Democrática e Timor), the main rival political party.

PURPOSE OF THE CAMPAIGN

The adult literacy campaign sought to raise people's awareness of the oppressive conditions of Portuguese colonialism and to foster participation in the political struggle for independence. Influenced by Freirean ideas, the pedagogy was built around such everyday words as *fós* (rice) and *tabaco* (tobacco). Learners discussed how and why they knew such words, as well as the kind of work that required their use. Tutors were involved in extended dialogue with learners about how to problematize and read the word and the world. The adults then learned how to write each word discussed. The approach was to take new adult students from simply identifying animals and learning to form letters, to a course in the nature of colonialism and the way forward to independence.

Influenced by Cabral's view that anti-colonial nationalism should draw upon popular and traditional values and reframe them as characteristics of a unified modern nation, familiar images and words were used to convey new political messages. The term *maubere*, for example, initially used by the Portuguese to describe illiterate members of the Mambai, one of the largest ethnic groups of East Timor, was reinvented as a badge of national pride to refer to all illiterates. Nationalist poets also composed lyrics depicting unjust colonial social relations to be sung with traditional East Timorese songs. *Foho Ramelau*, the national anthem, was sung widely in Tetum. The name refers to the highest peak in East Timor, which for the people symbolized their strength and independence. The words urged East Timorese to "Awake! Take the reins of your own horse / Awake! Take control of our land." The image of a hand holding the reins of a horse (*kaer-rasik kuda-tali*) would go on to become the FRETILIN logo during this period.

The literacy book that learners used had a cover depicting *maubere* women and children in the fields. It began with simple words for familiar animals and plants, along with accompanying drawings. Each group of referents emphasized different vowel and consonant sounds before moving on to traditional East Timorese objects of cultural significance. A map of Timor-Leste also allowed illiterate subsistence farmers to visualize the national territory and to find their own place in it. This was contrasted with the maps of Portugal that had hung in colonial schoolrooms, with the new map providing a renewed national frame of reference.

In the more advanced literacy lessons, tutors gave lessons on the nature of Portuguese colonialism and advocated for national unity. Text and accompanying diagrams indicated not only colonial exploitation but also groups of people from different districts holding hands. The historical lack of respect for East Timorese culture and language in the classroom was equally highlighted, as was the practice of forced labour. Soon, newly accomplished *letrados* (literates) were becoming party secretaries in the villages.

Phase 2

After invading, the Indonesian government sought to integrate East Timor into the Indonesian nation. To that end, it invested heavily in schools, expanded higher education, and insisted on the use of Bahasa Indonesia. FRETILIN, on the other hand, in its continued struggle for self-determination, sustained the adult literacy campaign in remote mountainous areas where its armed wing, the Forças Armadas da Libertacão Nacional de Timor-Leste (Armed Forces for the National Liberation of East-Timor), maintained control. Some who had achieved their initial training from the university students who had returned from Lisbon now trained a new cohort of literacy volunteers. However, there were few conventional writing materials available. Indeed, such was the deficit that it was often necessary to use charcoal and bamboo and to write in the sand.

Schools, medical care, and communal gardens were organized during this period, with the teaching of literacy embedded in associated activities conducted in the FRETELIN-controlled locations. Those who could read and write acted as *observadores* and wrote reports on the movements of the Indonesian Army. Eventually the military forced the majority of East Timorese to live in the Indonesian-controlled areas, but literacy classes continued, albeit now clandestinely. Conditions were such that the possibilities for translating into education practice the Freirean principle of "situating the word in the world" remained quite limited.

In the 1990s, a new generation of young student activists turned once again to the works of Freire and the Guinea-Bissau leader Amílcar Cabral for inspiration.[19] When the United Nations forced the government of Indonesia to agree to a supervised ballot in 1999, the overwhelming majority of the Timorese population chose independence. Some individuals then formed literacy groups yet again and went back into the districts as volunteers to restart the literacy campaign.[20]

Phase 3

We now turn to three of the most recent adult education programs in independent Timor-Leste to have been influenced by Freirean ideas.

THE CUBAN-DESIGNED *YO, SÍ PUEDO* (YES I CAN) PROGRAM

In December 2005, the FRETILIN prime minister Mari Alkatiri visited Havana to renegotiate Cuba's program of medical assistance. While there, he was offered the use of Cuban literacy advisers. That same month, an eleven-person team arrived in Timor-Leste from Havana. They had all been trained at the Institute of Pedagogy for Latin America and the Caribbean, a university established by the Cuban government in 1990. Adapting the program known as *Yo, Sí Puedo* (Yes I Can) that had already undergone trials in Venezuela, Bolivia, Ecuador, Mexico, and Nicaragua, they then trained over 400 local tutors to run classes in every part of Timor-Leste, using radio and audiovisual technology as part of a method they called "alphanumeric."[21] By September 2010, over 70,000 adults, or about one-fifth of the total illiterate population, had successfully completed a thirteen-week basic literacy course.

The Cuban pedagogical theory that influenced the alphanumeric method is based on a Freirean-style commitment to a deep egalitarian humanism conjoined with the writings of Havana-born José Martí, a leader of the nineteenth-century anti-colonial Cuban independence movement. Like Freire, Martí believed that education was a liberating force without which people could not realize their full human potential. His emphasis, however, was not so much on individualism as on "social solidarity," and not just in a single nation, but in all countries of the world.

Cuban pedagogy also held that for a literacy campaign to succeed it had to have the support of those working at all levels of society. In accord with that belief, the FRETILIN government created a national commission led by the minister of education and complemented by various local commissions. As the campaign progressed, villages, towns, and districts were to be declared free of illiteracy, and graduation ceremonies were to be organized by each local commission to celebrate the achievement.

The second phase of the campaign would focus on helping learners acquire literacy in a functional sense, and the third stage aimed at the establishment of post-literacy activities and courses. Along with more intensive literacy classes, there were to be literacy-based agricultural extension programs, health promotion, and human rights education.[22] The Cubans argued that these classes would, over a long period, come to form part of a fully articulated, non-formal adult education system. The overall notion was that only educated people can solve the problems faced by countries attempting to break free from colonial and neo-colonial dependency and to achieve intellectual, economic, and political independence.

An advancement on Freirean ideas was the use of a modified distance education model in classes during the first phase. This consisted of sixty-five one-hour lessons on DVD/videotape viewed under the supervision of local village-based "monitors" over a ten- to fifteen-week period. The Timor-Leste government bought each *suco* (local administrative unit) a TV monitor and DVD player, and every location without electricity was provided with a diesel generator and fuel so that no village would be excluded. Each on-screen lesson showed a class of adult students being taught literacy by an experienced teacher.

Under supervision, the local monitors were expected to help their students follow the video teacher's instructions and, using printed manuals and workbooks, complete oral and written exercises modelled for them on the screen by actors. The classes were based on what the Cubans described as an "analytic-synthetic" pedagogy, in which words and phrases are broken down into component sounds and letters and then reassembled. To facilitate the learning of the alphabet and the construction of words, each letter is associated with a number. This, the "alphanumeric" technique mentioned above, is based on an assumption that most non-literate or low-literate people have some familiarity with numbers through the operation of markets.

In line with the Freirean idea that instructors need to be seen by adult learners as authentic, they all lived and worked in the towns and villages. There they received a monthly allowance that was one-tenth the norm for international advisers. They rented rooms in local houses, shopped locally, and travelled via local transport. As a result, they won great respect in the localities and learned how to adjust their advice and supervision of the classes and monitors to local circumstances.

Deciding on what language of instruction to use was not easy given that the Timorese constitution recognizes two official languages, Portuguese and Tetum, and two further "working languages," Indonesian and English. When they first arrived, the Cubans chose Portuguese as they already possessed materials that had been developed in that language for use in Brazil. However, it soon became apparent that there were insufficient numbers of Portuguese-speakers in the local villages and towns able to work as monitors. Local manuals with Tetum were subsequently produced.

A change of government in July 2007 was followed by a restructuring of Timor-Leste's MoE. The new minister of education, Dr. Joao Cancio Freitas, returned overall leadership of the adult literacy campaign to his officials. An immediate consequence was a reduction in the number of *sucos* and the reduction of classes to thirty from a high in December 2007 of over two hundred. At that stage it appeared that some of the forces that had acted against the literacy campaign would prevail. The Cubans, though, following a principle of their model, remained strictly neutral.

In January 2009, Dr. Freitas changed course again when he agreed to pilot a more intensive phase of the campaign. By September 2010, classes were running in over 400 *sucos* and the number of people who had successfully completed the basic introductory classes had reached 73,600. Overall, then, the *Yo, Sí Puedo* project played a major part in the goal of trying to eliminate illiteracy in Timor-Leste.

The non-political character of the project and of the pedagogical model and materials used did, however, cause some Latin American educators to question its relationship to Freire's notions on popular education. Particular concerns were raised in relation to the basic teaching method that depended very much on the students and monitors closely following TV classes, manuals, and exercise books. That approach, it was argued, was much less participatory and dialogic than most people would expect in a Freirean campaign. Supporters, however, argued that Freire himself had been "realistic" and showed a willingness to compromise when he endorsed the use of similar manuals in Angola, Mozambique, Guinea-Bissau, and Nicaragua, even though that went against his "ideal world" scenario. The argument was that in most countries where illiteracy is a major problem, it is simply not possible to provide enough trained literacy teachers to utilize a totally participatory and transformative approach.

THE SECOND CHANCE EDUCATION PROJECT

The Second Chance Education Project[23] is based on an accelerated learning model aimed at improving literacy and numeracy and integrating academic and life skills through the provision of tailored support. In the initial stages of its operation, the World Bank and UNESCO provided the necessary funding. The Timorese MoE now runs it through community learning centres in eight municipalities. Unlike other adult literacy programs offered in Timor-Leste, it was designed as "a pathway for completing a high school equivalency programme or diploma,"[24] with the hope that one's employability would be maximized.[25] Novelli and colleagues[26] examined the influence of similar programs in other conflict and post-conflict settings, as well as in Sweden and Australia. Also, the evidence cited by Nordlund, Stehlik, and Strandh indicates that the challenges faced by adults, including those to do with age, lack of self-confidence, time constraints, and lack of purpose of study, can transcend context.[27]

The Second Chance Education Project was launched in Timor-Leste by the World Bank and delivers livelihood skills and small business and entrepreneurship training, along with important social and community development programs. It also emphasizes literacy, not only as a vehicle for poverty reduction through gainful employment, but also as a matter of political rights in the form of equal access to knowledge.[28] Furthermore, it is aligned with the nation's *Education Strategic Plan 2025* to "achieve universal completion of basic education by 2025, ensure gender parity by 2015 at all levels of education, … and eliminate illiteracy by 2015 among all age groups."[29] The focus is on three areas of learning: language skills in Tetum, Portuguese, and English (but not Indonesian); mathematics, natural science, and social science; and expertise in the trades. The Decree Law (30/2016) provides a framework for graduates to move into the formal education system.

A dearth of reading material for all ages has nonetheless been a challenge across the country, one that impedes engagement in lifelong learning. Nevertheless, since 2001, Care International has been producing and distributing such material developed not only for preschool and primary school children, but also for teachers and community members. Additionally, the Alola Foundation operates a mobile library service consisting of three vans in thirteen municipalities, again distributing reading materials developed, published, and donated by various organizations.

THE REFLECT-INSPIRED ADULT LITERACY PROGRAM

Oxfam GB, together with the FRETILIN women's organization, the Timor Women's Popular Organisation (Organisação Populár da Mulher Timor, or OPMT), initiated an adult literacy program in 2001, with assistance from the Popular Educators Network, Dai Popular, which had links with Brazil. It was based on the REFLECT methodology (Regenerated Freirean Literacy through Empowering Community Techniques). This entails a combination of Freire's literacy approach imported from Brazil, the ideas of Robert Chambers from the Institute of Development Studies in Sussex, in the United Kingdom, and such techniques as "participatory rural appraisal." The project's designers envisaged that, when used together, these approaches could help contextualize the literacy studies associated with development issues in various districts.[30]

Several of the OPMT facilitators had been involved in FRETILIN's literacy programs in the 1970s, and they recognized the value in what was being pioneered in independent Timor-Leste. Evaluators found that sometimes women were unsure about how their newly acquired literacy was going to help them and whether it would direct them away from their other tasks. They made recommendations to not just provide literacy classes but to also relate what is learned to women's practical needs.[31]

The program views non-formal education not just as an adjunct of the "education sector", but as a general public good that should permeate social services. For example, it recognized that participants can come to realize that the activities of the Ministry of Health could benefit enormously from an accompanying education strategy for dealing with such issues as malnutrition, malaria, and dengue fever. That has led to a growing appreciation that medical and therapeutic models need to be combined. The co-educational PermaScout movement, founded by PERMASCOUT'S-TL, has also responded by addressing the issues of food and cooking through education.

Conclusion

This chapter has sought to provide an exposition of adult literacy campaigns in Timor-Leste in relation to a number of periods. In doing so, emphasis has been placed not only on the adoption of Freirean ideas but also on their adaptation. It should not be forgotten that other types of adult literacy campaign having no association with Freire have also been conducted across Timor-Leste. For example, a formal six-years school curriculum for those in primary and secondary school has been collapsed into a two-year program for adults seeking an equivalency certificate. When it was commenced, this Brazilian-assisted, video-based program, called *Tele Escola*, was "Timorized" as *Telecurso*.[32] It is administered by the MoE's Recurrent Education Section. In 2010, the World Bank commenced an associated project to expand, replicate, and assist in the development of curriculum and the training of trainers so that the *Telecurso* program could be made available in all districts in the nation through community learning centres.

In nearly all the adult literacy programs offered, regardless of their philosophical underpinnings and assumptions about pedagogy, there is an appreciation that the aim is different from that pursued in formal education. In other words, it is recognized that adults want to understand "why" something is learned, along with the "what" and "how," and that they want to understand such information within the context of their lives, communities, and cultures. Through its involvement in the country, UNESCO has, concurrently, played a major role in promoting participatory citizenship by encouraging citizens to express their views and identities in public, especially in contexts where literacy acquisition is embedded in broader learning purposes. The central argument is that the cultural context shapes literacy, and that the closer and more relevant an adult literacy program is to the circumstances of learners, the more effective it will be.

The Freirean influence evident in the latter position has been far-reaching, even if it is not the only one. All indications point to the likely continuation of that influence. One challenge for the future, though, though is the fact that Timor-Leste is a multilingual society. To put that another way, people use literacies in different languages for different purposes. A multilingual approach to literacy, accordingly, is required, yet is difficult to provide that without compromising on one's total fidelity to Freirean positions.

Other practical constraints must also be kept in mind. Those include lack of state funds for education, poor infrastructure in education centres, and a lack of local teaching staff with the capacity to develop curriculum and modify programs and reading material for particular circumstances and locations. Additionally, adult learners themselves have very limited access to reading materials other than textbooks. Awareness of these factors, as well as the continuing dependence on donor development models, can help us understand why many adults in Timor-Leste have still not achieved "basic" or "functional literacy."

Finally, an argument circulating of late – that in adult education, the Freirean-derived ideas associated with the 1974–75 literacy campaign in Timor-Leste have recently been ignored by international agencies – is instructive. It is still reasonable to conclude, nonetheless, that over the long term, those concepts have continued to be persuasive, albeit alongside other ideas shaped by globalized discourses and a demand for functional literacy skills of benefit to those seeking paid employment. In particular, they have played a major part in promoting the notions that it is important to start from the existing situations of those being educated and to work with those individuals in considering what should they be; that a society in which the freedom of each citizen is respected and encouraged can only be built through cooperation; that those being educated should be provided not only with knowledge but also the opportunities to engage in reflection and action; that attention should be paid to the need for cultural awareness and freedom of action; and that those being educated should be brought to recognize that the future is not determined, but can be moulded through the cooperation of free individuals.

NOTES

1 Jonathan Kozol, "A New Look at the Literacy Campaign in Cuba," *Harvard Educational Review* 48, no. 3 (1978): 341–77.
2 Felipe Perez Cruz, "Paulo Freire and the Cuban Revolution," Proceedings of the Joint International Conference of the Adult Education Research Conference and the Canadian Association for the Study of Adult Education, Mount Saint Vincent University, Halifax, Nova Scotia, 2007.

3 P. Freire, "Thinking with Paulo Freire," recorded during Paulo Freire's 1974 visit to Australia for the ACC Commission on Christian Education, Move Records, Melbourne. Retrieved 14 November 2010 from http://www.move.com.au/disc.cfm/345.

4 Bob Boughton, "Cuba's Contribution to Adult Literacy, Popular Education, and Peace Building in Timor-Leste," in *The Capacity to Share: Postcolonial Studies in Education*, ed. Ann Hickling-Hudson, Jorge Corona González, and Rosemarie Preston (New York: Palgrave Macmillan, 2012), 197–214.

D. Durnan, "Popular Education and Peacebuilding in Timor Leste" (master's thesis, University of New England, Armidale, AU, 2005).

5 Estêvão Cabral, "Timor-Leste 1974–1975: Decolonisation, A Nation-in-Waiting and an Adult Literacy Campaign," *International Journal of the Sociology of Language*, no. 259 (2019): 39–61.

6 Colin Lankshear, *Literacy, Schooling and Revolution* (Lewes, UK: Falmer, 1987).

7 Jane Freeland, *A Special Place in History: The Atlantic Coast in the Nicaraguan Revolution* (London: Nicaraguan Solidarity Campaign/War on Want, 1988).

8 Caroline Kerfoot, "Changing Conceptions of Literacies, Language and Development: Implications for the Provision of Adult Basic Education in South Africa" (PhD diss., Centre for Research on Bilingualism, Stockholm University, 2009).

9 Christopher Stroud and Lionel Wee, "Introduction: Political Economies of Literacy in Multilingual South-East Asia," *International Journal of Bilingual Education and Bilingualism* 11, no. 2 (2008): 129–33.

10 David Barton and Mary Hamilton, *Local Literacies, Reading and Writing in One Community* (London: Routledge, 2012).

11 Barton and Hamilton.

12 Brian Street, *Literacy and Development: Ethnographic Perspectives* (London: Routledge, 2001).

13 Antero Benedito Da Silva, "Fretelin Popular Education 1973–1978 and Its Relevance to Timor-Leste Today" (PhD diss., University of New England, Armidale, AU, 2011).

14 Mary Kaldor, "Old Wars, Cold Wars, New Wars, and the War on Terror," *International Politics*, no. 42 (2005): 491–8.

15 Kaldor.

16 Margaret Sinclair, *Planning Education in and after Emergencies* (Paris: UNESCO, 2002).

17 Peter Buckland, "Post-Conflict Education: Time for a Reality Check?," in "Education and Conflict: Research, Policy and Practice," ed. David Johnson and Ellen van Kalmthout, supplement, *Forced Immigration Review* (July 2006): 7–8, https://www.fmreview.org/sites/fmr/files/FMRdownloads/en/FMRpdfs/EducationSupplement/full.pdf.

18 Clinton Fernandes, *The Independence of East Timor* (New York: Apollo Books, 2011).

19 Durnan, "Popular Education and Peacebuilding in Timor Leste."

20 Susan Nicolai, *Learning Independence: Education in Emergency and Transition in Timor-Leste since 1999* (Paris: International Institute for Educational Planning, 2004).

21   Bob Boughton, "Back to the Future? Timor-Leste, Cuba and the Return of the Mass Literacy Campaign," *Literacy and Numeracy Studies* 18, no. 2 (2010): 58–74.

22   Bob Boughton and Deborah Durnan, "The Political Economy of Adult Education and Development," in *East Timor: Beyond Independence*, ed. D. Kingsbury and M. Leach (Clayton, AU: Monash University Press, 2007), 209–22.

23   Tahmina Rashid, "Adult Literacy/Recurrent Education Programme in Timor-Leste," *Studies in the Education of Adults* 52, no. 2 (2020): 134–56.

24   Renira E. Vellos and Jennifer A. Vadeboncoeur, "Alternative and Second Chance Education," in *Sociology of Education: An A-to-Z Guide*, ed. J. Ainsworth (Newbury Park, CA: Sage, 2013), 35.

25   David H. Hargreaves, *Leading a Self-Improving School System* (Nottingham, UK: National College for School Leadership, 2011).

26   Mario Novelli, Sean Higgins, Mehmet Ugur, and Oscar Valiente, "The Political Economy of Education Systems in Conflict-Affected Contexts: A Rigorous Literature Review," Department for International Development, University of London, August 2014, http://eppi.ioe.ac.uk/cms/Portals/0/PDF%20reviews%20and%20 summaries/Political%20Economy%20Education%202014%20Novelli%20report. pdf?ver=2014-11-24-104035-650.

27   Madelene Nordlund, Tom Stehlik, and Mattias Strandh, "Investment in Second-Chance Education for Adults and Income Development in Sweden," *Journal of Education and Work* 26, no. 5 (2013): 514–38; Y. Take, "Participation in Municipal Adult Education in Sweden: Why and How Is the Second Chance Taken?," research report submitted to University of Gothenburg, spring 2015, https://gupea.ub.gu .se/bitstream/2077/52191/1/gupea_2077_52191_1.pdf; T. Stehlik and M. Christie, "The Relative Value of Investment in 'Second Chance' Educational Opportunities for Adults in Sweden and Australia: A Comparative Analysis," *Australian Journal of Adult Learning* 47, no. 3 (2017): 405–32.

28   Elizabeth Stanley, *Torture, Truth and Justice: The Case of Timor-Leste* (London: Routledge, 2009).

29   World Bank, "Implementation Completion and Results Report (IDA-H6330)," Report No: ICR00003631, 27 June 2017, p. 2, http://documents.worldbank.org /curated/en/529821498842746357/pdf/ICR00003631-06272017.pdf.

30   Roslyn Appleby, "'Not My Place': Gender Politics and Language Teaching in East Timor," in *Trends and Liberal Arts*, ed. K Ertuna, A. French, C. Faulk, D. Donnelly, and W. Kritprayoch (Bangkok: King Mongkut's University of Technology, 2007), 1–9.

31   V. Soriano, "Dreaming of a Different Life: Steps towards Democracy and Equality in Timor-Leste," *Journal of Lusophone Studies* 10 (2012): 35–53.

32   Durnan, "Popular Education and Peacebuilding in Timor Leste."

PART SIX

Epilogue

emerging presence continues

Alan Wilkinson

From Theory to Practice and Back Again

JAMES SCOTT JOHNSTON

Jurgen Habermas, in *Theory and Practice* (1972), once characterized the relation of the sciences as one of praxis. For Habermas, praxis contains both social and political arms. The social arm is the possibility of social insight or critical reflection on society (which I will discuss shortly). The political arm is the possibility of demonstrable transformation of existing governing institutions: the former manifests in critical *theory*; the latter in political *action*. The bridge from theory to practice must cover the expanse of reason, both theoretical and practical (in Immanuel Kant's sense). Put another way, it must connect theory (and science) with practical interest. This, of course, was the central task of Habermas's earlier work, *Knowledge and Human Interests* (1971). The complexity of building the bridge, however, necessitated more attention to the relationships between theoretical science (what Habermas calls "empirical analytic knowledge"[1]) and practical interest.[2] Specifically, it had to be shown that "there is a systematic relationship between the logical structure of a science and the pragmatic structure of the possible applications of the information generated within its framework."[3]

In *Knowledge and Human Interests*, Habermas notes "three categories or processes of inquiry."[4] These are the empirical-analytic, the historical-hermeneutic, and the emancipatory or critical.[5] As is well known, Habermas characterized the first as concerned above all with scientific method; the second with self-conscious reflection; and the third with social and political praxis. The methods of each are characteristically unique and cannot be superimposed onto, or collapsed into, one another. This has been the mistake of positivism, which attempts to reduce the social sciences in particular to empirical-analytic methods.[6] While the historical-hermeneutic sciences are able to see themselves as distinct from the empirical-analytic sciences, it is only through emancipatory means (critical theory and its corresponding praxis) that the distinction can be maintained. Otherwise, the historical-hermeneutic sciences themselves fall prey to positivistic temptations as long as they remain in pursuit of what

Habermas calls "nomological knowledge."[7] This is the attempt to produce law-like regularities from social contexts.

The bridge between theory and practice, then, can only be built if attention to the distinctive methodologies of the empirical-analytic sciences, the historical-hermeneutic sciences, and the emancipatory sciences (critical theory and its corresponding praxis) are kept in mind. This ensures that the program Habermas sets out is no tightly linked system. Nor is it a straightforward dialectical program, as is said to be the case with G.W.F. Hegel and Karl Marx. For Habermas eschews their approaches to methodology. In commenting on the self-reflection of the hermeneutical sciences, Habermas claims,

> The retrospective posture of reflection has the result that the enlightenment it offers does enable us to extricate ourselves from a (dialectical) interrelationship of distorted communication.[8] But to the extent to which the theory brings us enlightenment about our captivity within this interrelationship, it also disrupts the latter. Therefore the demand to *act* dialectically with insight is senseless. It is based on a category mistake. We only act within an interrelationship of systematically distorted communication as long as this interrelation perpetuates itself because it has not been understood in its falseness by us or anyone else. Therefore theory cannot have the same function for the organization of action, of the political struggle, as it has for the organization of enlightenment.[9]

As I understand it, Habermas's claim is that understanding distorted communication through a dialectical lens allows us to see ourselves as embedded in the distortion; however, the process of the movement of the dialectic destroys the interrelationship. Thus, any attempt at a solution to the problem of distorted communication through the dialectic is ultimately self-refuting. While a dialectical methodology is valuable for coming to see the distortion, it cannot salvage the interrelationships because its logical conclusions are self-destructive. Only critical theory (as the theoretical and practical arms of the emancipatory sciences) can instantiate political change. And if this is correct, the capacity of historical-hermeneutical sciences (including Marx and Hegel's "dialectical" sciences) is self-limiting with respect to social and political transformation. A systematic historical-hermeneutical program, in other words, can never manifest as a program for social and political action without at the very least a complementary critical-emancipatory program that results in the bridging of the expanse of theory and practice. Habermas suggests this himself in the following passage: "In contrast, strategic action oriented toward the future, which is prepared for in the internal discussions of groups, who (as the avant-garde) presuppose for themselves already successfully completed processes of enlightenment, cannot be justified in the same manner by reflective knowledge."[10]

Habermas's configuration of the empirical-analytic, historical-hermeneutic, and critical sciences is a useful tool to imagine the impact of Freire and Illich on historiography, as well as the practical contexts of education. For it suggests that the historical-hermeneutic is at the very least incomplete without its critical extension, and the prospect of its completion depends upon praxis. It is also a useful tool to engage with theory directly. Here, I attempt all three. I want to weave together various strands of argument as *themes* that emerge from the papers presented. The themes of these arguments emerge from what I label historiography, theory, and education. The nub of the thesis is that historiography informs the theories of Freire and Illich, and these theories in turn illuminate the practical dimensions – in this case, education – of their works. This practical dimension, in turn, illuminates the historiographies and theories. The relationship can best be described as *reciprocal*; an interrelationship of mutual reciprocity inhering between historiography, theory, and practice. In what follows, I gather a large cross-section of the papers presented at this conference. I will gather the papers together under these themes, and use the opportunities provided by the respective authors to engage the dialectic of theory into practice and back again, with the goal of demonstrating how these papers, taken together, embody the theory-practice continuum that Freire and Illich desire.

Theme 1: Historiography

Habermas's injunction towards a praxis-driven hermeneutic of the human sciences roughly characterizes the twin programs of Illich and Freire. Presumably, this extends to the historiography of our two subjects. The various papers self-consciously concerned with historiography *do* broadly bear this out. All of the conference papers are broadly historiographic, and it is somewhat arbitrary to select only a few for examination. Nevertheless, for this theme, I will be examining four papers in particular: Rosa Bruno-Jofré and Jon Igelmo Zaldívar's "*Pedagogy of the Oppressed and Deschooling Society* in the Long 1960s: A Contextualization," Gonzalo Jover and David Luque's "'The Wolf Shall Dwell with the Lamb': Traces of Prophetic Judaism in the Concept of Love in *Pedagogy of the Oppressed*," Veronica Dunne's "Sisters of Our Lady of the Missions and Paulo Freire: Weaving a Web of Life," and Ina Ghita's "In Support of Critical Thinking Education: Praxis and Dialogue in Digital Learning." While each of these papers deals with issues beyond historiography, together they demonstrate the importance of historiographic methods in their various analyses.[11]

The contexts in which Freire and Illich operated, together with the sources that informed their respective scholarships, are vast, and one of the merits of this symposium is bringing many of these to our attention. Some of these are better known than others, including the relationship of Freire to Fromm and Illich to Maritain. Others are not so well known, and it is a testament to the combined presentations that we see the vastness of the intellectual debt of these two authors. I am particularly interested in how the historiography is undertaken here; what particular methods are brought to the fore.

Bruno-Jofré and Igelmo Zaldívar note the pervasive influence of Maritain on Illich.

> Jacques Maritain had a lasting presence within Illich's way of thinking. Thus, he embraced Maritain's notion of an emancipatory engagement with the secular world, and Maritain introduced Illich to Thomas Aquinas's thought, which became an important frame of reference in his work, as reflected in *Deschooling Society*. Illich would pursue the line of moving beyond modernity and infusing society with the ancient ethos of the church. This explains his reluctance to identify himself with liberation theology or to link the church to any sociopolitical project. Illich's writing would be imbued, instead, with the notion of the church as the mystical body of Christ advanced by Belgium Jesuit Émile Mersch, and the vision that the life of Jesus on earth is prolonged in the church.[12]

Maritain's influence was also felt by Illich:

> His critique of the nation state has something to do with Maritain as well. Maritain agreed with Georg Moenious that a natural political order would be deeply federalist and pluralist, respecting natural hierarchies and local power structures rather than being centralized. Illich questioned the school not only as an institution, but as a societal ethos, as a cultural model that monopolized education. Thus, he asserted that it was not only education that had been schooled, but social reality as well, and that the institutionalization of values through schooling leads to a process of degradation and misery. He introduced the idea that schooling leads towards the modernization of poverty through its hidden curriculum and does so along with the idea of self-perpetuating progress.[13]

Maritain's investment in Transcendental Thomism cannot be overlooked here; to the extent that Illich was invested in Maritain's thinking, it is at least helpful to note the former's relationship with these Thomistic elements of the leading Catholic theologians; elements that were pervasive in the peri-Vatican II era. Freire's relationship with transcendental Thomism is also invoked through his intellectual association with Lonergan, well established in Darren Dias's paper, and we will discuss this in more detail in our exposition of this next theme.

Jover and Luque's paper discusses the relationship of Fromm to Freire, and specifically the importance of love to Freire's overall theoretic approach. Commenting on Fraser, the authors (correctly, in my opinion) claim that

> beyond approaches that brandish it as the chief motto of his educational proposals, little hermeneutic attention has been given to the strict meaning of love in Freire's work. To Fraser, this absence has to do with a general tendency to sidestep the theological underpinnings of Freirean pedagogy. But as Fraser warns, "ignoring spirituality, ignoring Freire's own power as a 'spiritual guide,' is both a distortion of his work and an unnecessary impoverishment of our own understanding of the world."[14]

Fromm is, of course, famously mentioned in the preface to *Pedagogy of the Oppressed*.[15] But Fromm is prominent elsewhere: Jover and Luque quote from Lake and Dagostino and Borgheti in establishing the influence of the former on the latter through the 1950s and '60s.[16] A somewhat weaker link is drawn between Freire and Buber regarding the understanding of love; one that draws on the scholarship of Löwy.[17]

Both Bruno-Jofré and Igelmo Zaldívar and Jover and Luque draw on historical sources as evidence for their claims. In contrast, Dunne draws on sources of narrative, such as this from Susan Smith, who comments on the general atmosphere of liberation theology at the time of Freire's writing:

> The 1973 publication in English of Gustavo Gutiérrez's *A Theology of Liberation* allowed many to see that history was where God was revealed. Exodus revealed a God who sees the misery of Israel in Egypt and resolves to liberate them. In hindsight, it can be seen that Vatican II still faithfully followed a banking model but it empowered Catholics, lay and clerical, to recognise that the world was the privileged arena of God's activity.[18]

This turn to narrative accounts helps us to better understand the context in which Freire was received by various members of the Catholic community.

Of course, this section cannot be considered complete without mention of the influence of Marx, Marxism, and critical theory, as it has historically come to be understood, on both Freire and Illich. Almost all of the papers discuss, or at least mention, this relationship. Indeed, it has become such a commonplace to locate Freire (especially) in the context of Marxism and neo-Marxism that the specific debt gets overlooked or passed by. Bruno-Jofré and Igelmo Zaldívar remind us that Freire's debt is particular, not general, and is but one of many that he owes to various figures in the milieu of Vatican II and the rise of populism in Brazil and elsewhere in Latin America. Freire's debt to the existential writings of Heidegger and Jaspers, and the personalism of Emmanuel Mounier, most evident in his writings of the 1950s and early 1960s, is well drawn out.[19]

Indeed, on reading the account of Freire in Bruno-Jofré and Igelmo Zaldívar's paper, one is tempted to say that an existentialism and phenomenology rooted in a *transcendental ontology* is the key ingredient of Freire's humanism, and not a straightforward Marxian account of dialectical materialism. I will pick up on this in our discussion of the next theme.

In sum, the two dominant historiographies of original sourcing and narratives help us readers to better grasp the context in which Freire and Illich operated, their various intellectual relationships, as well as how they were taken up and understood by various groups, including members of the Catholic community. These historiographies also play a role in the understanding of the theorization of Freire and Illich: an attempt, that is, to understand their relationships with the main intellectual currents of their time, including philosophy (Marxism, neo-Marxism, critical theory as it is historically understood) and theology (transcendental Thomism, the theological underpinnings of Vatican II, and liberation theology). It is to the relationship between historiography and these to which we now turn.

Theme 2: Theory

Here, I examine two papers of central interest to the topic of theory, which for my purposes includes theology and philosophy. These are Darren Dias's "Lonergan and Freire: An Initial Conversation," and Michael Attridge's "The Reception of Freire at the Second Episcopal Conference of Latin America in 1968." I will also draw some inferences from these, and the larger context in which Freire (and Illich) operated, to claim the importance of transcendental Thomism, the *au courant* liberation theology, and the "philosophies" of (humanist) existentialism for the thinker. I will also say something of the Vatican *aggiornamento* of Roman Catholic theology. Dias claims

> There are clear differences in discipline, context, and method between Lonergan and Freire. For example, Lonergan is concerned with mid-twentieth-century Roman Catholic theology and its place in the modern church and university, while Freire's concerns relate to the concrete liberation of the politically, socially, and economically oppressed. Lonergan's method is systematic and deductive while Freire's is inductive and rooted in praxis. However, there are also common themes in the two men's work. For example, economic analysis plays an important role in their social thought.[20]

Yet, they do share similarities. One is the rich context of existentialism, of which both partake. Whereas Lonergan's theological insights are front and centre, Freire's are more subdued.

> Freire's theology and spirituality is to be found peppered throughout his work, often latently, whether due to his personal faith, religious-cultural context, or

early experiences with activism, such as that practised by Catholic Action. His religious commitments are more obvious in his later writing. Theological tropes that could be compared and contrasted in Lonergan and Freire are legion, at least from a theologian's perspective. Some of these include phenomenology; social ethics; sin and grace; history and eschatology; Christian humanism; and theological anthropology.[21]

Lonergan's theology, as front and centre, has a strong impact on his anthropology, whereas Freire's is said to be secularized. Dias quotes from Stanley Aronowitz here: "Lonergan's anthropology is explicitly and clearly theological, rooted in the openness of the human person to question and the capacity to know and to love God. Freire's equally positive anthropology is grounded in what Stanley Aronowitz calls a 'secular liberation theology' with its categories of 'authenticity, humanization, and self-emancipation.'"[22]

All of this suggests that Freire was closer to Gutiérrez and to the liberation tradition, as well as *au courant* neo-Marxism, with its avowedly secular standpoint. Of course, Lonergan's tradition *was* transcendental Thomism: the relationship between the functional specialties, for example, of the dialectic are mediated by our consciousness, particularly our experiencing and understanding.[23] This experience and understanding together influence what Lonergan calls "conversion," which is a transcendental self-understanding; one that allows the person to rise above herself and to take a standpoint of love, not dissimilar to the description found in Fromm's and Buber's characterizations, as noted by Jover and Luque. This transcendental Thomist development, of course, had its genesis in Karl Rahner, and earlier, in the *nouvelle theologie* of Pierre Rousselot and others.[24] Interestingly, Gutiérrez, too, was influenced by transcendental Thomism, which he likely picked up while studying at Louvain in the early 1950s. Like Rahner, Gutiérrez thought the Gospel outlined the originary description of human existence and the overarching message for all political action. [25] In this respect, Lonergan, Freire, and Guttierez each inhabited a shared context.

Michael Attridge's paper is a fine blend of historiography and theological discussion. The Second Episcopal Conference of Latin America (CELAM II) took place in the immediate aftermath of Vatican II. Consonant with this was the spread of Freire's work across Latin America. Attridge focuses on the "theology of reception."[26] This notion of reception draws on the Vatican II theologian and historiographer Gilles Routhier. As Attridge writes,

> For him, reception is "a spiritual process by which the decisions proposed by a council are welcomed and assimilated into the life of a local church and become for it a living expression of the apostolic faith." It is not a top-down application, imposition, or implementation. Instead, he insists, it entails "assimilation,"

"actualization," "appropriation," or "inculturation" by the receiver. Furthermore, he adds, "the appropriation and assimilation involve the receiving party [in such a way that] the good assimilated is necessarily transformed. It is not just the one who receives it who is affected by the exchange, but also the *bonum recipiendum* (the good received)."[27]

Attridge uses the theme of reception to discuss the influence of Freire on four leading participants of CELAM II, and their influence on Freire, in turn. Through an examination of their various influences, Attridge ties Freire to the complex interrelationships between clergy and theologians (including Gutiérrez and Segundo) in Latin America. Freire's influence on CELAM II is profound, especially insofar as it militated for an embrace of liberation theology. Here, good historiographical work ties Freire clearly to the advent of liberation theology in Latin America, and not merely as a popularizer or pedagogue, but as a chief exponent. In suggesting that Freire was a founding member of liberation theology, Attridge quotes Gadotti and Torres, who claim he was a "founder."[28]

Scratching the surface of Freire's intellectual involvement with Lonergan and the members of CELAM II reveals his debt, not only to contemporary theologians and philosophers, but to the theological traditions they inhabited. And of course, in the context of Vatican II and the *aggiornamento* of Roman Catholic theology, this is transcendental Thomism. Rahner's unique "blend" of existentialism from Heidegger and others, together with his critique of the neo-Thomism of Gilson and others in favour of an account of revelation in which salvation and revelation exist throughout history, are subdued themes in Freire.[29] Freire's own invocation of transcendence is captured in his Christian *humanism*, which is an ontological commitment as well as a historical reality.[30] This transcendental Thomism – indeed, this existential humanism – is found in the conciliar documents of Vatican II, most famously in *Gaudium et Spes* (The Church in the Modern World), which stress the unity of the church through history, and specifically, the social role the church must take to participate in the modern world.[31]

Theme 3: Praxis (Education)

We now come to the topic that characterizes the bulk of the papers on Illich and Freire: praxis *through* education. There are a range of papers, here, all broadly historiographic. These run the gamut from school development in Latin America and Spain to Indigenous education. Unsurprisingly, most of the papers deal with the praxis or political commitment facet of the dialectic with theory, and this is likely for the simple reason that education in itself *is* a form of praxis. Of course, the dialectics of praxis has embedded within (as we see with Habermas) its own theoretical commitments, not the least of which are the phenomenological, existential, and experiential commitments to a corresponding philosophy of human nature. This is as true of Marx and Marxism as it is of Freire and Illich's "blended" anthropologies.

Here, I will examine five papers from the panoply on educational issues and concerns (though I will mention others). These are Josh Cole's "'The Time Has Come to Make the World Safe from Lifelong Education': John Ohliger, Ivan Illich, and Mandatory Continuing Education," Ana Jofre, Kristina Boylan, and Ibrahim Yucel's "Building Convivial Educational Tools in the Twenty-First Century," Christopher Beeman's "From *Nutrix Educat* to *Ju-jum Dakim*: A Possible Resolution for Illich's Forsaken Ritual," Jon Igelmo Zaldívar and Patricia Quiroga Uceda's "The Ideas of Ivan Illich in the History of the Homeschooling/Unschooling Movement and His Intellectual Relationship with John Holt," and finally, Leslie Morcom's "Reading *Pedagogy of the Oppressed* through the Lens of Indigenous Education: Reflections on Overlaps, Departures, and Social Developments." Though these papers range across a variety of issues and themes, they all share (at least) one dominant characteristic: praxis. And it will be praxis as political change with associated theoretical commitments that occupies me most fully in this section.

To say that education is praxis is (almost) a truism. In fact, education, as with praxis, has its theoretical side. On occasion, this is forgotten in the rush to characterize specific practices as materialistic. Freire's "critical" apparatus was of course materialist in the sense that he was concerned with this-worldly political events. But it was very much rooted in transcendence; an ontological commitment that drew from phenomenology, existentialism, transcendental Thomism, the characterization of love in the Gospel of John and the letters of Paul, and the overall role of the church in the world and in history. Indeed, Freire (and Illich) draw on such a complexity of intellectual traditions that it becomes very difficult to isolate, let alone ascribe chief importance to, any one of them, as the papers together attest.

All the papers discussing education mention Freire's and Illich's indebtedness to these traditions. Beyond this, they concentrate on the material and political aspects of praxis. But all do so with praxis firmly rooted in what Habermas calls the historical-hermeneutical sciences, of which theology and philosophy are most prevalent. Jofré, Boylan, and Yucel draw on Illich's critique of communication technologies to exemplify their particular thesis regarding the benefits of CITE:

> As Illich pointed out as early as 1983, using computing devices, particularly personal computing devices, has the potential to impoverish people's relationship with knowledge, just as enclosure impoverished people's relationship to the physical landscape. In his essay "Silence Is a Commons" he observes that access to

the microphone would determine whose voice shall be magnified. Silence now ceased to be in the commons; it became a resource for which loudspeakers compete. Language itself was thereby transformed from a local commons into a national resource for communication. As enclosure by the lords increased national productivity by preventing the individual peasant from keeping a few sheep, so the encroachment of the loudspeaker has destroyed the silence that had hitherto given each man and woman his or her proper and equal voice. Unless you have access to a loudspeaker, you now are silenced.

Many models of digital devices and learning replicate this problem. Pre-digested, searchable answers, and standardized, automated testing of them, drown out calls for other modes of enquiry and discussion of the results of the process of enquiry.[32]

Jofré, Boylan, and Ucel also invoke James Paul Gee, who draws on Freire in his own work. Gee is used to stress the affinities of community, sentiments that both Illich and Freire share. Ina Ghita's paper also shares a similar sentiment to Gee and to Jofré, Boylan, and Yucel.[33]

Christopher Beeman makes an interesting and provocative claim near the beginning of his paper: that the ritual of education is linked to the ritual of the church. For Illich, the figuration with the Catholic Church was apparently nausea-inducing:

From the perspective of a priest who was suddenly drawn into trying to understand the Puerto Rican government's devotion to universal public education despite its evident failure, Illich began to see the symbolic connection of public education to the kind of ritual that occurred in organized religion. The same faith was required to make it work. Through the idea of ritual, Illich began to make sense of the otherwise inexplicable hold that universal public education had on developed and developing societies.[34]

In Illich's early years, it was universal education, and not education per se, that was condemned. As with the church, the organizational matrix was problematic, though not the need to educate, for example, one's children. Only later, in Illich's last period, did the prospect of education itself come under heavy scrutiny, and the juxtaposition of the economics of scarcity with the education of children manifest.[35]

Some papers juxtapose Freire's and Illich's followers to Freire and Illich themselves, as Josh Cole does with respect to American educational theorist John Ohliger, suggesting that Ohliger thought American higher education could be reconstructed and the baby not thrown out with the bathwater:

Like Illich, Ohliger and McCarthy were eager to separate "education" from "learning," as the former short-circuits the latter. They also saw a clear and fruitful connection between what Illich famously called "learning webs" and pre-war modes of adult education, both characterized by "self-motivated" individuals freely participating in informal "learning networks." They did not agree with everything, however. They took exception to Illich's contention that education should be divested from the state and handed over to the marketplace. They opposed "the bureaucratic vampire," but argued that "the commercial vampire" would bring with it an entirely new set of anti-intellectual forces.[36]

Ohliger would perhaps change his mind about the capacity of higher education for emancipation and enfranchisement in his turn against lifelong learning, beginning with his paper "Adult Education: 1984." This satire, characteristically enough, would win the first Ivan Illich Dystopia Award.

Leslie Morcom's paper deals heavily with Freire's notion of "conscientization" in the context of pedagogy. Yet, this is not, Morcom claims, extended to Indigenous peoples in Brazil. Freire's approach assumes dialogue in the majority language, which is in itself an imposition of the settler colonial state.[37] Morcom's thesis relies heavily on critical race theory and theories of postcolonialism and Indigenization.[38] Conscientization and decolonization are said to be essentially the same, with education as the chief means of the latter. Interestingly, Freire's allegiance to Catholic theological and doctrinal thinking is (partly) at the root of the shortcomings of his conscientization:

> That dehumanization is present throughout history, starting with the issuing of papal bulls in the fifteenth and sixteenth centuries that set global colonialism in motion through evangelization and the Doctrine of Discovery, particularly the *Inter Caetera*, issued by Pope Alexander VI in 1493. It was present in the creation of arbitrary categories of race that divided society and offered distorted views based in contempt and pity for those categorized as "other." It was present in the creation of the Indian Act and other racist legislation aimed at aggressive assimilation through both physical and cultural force. And it is present today across our society and clearly visible in our Euro-normative school system and curricula, which all but ignore Indigenous knowledges and perspectives prior to and after colonization, and which continue to serve Indigenous learners extremely poorly. The process of societal conscientization in Settler colonial contexts, then, begins with acknowledgment that the dehumanization of Indigenous people, and the processes of genocide and aggressive assimilation that this dehumanization enables, are pillars of the Settler colonial state.[39]

This seems to suggest that Catholic doctrine and dogma, pervasive since the Counter-Reformation of the sixteenth century, at least contributed to Freire's understanding of conscientization, and that this understanding is riddled with colonialism. In fact, little mention is made of the *nouvelle theologie*, transcendental Thomism, or the liberation theology that (at least in part) grew out of these. Yet, it was these that formed the nucleus of Freire's theological understanding of humanism, of transcendence, and of the ontological basis of praxis.[40]

Igelmo Zaldívar and Quiroga's paper examines the various interpretations of Illich's *Deschooling Society* at its inception. One of these was to portray Illich as some sort of libertarian. Another concentrated on his "learning webs" and saw him as an early proponent of what would become network education. Still another drew him into the theory of the homeschooling movement. And of course, John Holt was instrumental in this last appropriation. As with Beeman, Igelmo Zaldívar and Quiroga note Illich's increasing radicalization as he aged; a radicalization that would move him from a general antipathy towards organized and bureaucratic systems of education (modelled performatively on the church) to a condemnation of education itself as a form of economic scarcity. As the authors note, quoting Illich, homeschooling itself came under criticism for perpetuating this performativity:

> A short while ago I was back in New York in an area that two decades ago I had known quite well: the South Bronx. I was there at the request of a young college teacher who is married to a colleague ... In the evening, at dinner in my colleague's home, I suddenly understood ... [that] this was no longer a man but a total teacher. In front of their own children, this couple stood *in loco magistri*. Their children had to grow up without parents – because these two adults, in every word which they addressed to their two sons and one daughter, were "educating" them. And since they considered themselves very radical, off and on they made attempts at "raising the consciousness" of their children.[41]

The historiography of these various papers captures the image of praxis common to both Freire and Illich. In each case, praxis is rooted in a deep and abiding mistrust of the prevailing economic system, and this extends to its performative and ritualistic dimensions. Equally apparent is the fact that praxis is rooted in an antipathy towards the bureaucracy, doctrine, and dogma of the Catholic Church (Illich). Other papers (Ghita, Mohammad Abul Fateh) make it clear that praxis, especially for Freire, has its roots in Marxist and neo-Marxist critiques of capitalism, together with the sociality and community that is manifest in communist rhetoric. (This latter is, of course, very well known.) Something like Habermas's understanding of critical theory, in which only critical theory (as the theoretical and practical arms of the emancipatory sciences), can instantiate political change, seems evident. Nevertheless, this praxis often seems disconnected from the theoretical standpoints of Freire and Illich. Therefore, in my final section, I want to pull together theory and praxis, first by discussing how theory informs praxis, and second (and perhaps most importantly), by looking at how praxis complements and completes theory. This will be my "Habermasian" contribution to this fine set of papers.

Conclusion: From Theory to Practice and Back Again

In this final section, I want to highlight what I see as the chief characteristic of these papers, taken together. As I see it, this consists in a movement. The movement I want to suggest is one from theory (as the historical-hermeneutical sciences, in Habermas's terms) to praxis (critical theory as action) and back again. This "renewed" or "reconstituted" historical-hermeneutical science is infused with praxis, and the theory that informs it is bolstered as a result. Specifically, though we see our presence in the distortions created by the "distorted communication" of economic systems, we cannot emerge from the dialectic of the historical-hermeneutical sciences. Only critical theory allows us the opportunity for escape. And this is tantamount to *political change*. When we examine the historiographic theme of the papers (all of which, incidentally, share in this theme), we find that political change is at the base of the various characterizations of Freire and Illich. It is a truism to say that both thought political change the proper means of fostering emancipation. Of course, this political change *was* buttressed by a critical theory that was in turn theoretically informed for both, in part through the dialectics of Marxist and neo-Marxist thought and through the theology of transcendental Thomism and Vatican II, as well as through myriad other influences. This is especially evident in Bruno-Jofré and Igelmo Zaldívar's treatment of the various intellectual currents of the 1950s and '60s. Yet, all the papers dealing predominantly with historiography make this clearer.

The papers concentrating on theory (theology and philosophy) also serve to drive Freire and Illich towards praxis. For example, as Lonergan's transcendental Thomistic philosophy intersected with Vatican II's push towards the modern world as exemplified in *Gaudium et Spes*, so, too, do these authors move the theoretical commitments of Freire and Illich towards their practical conclusions in a socially adjusted world. Yet, their respective theoretical commitments remain; for example, Freire's connection to Lonergan and Gutiérrez, and through them, to Rahner and transcendental Thomism, is well manifest. The papers serve to push Freire from his theoretical commitments to praxis and from praxis back to his theoretical commitments, exemplifying the bridge between the historic-hermeneutical science of theory and the critical theory of praxis.

Finally, the papers concentrating on education bear witness to this movement from theory to praxis and back again. Almost all examine the specific contexts from which both Illich and Freire wrote their educational treatises, and in some cases, pushed these leading ideas into new contexts, new formats.

The critical theory of education was front and centre in these examinations. Nevertheless, significant theoretical commitments of both were elucidated, and the connections between them as well. There is a back-and-forth evident in the discussions of the theoretical commitments to their praxis; a commitment that demonstrates that praxis informs the theory as much as the theory informs the praxis. For example, that the Marxist and neo-Marxist critiques of capitalism, extended to economic systems more generally, are for Freire the historic-hermeneutic counterpart to praxis, which consists in political change. The movement to even deeper radicalization in Illich, wherein all economic systems lead inexorably to scarcity, is a theoretical claim informed by the consequences of political change (praxis). All the papers under this theme respect this basic relationship.

In summary, I believe these papers exemplify in the cases of Illich and Freire what Habermas is calling critical theory: a praxis that contains both social and political arms. Together, there is critical reflection on society, as well as political change. The former consists in theory, the latter in action. What makes theory critical is not merely its suspicions of capitalism or other economic systems; it is, rather, the operations of theoretical commitments that are built into its praxis, and the receptivity of these commitments to the practical, political changes that they instantiate. Taken together, these papers lead one to the conclusion that Illich and Freire are operating with an informed praxis; one whose theoretical commitments are brought to bear on political change, and importantly, one whose political change bears back on its theoretical commitments.

NOTES

1   Jürgen Habermas, *Knowledge and Human Interests*, trans. Jeremy Shapiro (Boston: Beacon Press, 1971), 308.
2   Jürgen Habermas, *Theory and Practice*, trans. Jeremy Shapiro (Boston: Beacon Press, 1972), 8.
3   Habermas, 8.
4   Habermas, *Knowledge and Human Interests*, 308.
5   Habermas, 308.
6   Habermas, *Theory and Practice*, 275.
7   Habermas, *Knowledge and Human Interests*, 310. By "nomological" Habermas has in mind rule-governed (scientific) knowledge.
8   The context of "distorted communication" is that in which Habermas is operating here. Distorted communication is first and foremost a diagnosis of the emancipatory sciences; though historical-hermeneutical sciences have historically broached social problems as linguistic-pragmatic (we can think of Hegel's claim regarding language as the form of all categories at the very beginning of

the *Science of Logic*). The solution to the problem of distorted communication does not lie in the historical-hermeneutical sciences; it lies in praxis, and this is Habermas's larger point.

9 Habermas, *Theory and Practice*, 38. Italics mine.

10 Habermas, 38.

11 Indeed, the same can be said for the bulk of the papers; all of them range across historiography, theory, and praxis. In choosing papers for the themes, I am conscious of this. It is to the preponderance of the criteria of one or another that determines into which theme the papers are slotted.

12 See chapter 1 in this volume, p. 20.

13 Chapter 1, p. 25.

14 Fraser, "Love and History in the Work of Paulo Freire," 175, quoted in chapter 5, p. 105.

15 Paulo Freire, *Pedagogy of the Oppressed*, trans. Myra Bergman Ramos (New York: Seabury, 1970), 58.

16 Chapter 5, p. 108.

17 Chapter 5, p. 111.

18 Susan Smith quoted in chapter 6, p. 129.

19 See chapter 1. Something like this inhabits Illich's *Deschooling Society* as well. The turn to the "Epimethean" in the final chapter is redolent of the trans-valuation of existing values and suggests a strong existentialist motif. One could even say the turn is transcendental. See Ivan Illich, *Deschooling Society* (New York: Harper and Row, 1972), 114–15.

20 Chapter 4, p. 88.

21 Chapter 4, p. 89.

22 Aronowitz, "Paulo Freire's Radical Democratic Humanism," 12, quoted in chapter 4, p. 89.

23 See Bernard Lonergan, *Collected Works of Bernard Lonergan*, vol. 14, *Method in Theology*, ed. Robert M. Doran and John D. Dadosky (Toronto: University of Toronto Press, 2017). This is also taken up in Maritain's work, though less prominently.

24 Enrique Dussel, *A History of the Church in Latin America: Colonialism to Liberation* (Grand Rapids, MI: William B. Eerdmans Publishing Company, 1981), makes this quite clear.

25 Rahner Gutiérrez, *A Theology of Liberation: History, Politics, and Salvation* (London: SCM Press, 2002), 134.

26 Chapter 2, p. 53.

27 Routhier, "La reception d'un concile," 128, cited in chapter 2, p. 54.

28 Chapter 2, p. 61.

29 Karl Rahner, *Foundations of the Christian Faith* (New York: Crossroads, 1978), 62.

30 Freire, *Pedagogy of the Oppressed*, 25.

31 *Vatican II: The Conciliar and Post-Conciliar Documents*, Pastoral Constitution, section 5, ed. A. Flannery (Grand Rapids, MI: William B. Eerdmans Publishing Company, 1994).

32 Chapter 8, p. 158.

33 See chapter 9.

34 Chapter 12, p. 225.

35 Chapter 12.

36 Chapter 11, p. 208.

37 Chapter 13, p. 243.

38 E.g., Céleste Kee and Davin J. Carr-Chellman, "Paulo Freire, Critical Literacy, and Indigenous Resistance," *Educational Studies* 55, no. 1 (2019): 89–103; Graham Hingangaroa Smith, "Indigenous Struggle for the Transformation of Education and Schooling" (keynote address, Alaskan Federation of Native Convention, Anchorage, AK, October 2003); Smith, "Mai te Maramatanga, ki te Putanga Mai o te Tahuritanga: From Conscientization to Transformation," *Educational Perspectives: Journal of the College of Education/University of Hawai'i at Mānoa: Indigenous Education* 37, no. 1 (2004): 46–52.

39 Chapter 13, p. 241.

40 Morcom insists, "Still, the roots of *Pedagogy of the Oppressed* are firmly planted in the context of mid-twentieth-century Latin America, in which issues and philosophies surrounding land reform and classism were at the fore, and it is also informed by primarily European philosophies. These include post-Enlightenment principles such as progressivism, individualism, and democratization of society, as well as Marxist and Christian philosophies. The text does not address in detail the realities of colonial oppression as a cause of class inequality (and other forms of oppression) in Brazil as a Settler colonial state, or the need to adapt Freire's approach based on differences in cultural philosophies, values, and goals." chapter 13, p. 238.

41 Illich, "The Taught Mother Tongue," quoted in chapter 10, p. 195.

Contributors

Dr. Rosa Bruno-Jofré is a professor and former dean (2000–10) of the Faculty of Education, cross-appointed to the Department of History, Faculty of Arts and Science, at Queen's University. She is a fellow of the Royal Society of Canada in the Humanities Division. She is the co-founding editor of *Encounters in Theory and History of Education* and founding coordinator of the Theory and History of Education Group (Faculty of Education, Queen's University). Her most recent authored books are *Our Lady of the Missions: From Ultramontane Origins to a New Cosmology* (University of Toronto Press, 2020) and, co-authored with Jon Igelmo Zaldívar, *Ivan Illich Fifty Years Later: Situating Deschooling Society in His Intellectual and Personal Journey* (University of Toronto Press, 2022). She has published articles in the *Journal of the History of Ideas, American Catholic Review, Journal of Ecclesiastical History*, and *Historical Studies*, among other journals. She received the 2018 George Edward Clerk Award from the Canadian Catholic Historical Association.

Michael Attridge is an associate professor in the Faculty of Theology, University of St. Michael's College in the University of Toronto. His areas of teaching and research include ecclesiology, nineteenth- and twentieth-century theologians and theological movements, Catholic modernism, and Vatican II. He is the director of the Institute for Research on the Second Vatican Council in Canada. His current research project is a comparison of the receptions of Vatican II in Quebec and Ontario from 1965 to 1985.

Jon Igelmo Zaldívar is an associate professor in the Faculty of Education, Complutense University of Madrid. His areas of research include the historiography of education and the history of educational ideas. He is co-editor of the journal *Encounters in Theory and History of Education* and associate editor of *Bordón. Revista de Pedagogía*. He is co-coordinator of the Theory and History of Education International Research Group and the group Cultura Cívica and Políticas Educativas.

Cristóbal Madero is an assistant professor in the School of Education at Universidad Alberto Hurtado, the Jesuit university in Santiago, Chile, and a research affiliate in the International Education Research Initiative at the University of Notre Dame, Indiana. His research interests are at the intersection of religion and education in the public system, with a particular focus on catholic schools in Latin America, inclusion policies, and schoolteachers' attraction and retention policies.

Darren Dias is the executive director of the Toronto School of Theology and an associate professor in the Faculty of Theology, University of St. Michael's College in the University of Toronto. His current research explores the implications of decolonial theory and method for Christian theology and church praxis. He is also working on two funded research projects: the Metaphysics of Contemplation and Lonergan and Postcoloniaity.

Gonzalo Jover is a full professor and dean at the Faculty of Education of the Complutense University in Madrid. He is president of the Spanish Pedagogical Society and a member of the Councils of the European Educational Research Association and the World Educational Research Association, in addition to his roles as associate co-editor of *Revista Internacional de Teoría e Investigación Educativa* and honorary co-founding editor of *Encounters in Theory and History of Education*. He served as adviser for the Spanish Ministry of Education during the ninth parliamentary term. His major research areas are educational theory and history, politics of education, and citizenship education.

David Luque is an assistant professor in the Faculty of Education, Complutense University of Madrid, and belongs to the research group Civic Culture and Educational Policies. His current research is in the field of educational theory, and more specifically is aimed at understanding the implications of liberal education and religious education for the formation of identity. In recognition of his academic career, he has been awarded the Extraordinary Bachelor and Doctoral Award of the Facultad of Educación at the Complutense University of Madrid, the Complutense Humanities Award, and the first National Award for Academic Excellence.

Veronica Dunne is a Sister of Our Lady of the Missions (Religieuses de Notre Dame des Missions, RNDM), who has primarily worked as an educator and counsellor in institutional and community-based settings in Canada. She has also served with the RNDMs in Senegal, Peru, and Aotearoa, New Zealand.

A 2002 doctor of ministry graduate from the University of St. Michael's College in the University of Toronto, she subsequently served as director of the Doctor of Ministry Program at St. Stephen's College at the University of Alberta in Edmonton. She is presently in leadership with the RNDMs in Canada. Her current research interests are in eco-theology and cosmology and their intersections with Indigenous cosmologies and spiritualties.

R.W. Sandwell is a social historian and a professor emerita at OISE and the Department of History at the University of Toronto. Her areas of teaching and research have included the history of education, the history of rural Canada, and the history of energy. Her current research explores the history of energy use in the Canadian home. She is the editor of *Powering Up Canada: A History of Fuel, Power and Energy from 1600* (McGill-Queen's University Press, 2016) and co-editor, with Abigail Harrison Moore, of *In a New Light: Histories of Women and Energy* (McGill-Queen's University Press, 2021).

Ana Jofre is an associate professor at State University of New York Polytechnic Institute, where she teaches design and creative practice. Her research and creative interests include data visualization, web development, cultural analytics, and user-experience design. She has a PhD in physics from the University of Toronto and an MFA from OCAD University. Her art has been exhibited internationally, and her articles have been published in the *Journal of Cultural Analytics* and *Digital Humanities*, among other venues.

Kristina A. Boylan is an associate professor of history in the Communications and Humanities Department and the Interdisciplinary Studies Program at the State University of New York Polytechnic Institute. Her historical research has focused on gendered identities in Catholic activism in revolutionary Mexico; additional streams of research and teaching areas include humanitarian engineering/studies and inclusive learning environments, creativity pedagogy, and community food and gardening projects.

Ibrahim Yucel is a scholar of games studies, virtual reality, new media, digital culture, and online communities. His research currently focuses on the evolving forms of gamification and mixed realities. He is the coordinator of the Interactive Media and Game Design Program at the State University of New York Polytechnic Institute. He also teaches in the Communications and Information Design Program at SUNY Poly, where he is an adviser for the Information Design and Technology Master's Program.

Ina Ghita is an independent scholar in the areas of motivation, engagement, and critical thinking in e-learning. She holds a PhD in education and society from the University of Barcelona, an MA in education from Queen's University, and a second MA in cognitive sciences and interactive media from Universidad Pompeu Fabra, Spain. She collaborates with the Open University of Catalonia as an associate professor in the areas of qualitative and quantitative user research and works as a user-experience researcher in a global e-learning company.

Patricia Quiroga Uceda is an assistant professor in the Faculty of Education, Complutense University of Madrid. Her areas of teaching are the history and theory of education. Her main research interests include alternative education, such as Waldorf, Montessori, and Pikler pedagogies, from a historical perspective. She is co-editor of the journal *Espacio, tiempo y educación*.

Josh Cole holds a PhD in history from Queen's University. His research interests include twentieth- and twenty-first-century Canadian, American, and global intellectual and cultural history. He is the author of *Hall Dennis and the Road to Utopia: Education and Modernity in Ontario* (McGill-Queen's University Press, 2021) and numerous peer-reviewed journal articles published in North America and Europe on education, journalism and media, and other public policy issues.

Chris Beeman, PhD, is a professor in the Faculty of Education at Brandon University in Manitoba, Canada. His research and teaching focus on understanding the epistemological and ontological ties between ecologically interconnected being states and Indigenous perspectives. His current endeavours explore these through interactions with the more-than-human world, occurring predominantly through long-duration and long-distance journeys in less human-controlled places

Dr. Lindsay A. Morcom is an associate dean, graduate studies in the Faculty of Education at Queen's University, as well as Canada Research Chair in Language Revitalization and Decolonizing Education in the Faculty of Education at Queen's University. She earned her master's degree in linguistics at First Nations University through the University of Regina in 2006. She then completed her doctorate in general linguistics and comparative philology as a Rhodes Scholar at Oxford University in 2010. She is an interdisciplinary researcher with experience in education, Indigenous languages, language revitalization, linguistics, and reconciliation. She is of Anishinaabe, German, and French heritage and embraces the distinct responsibility this ancestry brings to her research and to her contribution to reconciliation. She is an active member of Ardoch Algonquin First Nation and the Kingston urban Indigenous community, and she works collaboratively with other organizers of the Kingston Indigenous Languages Nest for urban Indigenous language revitalization.

Mohammad Abul Fateh is a PhD candidate and R.C. McLaughlin Fellow at the Faculty of Education, Queen's University, Canada. His present research interests include critical pedagogy, adult literacy, curriculum theories, and the education programs of development NGOs in the Global South. At present, Mohammad is working on the co-option and desertion of Brazilian pedagogue Paulo Freire's critical literacy, liberating process, and education method by the world's largest "hybrid" NGO, Building Resources Across Communities (BRAC), which operated in Bangladesh in the 1970s and '80s. He is also taking up some work on why NGOs in Bangladesh largely shifted their focus from education to micro-finance at the wake of neoliberalism in the 1980s. Mohammad is interested in contributing to NGOs and the third-sector initiatives to fight poverty and oppression with a view to transforming society and establishing social justice.

Tom O'Donoghue is a professor emeritus and senior research fellow at the University of Western Australia. He is also an elected fellow of both the Academy of the Social Sciences in Australia and the Royal Historical Society (UK). He has worked in Ireland, Papua New Guinea, Australia, Singapore, Hong Kong, Malaysia, and the Philippines. The foci of his research are the history of Catholic education internationally and the historical antecedents of contemporary issues in education.

James Scott Johnston is a jointly appointed professor in the Faculty of Education and Department of Philosophy at the Memorial University of Newfoundland, Canada. He completed his PhD at the University of Illinois Urbana-Champaign in 2004. He has published in journals such as the *International Journal of Philosophy/Con-Textos Kantianos*, *Transactions of the Charles S. Peirce Society*, *Educational Theory*, *Educational Studies*, *Studies in Philosophy and Education*, and the *Journal of Philosophy of Education*. He has authored five books, most recently *John Dewey's Earlier Logical Theory* (SUNY Press, 2014). In addition, he has co-authored (with R. Bruno-Jofré, G. Jover Olmeda, and D. Troehler) *Democracy and the Intersection of Religion and Tradition: The Reading of John Dewey's Understanding of Democracy and Education* (McGill-Queen's University Press, 2010) and co-edited (with R. Bruno-Jofré) *Teacher Education in a Transnational World* (University of Toronto Press, 2014). He is associate editor of the journal *Dewey Studies*.

Index

Milton Keynes UK
Ingram Content Group UK Ltd.
UKHW011410160124
436131UK00009B/43/J